PENGUIN BOOKS

999

THE JOURNALS OF ARNOLD BENNETT

EDITED BY FRANK SWINNERTON

THE JOURNALS
OF ARNOLD BENNETT

SELECTED AND EDITED BY
FRANK SWINNERTON

PENGUIN BOOKS

MELBOURNE · LONDON · BALTIMORE

Arnold Bennett's *Journals* were originally published in four volumes:
the first and second, covering the period 1896–1921, in 1932;
the third (1921–8) in 1933;
the fourth (1929) in 1930, during the author's lifetime.
This selection first published 1954

Made and printed in Great Britain
for Penguin Books Ltd, Harmondsworth, Middlesex
by The Whitefriars Press Ltd
London and Tonbridge

INTRODUCTION

THE first twenty-one years of Arnold Bennett's life were spent in his native county of Staffordshire; and once he left the county he never lived there again. In 1927, three and a half years before his death, when he had been to Manchester for a theatrical production, he wrote in his *Journal*: 'I took the 12.5 back to London, which went through the Potteries. The sight of this district gave me a shudder.'

You could draw several conclusions from that entry, by contrasting it with the views of industrial beauty expressed early in *Anna of the Five Towns* or the *Journal*, or by adopting the rigour of those who search Bennett's writing for betrayals of a spiritual deterioration proper to successful authors; but the shudder privately confessed the pain of a lifetime's memories and the abnormal sensitiveness which he hid from all but his true intimates. 'We are of the North,' he said; 'outwardly brusque, stoical, undemonstrative, scornful of the impulsive; inwardly all sentiment and crushed tenderness.'

'Crushed' is an embarrassing word for modern readers; a truer, in Arnold Bennett's case, would be 'repressed'. He gave superficial people the thought of immense self-confidence, of severely practical intelligence and pugnacious commonsense. The staccato abruptness of articles written for popular understanding – and sometimes collected into little books for unself-disciplined noodles – deceived men priding themselves upon exquisite taste. He was declared to be a vulgarian who 'stank of brass' – in Virginia Woolf's word, a tradesman. In reality he was an artist to whom the expression of strong feeling was wellnigh impossible, whose stammer checked him throughout life and communicated itself to his limbs and pen, and whose work should be searched, not for corruption, but imaginatively for the impulsive tenderness which he was too proud to display.

If this is understood, Bennett's character becomes clear. He was not preoccupied with money. He was not the little fat man of caricature who was 'in books' for what he could get out of them. He was not a snob. He was not enraptured, although he was amused, by the magnificence of gilded hotels. He was not worried by the sense that he had been born in the Provinces, and that he must toil after gentility and culture. On the contrary he was simple, modest, indifferent to class, free from avarice; and unimpressed by splendour. His notion of a good hotel was one where, without getting out of bed, he could switch on a light which enabled him to read while wakeful. His integrity was perfect; his humour all-pervading; his magnanimity beyond the dreams of his adverse critics.

Arnold was the eldest of six children; and his father, before becoming a solicitor, had been a potter and a schoolmaster. A small pawnbroking business was also carried on in part of the Bennett home at 90 Hope Street, Hanley; but all the child knew of this was that it was a place full of black bundles. He remembered being virtuously indignant when, at the age of three, having found a single printed leaf, and being busy in pretending to read its mysteries, he heard the brother next to him in age crying noisily at the end of a long passage leading to the pawnshop. He also remembered having on this occasion washed his own face so imperfectly that his eyes smarted with soap. Independent, observant, concerned with literature, and appalled by the uncivilized row the baby was making, he was already a formed character.

He stammered, whether as the result of a fall, or because his fingers had been pinched in a mangle, or because he was naturally handicapped, is not positively known. Also, as the eldest child, he was early conscious of responsibility towards his juniors. This sense of responsibility never left him. It was his nature to look after others, to protect them, often to advise, sometimes to lecture. In his little 'pocket philosophies' he lectured the lazy and illiterate of a much larger human family, doing them, I feel sure, much good, always from kindness and without any of that odious sense of superiority which we associate with the term 'highbrow'. In boyhood he was called 'Enoch'. His full name was Enoch Arnold Bennett; and he was born on May 27th, 1867, a good Victorian Wesleyan Methodist of the North Midlands, destined, it seemed, to become like his father a solicitor.

What Arnold Bennett's earliest schooldays were like is not known; but by 1877, when he was ten years old, he was at the Burslem Endowed School, where the headmaster, a man of character, taught pupils to fence; played them into school on a harmonium, to a march of his own composing; made them do gymnastics; and, according to Bennett, talked about their honour, 'audaciously leaving many things to its care'. A debating society and an amateur dramatic club were other enterprises of the greatest possible novelty at that time; and this original headmaster went so far as to offer a prize to the pupil who wrote the best poem on Courage. Arnold, aged eleven, hammered out the only original poem submitted; and received the prize, a shilling. 'No man but a blockhead ever wrote, except for money,' said Dr Johnson: can it be that this first payment for literary work ruined the boy's literary character?

As I have mentioned Dr Johnson, it will be in place to remind readers that Johnson also came from Staffordshire, although from farther south than Arnold Bennett, from Lichfield. It was Johnson who said that the natives of Lichfield were 'the most sober, decent people in England', who 'spoke the purest English'. It was Johnson, according to James Boswell, who retained through life the habit of pronouncing certain words as they were pronounced in Staffordshire. Johnson said 'theer', 'woonce', 'poonsh' for 'there', 'once', and 'punch'. Bennett said 'rheum' for 'room', and always gave the 'a' in 'dance' or 'bath' the flat provincial sound. He also, when, in spite of every effort to arrive with exact punctuality, he was once again too early, exclaimed ruefully in the tone of the Potteries, 'We shall look a bit soft.'

There were many resemblances between Johnson and Bennett. Both expressed themselves with finality; both detested cant and pretentiousness; both were honest to the bone; and both – although their reputation was otherwise – were models of sweetness. 'You may observe,' remarked Johnson to Mrs Thrale, 'that I am well-bred to a degree of needless scrupulosity.' 'I don't care what anybody says,' observed Bennett, after contemplating a portrait of himself; 'I am a nice man.'

From the Burslem Endowed School Bennett went in 1882 to the Newcastle Middle School, for the headmaster of which, a Mr Hurley, he felt lasting veneration; and when he left the Middle School some time between December 1883 and April 1885, he studied art locally; and tried his hand at a short story and a horrifying serial to illustrate the evils of drink. His favourite author in those days was Ouida; but he had just read Zola's *L'Assommoir* in translation and no doubt was under the influence of it. Both these attempts at fiction were made for the sake of possible prizemoney. He had no natural facility in writing, and no wish to write. He was to study law, sit for a legal degree (he never did this), and become a solicitor.

He was twenty-one. He left the Potteries. He became a shrewd clerk in the office of some London solicitors. But in this office he met a bibliophile, and outside it he made friends with a number of youngsters of his own age who were given to practising the arts. It was with astonishment that he learned, presently, how sure these young people were that he was destined to become not only a writer but a very good writer. Under his air of authority, Bennett was so modest that such a thought had never occurred to him; but once he had grasped it he at once promised to surpass their expectations. This was his habit; a sort of bravado which made him say 'of course' and prophesy his own grandeurs. He said, not in the least meaning it, but being later forced by pride to fulfil his boast, that he would write a highly original novel. He sat down to the task; and, having substituted George Moore and the de Goncourts for Ouida and Zola as his models in the art, he was determined, at the age of twenty-seven, to make his book 'grey, sinister, and melancholy'. 'There was to be no bowing in the house of the Rimmon of sentimentality.' The book 'was to be the Usual miraculously transformed by Art into the Sublime'.

I have begun the present selection from Arnold Bennett's

Journals with entries relating to this novel, *In the Shadow,* which was afterwards called *A Man from the North.* You will be able to read for yourselves what he wrote about it, and how it was accepted for publication by John Lane on the recommendation of John Buchan. In a preface to *The Grand Babylon Hotel* I have explained how the grey, sinister, and melancholy realism of *A Man from the North* came to be compensated by the much more sinister sensationalism of another kind of writing; and that there were always two elements in Bennett's nature which, though not at war with each other (that would suggest a conflict which he did not feel), struck those who did not know him as incongruous. One of these elements was the scrupulous integrity already mentioned; the other was a larkish and uncontrollable inventiveness.

He rarely had any difficulty in the invention of stories. He went for a walk, or to a picture gallery, or to a concert, in search of 'ideas' for the work of the day. He always in the end found those ideas. He did not feel the passion for writing or preaching that more evangelical authors have felt. He was too naturally modest to believe in his own genius or to suppose that, as Sterne pretended to do, he caught in the air inspirations intended for other men. Only the confidence of his friends had started him on the writing of novels; only that delightful but to himself sometimes inconvenient optimism of forecast led him to engage in the writing of sensational serials; only the requests of editors, and, in time, their pressing offers of ever-rising remuneration, carried him forward to prolificity and renown.

He was for some time assistant editor and then editor of a weekly journal named *Woman.* He wrote the reviews and articles he enjoyed writing for *The Academy* when it was edited by Lewis Hind, and when its contributors included Lionel Johnson, Elizabeth Robins, E. V. Lucas, and Wilfred Whitten. He advised a firm of publishers about what they should publish. And, after consulting his father, he abandoned the editorship of *Woman* and went to live by himself in Paris. In this he was following the example of George Moore, whose novel, *The Mummer's Wife,* with its scenes in the Potteries, had first suggested that he might use the familiar backgrounds of boy-hood for serious fiction.

I assume, although I do not know, that before leaving England he had entered into some arrangement with Wilfred Whitten, then acting editor of a popular literary journal nomi-nally edited by T. P. O'Connor and called *T.P.'s Weekly*; for he contributed to that paper innumerable articles about books, and how to develop mental efficiency, literary taste, and a full use of the day's twenty-four hours. He collaborated in plays with Arthur Hooley and Eden Phillpotts, and with Phillpotts in novels, one of which was serialized in *T.P.'s Weekly*. He continued the thrillers he had begun to tire of writing. He produced other novels, grave or gay according to mood, from one about a no-longer-young heroine, *Leonora*, to the sportive tale of a naïf careerist, *A Great Man*. These books were not striking successes: they were the productions of a man who, although aware of his own talent, had never imagined him-self in a position of eminence. Bennett, in fact, though not a hack, was now, as always, a professional writer. He says some-where in the *Journal*: 'On my principle of never declining work I am practically challenged to do, I accepted.' It was not a principle; it was an unwillingness to disappoint by refusal, and perhaps the result of an early struggle with intense diffi-dence. Pride in 'delivering the goods' accompanied him throughout life.

The habit of work grew. It became a disease. He no sooner finished one book, one play, one short story, than he began another. He was full of ideas for books; he was always being invited to contribute to periodicals, or to write plays in colla-boration or for a particular theatre or actor. He wrote all the time. It is said that he did this according to plan; that in youth he told companions at lunch or dinner that he intended to write pot-boilers until he was forty and then produce a master-piece; that he would marry a Frenchwoman; that he would own this or that. He once assured me that not one of these journalistic stories was true. He never deliberately wrote pot-boilers; he merely wrote, as he thought Balzac must have written, one book after another. He had no fixed notion of writing a masterpiece at the age of forty. He merely wrote a masterpiece, which he thought dull; but into which he put that extra effort, that extra genius, with which the subject inspired him. He married a Frenchwoman after having been rejected by an American.

However, one day (as you will read in the *Journal*) he went to his cheap, customary Duval restaurant in Paris; and there saw a ridiculous and fussy old woman who changed her place several times and made the waitresses snigger. Bennett's natural compassion was roused. He thought to himself that this old woman must once have been a girl, very likely pretty and hopeful; and in thinking of her again and again he saw the theme of a poignant short story. As foil, he thought of a sister. And very soon he had the whole plan of *The Old Wives' Tale* in his head, ready for imagination to work on.

The Old Wives' Tale was the turning point in Arnold Bennett's career. Its length alarmed publishers accustomed to receiving short books from him. Its sales were not, in the beginning, very large. Nevertheless it was admired; its reputation grew; Bennett jumped from the position of one writer among many writers to the position of a leader. Thomas Hardy had abandoned novels for poetry; in the theatre Shaw and Barrie were in their prime and Granville Barker was a star in the East. Wells had written *Kipps* and *Tono-Bungay*; Galsworthy *The Man of Property*, *The Silver Box*, and *Strife*; Conrad, not yet made distasteful to snobs by the success of *Chance*, was still a master who had produced *Lord Jim* and *Youth*; Henry James was becoming 'The Old Pretender' of Philip Guedalla's gibe at his third manner. Bennett was considered the peer of them all.

Once again he was astounded; once again he pretended not to be astounded. The news spread about London that he was to receive advances of a thousand pounds apiece for three new novels about the Five Towns. The sums were grossly exaggerated. They were not extorted by himself; they were proposed by the publisher. Bennett accepted them in wonder. He was writing gratuitously, over the pseudonym Jacob Tonson, for a brilliant weekly review, edited by A. R. Orage, called

The New Age, some notes about books and authors. He was making acquaintance with his contemporaries and his juniors. He visited London; he decided to settle in England; he bought a house in Essex in order to be near the Thames Estuary; and he bought a barge-built yacht in which to rove around the coast, through Continental canals, and even up the Tiber to Rome. He had married his French wife; he had been 'discovered' in the United States; money was poured upon him; the modest success of *The Old Wives' Tale* had begun an avalanche of worldly prosperity.

Still so modest that he could not stand, as lesser men do, upon his dignity, he continued to produce, besides *Clayhanger*, the shorter, cheekier comedies such as *Buried Alive* and *The Card*. He not only continued to write the homiletic articles which seemed to link him (censorious persons thought) with the author of *Self-Help*, but to bring them out in book form. He dramatized *Anna of the Five Towns* under the title of *Cupid and Commonsense*; and presently, in collaboration with Edward Knoblauch, he wrote *Milestones*, which was the rage of London.

Worldly success is never forgiven by the envious. Bennett's worldly success has never been forgiven. And it is true that he did write on several levels. He did this, however, from fecundity of talent, from, as I have said, inability to take seriously either that talent or the priggish generation which grew up before the 1914–18 war and became vocal in peacetime. He did not refuse editors; being 'practically challenged' by them, he accepted the challenge. He wrote his best in words that all could understand. Sometimes he wrote platitudes. He never consciously wrote what was false or vicious. He never wrote for the sake of the money his work would bring.

Much of what I have said applies to the journalism which he produced during the 1914–18 war. That war, with its excesses of brutality, was an overwhelming shock for liberal Victorian minds, where the notion of a progressive civilization had taken root. Bennett, refusing to show the quite desperate horror which he felt at the return of barbarism, was applied to for service in the maintenance of civilian morale. He accepted this task as a public duty. He wrote pungent articles which enjoyed immense réclame. So did Wells. So did Belloc. So, alas, did Horatio Bottomley. One saw the names of all these men on posters everywhere. And, since it was an hour when, for their own reasons, newspaper proprietors greatly rewarded 'star' contributors, all were lavishly paid, both in Britain and in the United States.

In the end, having been sought out by Lord Beaverbrook, the owner of the *Daily Express* and the *Evening Standard*, who had been made Director of the Ministry of Information, Bennett was invited to become head of the section devoted to propaganda in France. You may read what he thought of his contacts with the political world in the novel, *Lord Raingo*. You may also read in that book, which was published in 1926, an ante-dated picture of Bennett as he was when he wrote it, ill, depressed, and in love.

While engaged in the wartime work, he slowly completed, at his home in Essex, or in rooms at the Royal Thames Yacht Club, the trilogy which had begun with *Clayhanger*. This trilogy had been dreamed of as a companion piece to *The Old Wives' Tale*, showing how, instead of two sisters, two young lovers grew up, came together, and affected each other in married life. *Clayhanger*, spreading rather than condensing time (as *The Old Wives' Tale* had done), had been an artistic success; its sequel, *Hilda Lessways*, owing to a too mechanical mirroring of *Clayhanger*, a disappointment. The third book, *These Twain*, was about a different Hilda. It in some respects recorded a conflict which was being enacted in Bennett's own life; and although its scenes were set in the Potteries, and Auntie Hamps had her greatest days in it, there was no continuity of mood between the three books. The determined integrity of the writing of *These Twain* gives it importance in the study of Bennett's work: the *Clayhanger* trilogy as a whole, together with a kind of supplementary volume entitled *The Roll Call*, missed the acclaim which it might have received if there had been no war.

The war ended; and in the following years Bennett's health

was a cause of great anxiety to his friends. Domestic stresses were added to the strains of overwork and over-responsibility during the war. He had become the friend and guardian of many young writers, whom he helped; the concerns of others who applied to him for help and money and advice were particularly exacting; his physical reserves were unequal to the demands he made upon them. It has been suggested by the censorious that he loved being 'in the swim', and that the company of lords and Cabinet Ministers went to his head. I was constantly with him from 1914 until his death, and indeed persuaded him in 1920 to take a month's holiday in Portugal in my company. I hope to be believed, therefore, when I say that the suggestions are untrue. His behaviour to lords and Cabinet Ministers was identical with his behaviour to club waiters, taximen, and casual acquaintances. That is, it was benevolent. No man was less of a snob.

In these years Bennett was still the inveterate author as well as the man about town. He wrote *Riceyman Steps*, to the composition of which he was led by discovery of an old book about misers in a little secondhand shop in Southampton; he was invited by Lord Beaverbrook to contribute each week to the *Evening Standard* an article about books in the vein of those old notes for *The New Age*; and at length, after much consideration and laborious accumulation of facts, he undertook the immense novel *Imperial Palace*.

This was his last ambitious work. With it, he may be said to have completed the circle which (on the strength of a single visit to the Savoy Hotel as a young man) he began with his sensational serial story, *The Grand Babylon Hotel*. Even in that earlier book he attributed to Theodore Racksole, the American millionaire, his own zest for the organization of so vast a concern. This was a world in little, a complexity in which, while every individual was hardly more than a cog in the machine, each human cog had his or her exquisite secrets. For him, the hotel was a background; the hearts and minds of its servants supremely important. And so, whereas, in *The Grand Babylon Hotel*, murder and kidnapping played their parts, in *Imperial Palace* character was the key to all.

As it happened, character was swamped by detail. He was tired. Having overworked for thirty years, he was driven back upon his will; and his will, though it functioned, had lost resilience. A few more minor novels, much travel and activity in the theatre (where his own plays failed and the dramatic enterprises of others absorbed yet more of his small remaining energy); and, during a last visit to France, he was attacked by typhoid fever. He came back to London; Baker Street and Marylebone Road were strawed as he lay dying in the great flat over Baker Street Station; his friends gathered around him after he had lapsed into delirium; and at last the greatly loved man was gone. For weeks afterwards his old companions at the Reform Club looked up from the lunch table, half expecting him to join them as he had so often done.

He had joined them, moving rather stiffly, with his head on one side and a single shoulder raised as he maintained the swagger of a lifetime. His northern nod to friends and waiters, which was as slight as the wink with which he received praise which he thought excessive, left smiles in its wake. As he reached the table he spread benignity upon it. He was teased – because he was loved – and he retorted upon the teasers, without stammering, and with a quickness which was generally appreciated. One teaser would say: 'Well, Bennett, how is the play going?' and he would candidly answer: 'It . . . is a failure.' Or another would ask: 'Are you working?' To which he would reply: 'I . . . have written seven hundred words this morning. All of the best.' For the rest of the time the simplicity and integrity of his character caused those present to be happy and as witty as Nature allowed.

Here is a book full of that simplicity and integrity. The *Journal* was kept daily, with brief gaps, from 1896 to the end of Bennett's life in 1931. It originally contained a million words. Even Sir Newman Flower's selection, from which the present volume is solely derived, ran to more than four hundred thousand words. The volume for 1929, published by Bennett in his lifetime, had obviously been amplified by the author, and jocularized. Therefore I have taken comparatively little from it. All through, however, the book shows

Bennett's gift of observation, his power to appreciate all kinds of writing, painting, and music, his industry, and in some small degree his character. Some things have gone which I should have liked to keep, and so have some of the daily records of work, insomnia, and neuralgia. What remains, I hope, is an impression of the writer's unremitting candour. I have omitted nothing from malice or defensiveness. I have tried to offer you an interesting book.

FRANK SWINNERTON

1953

·1896·

Friday, May 15th. – At noon precisely I finished my first novel, which was begun about the middle of April last year; but five-sixths of the work at least has been performed since the 1st October. Yesterday, I sat down at 3 p.m. to write, and, with slight interruptions for meals etc., kept at it till 1 a.m. this morning. The concluding chapter was written between 9 and 12 to-day.

My fears about *In the Shadow* [published as *A Man from the North*] are (1) that it is not well-knit, (2) that it is hysterical, or at any rate strained in tone. Still, I should not be surprised if it impressed many respectable people. The worst parts of it seem to me to be in front of my *Yellow Book* story ['A Letter Home'], which came in for a full share of laudation.

Thursday, May 28th. – John Lane showed me John Buchan's report on my novel. It was laudatory and kind, but not (I thought) critically appreciative. He had no fault whatever to find with the novel *qua* novel, but he said it would probably not be popular and that the same sort of thing had often been done before. Although it probably will not be popular, the same sort of thing has not been often done before; it has never been done before – in England. I can recall no novel of which either the essential material or the treatment is at all similar. The man is most honest, and anxious to do justice, but he clearly has not been able quite to sympathize with the latest disciple of the de Goncourts. Lane said, 'I will publish it,' and I said, 'That is very good of you,' or something like that, and that was really all that passed in the matter of the book.

(*Margin Note.*) I find on reading more carefully a copy of the report that Buchan said no such thing. – June 6th.

Friday, June 5th. – *The Meistersingers*, Covent Garden. From a side box on the top tier I could see all the furtive activities which in an opera performance are hidden from the bulk of the audience: Screened by his wooden hood, the prompter's head appears just above the level of the stage; he follows the score untiringly with his left hand while beating time, giving cues, gesticulating with his right; he is never for a moment at rest; he seems to know instinctively when an actor will be at fault, and his low clear voice is heard exactly at the second when its help is imperative, and not till then. Compared to the prompter the conductor seems almost insignificant. In the wings a couple of chorus masters, with book in hand, direct and inspire the sheep-like masses of men and women who cluster round the principals. Several other men, one in a straw hat, move mysteriously to and fro in the wings. A fireman and a footman stand guard over the curtain ropes. Right at the back of the stage dim shadows with lamps pass and repass. High up, even higher than the top tier, are men in their shirt sleeves moving amid a multitude of ropes, winches and blocks. . . .

Consider the order and discipline which is necessary to the harmonious interworking of all these different forces for an hour and a half at a time. A slight forgetfulness on the part of any one of them might bring the performance to a standstill, and cover the entire organization with disgrace. When once the first chord of the 'vorspiel' has been sounded, the boats are burned, as it were, and all depends on courage and presence of mind. In an opera like *The Meistersinger* systematization must indeed be carried to extremes. Now and then even the audience gets a hint of this; as witness the first and second bells for the raising of the curtain, each struck firmly and decisively at a particular bar of the score; with what marvellous obedient promptitude the immense stretch of canvas vanished into the ceiling on the stroke of the second bell!

At the end of an act, while the 'principal' principals are

taking their calls, all sorts of people crowd into the wings to watch their demeanour; even the principals of the second rank (Corsi, Gilibert, de Bars etc.) press forward with childish curiosity to watch the de Reszkes, Plançon, Eames, Bispham etc, receive the adoration of the audience. This is surely a significant manifestation of what may be called the 'operatic temperament'.

Monday, June 15th. – Fulham Road is dotted with the aged male inmates of the workhouse in their brown coats and corduroy trousers, out on leave. (The clean, soft pinkiness of their gnarled, work-worn hands seems curiously inapposite.) One sees a few of them in every public-house along the street. Strange that the faces of most of them afford no indication of the manner of their downfall to pauperdom! I looked in vain for general traces either of physical excess or of moral weakness. Must their helplessness in old age, therefore, be attributed mainly to mere misfortune, adverse fate? Or does society as at present constituted force them to this ignominy? Or is it that the regular, healthy existence of the workhouse removes or obscures those signs of physical excess or moral weakness which would account for their failure in life?

Tuesday, June 23rd. – At John Lane's I met John Buchan, just now principal 'reader' to the Bodley Head. A very young, fair man; charmingly shy; 'varsity' in every tone and gesture. He talks quietly in a feminine, exiguous voice, with the accent of Kensington tempered perhaps by a shadow of a shade of Scotch (or was that my imagination?). Already – he cannot be more than 23 – he is a favourite of publishers, who actually seek after him, and has published one book. He told me that his second novel, a long Scotch romance, was just finished, and that he had practically sold the serial rights. ... A most modest, retiring man, yet obviously sane and shrewd. Well-disposed, too, and anxious to be just; a man to compel respect; one who 'counts'.

Wednesday, July 8th. – Miss Symonds lamented the decadence of the novel since Thackeray and George Eliot, and I retorted that in future years the present would be regarded as a golden age of fiction. She regretted the lapse of that custom which made it lawful for authors to intersperse their narratives by personal reflections, opinions, moralizings. In the case of a great author, she said, these constituted for her frequently the chief charm of a novel.

Which shows that sensible people are capable of holding the most bizarre views.

Wednesday, July 22nd. – At 10 o'clock, Piccadilly pavements were loosely thronged with women in light summer attire – cool, energetic, merry, inquisitive, and having an air of being out for the day. Their restless eyes were on everything at once: on each other; on the great houses of Piccadilly decorated with bunting [for a Royal wedding], where workmen even then were erecting stands and gaspipes curved into mono-grammatic designs, and nailing festoons of gold fringe upon red cloth; on the patient vendors of elevated standing room behind the railings of the Green Park; on the mounted police who, disposed in companies, dismounted like automata at the word of command.

Happy, infantile faces, most of them had, faces expressive of a childish intention to enjoy; faces unmarked by thought and showing but slight traces of care; the faces of those to whom life is a simple, orderly affair, presenting few problems. Here and there was a family group – husband, wife, and tall young girls with long loose hair. And how transparently naïve these last! Essentially as untutored as the veriest village maid, and offering a sharp contrast to the men of business, young and old, who in cabs and omnibuses and on foot were wending to the city just as though this had been a common day! Judging from the ordinary occupants of the streets, one is apt to think of London as a city solely made up of the acute, the knowing, the worldly, the blasé. But, hidden away behind sunblinds in quiet squares and crescents, there dwells another vast population, seen in large numbers only at such times as this, an army of the Ignorantly Innocent, in whose sheltered seclusion a bus-ride is an event, and a day spent amongst the traffic of the West End an occasion long to be remembered.

At one o'clock, as I rode home on the omnibus, all the streets were so many seas of faces, so many gardens of hats. Most of the shop-windows and balconies were already occupied in anticipation of a spectacle yet two hours distant. And though hundreds of women sat contentedly on the pavements with their feet in the gutter, none looked fatigued or bored.

August 20th. – At Ostende:

The Quai des Pêcheurs, where one lands, is a street of houses that look like lanky overgrown cottages. Nearly every dwelling is an *estaminet*, in the sanded, pine-dressed taproom of which fat, enceinte, good-humoured women move loosely and languidly to serve sailors and quay-loafers with bock and cheap tobacco.

Along the front lounge sailors in English blue (looking precisely like English sailors in face, gait, manner and dress); children clatter their loose sabots; fishwives are carrying fish from a brown and yellow tangle of smacks to waiting carts; occasionally a woman porter goes by, sweating in the sunshine, with her elongated barrow curving downwards to one little wheel at the extremity.

In the afternoon Brown squatted down on his stool, *en pleine rue,* to paint the smacks and lighthouse behind. He had no water. We interrogated small boys, and afterwards men in French, but only Flemish is spoken on this quay. At last a sailor comes who can speak French, and he sends a child for a glass of water. But the child never returns, and the French-speaking sailor has gone. Then a boy takes off his sabot, holds it up to me suggestively, rushes off with a clack-thud, clack-thud, and comes back with the sabot full of water.

Brown's audience gets larger, and it is difficult to keep them in order. Then he discovers that German is near enough to Flemish to be understood, and begins to talk to a short, thick-set young sailor with an honest, amiable face who thereupon constitutes himself policeman of the crowd. We make friends with the sailor, and when the picture is done take him to an *estaminet* for bock. In the corner of the taproom is a primitive bagatelle-table; we play and beat him easily, while the fat and pregnant women of the establishment, three in number, look on good-humouredly and yet with a distant air of tolerance.

Turning to the left at the end of the Quai des Pêcheurs, one is on the Digue – a vast, straight expanse of promenade paved with small, diamond-shaped, corrugated brown tiles, and dedicated to pedestrians and cyclists only. This promenade, overlooking the immense sands and the dazzling sea, is flanked by lofty buildings of florid modern architecture, painted white or yellow – lodging-houses, restaurants, hotels, and the white Kursaal (all curves) in the centre – flashing in the brilliant sun so that one can scarcely bear to look on them.

The lodging-houses are peculiar, and seem to be all made to one pattern. The front room of the *rez-de-chaussée* has a sliding glass front, giving by a broad flight of steps directly on to the street. At the top of the steps is invariably mounted a large brass telescope, polished to blindingness. This front room is furnished with garish theatrical magnificence: highly decorated walls, elaborately carved furniture, a chandelier fit for a ballroom scene at the Haymarket, gaudy transparent paper screens. In the rear of this room wide doors folded back disclose another room – the *salle-à-manger* – treated in the cool shadow of drawn blinds. One's impression is that the occupiers of these apartments conduct their existences for the delectation of the public eye. After lunch, during the siesta, one observed stout men, carefully attired in flannels, smoking or drowsing in the front rooms, while further back in the picture fashionably-dressed women with closed or half-shut eyes waved their fans dreamily.

All day, visitors perambulate the promenade and treat each other punctiliously.

This part of the town reaches the very summit of artificiality. The back streets and market-places are different in character, quaint, with Flemish signboards, dogcarts, bargaining wives, and a free, unhampered stir and movement of old, mellow colours – amidst all which the visitors, whose natural resting place is the Digue, seem out of key.

Tuesday, September 29th. – To-night I am to begin my new novel, *Sir Marigold* [afterwards *Anna of the Five Towns*], a study of paternal authority. All the old timidities, banished for a time by the prompt acceptance of my first book, have returned, have crept back again imperceptibly, until misgivings, intensified perhaps by experimental knowledge of the difficulties to be overcome, seem to hem me in on every side. My one chance of security lies in fixing attention solely on the first chapter and ignoring all else. Enthusiasm, after a week of suppressed expectant anxiety and wakeful nights, has stealthily withdrawn itself, or fallen away and left me naked. I have no desire to write, and at intervals an impulse arises to put off the beginning till another day. And yet through it all, I know that I shall somehow accomplish a sketch, more or less unsatisfactory, of the first chapter to-night – delve it up from somewhere. And then the rest will be easier for a time.

The main outline of the book is well settled, and appears to me to be safe and good. But not a vestige of material useful for incident presents itself. I have hold of nothing but the bare leading facts. I suddenly realize that I know none of the five principal characters – neither by face nor voice. I have forgotten all the maxims and rules of technique carefully evolved during the last few months. Moreover, I have unwisely been reading books by George Meredith and Mrs Humphry Ward, and at first my work will certainly reflect their methods – methods which – the one splendidly fantastic, the other realistic by dint of laborious and carefully ordered detail – are both at variance with my natural instincts towards a *synthetic impressionism*. I ought during the past month to have read nothing but de Goncourt.

Monday, October 12th. – I have been re-reading *Virgin Soil*, and it occurs to me, is indeed forced on me, that I know practically nothing yet of *development* of character.

In drawing character, Turgenev generally begins by sketching the previous history of the person almost from birth, with piquant gossipy detail. The reader, therefore, is made personally acquainted with the character to start with. A simple trick

23

this, in essence. Yet what perfect art Turgenev puts into the composition of these little biographies! There is no doubt in my mind that he is the greatest master of the modern novel. I can divine, even through a mediocre translation, that his style was simple, natural, graceful and effective. Probably he took no pleasure in the mere arrangement and nice choice of words – I mean no 'technical' pleasure in the labour itself of composition – such as Flaubert, the de Goncourts, Stevenson and Pater found.

Thursday, October 15th. – Does there, I wonder, exist a being who has read all, or approximately all, that the person of average culture is supposed to have read, and that not to have read is a social sin? If such a being does exist, surely he is an old, a very old man, who has read steadily that which he ought to have read sixteen hours a day, from early infancy. I cannot recall a single author of whom I have read everything – even of Jane Austen. I have never seen *Susan* and *The Watsons*, one of which I have been told is superlatively good. Then there are large tracts of Shakespeare, Bacon, Spenser, nearly all Chaucer, Congreve, Dryden, Pope, Swift, Sterne, Johnson, Scott, Coleridge, Shelley, Byron, Edgeworth, Ferrier, Lamb, Leigh Hunt, Wordsworth (nearly all), Tennyson, Swinburne, the Brontës, George Eliot, W. Morris, George Meredith, Thomas Hardy, Savage Landor, Thackeray, Carlyle – in fact every classical author and most good modern authors, which I have never even overlooked. A list of the masterpieces I have *not* read would fill a volume. With only one author can I call myself familiar, Jane Austen. With Keats and Stevenson, I have an acquaintance. So far of English. Of foreign authors I am familiar with de Maupassant and the de Goncourts. I have yet to finish Don Quixote!

Nevertheless I cannot accuse myself of default. I have been extremely fond of reading since I was 20, and since I was 20 I have read practically nothing (save professionally, as a literary critic) but what was 'right'. My leisure has been moderate, my desire strong and steady, my taste in selection certainly above the average, and yet in ten years I seem scarcely to have made an impression upon the intolerable multitude of volumes which 'everyone is supposed to have read'.

Essential characteristic of the really great novelist: a Christ-like, all-embracing compassion.

Saturday, October 17th. – Foyer of the Haymarket Theatre. First night of *Under the Red Robe.* Newnes and Harmsworth, chiefs of the two greatest 'popular' journalistic establishments in the kingdom, each controlling concerns which realize upwards of £100,000 net profit per annum, talking together. Newnes, the very type of the middle-aged prosperous bourgeois, with full, flamboyant brown-grey beard, and greying hair; a pleasant, comfortable face, not strikingly shrewd. Harmsworth (director of 14 weeklies reaching 3,300,000 copies, and 3 daily papers) with the head of a poet and thinker; blond hair; quiet, acute, self-contained; a distinguished look about him. One would take him for a *Saturday Reviewer* or the editor of some *Yellow Book*, a young lion of the people-despising kind, a contemner of popular taste and of everything that caught the public fancy. Never did a man's appearance so belie his true character. He cannot be more than 30. He too had a pleasant, good-natured face. One felt that it would be good to talk to him.

Wednesday, November 4th. – Last night, in order to enliven a drowsy liver, I walked the streets of the West End, for three hours, 8.30 to 11.30, from Tottenham Court Road to Hyde Park Corner; and noted nothing beyond the extraordinary number of policemen, stationed every few score yards on either side the road, in Coventry Street and neighbouring thoroughfares. Everything was quiet and I puzzled in vain to account for them. Only the fear of a snub prevented me from inquiring of one of them direct.

Thursday, November 5th. – Two ideas for new books have occurred to me:

1. A novel of which a character drawn mainly and fully from Emily Brontë shall be the heroine. In reading Clemer

Shorter's *Charlotte Brontë and her Circle*, the sombre splendours of Emily's character have again attracted me, and I seem to see in the short and vague history of her life the most superb material for fiction.

2. 'My adventures in London'; a sentimental, Leigh-Hunt sort of book. Short, about 25,000 words; dealing with a dozen 'adventures'.

Friday, November 13th. – At the Press View of the New English Art Club, Egyptian Hall. About ten people, half women, in the one gallery sparsely hung with eccentric landscapes imitative of early Italian and Dutch work, a few soft hazy portraits, a few intelligent originalities, a few sterile meaningless absurdities, and one striking, shouting, insistent, dominant nude by Wilson Steer. In the centre of the gallery a table with sandwiches, wines and cigarettes, which everyone carefully avoided in spite of whispered invitations from a middle-aged male attendant.

Seated in front of the nude – a slim woman of 30, with full breasts and red cheeks sitting up in a very large bed – were a man and a woman talking in loud Kensingtonian tones which outraged the prim silence of the gallery. Near them an old and shabby art critic, to be seen everywhere, was writing in a notebook, his red nose and small peering eyes bent down close to the page. After a long time he joined in the conversation of the other two, and they began even more loudly to discuss the nude, dispraising it in a few light easy sentences of condemnation. It certainly was not a masterpiece, with its hard, laboured, unreal flesh-painting, but the manner of this condemnation almost made me like it.

When I next turned round, the art critic had withdrawn and the other man was elaborately raising a silk hat from his grey head to the departing woman. She left him to talk to another woman in a corner, and then stood alone staring round the gallery. She was a well-developed woman of 34 or less, with the face and bearing of a Sunday-school teacher; her thick mouth worked in that calculating contemplative way that I have noticed in Sunday-school teachers with a passion for gossip at sewing meetings. To see her in the street none would have dreamt that she was a professed art critic, capable of discussing – however foolishly – an uncompromising nudity with her male acquaintance for half an hour at a time.

The total conglomerate effect – loud voices falling coarsely on the silence; untouched sandwiches; silk-hatted man; dowdyish self-possessed woman; inured, quiet art critic practising his trade in the spirit of a tradesman; and the rank, calm, supercilious, harsh nudity – the effect was bizarre and memorable.

Wednesday, December 9th. – I have just finished reading J. M. Barrie's account of his mother, *Margaret Ogilvy*. This book is a picture of a grave, mighty, passionate family of men and women. Instinctively, and all the time, I was comparing it with my own, and in particular comparing Margaret Ogilvy and J. M. Barrie with my mother and myself. Again and again, I had to acknowledge inferiority – inferiority of essential 'character', apart from inessential talent – a lack of bigness, and a presence of certain littlenesses. Yet at the same time, I found us sturdy enough not to be ashamed of shortcomings. What we are, we are! 'I exist as I am, that is enough.' To hold such a creed religiously is in one way to be great.

A proud, self-unconscious self-esteem: that is what few people have. If at times it deserts me and mine, it always returns the stronger for having retreated. We are of the North, outwardly brusque, stoical, undemonstrative, scornful of the impulsive; inwardly all sentiment and crushed tenderness. We are of the North, incredibly, ruthlessly independent; and eager to say 'Damn you' to all the deities at the least hint of condescension.

Monday, January 11th. – The novelist of contemporary manners needs to be saturated with a sense of the picturesque in modern things. Walking down Edith Grove this afternoon, I observed the vague, mysterious beauty of the vista of houses and bare trees melting imperceptibly into a distance of grey fog. And then, in King's Road, the figures of tradesmen at shopdoors, of children romping or stealing along mournfully, of men and women each totally different from every other, and all serious, wrapt up in their own thoughts and ends – these seemed curiously strange and novel and wonderful. Every scene, even the commonest, is wonderful, if only one can detach oneself, casting off all memory of use and custom, and behold it (as it were) for the first time; in its right, authentic colours; without making comparisons. The novelist should cherish and burnish this faculty of seeing crudely, simply, artlessly, ignorantly; of seeing like a baby or a lunatic, who lives each moment by itself and tarnishes the present by no remembrance of the past.

Tuesday, January 12th. – I took up my neglected novel *Sis Tellwright* [*Anna of the Five Towns*], and sketched out a chapter, with difficulty re-creating the atmosphere. The portions already drafted seemed good, more than satisfactory as the result of the 'first process' in the manufacture of my fiction. The 'first process' (imagine the building of a house on a hill) is to get the materials, pell-mell, intermixed, anyhow, to a certain height. Having carried them there, I have found that what remains to be done is somewhat less difficult, at any rate requires less *brute power of brain*.

Wednesday, January 27th. – At a City branch of a certain bank yesterday morning two golden-haired girls, with large feathered hats, presented a piece of paper bearing a penny stamp and the words 'Please pay bearer £2 10/–. Henry T.

Davies.' The cashier consulted his books and had to inform the ladies that Henry T. Davies had no account there. 'I don't know about that,' said one of them, 'but he slept with me last night, and gave me this paper because he hadn't any cash. Didn't he, Clara?' 'Yes,' said Clara, 'that he did, and I went out this morning to buy the stamp for him.' The cashier commiserated them, but they were not to be comforted.

Thursday, January 28th. – I cannot conceive that any author should write, as the de Goncourts say they wrote, 'for posterity'. An artist works only to satisfy himself, and for the applause and appreciation neither of his fellows alive nor his fellows yet unborn. I would not care a bilberry for posterity. I should be my own justest judge, from whom there would be no appeal; and having satisfied him (whether he was right or wrong) I should be content – as an artist. As a *man*, I should be disgusted if I could not earn plenty of money and the praise of the discriminating.

During these weeks of indolence (in the matter of creative work) I can feel, with a sense of satisfaction, the tide of *unexpressed sensation* rising higher and higher; soon, I know, it will break the dam of inactive habit which circumstances and a somewhat weak purpose have erected, and pour forth over a thousand sheets. It grows and rises of itself, and I watch it lazily.

Monday, February 1st. – To-day I took up my novel again, and after roughly scribbling 2,300 words in three hours, began actually to have a dim vision of some of the characters – at last. To 'get way on', there is nothing like seizing the pen and writing something, anything about one's characters.

If I could spend every day as I have spent to-day, happiness would almost be within grasp. A couple of hours' editorial work at the office in the morning. After dinner I read myself to sleep with d'Annunzio's *Annales d'Anne*, and when I awoke I went to pay some money into the bank. Then I schemed out in my head the next chapter of my novel. Before tea, Mrs Sharpe came upstairs for a talk, a talk which continued till some time after tea was over. From six to nine I worked fairly easily at my novel, drafting 2,300 words – a complete chapter. After supper, I opened a new copy of Arnold's *Essays in Criticism* (Second series) and read the essay on Tolstoy. I shall read myself to sleep (for the second time to-day) with Maria Edgeworth's *Belinda*. In spite of the laziest liver in the world, I am well nigh content with myself to-night.

Saturday, February 20th. – Another Promenade Wagner concert. At the interval, when the Wagner music was finished, Brown and I tortuously picked our way to the orchestra room, where he has many acquaintances. From a little conversation with Busby, the hornplayer, I learned a lot about rehearsals, the *personnel* of the band, and the conductor's popularity. Then we went into the orchestra and sat down by the drums. The serious part of the programme was now over, and both conductor and orchestra were larkish for the *Pinafore* Fantasia. The conductor raps, consults each leader of a section in turn with a questioning nod and wink, and then, lifting both arms, he starts the great machine. The mere noise is cosmic! The booming of the tympani shakes the floor, the brass splits your ears, and the heavy, piercing crepitation of the (kettle) drum almost frightens you into running away. It seems as if the unfortunate conductor had created suddenly a monster impossible to control. ... Then someone makes an utterly wrong attack, and a loud wave of laughter unsubdued runs across the orchestra. One wonders that the audience isn't shocked, but the audience can't hear it. Even the conductor laughs, winking at the delinquent – this piece is only fun. Yet it won't do to be too slack, and one sees the men bracing their faces to seriousness. They are at work, earning a livelihood. Beneath the mirth of Sullivan's music, there is a perceptible under-effect of solid workaday endeavour by industrious and capable men. When the end came, with a prodigious rattle of kettledrums, a bassoon player said to the kettledrummer, 'You enjoy yourself, no mistake.'

'I do,' was the answer, in great broad tones, 'and I work hard.'

'No one seemed to know where anybody was that time!' another player said, passing me to leave the orchestra; he was charging a pipe.

Tuesday, June 16th. – Never since first I came to London has the West End been so crowded with sightseers, so congested by the business of pleasure: lines of women, gay and perspiring in the hot sun, recklessly ruffling their light thin frocks in scrambles for seats on the tops of buses; straw-hatted and waistcoatless men continually discussing the prices of seats to view the [Diamond Jubilee] procession, and the fortunes made and lost thereby; the thoroughfares packed with vehicles six and eight deep, and the drivers in their grey felt hats as imperturbable as ever, save for a stronger tendency to quarrel cynically among themselves for right of way. On all sides the sound of hammers on wood, and the sight of aproned carpenters working with the leisurely content of men earning eighteenpence an hour. In all the gutters poles springing up, decorated with muslins and streamers and gilt apexes, and here and there patches, daily growing bigger, of red and blue draperies covering the yellow wood of jubilee stands. Everything, taken separately, ugly and crude, yet in combination, by sheer immensity and bold crudity, certain in the end to produce a great spectacular effect.

Saturday, July 3rd. – At Earl's Court Exhibition. It is good to bear in mind that all these vast vulgarized crowds of people are being subjected to the same influences which one feels oneself – the influences of bright colour and music, al fresco gaiety, and sex; that all the men enjoy more or less the close presence of these thousands of girls in their summer attire and white shoes, the smiles and light laughter coming from behind veils of spotted muslin; that this assemblage has not got itself together simply to provide a pleasurable humanizing sensation for *you*, but that each unit of it revels in just that same sensation and will go away the better and the happier for it.

Sunday, July 11th. – I rode up to the Tower Bridge starting at 6.30 a.m. The streets, not yet cleansed, had a sallow look in the strong hot sunlight. In the course of an hour the description of the occupants of stray hansoms changes from people who have obviously been awake all night to people who are away on some excursion with all the fresh energy of morning.

In Piccadilly; two Rothschild servants starting out for a bicycle ride; the older, a woman of 45, brisk, alert, who smiled profusely and self-consciously on the policeman at the corner, the other a young thin girl.

Woman cleaner unlocking a church door.

In Newgate St.; the night guard of soldiers returning from the Bank to their quarters.

Soho, with all its side alleys and lanes, was quite deserted; littered with the refuse of Saturday night.

By seven o'clock there were plenty of people about with provision baskets and hampers setting forth for a day on the river and elsewhere.

Tuesday, July 13th. – I lunched at the Rainbow, a type of City restaurant which is passing away. A large dark room, sombrely furnished in mahogany, and gaslighted, even in the sunshine of a hot July day. In the centre a table at which a stout carver in white cap, coat and apron, carves the saddle of mutton and the sirloin of beef – dishes which are never varied, and of which the customers seem never to tire. Here come lawyers and other *hommes d'affaires* of middle-age to whom luncheon is a serious meal, not to be ordered without minute instructions to the obsequious waiter. 'Do you call this underdone?' a portly customer asks sharply. 'Yes, sir.' 'Well, I don't. Take it back.' 'Yes, sir.' Here one drinks either stout from a tankard, or some sound wine; but if one orders wine, one gives the waiter directions as to the temperature. It is *de rigueur.* The door leading into the dining-room is labelled 'coffee room', and there is a significant notice 'Ladies' dining room upstairs'. Ladies are not willingly admitted to the ground floor, and those women, if any, who dared to pass that door labelled 'coffee room' would be requested to leave, or at least pointed at as unwomanly. This is one of the last strongholds of the conservative male. Yet here we males respect ourselves; we have a regard for the decencies. 'Gentlemen are requested not to smoke pipes in this establishment.'

Saturday, August 1st. – Watson, the late registrar of the Royal College of Music, went to get shaved in a provincial town. 'How easy it would be for me to cut your throat, sir!' said the barber as he was stropping the razor. Watson considered a moment and fled. The next day the barber did cut a customer's throat. He had become a homicidal maniac.

Lincolnshire, Sunday, August 2nd. – Riding through the heart of England, the general impression is one of decent prosperity and content. One sees nothing of that agricultural distress of which one reads so much in towns. It is an endless succession of picturesque and cleanly rural activities punctuated by neat towns, where old-fashioned inns seem to dominate and represent the municipal architecture. The worst roads are passable, and every village has the air of being well-tended. But then one rides only in summer and fair weather.

Doncaster, Sunday, August 2nd. Evening. – The landlord of the Reindeer told us at length of his difficulties with the swell-rough in race-weeks, and it appeared that at these times a loaded revolver always formed part of his personal outfit. 'This place is simply hell,' he said. 'We have two policemen continually at the foot of the stairs, and at any moment eight more can be summoned in 15 seconds.'

Friday, September 10th. – During this week, when I have been traversing the district after dark, the grim and original beauty of certain aspects of the Potteries has fully revealed itself for the first time. Before breakfast, on the heights of Sneyd Green, where the air blows as fresh and pure (seemingly) as at the seaside, one gets glimpses of Burslem and of the lands between Burslem and Norton, which have the very strangest charm.

The stretch of road on which one stands, used by men and young women on their way to work, is sufficiently rural and untouched to be intrinsically attractive. It winds through pretty curves and undulations; it is of a good earthy colour and its borders are green and bushy. Down below is Burslem, nestled in the hollow between several hills, and showing a vague picturesque mass of bricks through its heavy pall of smoke. If it were an old Flemish town, beautiful in detail and antiquely interesting, one would say its situation was ideal. It is *not* beautiful in detail, but the smoke transforms its ugliness into a beauty transcending the work of architects and of time. Though a very old town, it bears no sign of great age – the eye is never reminded of its romance and history – but instead it thrills and reverberates with the romance of machinery and manufacture, the romance of our fight against nature, of the gradual taming of the earth's secret forces. And surrounding the town on every side are the long straight smoke and steam wreaths, the dull red flames, and all the visible evidences of the immense secular struggle for existence, the continual striving towards a higher standard of comfort.

This romance, this feeling which permeates the district, is quite as wonderfully inspiring as any historic memory could be.

And if the effects of morning are impressive, what shall be said of the night scenes – of the flame-lit expanses bearing witness to a never-ceasing activity; the sky-effects of fire and cloud; and the huge dark ring of hills surrounding this tremendous arena.

Thursday, September 30th. – This morning John Lane gave a definite undertaking to publish my novel *A Man from the North*, on or before the 1st of February next.

As an excuse for delay, he said that the past season had been incredibly bad for publishers, and that he had been obliged to postpone publication of so many volumes that everything was in arrears.

Speaking of his approaching marriage, he said: 'I want it to come; I want it to be soon; I must settle down; one needs a woman in the house. I am tired of my present life, have been tired of it for a long time.'

This from a bachelor aged *circa* 40.

Tuesday, October 5th. – To wake up at midnight, after an hour's sleep, with a headache, slight but certainly indicative of the coming attack; to hear the clock strike, every note drilling a separate hole into your skull; to spend the rest of the night uneasily between sleeping and waking, always turning over the pillow, and tormented intermittently by idiotic nightmares, crowded with action, which fatigue the brain: this is a disturbed liver. Towards morning comes the hope, caused by the irregularity of the pain, that the headache will pass away on getting up. But it never does so. Then one comes downstairs, eyes as it were in red-hot sockets, and gulps some effervescing saline. One rises from breakfast with a mouth full of reminiscences – butter, cocoa, porridge, and the headache remains. One walks to the office in the fresh autumn air; the headache remains. Towards noon, one seeks the last remedy, a draught which weakens the action of the heart. It is effective, and after half an hour's somnolence in a chair, one recovers, half-dazed, but without the headache; weak, silly, nerveless, but without the headache. The impulse to work is alive again, and one accomplishes an hour. But after lunch and dinner one has a consciousness that a new headache is lying in wait, and, one's resolves worn away by the constant sense of fatigue in the eyes and of rapid pulsation round the back of the head, one weakly lapses into idleness, trusting that to-morrow will be different.

Wednesday, October 6th. – At times, and in some fortunate aspects, London will look as quaint, picturesque, and mediaeval, as any old-world continental city. But it must be regarded with a 'fresh' eye, an eye unprejudiced by custom and associations. When I catch the town in such an aspect, I understand how the inhabitants of these old-world continental cities can be oblivious to the attractiveness which surrounds them, as they certainly are, and I suddenly see eye to eye with the appreciative foreigner in London.

This morning, as I walked through the Green Park in an October mist, it occurred to me that the sheep grazing there, and the soldiers practising flag-signals, would, if seen by me in an unfamiliar city, have constituted for me a memorable picture of pure quaintness. Then, walking in the Strand as the sun overpowered the fog, what mellow picturesque was there in the vista of churches, backed by the roofs of the Law Courts and further away a tower for all the world like the Beffroi at Bruges. Observed five hundred miles away, a scene less striking than this would be one to talk about and grow enthusiastic over, one to buy photographs of. ... But it happens to be in London.

Thursday, October 7th. – Criterion Theatre. Whenever I see Charles Wyndham in a new part, I come away from the theatre full of a desire to conduct my life as invariably he conducts his, on the stage: with good humour, kind cynicism, adaptability, and at back of these a strain of real faith in the 'ultimate decency of things'; but perhaps most of all I envy his *savoir faire*, his equality to any *contretemps* that may arise, and his unfailing presence of mind. Whatever his dramatists may have intended, Charles Wyndham always plays exactly the same character, a character which has the qualities I have named and which sets me buzzing with insane aspirations.

Thursday, October 21st. – Lunch with Eden Phillpotts, H. D. Lowry, Bayly and another. The conversation came round to author's receipts. Phillpotts said that he, one of the original band of contributors, was suing the *Idler* for (I think) twelve guineas, and that he had recently lost fifteen guineas due from the *Minster Magazine*. The fifth man told how G. A. Sala had got him to work for six months without paying a penny.

Referring to defaulting journals, I told them that I had only lost money once. For years the *Star* has owed me 3/6 for a paragraph, which I have never been able to obtain.

Paris, Saturday, October 23rd. – As the train swaggered through Dulwich, we caught a glimpse of a platform full of city men and city clerks and a few girls, waiting for an up-local.

It was impossible not to feel uplifted by a feeling of superiority. In the minds of how many on that platform is not the continental train, as it thunders past every morning, the visible symbol of pleasure, adventure and romance! ... I remembered my emotions years ago at Hornsey, as I stood on the platform there and saw the Edinburgh express sweep swiftly and smoothly by. ... And the Edinburgh express was not the Continental boat train, though it moved more proudly, with its gorgeous Pullman in the centre of it.

Dover and Calais. What mean, amorphous entrance portals to great kingdoms! Mere grimy untended back-doors!

As we left Dover harbour, the lines of greyish-yellow official buildings on the grey-green hillside spread out clear, and then disappeared in the vague distance. The sea was rough. I closed my eyes and prepared to be uncomfortable.

Paris train: The carriage was full of silent Frenchmen, and as we flew along through a flying sea of yellow leaves glinting in the sunlight, I remembered tales of the sociability of Frenchmen – how, unlike Englishmen, they beguiled their journeys by courteous and cheerful dialogue. Perhaps on this line the native public has suffered by the example of our insular manners.

For many miles the landscape was bare, greyish and uninteresting. Then, as we increased our distance from the sea southwards a change of temperature and of atmosphere became more and more perceptible, until the warmth and brightness made almost an English summer. Presently the character of the landscape altered. Water was everywhere in large quiet pools bordered by trees delightfully tinted, and we passed by picturesque towns with fine churches and wonderful crooked white streets.

We entered Paris, as one enters London, by boring a way into the city through ravines with windowed walls. On the right was a single impressive feature, the hill of Montmartre surmounted by a great cathedral under scaffolding.

It was dusk as we drove to the hotel through traffic less crowded than that of London, but noisier, more gesticulating, and far more bewilderingly mazy.

As we came out of the Opéra, men were crying the *Journal*, with the first feuilleton of Zola's *Paris*. Zola and the *Journal* and Steinlen's poster thereof seem just now to flame in the forehead of the City.

Monday, October 25th. – Ascended the tower of Notre Dame in order to see the Devils, which surpassed expectations. It struck me that these twelfth century devils gazed over Zola's Paris with a certain benign satisfaction.

Gardens of the Luxembourg. It is here that Bohemian Paris takes the air. This part of the city has an effective significance which is missing in the neighbourhood of the cosmopolitan Boulevard des Italiens. Here is some Doing. People are less self-conscious and more purposeful; more truly lighthearted and yet more earnest. ... A beautiful afternoon, absolutely cloudless sky, gentlest breeze just moving out of the perpendicular the high fountain-spray in front of the Palace. ... A large, apparently but not really shapeless space, gravelled and sown with brown trees and yellow chairs, and untidy with autumn leaves.

As to the people:

Nursemaids, whose large white or blue aprons and white caps seem to strike the *note* of the scene; scores of children, many just able to walk, others learning to skip or clumsily trundling hoops, others in arms; the last seemed always to be receiving clean napkins from their plump, comfortable nurses.

Students in fine black hats and vast neckties, walking about or sitting in groups.

The chairwoman, a buxom young woman, capless, with a large black apron. She goes to a group of young students who are talking and laughing among themselves. Without apparently noticing her, they throw her a few words, still laughing, a colloquy ensues, and then for some reason she goes away without exacting pennies from them.

Young women, carelessly *chic*, some powdered, all talkative, sitting about in pairs, with looks on their faces of invitation.

Here and there a few sedater groups, well-dressed; *papa,*

mama et bébé, or perhaps several old women full of volubility and gesture.

A few inquisitive dogs.

In the distance, the tooting of tram cars, and the vague roar of traffic.

The traveller, however virginal and enthusiastic, does not enjoy an unbroken ecstasy. He has periods of gloom, periods when he asks himself the object of all these exertions, and puts the question whether or not he is really experiencing pleasure. At such times he suspects that he is not seeing the right things, that the characteristic, the right aspects of these strange scenes are escaping him. He looks forward dully to the days of his holiday yet to pass, and wonders how he will dispose of them. He is disgusted because his money is not more, his command of the language so slight, and his capacity for enjoyment so limited. His mind goes forward to speculate as to his future career, which seems one of but narrow possibilities, and he foresees failure. The newness of things grows monotonous; he desires the known, the expected.

Wednesday, October 27th. – The *Journal* stated to-day that last Saturday one hundred *voitures-réclames* visited every place within 20 kilometres of the fortifications, to distribute Steinlen's *affiche* of Zola's *Paris*; also that 30 *voitures-réclames* had been circulating continuously for 10 days previously; also that the cost of launching the novel had been 150,000 francs.

I walked the length of the Champs Elysées and back again to-night between 10 and 11. The immense thoroughfare had a depressing deserted appearance. In the side alleys under the trees a light mist hung low, and through this the forms of empty chairs were made spectrally visible by the gas-lamps. Down the road at intervals passed cyclists with Chinese lanterns, swiftly overtaking the few fiacres. Occasionally the light of a flying lantern lit up the face of a girl pedalling hardily in her neat knickerbockers over the perfect surface of the gloomy thoroughfare.

Thursday, October 28th. – At the Post Office in the Avenue de l'Opéra, where I was sending off a telegram, two men came in and wrote a letter in consultation *'Chère Amie* – no – *ma chère petite amie ... mille baisers. ... Ton Albert.'* ... Every word of the assignation was minutely discussed before being set down. An incident, I thought, characteristically French.

Saturday, October 30th. – Montmartre. 'Cabaret du Conservatoire (Ancienne abbaye de la Butte – 12th cent.).'

There was an attractiveness in the simple exterior of this café of the Boulevard Rochechouart. When we went in, the *salle du concert* was not yet opened. While waiting we ordered cognacs, and looked at the very clever pencilled portraits which covered the walls. The café proper, or outer court, was a long low narrow room, narrowing still more at the back to the door giving on the *salle du concert*. There were perhaps a dozen *consommateurs*, none of them apparently different from the *consommateurs* of any other café. At about 9.30 it was quietly announced that the concert would commence at once, and we went forward, rather surprised at the charge of 2 francs for entrance to the show. The *salle* was a room of irregular shape, roughly painted to represent a crypt, with a groined roof. Down the middle of it were three narrow trestle-tables with seats at either side of them. In one corner a clumsy tapestry arrangement of a proscenium, very small and toy-like, and near this a piano. At the back were several toy *loges*, a comical imitation of a theatre. The walls were hung with copies of ancient standards and with old brass musical instruments, and here and there they were frescoed.

The pianist came and moved his fingers lightly over the keyboard, and drifted into a march. Then the proprietor at the back announced *'mon bon camarade'* So-and-so. A dark little man of about 35 with a keen pleasant face, dressed in blue serge, came forward, and leaning negligently on the piano, sang very prettily, in a thin voice, a sentimental song about Venice. His tone suited the small room (which 80 people filled) to perfection. Then another *'bon camarade'* was announced, an older heavier man, very dark and self-contained, and with a face something like Verlaine's in its torpor and pallor. He sang a humorous song, and in the last verse, after

3 verses of utter impassivity, disclosed a twinkle and a smile to show that he also was enjoying the joke. The applause was immense. This man sang twice, and each time hoisted himself on to the low platform by clinging to the piano. Others followed him, all roughly dressed – one man had brown gloves sticking up from the breast pocket of an old frock coat, and among them two women ('*ma bonne camarade*') both charmingly unaffected and good-natured and clever, dressed in black or dark blue, with none of the conventional stage airs. Before the entertainment had proceeded ten minutes, the artistic feeling which permeated it was most apparent. The audience was of the lower middle class, seemingly quite ordinary, but nevertheless appreciating what was set before them. One woman, not at all fashionably dressed, wore an exquisitely embroidered stomacher in blues and purples.

The songs were varied by some scenes from the little *théâtre de l'ombre*, in which cardboard figures throw a shadow against a background thrown from a magic lantern. Then, after more songs, came the piece of the evening, for *théâtre de l'ombre*, *pièce en dix tableaux*, entitled *La marche à l'étoile*. The lights were turned down, and the *auteur-compositeur*, looking like an intelligent carpenter, came forward to sing the lyric accompaniment to his shadow-drama. The play proved to be a rendering of the story of the Cross, and, as rendered, it was remarkably effective, even moving; certainly the theme was treated with singular poetic breadth. I could not judge either the words or the music, but there could not be a doubt that the intelligent carpenter was some sort of an artist.

Monday, November 22nd. – At the Grieg Concert, St James's Hall. A crowded house, mainly filled with hordes of those idle, well-dressed, supercilious, unintelligent women who inhabit the West End and the more expensive suburbs; their hats, though it is Autumn, made a garden.

Grieg came on in a short jacket of black velvet which serves to decrease still further his short stature. He has a large head with white hair and a bald patch, and the shrewd wrinkled face of a thinker. A restless man, weary and yet the victim of an incurable vivacity. The concussion of his hands on the keys jerked back his head at every loud chord. Between the movements of a sonata he bowed almost imperceptibly and wiped his face every time with the same mechanical movement. He looked like one who has exhausted the joys of fame and of being adored.

In the orchestra, full of hero-worshippers, I noticed particularly two girls, friends, who must have stood hours at the door to gain their unique position in the first row. One smiled ecstatically and showed her teeth (I think she was American) throughout the concert. The other had a fixed and mournful face. She never stirred and seldom spoke; she did not join in the applause, which was frantic in those seats. Her thin lips were set, and her dark eyes set. She was the Serious Student, never happy, never even passably content, always reaching for the unattainable; without doubt she had little talent, but an immense purpose and energy. I fancied I could see her in her daily existence, secretive, self-contained, and occasionally, only occasionally, opening the gates of her soul to some companion in a sudden abandonment.

Saturday, November 27th. – Indirectly I heard news of Simeon Solomon through a picture dealer in Regent Street, via Marriott. Simeon Solomon was once one of the lights of the Pre-Raphaelite School, the friend of Rossetti and of Burne-Jones, who both had sincere admiration for his work. The dealer said that he was now in a lunatic asylum. 'At one time,' he said, 'I gave him £2 a week and took his sketches. The money was paid daily, for he was always penniless.' Marriott asked where Solomon lived in those days. 'He didn't live anywhere,' the dealer said; 'he had no home. If he could afford it, he slept at a common lodging-house; if not, on the Embankment.'

Marriott said that Solomon had really been mad for years, and that many years ago, it was stated that he was reduced to doing sketches for pots of beer.

Monday, December 6th. – On Saturday night I finished my second book, *The Art of Journalism for Women*. This afternoon,

reading in the *New Review* (which this month ceases to exist)
the conclusion of Joseph Conrad's superb book, *The Nigger
of the Narcissus*, I had a mind to go on at once with my Staffordshire novel, treating it in the Conrad manner, which after
all is my own, on a grander scale.

Tuesday, December 7th. – At Louis Parker's new play *The
Happy Life* at the Duke of York's. During passages of rank
sentimentality at the theatre, I am affected like a puritanic
provincial lady when first she sees a woman in tights. I am
obliged to look away, at the ceiling, at the boxes, anywhere
but on the stage.

Now and then during the evening Tertia and I could not
help smiling at the naïve comments and appreciation of
pseudo-tenderness, of two middle-aged people who sat behind
us. I thought they must be well-to-do farmer people in town
for the Agricultural Show. As we went out, I caught sight of
them – Genevieve Ward and W. H. Vernon. I have noticed
before that no amount of being behind the scenes dulls the
actor's appetite for the simple emotions of the stage.

Thursday, December 16th. – At my dentist's, a strangely
Bohemian cockney, who called me 'Mate' at the second interview, and referred intimately to the missis and the kids.
Nevertheless a good dentist. In his own jargon he said: 'I
have put in two uppers and a lower to-day.' He told me also
of a curious domestic custom: 'My missis,' he said, 'has
extraction money and toothpowder money for 'er perks.'

Friday, December 17th. – I had imagined that leader-writers
on the morning dailies received munificent salaries. But at
lunch to-day, discussing with Lowry the murder of Terriss, on
which the previous evening he had written a column leader
in 70 minutes, I learnt otherwise. Lowry is on the *Morning Post*,
and he is paid by the piece, receiving 2 guineas for a column,
1 guinea for half a column, and half a guinea for a quarter
column.

Sunday, December 19th. – A story told to me to-day reminded me of a confidence of my Aunt's, made some years ago, concerning my maternal grandfather. It was given in the horrified tones of a daughter whose Puritan susceptibilities had been lacerated. My grandfather, it appears, at the age of seventy and odd, and after having been a long time a widower, began to pursue servant girls upon the outskirts of Burslem; and not all the shocked remonstrances of his daughters could bring him back to the narrow path. He never succeeded in enchanting any of these girls, but the intention was, I was told, only too obvious. It is curious that at such a time of life, the long-repressed instincts of a man who had lived as a strict Wesleyan-Methodist, should at last have become unmanageable. Shortly after the episodes of the servant girls he married a buxom woman forty years his junior, a plump-faced pleasant woman who had the greatest difficulty not to call me '*Mr* Arnold'.

Tuesday, December 21st. – The constant unsleeping watchfulness for verbal mistakes and slips and clumsiness in composition, necessitated by my post as editor of women's journalism, has sharpened and exasperated my susceptibilities to such a point that only by a great effort can I read anything now without noting such slips, however trifling. In spite of myself, my mind registers them as they occur, in no matter what writer's work. Such preposterous attention to the superficialities of style seriously interferes with the enjoyment of literature. There is scarcely an author – unless it be Henry James – whom I find flawless, and whom, therefore, I can read in perfect comfort.

·1898·

Tuesday, January 11th. – It seems to me that only within the last few years have we absorbed from France that passion for the artistic shapely presentation of truth, and that feeling for words as words, which animated Flaubert, the de Goncourts, and de Maupassant, and which is so exactly described and defined in de Maupassant's introduction to the collected works of Flaubert. None of the (so-called) great masters of English nineteenth-century fiction had (if I am right) a deep artistic interest in form and treatment; they were absorbed in 'subject' – just as the 'anecdote'-painters of the Royal Academy are absorbed in subject, and in my view they are open to the same reproach as these. Certainly they had not the feeling for words to any large degree, though one sees traces of it sometimes in the Brontës, – never in George Eliot, or Jane Austen, or Dickens, or even Thackeray or Scott.

Yet that this feeling for words existed independently in England is proved by the prose of Charles Lamb and John Ruskin. The novelists cared little for form, the *science* of construction, – *Composition*. They had not artistic taste; they lacked this just as Millais lacked it. Millais may have been a great painter; these novelists may have been great writers, but neither (to use de Maupassant's distinction) were great artists in the sense in which I understand the word. An artist must be interested primarily in presentment, not in the thing presented.

Wednesday, January 12th. – In accordance with an urgent message from Lane, I called this morning to see him about my second book, *Journalism for Women: a Practical Guide.* He was unwell and in bed, and the interview passed in his bedroom. He beamed on me, made attentive inquiries about my affairs, and sent for cigarettes. Then he showed me the glowing report made by Miss Evelyn Sharp upon my book, and said that he wanted to publish it at once – within three weeks. He offered me a 10 per cent royalty; I suggested 15 per cent, and he agreed at once. Title, shape, type, paper, and price were settled there and then and Chapman received instructions to draw the contracts. In another five minutes the contracts were signed and exchanged, and the manuscript was made up to go to the printers that morning – within the hour.

How different the reception of this book from the frigid welcome given to *A Man from the North*! The latter, a serious and laborious work, has waited, after acceptance, nearly two years for publication. *Journalism for Women*, thrown off in about eight weeks, is to be printed and published in less than a month.

Tuesday, February 15th. – The preoccupation of removing to a new house (9 Fulham Park Gardens) is now almost over, and after three days of incessant manual work, arranging books, clothes, furniture, and pictures, a householder for the first time, I find myself wandering without aim through the house, staring at finished rooms, and especially at the terra cotta effects of my new study, with a vague satisfaction. But stronger, more insistent than this satisfaction, is the feeling of graver and complicated responsibilities, and a sort of anxiety for the future.

And I wonder, at the age of 30, whether the great game is worth the candle. I return with regretful fancy to the time when, with the lighter cares and the highest hopes that ignorance could induce, I lived in Raphael Street, and in Cowley Street, on about 15s. a week.

To-night I have set to work on a long criticism of George Moore.

Wednesday, February 16th. – As I opened the front door this morning to leave for the office, the postman put a parcel in my hand. It was from John Lane, and it contained the first copy of my first book. I untied it hastily, and after glancing at the cover, gave it to Tertia to read. To-night I looked through the tale, picking out my favourite bits. The style seemed better than I had hoped for.

Wednesday, February 23rd. – Sitting with me in his dark little office at *Black and White* after lunch, Eden Phillpotts, heavily wrapped up and pale after a long attack of influenza, told me something of his life. After leaving school at 17, he came to London and entered an insurance office. His first idea was to be an actor. He studied elocution etc. at the School of Dramatic Art, and after two years found he was unfitted entirely for acting. Then, having already written a little, he turned to literature with seriousness. For eight years he wrote from 6 to 9 in the evening. At the end of that time he could earn £400 a year by his pen. He left the insurance office, married, and lived by his pen comfortably till *Black and White* offered him, through his agent, the post of assistant editor. As this meant an assured revenue, he accepted it. He works three days a week, machine-writing, free from responsibility, and the rest of his time he gives to novels and short stories.

To-day is published my first book, *A Man from the North*. I have seen it mentioned in several papers among 'Books received'. Beyond that, I have scarcely thought of it. The fact has not at the moment interested me. But during the last few days I have been several times naïvely surprised that some of my friends are not more awake and lively to the fact than they seem to be.

Tuesday, March 1st. – A lady who wished to write a palmistry column for *Woman* read my hands. She was very accurate in describing my character, and told me several facts about my past. She said that I should live long, make money, and enjoy much domestic happiness; that Friday was a lucky day for me; that I should marry 'soon', but not till after some difficulty as regards the lady had been smoothed over; that I should have a prescience of coming disaster or good fortune. Also – most remarkable – that I had not long since suffered a shock through some female relative. She seemed a clever and capable woman, and it was difficult for me not to believe that her predictions had [not] some reasonable foundation. She gave me some particulars, marvellous enough, about the healing of nervous diseases by will-power, in which subject she is interested, and invited me to investigate one case.

Saturday, March 12th. – On my way to seeing Mrs L. [who had a 'cure' for stammering] I called at a bread-shop in Holborn. To judge from the exterior one could desire no place of refreshment more fastidiously neat and dainty. But when I was inside I found the shop and the room at the back occupied by women and girls in various conditions of *déshabillé*. The place was being cleaned, and the hour being only 11 a.m. customers were clearly not expected. The girls all looked up surprised, and with a show of indifference I picked my way amongst kneeling figures into the inner room. When I had sat down, I heard a rummaging noise under the table, and presently a fat young girl appeared therefrom. She hurried away laughing, but came back shortly and produced from under the table a tin bowl of dirty water which she carried away, with a giggle. I ordered a glass of milk and a sandwich, and then waited. A girl, tall, thin and vacuous, ran upstairs and came down soon afterwards pinning on an apron at the back. She brought me my food. I ate it, while looking at a dirty newspaper placed to protect the newly-washed floor, and at the crimson petticoat showing through the placket-hole of a girl who was washing the floor behind the counter. I could feel about me the atmosphere of femininity. The dirt and untidiness spoilt the taste of my food, and I thought: 'This is a bad omen for the result of my interview with Mrs L.'

The room into which I was shown in Gower Street was, I think, the ugliest, the most *banal* I have seen. From the twisted columns of the furniture to the green rep of the upholstering, everything expressed Bloomsbury in its highest power. This was a boarding-house. My hopes sank, and they were not raised by the appearance of Mrs L. who combines the profession of a landlady with that of a 'mental healer'. She looks the typical landlady, shabbily dressed, middle-aged, and with that hardened, permanently soured expression of eyes and lips which all landladies seem to acquire. She fitted with and completed the room.

She asked me about my stammering and my health generally, talking in a quiet, firm, authoritative voice. I noticed the fatigue of her drooping eyelids and the terrific firmness of her thin lips. She told me how she had been cured of nervousness by Dr Patterson of America, and gave a number of instances of his success and her own in 'mentally treating' nervous and physical disorders. Some of them were so incredible that I asked myself what I, notorious as a sane level-headed man, was doing in that galley. However, as Mrs L. talked I was rather impressed by her sincerity, her strong quietude, and her sagacity. I asked what the patient had to do. 'Nothing,' she said. I explained my attitude towards 'mental healing' – that I neither believed nor disbelieved in it, that certainly I could not promise her the assistance of my 'faith'.

'Can you cure me of my stammering?'

'I am quite sure I can,' she answered with quiet assurance, 'but it will take some time. This is a case of a lifelong habit, not of a passing ailment.'

'Shall you want to see me often?'

'I shall not want to see you at all; but if you feel that you want to see me, of course you can do so. I shall look after your general health too. If you have a bad headache, or a liver attack, send me a word and I will help you.'

I nodded acquiescence but I was nearly laughing aloud, and telling her that I preferred to dispense with these mysterious services. As I was arranging terms with her, I marvelled that I should be assisting at such an interview. And yet – supposing there were after all something in it! I was not without hope. She had distinctly impressed me, especially by odd phrases here and there which seemed to indicate a certain depth of character in her. I went away smiling – half believing that the whole business was a clever fraud, and half expecting some happy result.

To-night I sent her a cheque. I wondered, as I wrote it out, whether twelve months hence I should be wanting to burn these pages which recorded my credulity, or whether with all the enthusiasm of my nature I should be spreading abroad the report of Mrs L's powers.

Tuesday, May 10th. – Phillpotts, who has just finished a novel, *The Children of the Mist*, told me that his publisher was moaning about the length of it – 180,000 words. He said that he had cut a lot out of the typewritten copy, and should probably cut more from the slip proofs. He appeared to see nothing extraordinary in this. To me it was very extraordinary. Having finished a novel I could not cut it down, because I should have satisfied myself that it contained nothing inessential. Phillpotts admitted that he was uncertain whether some parts of the book were not redundant. If I cut out I should be obliged to rewrite. The notion that anything can be taken from a finished work of art without leaving a gap seems to me monstrous.

Sunday, May 15th. – It occurred to me that the reason of Nietzsche's defection from Wagner was that he expected a different kind of beauty in the *Ring* from what he found there. Only that. The philosophic account of the defection could have amounted to nothing but that. The worst of critics is that they will not allow artists to choose their own kind of beauty. Those critics are excessively rare who have learnt that the kind of beauty is immaterial, and who have had the wit and restraint not to pledge themselves to any particular kind. Critics who *have* so pledged themselves, and who are excellent critics of their chosen kind of beauty, are common enough.

Thursday, June 9th. – While reading George Moore's new novel *Evelyn Innes*, I was struck by the magnificence of the career of a *prima donna* as a theme for fiction. In Moore's book the vocal side of the *prima donna*, her triumphs etc., is scarcely more than incidental. I would make it central. There is nothing more marvellous, more all-compelling, more inscrutable in the world than a great soprano voice. And the emotions of the *prima donna* in the hour when she dominates her audience must be unique. Probably I shall never be able to write such a novel – from lack of material. But if I could wander about Covent Garden stage during a season, and could have a few afternoon teas with a *prima donna*, I would attempt the book.

The old age of the *prima donna* and her death might make a superbly cruel contrast to the rest of the story – astringent, chilling, unbearably hopeless and bitter with reminiscence.

Saturday, June 11th. – Aunt Longson said to Tertia: 'I can't do with young A—. The very day after his father died suddenly of heart disease, he was going his father's rounds in a cab, and he stopped at a house opposite us, and as he was getting into the cab again – you know it was Sunday – I saw him buy a *Pink Un*, a *Sporting Times*! Now, Tertia, should *you* like to be attended by a young man who bought the *Pink Un* in the street the day after his father's death – and Sunday too?'

Friday, June 24th. – When Lewis Hind gave me George Moore's *Evelyn Innes* to review for the *Academy* I was careful to explain to him my attitude of admiration towards George Moore, and he told me to write exactly what I thought, without considering him. He explicitly gave me *carte blanche*. For once, therefore, I *expressed myself* as regards fiction in general and George Moore in particular. I sent in the article 11 days ago. To-day Hind writes me that 'while fully acknowledging the excellence' of the article he will not use it, though he will pay for it! The timidity of people in the matter of George Moore's work is almost incredible. My article was indeed an excellent one, and I was intensely annoyed that it should be lost to the public. For the sake of English fiction such articles are sadly needed.

Monday, September 12th. – Partly owing to the influence of Phillpotts, I have decided very seriously to take up fiction for a livelihood. A certain chronic poverty had forced upon me the fact that I was giving no attention to money-making, beyond my editorship, and so the resolution came about. Till the end of 1899 I propose to give myself absolutely to writing the sort of fiction that sells itself. My serious novel *Anna Tellwright* with which I have made some progress is put aside indefinitely – or rather until I have seen what I can do. To write popular fiction is offensive to me, but it is far more agreeable than being tied daily to an office and editing a lady's paper; and perhaps it is less ignoble, and less of a strain on the conscience. To edit a lady's paper, even a relatively advanced one, is to foster conventionality and hinder progress regularly once a week. Moreover I think that fiction will pay better, and in order to be happy I must have a fair supply of money.

Also I have decided very seriously to aim at living in the country, to the entire abandonment of London. A year ago I could not have contemplated the idea of leaving London, but I have developed since then.

·1899·

Sunday, January 1st. – During the last quarter of 1898 I produced about twice as much work as in any previous similar period. I wrote two-thirds of a serial story, four or five short stories, a lot of reviews for the *Academy*, and all my usual stuff for *Woman* and *Hearth and Home*.

Mrs Kennerley was here to-day to have tea with Ma. She said, speaking of the diseases of children: 'We never used to *think* of having the doctor for measles. I had all my children down at once. We kept them in the sitting-room during the day, and carried them upstairs at night. They went on quite well. It is different now. People seem to be more afraid, but we never used to *think* of the doctor in those days.'

'Those days' would be 15 or 16 years ago.

Monday, January 2nd. – If I gained nothing else last year, I gained facility. In the writing of sensational fiction I made great strides during the last few months, and with ordinary luck I could now turn out a complete instalment (about 4,000 words) after 3 o'clock in an afternoon. For critical work too, I have become much faster and more adroit.

Tuesday, January 3rd. – At the Burne-Jones Exhibition. The sight of Burne-Jones's aloofness, of his continual preoccupation with the spiritual, to the ignoring of everyday facts, served to complete in me a modification of view which has been proceeding now for a year or two. The day of my enthusiasm for 'realism', for 'naturalism', has passed. I can perceive that a modern work of fiction dealing with modern life may ignore realism and yet be great. To find beauty, which is always hidden; that is the aim. If beauty is found, then superficial facts are of small importance. But they are of *some* importance. And although I concede that in the past I have attached too high a value to realism, nevertheless I see no reason why it should be dispensed with. My desire is to depict the deeper beauty while abiding by the envelope of facts. At the worst, the facts should not be ignored. They might, for the sake of more clearly disclosing the beauty, suffer a certain *distortion* – I can't think of a better word. Indeed they cannot be ignored in the future. The achievements of the finest French writers, with Turgenev and Tolstoy, have set a standard for all coming masters of fiction.

What the artist has to grasp is that there is no such thing as ugliness in the world. This I believe to be true, but perhaps the saying would sound less difficult in another form: All ugliness has an aspect of beauty. The business of the artist is to find that aspect.

Thursday, January 5th. – You can find a certain wide romance even in the January Sales at the draper's shop. My mother bought some very large unbleached linen sheets to-day for our cottage at Milford. They cost 1s. 11½d. each, and are 3¾ yards in length. She was told that these sheets are woven by Russian peasants by hand. They are sold to the French War Office, used during the annual military manoeuvres, and after the wear of a month or so, are sold by the French Government to English traders. So it comes that I may sleep between linen that has passed through the hands of the most miserable and unhappy people in Europe – Russian peasants and French conscripts.

Friday, January 6th. – To-day during breakfast, I happened to collect some ideas for that book on modern fiction which I am to do when I have time. I would call it *Our Novelists*. There would be chapters on 'conscious pleasure in technique', which was apparently unknown to the earlier generation; illiteracy among our leading writers; the real position of Dickens, Thackeray, George Eliot and others whom everyone has (ridiculously) agreed are above criticism; Turgenev, and the relation of English to continental fiction; the courageous exploitation of the author's personality in fiction, with special reference to George Moore; an essay on Eden Phillpotts, the greatest of our younger writers, yet very imperfectly recognized at present; the conjuncture of realism with idealism.

Tuesday, January 24th. – Last night I finished my sensational novel, *The Curse of Love* [*For Love and Life*; in book form *The Ghost*], 50,000 words in exactly three months, with all my other work. The writing of it has enormously increased my facility, and I believe that now I could do a similar novel in a month. It is, of the kind, good stuff, well written and well contrived, and some of the later chapters are really imagined and, in a way, lyrical. I found the business, after I had got fairly into it, easy enough, and I rather enjoyed it. I could comfortably write 2,500 words in half a day. It has only been written once, and on revision I have scarcely touched the original draft. Now I want to do two short sensational stories – and then to my big novel.

Friday, January 27th. – A few nights ago – we had been to the Empire, Sharpe, Mater, Sep and I – there was a gale. In the usual midnight altercation at Piccadilly Circus for the inside seats of omnibuses we had suffered defeat; we sat on the inclement top of the vehicle, a disconsolate row of four, cowering behind the waterproof aprons (which were not waterproof), and exchanging fragments of pessimistic philosophy.

We knew we were taking cold; at first we were annoyed, but with increasing numbness came resignation. We grew calm enough to take an interest in the imperturbable driver, who nonchalantly and with perfect technique steered his dogged horses through the tortuous mazes of traffic, never speaking, never stirring, only answering like an automaton to the conductor's bell. Some drivers will gossip, but this one had apparently his own preoccupations. We could see only his hat, some grey hairs, his rotund cape, and his enormous gloved hands, and perhaps we began to wonder what sort of man he was. For mile after mile he drove forward in a Trappist silence till we were verging upon Putney, and the rain-washed thoroughfares reflected only the gaslights and the forbidding façades of the houses. Then at last, but without moving his head, he suddenly joined the conversation.

'I've been out in worse,' he said. 'Yes, we gets used to it.

But we gets so that we *has* to live out of doors. If I got a indoor job I should die. I have to go out for a walk afore I can eat my breakfast.'

A pause, and then:

'I've driven these roads for eight-and-twenty year, and the only pal I've found is Cod Liver Oil. From September to March I takes it, and I never has rheumatism and I never has colds nor nothing o' that sort. I give it my children ever since they was born, and now I'm blest if they don't cry for it.'

He finished; he had imparted his wisdom, delivered his message, and with the fine instinct denied to so many literary artists, he knew when to be silent. We asked him to stop, and he did so without a word. 'Good night,' we said; but he had done with speech for that evening, and gave us no reply. We alighted. The bus rolled away into the mirror-like vista of the street.

Saturday, January 28th. – The hypnotized audience, crowded tier above tier of the dark theatre, held itself strained and intent in its anxiety not to miss one gyration, one least movement, of the great dancer – that dancer who had enslaved not only New York and St Petersburg but Paris itself. Swaying incorporeal, as it were within a fluent dazzling envelope of endless drapery, she revealed to them new and more disturbing visions of beauty in the union of colour and motion. She hid herself in a labyrinth of curves which was also a tremor of strange tints, a tantalizing veil, a mist of iridescent light. Gradually her form emerged from the riddle, triumphant, provocative, and for an instant she rested like an incredible living jewel in the deep gloom of the stage. Then she was blotted out, and the defeated eye sought in vain to penetrate the blackness where but now she had been. . . .

It was a marvellous and enchanting performance. Even the glare of the electric clusters and the gross plush of the descending curtain could not rob us all at once of the sense of far-off immaterial things which it had evoked in our hearts. We applauded with fury, with frenzy; we besieged the floor with sticks and heels, and clapped till our arms ached. . . . At length she came before the footlights, and bowed and smiled and kissed her hands. We could see she was a woman of thirty or more, rather short, not beautiful. But what dominion in the face, what assurance of supreme power! It was the face of one surfeited with adoration, cloyed with praise.

While she was humouring us with her fatigued imperial smiles, I happened to look at a glazed door separating the auditorium from the corridor. There, pressed against the glass, was another face, the face of a barmaid, who, drawn from her counter by the rumour of this wonderful novelty, had crept down to get a glimpse of the star's triumph.

Of course I was struck by the obvious contrast between these two creatures. In a moment the barmaid had departed, but the wistfulness of her gaze remained with me as I listened to legends of the dancer – her whims, her diamonds, her extravagances, her tyrannies, her wealth. I could not banish that pale face; I could not withhold from it my sentimental pity.

Later, I went up into the immense gold refectory. Entrenched behind a magnificent counter of carved cedar flanked on either side by mirrors and the neat apparatus of bottles and bon-bons, the barmaid stood negligently at ease, her cheek resting in the palm of one small hand as she leaned on the counter. I noticed that she had the feeble prettiness, the voluptuous figure, the tight black bodice inexorably demanded of barmaids. In front of her were three rakish youths whom I guessed to be of the fringe of journalism and the stage. They talked low to her as they sipped their liqueurs, frankly admiring, frankly enjoying this brief intimacy. As for her, confident of her charms, she was distantly gracious; she offered a smile with a full sense of its value; she permitted; she endured. These youths were to understand that such adulation was to her an everyday affair.

In the accustomed exercise of assured power her face had lost its wistfulness, it was the satiated face of the dancer over again, and so I ventured quietly to withdraw my sentimental pity.

Wednesday, February 22nd. – To-day Tillotsons offered me £60 for the serial rights of *For Love and Life*. I have asked them for £80, but £60 was the price I had myself thought of.

Thursday, March 2nd. – I accepted £75 from Tillotsons for the serial, and have adopted the pseudonym, 'Sampson King'.

Tuesday, April 18th. – I finished the draft of *Anna Tellwright* just before Easter – having written it at the rate of eight or ten thousand words a week – and till that was done I had no leisure for keeping a journal or spare energies for observation. I went home at Easter in order to collect facts useful for the novel, and I got what I wanted. The novel however is to rest till after Whitsuntide. In the meantime I am doing a one act farce, *The Arrival*, and some short stories – one called *Marooned in London*, and a great deal of work for the *Academy*.

As the draft of my novel progressed I got thoroughly interested in it, and I finished it with good hopes of the excellence of the complete thing. It was with difficulty that I resisted the temptation to proceed with the second writing immediately after Easter.

To-day I sat on a Coroner's Jury at Fulham and heard four cases, including one suicide through religious mania. I was struck by several things:

The decency of people in general.

The common sense and highly-trained skill of the coroner.

The dramatic quality of sober fact. In two instances, the deceased persons had died from causes absolutely unconnected with the superficial symptoms. Thus a woman who had brought on a miscarriage and died, had died from heart disease.

The sinister influence of the ugliness amid which the lower classes carry on their lives.

The enormous (as it were) underground activity of the various charitable and philanthropic agencies which spread themselves like a network over London. It would seem that nothing could happen, among a certain class of society, without the cognizance of some philanthropic agency.

The dullness and the conscientiousness of a jury.

The absolute thoroughness with which suspicious deaths are inquired into.

Tuesday, May 30th. – I went to the Ysaye concert this afternoon. Ysaye, aged apparently about 45, has the unkempt, bleary look of a well-seasoned music-hall comedian. From my distance, I could not detect any sign of distinction in his head or face. His hair was neither long nor short; there were queer little locks, over the ears, which waved constantly to and fro as he played. To me he was the greatest of all violinists.

Balzac thoroughly enjoyed building up the social atmosphere of a place – and taking his full time over the business. Witness *Ursule Mirouet*, in which a third and more of the book is 'preparation'. *The Country Doctor* contains, strictly speaking, no 'story'; the sole concern is a change of atmosphere.

Monday, July 3rd. – The *Academy* sent me the MS. of an article by Elizabeth Robins on Ibsen, to which I am to write a companion article. I was struck by the lack of 'literari-ness' which the MS. disclosed: large, slow caligraphy, uncertainty in spelling and punctuation, and a hundred little things which mark the beginner. Yet she has written several books, one of them quite first rate and notable.

I have bought the hundred books which Bells allow you to select from the six hundred volumes of Bohn's Libraries. They stand in a long beautiful row, houseless on the top of my shelves. Arriving late last night from Witley, eager to view them – they had been delivered in my absence – I cut several of them and looked through Juvenal, Suetonius, and da Vinci. I found that the celebrated and marvellous passage in Beaumont and Fletcher's *Philaster*, about marrying 'a mountain girl', in which occur lines

> And bear at her big breasts
> My large coarse issue

must certainly be based on a passage in Juvenal's Sixth Satire.

To-day I began to read Benvenuto Cellini. He seems to have

been less absolutely reprobate than I had imagined. The mark of the truly great man is on every page. I was enchanted with a phrase attributed to Benvenuto's father. Benvenuto was in trouble with the magistrates, and his father was defending him with moral support. 'My father, in answer to these menaces, said, "You will do what God permits you, and nothing more." The magistrate replied that nothing could be more certain than that God had thus ordered matters. My father then said boldly to him, *"My comfort is that you are a stranger to the decrees of Providence!"* '

Thursday, August 10th. – I have just remembered a saying of Mrs Dunmer, our new housekeeper at Witley. She said to me: 'There's a lot of old maids in this village, sir, as wants men. There was three of 'em after a curate as we had here, a very nice young gentleman he was, sir. No matter how often the church was opened those women would be there, sir, even if it was five times a day. It's a sign of a hard winter, sir, when the hay begins to run after the horse.'

Monday, August 21st. – I rode up from Witley to Hindhead with Ravenshaw on his motor-car. He said that he did not have pneumatic tyres on his wheels because a set cost £40 and would only last 3,000 miles. The cost for tyres alone would therefore be over 3*d.* per mile. In 20 years this fact will acquire quaintness.

Tuesday, August 22nd. – Finished *Memoirs of Cellini.* What it leaves most clearly on my mind is an impression of the intense interest which princes and people showed in the fine arts in the sixteenth century. Of course Cellini sees nothing extra-ordinary in this interest.

Wednesday, October 18th. – To-day I made an arrangement with Bayly by which I am only to attend at the office four half days and one whole day in the week. As I never count office work as real work, this means that I can do five full days of my own work at home, excluding Sunday. It is a great stroke of business, well managed by me, and I feel like a man suddenly enriched who is not quite ready with a scheme for spending. I hope to devote at least three whole days a week to *Anna Tellwright* and to resume this Journal with regularity. I shall cease now to work at such high pressure as I have been driving at during the last six months.

Saturday, October 21st. – This morning, leisurely reading up for a 3,000-word article with which I am to celebrate for the *Academy* the approaching completion of Mrs Garnett's translation of the works of Turgenev, I spent four hours in what seemed to me almost an ideal way. I was not hurried; I had books heaped about me; and I allowed ideas slowly to germinate in my head. It was calmer, less exciting than creative composition. To-night, for a change, I composed the crudest funny song which Marriott is to sing at Christmas to make us laugh at Burslem – a lyric about Sissie's baby.

Tuesday, October 24th. – Richter Concert. I sat in the orchestra, between the kettle-drums and the side-drum. You can't be too close to an orchestra. The sound is quite different, more voluptuous, more significant, when you are in the middle of it. Everything takes on a new aspect. The orchestra becomes a set of individuals delicately inter-related, instead of one huge machine.

Richter has all the air of a great man. He seems to exist in an inner world of his own, from which, however, he can recall himself instantly at will. He shows perfect confidence in his orchestra, and guides them by little intimate signs, hints, suggestions. When pleased he shows it in a gay half-childlike manner; smiling, nodding and a curious short wave of the fore-arm from the elbow. Having started his men, he allowed them to go through the second movement of Tchaikowsky's *Pathétique* Symphony without conducting at all (I understand this is his custom with this movement). They played it superbly. At the end he clapped delightedly, and then turned to the audience with a large gesture of the arms to indicate that really he had nothing to do with that affair.

Sunday, November 5th. – I have now decided, acting on Phillpotts's advice, to write a short story *every* month. I finished my November story this morning: 'The Phantom Sneeze,' a humorous ghost tale, 4,500 words.

Tuesday, November 7th. – Yesterday and to-day I have been reading through the draft of *Anna Tellwright*. It came fresh to me. Some involutions of the plot I had quite forgotten. On the whole I was pleased with it. Much of it impressed me to a surprising extent, but the end will have to be approached more slowly; it needs to be 'prepared'; and when it comes it must be described with much greater detail.

I tried very hard to make a satisfactory beginning of the final writing of *Anna Tellwright* this afternoon, and could do absolutely nothing, couldn't get a sentence that wasn't drivel.

Friday, November 10th. – After cogitating off and on all through the night I decided upon what will probably be the first sentence of my novel: 'Bursley, the ancient home of the potter, has an antiquity of a thousand years' – and also upon the arrangement of the first long paragraph describing the Potteries.

This evening, at his request, I called to 'have a chat' with Cyril Maude at the Haymarket Theatre. I saw him in his dressing-room, a small place with the walls all sketched over by popular artists. Round the room was a dado-border of prints of Nicholson's animal drawings. Although the curtain would not rise for over half an hour Maude was made-up and dressed. He was very kind and goodnatured about my one-act play *The Stepmother*, without overflowing into that gush which nearly all actors give off on all occasions of politeness. He said that he and Harrison would certainly consider seriously any 3 or 4 act play of mine. He advised me against doing any more curtain-raisers. He suggested that any man, not perfectly familiar with the stage, who wished to write a play, should study Dumas and – Boucicault.

Speaking of Phillpotts, he asked me if he was doing well.

'Very well indeed for a novelist,' I said, 'but a novelist never makes much money compared with you folks.'

'Except,' interrupted Maude, 'when he writes a good play. I have a vivid recollection of sending Barrie a cheque for over £1,000 for the first six weeks of the provincial tour of *The Little Minister*.'

As I was leaving, he said: 'Shall you begin the play at once?'

'I can't,' I said; 'I've too much on hand, but I shall do it within a year from now. Good-bye.'

'And let us see it?' he called out anxiously. If it was acting it was incredibly fine acting. If it wasn't, he is really anxious to consider a piece of mine.

'Rather!' I replied, 'I should think so – after your kindness.'

Sunday, December 24th. – Thomas Arrowsmith called on John Beardmore for a subscription to the Burslem Wesleyan Chapel. Beardmore declined to contribute, and explained how he was losing money on all hands and had in fact had a very bad year. He went to such lengths of pessimism that Arrowsmith at last interrupted:

'If things are so bad as that, Mr Beardmore,' he said, 'we'll have a word of prayer,' and without an instant's hesitation he fell on his knees.

Beardmore began to stamp up and down the room.

'None o' that nonsense,' he shouted. 'None o' that nonsense. Here's half a sovereign for ye.'

Sunday, December 31st. – This year I have written 335,340 words, grand total. 228 articles and stories (including 4 instalments of a serial of 30,000 – 7,500 words each) have actually been published.

Also my book of plays – *Polite Farces*.

I have written six or eight short stories not yet published or sold.

Also the greater part of 55,000 word serial – 'Love and Life' – for Tillotsons, which begins publication about April next year.

Also the whole draft (80,000 words) of my Staffordshire novel *Anna Tellwright*.

My total earnings were £592 3s. 1d., of which sum I have yet to receive £72 10s.

Tuesday, January 9th. – I finished Balzac's *A Second Home* in the middle of last night, being sleepless, and thought it among his very best short stories, though absurd here and there with its Byronic flavours – 'The Stranger', 'The Unknown', and the whole attitude of Roger de Granville towards his mistress. The last two pages are great – a superb example of Balzac's instinctive knowledge of how to leave out everything but essentials. The relations between the Comte and his children are not explained at all, but the first words between father and son in the former's room explain what these relations have been in an instant. ... One phrase struck me as comic: 'The babe awoke and craved its limpid nourishment.'

Sunday, March 4th. – At the musical evening at Marriott's last night, Sharpe led a great demonstration of patriotism, apropos of Ladysmith: – flag-waving, portrait of Buller, reading aloud of a leading article from the *Telegraph*, cheering, singing of *Rule Britannia*. It was distinctly an exhibition of insularity. I must say that I have been quite unable to join with any sincerity in the frantic and hysterical outburst of patriotic enthusiasm of the last few days. Such praise of ourselves as a nation, such gorgeous self-satisfaction and boastfulness are to me painful.

Tuesday, April 10th. – I discussed with the Pater last night the advisability of my leaving *Woman*. He was thoroughly in favour of my doing so, and the stroke was then and there finally decided.

Tuesday, January 1st. – Last year I wrote three plays.

The Postmistress (1 act).

Children of the Mist (4 acts – in collaboration with Eden Phillpotts).

The Chancellor (4 acts – in collaboration with Arthur Hooley).

Also a serial *The Grand Babylon Hotel,* of 70,000 words.

Also the draft of my Staffordshire novel, *Anna Tellwright,* 80,000 words, and part of the final writing.

Also half a dozen short stories.

I also wrote and published 196 articles of various length.

I also collected, revised, and wrote a preface for a series of my articles from the *Academy,* to be called *Fame and Fiction, an inquiry into certain popularities.*

I also edited *Woman* till 30th Sept. – when I resigned, and came to live in the country with Pater, Mater, and Tertia.

I also advised Pearsons on 50 MSS. books.

From April till the third week in December I was working almost continuously at very high pressure, and had no energy to spare for this journal. Since I came here I wrote both *Children of the Mist* and *The Chancellor* in collaboration; and I was, moreover, very much preoccupied and fretted in the superintendence of the repairs to this house.

On the completion of *The Chancellor,* I vowed never again to work so hard, but in future to find time to read poetry regularly, to gather materials for a work on the fiction of nineteenth century, and – ? – to study Latin.

Friday, January 18th. – Last night I read and re-read a lot of Dr John Brown's *Horae Subsecivae,* and was much impressed by it. The pictures of Scottish character give one to see why the Scots prevail everywhere; and what a number of great men there are in the world who never achieve wide fame. The 'Letter to Dr Cairns' is one of the best biographical sketches

I have ever read; the records in it of fine scholarship in humble places are amazing, and humiliating to one who has been forced into the habit of taking seriously the facile reputations of literary London. Dr Brown himself was a passably big man, but his father, grandfather, great-grandfather, uncle and great-uncle were at least as big, if not bigger. He is the best known of all the family, by reason of these essays and sketches which have been popular for 30 or 40 years, but perhaps he marks the beginning of the decline of a great family; he was a light *littérateur*, an amuser and diverter.

What a difference between that and his father's immense and erudite work *On Civil Obedience* – of which I had never heard before!

With the history of the Browns fresh in my mind this morning, I was able to estimate at its proper unimportance the circular which the *Graphic* people have issued about my serial *The Grand Babylon Hotel*, to appear in the *Golden Penny*, which they sent me this morning, and which in a whirl of adjectives describes the thing as 'the most original, amusing and thrilling' serial written this decade – the best thing of the sort since *The Mystery of a Hansom Cab*. Fancy writing a story as good as *The Mystery of a Hansom Cab*!

Tuesday, February 26th. – The latter half of *The Queen's Necklace* is one of the finest examples of Dumas's skill, supreme skill, in handling a purely artificial intrigue. The complexity of it is only equalled by its perfect clearness, its diversity only by its unity and coherence. Beginning with a Dromio-like similarity of face between Marie Antoinette and a country girl of loose morals, he gradually builds up a dazzling erection of misunderstanding, and, what is more, his sheer creative power is such that he forces you to believe in the gigantic impossibility.

I have been reading Gaboriau's *Lecoq* and its sequel (which is not a sequel but the solution of the problem) for the *Academy*. It struck me as among the best of all detective stories. And the sequel had a touch of Dumas at his most melodramatic and 'plotty'.

Friday, May 17th. – I finished *Anna Tellwright* [*Anna of the Five Towns*] this morning at 2.45 a.m., after 17 hours' continuous work, save for meals, on the last 5,000 words. I was very pleased with it; slept well for 4 hours, got up with a frightful headache, and cycled through Hemel Hempstead to St Albans, lunched at the George, and home – 42 miles. 'A.T.' is 74,000 in length.

Wednesday, May 22nd. – Rickards and I, in the evening, went over the vast, unfinished Roman Catholic Cathedral in Victoria Street, and found it distinguished, impressive, a work of great and monumental art. Bentley, the architect, was wandering under the dome, examining and enjoying his mighty production, the realization of a conception which must live for many centuries. It was an impressive sight to see him, an impressive thought to think that one has seen him so, this magnificent artist, who started life as a stonemason, and is now slowly dying of cancer on the tongue. He wore a frock-coat and silk hat, but a necktie of black silk tied in a loose bow.

Sunday, May 26th. – Talking about the Potteries with me, Billy Bennett told me that his father had once pointed out to him, that no potting firm, except Wedgwoods, had survived to the third generation. The first generation was of the people, industrial, simple; the second, though raised in the social grade, was still plodding and energetic and kept the business together; the third was a generation of wastrels coming to grief. He said that the usual condemnatory phrase of potters for bad clay was 'Nowt but moss-muck'.

·1903·

Monday, September 28th. – Illustration of the *sans-gêne* of Montmartre. As I was sitting on the terrace of the Café de la Place Blanche, a *voiture* drove up containing two men, two women, and a white puppy. One of the men was clearly an actor or singer of some sort, he had the face and especially the mouth; one of the women, aged perhaps 25, short, getting plump, and dressed with a certain rough style, especially as to the *chic* hat and the *jupon*, was evidently his *petite amie*; the other woman was a servant, *nu-tête*, and wearing a white apron; the other man had no striking characteristic. The two men and the *petite amie* got out and sat near me. The driver turned away.

'Où allez-vous?' the *petite amie* shouted curtly in a hoarse vulgar voice. Whereupon the driver gave a shout of laughter and the servant, who was nursing the puppy, laughed too. 'Oh! Il tourne,' murmured the *petite amie*, grimly enjoying the joke at her expense. The driver was only turning round to a quiet corner where he might wait without impeding the traffic. Having drawn up his vehicle, he got down and sat in the carriage and produced a coloured comic paper, and shared his amusement over it with the servant. From time to time the *petite amie* from her table shouted remarks to the servant.

Afterwards, I dined with the Schwobs [Marcel Schwob was a critic and translator of Shakespeare's *Hamlet* for Sarah Bernhardt]. First night of Jean Aicard's drama in verse, *La Légende du Cœur*, at the Théâtre Sarah Bernhardt in which Mme Schwob [Marguerite Moréno] plays the hero-troubadour. Schwob ill and very pale and extremely gloomy and depressed. Neither of them could eat and each grumbled at the other for not eating. Before dinner Schwob had described to me the fearful depression of spirit accompanied by inability to work, which has held him for several months. Every morning he got up feeling, 'Well, another day, and I can do nothing, I have nothing to look forward to, no future.' And speaking of my novel, *Leonora*, he said: 'You have got hold of the greatest of all themes, the agony of the older generation in watching the rise of the younger.' Yet he is probably not 40.

Tuesday, September 29th. – Last night, in talking of Kipling's literary power, Marcel Schwob said that an artist could not do as he liked with his imagination; it would not stand improper treatment, undue fatigue etc. in youth; and that a man who wrote many short stories early in life (Schwob seemed to think short-story-writing very exhausting to the imaginative power) was bound to decay prematurely. He said that he himself was going through this experience. He was in a very black and despondent mood when he said this. The observation seemed to me to be interesting, but it did not convince me.

Thursday, October 1st. – *Leonora* appeared, my tenth book, and my fifth published novel. But Chatto has two novels in hand, *Love and Life* and *Teresa*, which, I hope, never will be published.

Sunday, October 4th. – In the afternoon Schwob called unexpectedly. We went up to the Moulin de la Galette, which he said was the last genuine *bal* of the lower classes left in Paris, and even that genuine only on Sunday afternoons. In the evenings it was the resort of whores like the other *bals*. A tremendous climb (we had a difficulty in getting a driver to take us). Inside: stuffy. All the walls seemed to be covered with trellis work on which creepers grew very sparsely. Crowded dancing hall, with a sort of aisle for drinking on either side. The *monde ouvrier* was certainly there, dancing clumsily and perspiringly, and colliding with itself. Not nearly so graceful as the Bal Bullier. Band very brassy. Schwob said there were plenty of scoundrels – *maquereaux*, thieves, *apaches*, till-robbers etc. but I doubt it. The company looked innocent on the whole, though I thought I saw a few wrong 'uns (men). Afterwards we climbed up into the garden, and I saw the old wooden windmill (with its date 1295) garlanded with electric light apparatus. A solitary gendarme up there was glad to talk to Schwob. He began by saying that the weather was turning colder; he did not disguise that he was bored, but 'On est tranquille,' he said, shrugging his shoulders. He was a rather cynical philosopher, and referred slightingly to the clients of the *moulin*, and dashed the respectability of the women with a single grimace. But when the cakewalk began he descended part of the stairs to get a glimpse of it.

Monday, October 5th. – You can divide the restaurants of Paris, roughly, into two classes, those where the customers eat to live, and those where the customers eat to enjoy themselves. The Duvals are the great type of the former. Everything is stern, business-like, sharp, and no extra-food luxuries at all. In the second class there is always leisure, and the waiters seem to be in a charming conspiracy to anticipate your wishes, and everything is done for you (quite apart from eating) that you could desire. In a word, the attitude of the restaurant to its customer is: 'You are here to enjoy yourself. Do so. Command us in anything. We will do all we can to produce an atmosphere of gaiety.'

Wednesday, October 14th. – We went to see *Faust* at the Opéra. A performance exquisitely free from any sort of distinction. But between the acts, from the balcony, we had amazingly good views of the illumination of the Avenue de l'Opéra for the King and Queen of Italy. It was only a trial illumination and was 'out' at 11 p.m. I noted the effect of the masts lighted perpendicularly. The only part of the Opéra that we enjoyed was the ballet. I noted the business-like air and habits of the *corps de ballet*; how they calmly tested shoes and hair in the middle of the stage; and the enormous potential activity of their legs – strong, muscular, and elegant, but not exactly pretty, animals. And how the whole 'convention' of the piece was changed, and cleared of all sentimentality and make-believe, and sickliness, while the ballet lasted. As if the corps said: 'Now understand, no mistake, no pretence, this is a ballet and nothing else, a thing by itself, complete in itself, and we shall execute it regardless of everything except the rules and conventions of the ballet. You must forget *Faust* for a while.' I was much struck with this.

Monday, October 19th. – Yesterday there were two alarms of fire (false) at French theatres. The Opéra Comique and the Français. A reporter of the *Debâts* stated that, at the latter, nearly everyone ran for the doors, and that when they came back some were still *tout émues*. One lady was sure that the auditorium was full of smoke. 'Can't you see it, Monsieur?' she said to him. 'You can see it very well.' Another had *seen* flames round the chandelier. Yet there had been no fire at all. The alarm had been caused thus: A spectator, feeling ill, had gone out into the *couloir* of the fourth gallery to take the air. He fainted, fell against the door of a *loge*, and the door being forced open had upset some chairs.

Tuesday, October 20th. – Talking about wages in Paris, C. said that everyone was badly paid and that everyone was 'on the make'. She told me that when she was in the chorus at the Variétés, the fines were simply an organized swindle by the *régisseur* at the expense of the choristers. Fines were levied for the most absurd trifles, and her month's bill for fines would sometimes amount to 30 francs, out of a total of 90 francs wages.

I began to read Boswell again, sixth vol. and couldn't leave it. I also read two acts of Donnay's *L'Autre Danger*, and was surprised at the absence of technical or verbal pretentiousness in it, and to find that it did not move entirely in circles of the greatest wealth. I was impressed by its simplicity and sincerity, and perhaps also by a certain stiffness in the working of the first act. *Two* chance meetings of old friends separated for years seems rather too much of an allowance for one act.

Wednesday, October 21st. – In the reviews of *Leonora*, what strikes me most is the inability of the reviewers to perceive that the life therein described (with its 'meat teas' – which they always fasten on to) is no more vulgar than any other sort of life. The *Scotsman* says: 'The smug prosperity of the home, with its six-o'clock "meat-teas" and its subservient attitude to the blustering head of the house.' As if that kind of thing was not tremendously prevalent everywhere in England and Scotland. No, what really abrades them is not the life described but what the *Scotsman* calls 'the fearless strength of description' of it.

C. told me that, by an order of police, gas was forbidden on the stage in Paris. All lighting must be done by electricity. Also that there was a decree against cigarettes or matches in the dressing-rooms. When I told her that I had seen smoking in dressing-rooms, she said: 'Oh, yes, of course. Everyone does it. But there is an official search of all dressing-rooms etc., once a month by the firemen, and before that, an attendant comes round and says to the artists: "Kindly hide your matches etc., as the pompiers will be here directly." ' The extraordinary humour of this did not seem to occur to her. 'C'est bien Parisien, ça!' I said, and she cynically and bitterly agreed that it was. But she could not see the joke.

Saturday, October 24th. – I could not work to-day. I think I find my nerves more sensitive every day, really. I wish letters came just before dinner instead of just after breakfast; then they could not interfere with and disarrange the general 'lay' of one's thoughts for the day's work.

Sunday, October 25th. – Schwob had been reading G. B. Shaw's plays, and broke out into invective against Shaw and all his works. He could see nothing in them at all. He said he could see what *we* saw and took for *esprit*, and what to us *was esprit*, but to the French mind it was nothing but foolishness. He denied that the characters had any reality, even the reality of fantasy, and said that Barrie's plays were much better. I was much inclined to agree with him, but then I always find French criticism of English work very instructive, disconcerting, and tonic.

Tuesday, October 27th. – I worked very late again, though with an incipient headache, and much dissatisfaction with the work done. You may perceive intellectually that a sensational story may also be artistic, but it does not follow that you can sit down and produce the thing, unless you have a natural bent for it. I have been under the mistaken idea that, because I saw the possibility of it being done, therefore I could do it.

Tuesday, November 3rd. – I was told to-day that, as I thought, the most distinguished of the music-hall *cocottes* went to the Casino de Paris; and also that they did business comparatively infrequently, but what they did was very remunerative. This latter statement I regarded with suspicion, as also the following: That a particular woman, tall, very distinguished, and well-dressed and well-jewelled, whom I had often admired in various resorts, had an absolute minimum of 250 francs. It seems she goes about in a pair-horse carriage in the evening, by some sort of arrangement with the coachman. I was told that many *cocottes* pay their coachmen either partly or wholly in love. This woman, by the way, sometimes brings to the Casino her young child, of 7 or 8 years old perhaps. I have seen them together there, and the effect was certainly effective.

Wednesday, November 4th. – At the Montmartre Fair, now in progress, I was much struck by the charming effect of the roundabout opposite the Moulin Rouge: The machine in full swing, the pigs galloping one way and the ceiling of the machine going the other brilliantly lit by electric light in clusters and in single arc lamps. Two young, fair, and pretty *cocottes* with red lips and white teeth, brilliantly dressed, sitting *sans gêne* in one of the cars, in the full glare, showing well against red velvet cushions of the car, and throwing those peculiarly French coloured paper-streamers into the crowd; these streamers have the effect of fireworks, rockets, in the sky – a line of fire. The whole machine is gradually covered with them, and becomes a sort of cocoon, and they stream round after it in thousands and lie thick in the road.

Thursday, November 5th. – I had a chill, and all day I failed to concentrate my thoughts on my third *Windsor* story. But I had one good idea in the night.

In the afternoon I walked down the whole length of the Fête de Montmartre as far as La Chapelle, and then back on the other side of the road, incidentally inspecting the immense shop of Dufayel. I only saw one episode that interested me – a horse falling down as it turned too sharply from the boulevard into one of the steep streets north. This accident, like many others here, was due to the practice of balancing really large and heavy carts (the cart was loaded with bricks) on two wheels only. The strain on the shaft-horse must sometimes be enormous. The leader had stumbled several times on to his knees in the boulevard, but he got round the corner in safety. It was the shaft-horse that fell. The teamster gave a little fatalistic nod. The horse, after a brief struggle, resigned himself. Of course, a crowd gathered immediately; a busy, interfering, wishful-to-help crowd. I was much struck by the stink of the crowd, the low type of face, the squints, the bulletheads, the misshapen features. The getting up of the horse was mismanaged for a long time; but in the end it was accomplished without injury to the horse or cart. No gendarme appeared until just before the end, and then he stood amiably smiling and watching – an oldish man. At least a dozen men gave active assistance, and dozens gesticulated and shouted advice. It was rather melancholy, this exhibition in the mass of the French *man*'s ineptitude. A crowd of French *women* would have managed it better. I was out an hour and a half, and at the end, as I came in, the noise of the scores of sham orchestras had got fearfully on my nerves.

Sunday, November 8th. To-day I managed to concentrate pretty nearly all day till 9.30 p.m. on my story, and I collected a few decent ideas for it. I saw no one to speak to except my *domestique*, in the morning, and the waitresses at my restaurants. Last thing, I began to read *Don Quixote*.

To-day I spent such a day as ought to satisfy a man of letters. Having done my correspondence, I went out at 10.15 for a walk, and to consider the plot of my story. I strolled about the Quartier de l'Europe till 11.30, and then lunched at my usual restaurant where I am expected, and where my maternal waitress advised me in the selection of my lunch. During lunch I read *Le Journal*. I came home, finished *Le*

Journal, read *Don Quixote* and fell asleep. Then at 1.30, I amused myself on the piano. At 2 I began, in my Bruges chair, to ponder further on my story, and the plot seemed to be coming. At 3.30 I made my afternoon tea, and then read more *Don Quixote*, and fell asleep for about a minute. The plot was now coming faster and faster, and at 5 I decided that I would, at any rate, begin to sketch the story. At 6.45 I had done a complete rough draft of the whole story.

Then I dressed and went to dine at my other restaurant in the Place Blanche, where the food and wine are good, and the waiters perfect models, and the *chasseur* charming, where men bring their mistresses, and where occasionally a 'mistress' dines alone, and where the atmosphere is a curious mixture of discretion and *sans gêne* (the whole place seems to say: 'You should see what fun we have here between midnight and 3 a.m. with our Hungarian music and our improvised dancing, and so on and so on'). I *dined* slowly and well, while reading *Le Temps* and *The Pilot*, and also while watching the human life of the place.

Thursday, November 12th. – *Bostock's Great Animal Arena* at the Hippo. Palace. First night. Vast crowd, very badly controlled. The whole performance consisted of wild-animal tricks. The principal *dompteur* had some exciting moments in the vast cage with lionesses, a tiger, several bears, a hyena, a leopard, two superb dogs, and other animals. When a crisis arrived the Frenchmen around me were as impressed as children. 'Ils ne sont pas commodes', 'Il a du sangfroid! Il a du sangfroid!' And, when their nerves were getting strained, 'Assez! Assez!' in a nervous tone. Some of the crises were apparently somewhat dangerous. During a long bout of opposing wills between the trainer and the tiger, the tiger chewed up a good part of a wooden seat and splintered the gate over which he had to jump. And if, at the end of that bout, the trainer was only acting when he wiped his brow, he was acting very well. At the beginning the crowd was captious and fractious, owing to delays and bad arrangements, but the applause was now tremendous. The performance was really rather out of the way, and I appreciated more than I have done before the charm of danger in a show, real danger.

Saturday, November 14th. – Last night *Le Sire de Vergy*, Variétés, with the 'artistes' Brasseur, Anna Tariol, Claudius, Max Dearly etc., I was extremely disappointed with the whole thing. I found this fashionable theatre (like most of the rest) dirty, dingy, uncomfortable, dear, and badly managed. The first row of the balcony is 12 francs exclusive of booking-fee. Everything began late, and the thing was not over till 12.15. Our seats, 2nd row of balcony (10 francs) were very badly stuffed and very uncomfortable, and there was no room. A boulevard swindle. The orchestra was vile, but for opera bouffe, I found the music really rather good – certainly fresh and clever. It was less the piece than the whole thing that I objected to, the general *sans gêne* and brazenness of the swindle. C. told me that this was quite a theatre apart, a genre of its own, where there was no discipline, except for the chorus-girls. She has performed there. The chorus-girls, at rehearsals, have to wait 1 or 2 hours for the 'artistes', but if they are 5 minutes late – a fine! In the green-room drinks are ordered *ad lib*. Speaking of the lateness of everything, and the long entr'actes, C. said: 'Ici on se moque du public. *On travaille quand on a le temps.*' And she referred me to Zola's *Nana*, and the various places where the public is kept waiting for Nana's pleasure. She said that Zola had given an exact description of the green-room of the Vaudeville, and that he must have studied his scenes from this theatre. How true this is I don't know. But I certainly came away with the impression that I had seen the worst side of *soi-disant* high-class theatrical entertainment in Paris.

Wednesday, November 18th. – Last night, when I went into the Duval for dinner, a middle-aged woman, inordinately stout and with pendent cheeks, had taken the seat opposite to my prescriptive seat. I hesitated, as there were plenty of empty places, but my waitress requested me to take my usual chair. I did so, and immediately thought: 'With *that* thing opposite to me my dinner will be spoilt!' But the woman was evidently also cross at my filling up her table, and she went away, picking up all her belongings, to another part of the restaurant, breathing hard. Then she abandoned her second choice for a third one. My waitress was scornful and angry at this desertion, but laughing also. Soon all the waitresses were privately laughing at the goings-on of the fat woman, who was being served by the most beautiful waitress I have ever seen in any Duval. The fat woman was clearly a crotchet, a 'maniaque', a woman who lived much alone. Her cloak (she displayed on taking it off a simply awful light puce flannel dress) and her parcels were continually the object of her attention and she was always arguing with her waitress. And the whole restaurant secretly made a butt of her. She was repulsive; no one could like her or sympathize with her. But I thought – she has been young and slim once. And I immediately thought of a long 10 or 15 thousand words short story, 'The History of Two Old Women'. I gave this woman a sister, fat as herself. And the first chapter would be in the restaurant (both sisters) something like to-night – and written rather cruelly. Then I would go back to the infancy of these two, and sketch it all. One should have lived ordinarily, married prosaically, and become a widow. The other should have become a whore and all that; 'guilty splendour'. Both are overtaken by fat. And they live together again in old age, not too rich, a nuisance to themselves and to others. Neither has any imagination. For 'tone' I thought of *Ivan Ilyitch*, and for technical arrangement I thought of that and also of *Histoire d'une fille de ferme*. The two lives would have to intertwine. I saw the whole work quite clearly, and hope to do it.

Thursday, November 19th. – Yesterday I had a nervous dyspeptic-headache, due to the labours of Monday. I did nothing but perambulate the city, and collected a few ideas for my next story. I did well to collect any at all.

I certainly ought to have been sure from the first that my waitress at the Duval, fat, fifty, and apparently the image of shrewd content, was really a *névrosée*, given to crises and sudden violent feelings of an irrational character. I ought to have known it from the day when, after a few days' absence from the restaurant, she greeted me bluntly with the question: 'Is she prettier than I am, then?' I only made sure of her nervous temperament yesterday, when she cried violently about some undisclosed thing, at lunch. One meets an extraordinary large number of *névrosés* of all sorts in Paris.

Sunday, November 22nd. To the annual banquet of *La Plume* at the restaurant of the Sociétés Savants. About 200 guests, I should imagine, including a dozen or so 'movement-y' women, sloppy, of the sort that I detest – Stage Society, Fabian Society sort, almost exactly as in London. A big, badly-arranged, too-crowded banquet, mediocre as a meal. I was introduced to Auguste Rodin, a little man with a fine long grey beard and a big nose over it, and very vivacious. He was in evening dress (against the rule) with the rosette. He seemed a simple man; he talked to me for a few minutes quite naturally and without any sort of pose. Afterwards I came home with Kozakiewicz, and found him an ardent Wagnerian. He told me he had sold 300,000 copies of the French translation of Sienkewicz, and had paid the author over 80,000 francs.

Monday, November 23rd. – I called on the Schwobs yesterday afternoon and found [Henri] Davray and his wife there. Schwob a little better, but very listless, and those terrible piercing eyes which he has when he is ill. They were talking of Rémy de Gourmont's new book on the sexual instinct. Moréno said she supposed she ought not to admit that she had read it, and she forbade me to read it. She said that all the pornography was interlarded with reflections in the style of *Paul and Virginia*.

Les trois filles de M. Dupont, by Brieux, at the Comédie Mondaine. House packed. I found this well-known piece interesting enough. Thoroughly serious, and marked by great 'justice of observation'. But of course clumsily constructed. Too much 'means' for too little 'end', and the big situation between the three sisters at the close, where even unsuccessful marriage is justified, and one sister persuades Julie against a life of solitary industry, and the other against a life of vice – this situation is badly 'forced'. But the play is the sort of play that makes you think. It made the audience think. It angered them and it pleased them, and on coming out they discussed the problems raised. It is not a good work of art, but it is a serious work of art. I thought of it so much on coming out, that I quite forgot that I had meant to go to a café at midnight to meet a friend. I went straight to bed.

Wednesday, November 25th. – It was a thoroughly wet and rotten day yesterday. After noon the streets became impossible. I did not work at all, couldn't concentrate in the least. I had to go out and lunch with a companion, and to suffer all sorts of sentimental worries, and to argue closely in French, and to write a long letter in French. Afterwards I played Bach's preludes and fugues till I couldn't play them any longer. I read Casanova, *L'Étui de Nacre*, Maupassant's *La Vie Errante*, and *Le Mercure de France*. I went to bed at 10.15 and arose at 8.30 this morning thoroughly well in all ways.

Friday, November 27th. – At the restaurant in the Hippodrome I saw the notorious 'Pipe-en-bois' with two young and naïve and rather ugly girls, sisters. 'Pipe-en-bois' is a corsetmaker in a large and successful way of business, and a shareholder in many Parisian theatres. He is a perfectly ordinary common-looking man, quite without *chic*, a long spreading auburn beard, and bad neckties; rough hair, short of stature. He has keen eyes. He is a *coureur*; enjoys himself every night. Known in all the *coulisses*, of which he has the run; favourite of all the chorus girls. They say he is extremely keen in business, and a grudging taskmaster. His wife takes a large share in the management of the business. They understand each other, these two, and go their own separate ways. Certainly a 'type' this man. Age between 45 and 50.

Tuesday, December 1st. – This year I have written 12 short stories, and as some of my stories are apt to disappear from view absolutely in the files of the periodical press, I will make a list of them:

'The Hungarian Rhapsody' (*T.P.'s Weekly*)   good.
'Midnight at the Great Babylon' (Tillotsons).
'The Clock'   (Tillotsons).
'Phantom' (*Hearth and Home* Xmas No.)   fairly good.
'Loot of Cities' series.

All good on their plane { 'The Fire of London' / 'Comedy on the Gold Coast' / 'A Bracelet at Bruges' / 'A Solution of the Algiers Mystery' / 'The Capital of the Sahara' / 'Lo! 'Twas a Gala Night' } (*Windsor*).

'The Railway Station'   (Tillotsons) facetious.
'Saturday to Monday'   (Tillotsons) fairly good.

Besides these, several stories have appeared this year which I wrote last year – but I cannot remember all their titles – in *Sphere, Queen, T.P.'s Weekly*, and elsewhere.

Wednesday, December 2nd. – It snowed all yesterday morning. I walked out three miles in it to make purchases; amongst other things the *Mercure de France*, where I found 3 pages concerning myself by Davray, – all that was most amiable and appreciative, and yet sober too.

I dined with C.L. at Maire's, corner of Boul. de Strasbourg, and really enjoyed myself. The place is very *chic*, and I hit on a Burgundy at 3.50 which was really fine. Naturally I drank too much of it. I finished the dinner with 'fruits rafraîchis', refreshed, that is, with abundant liqueurs such as kirsch; I also had a little cognac. The consequence was that I was extremely unwell in the night. However, the attack, which in other days would have lasted 48 hours, cleared away this morning, and I was able to go out and buy a closed French stove – 45 francs, second hand, a bargain. I now hope to get, and keep, the *appartement* warm.

After the dinner, Antoine's. And I saw for the first time Henri Becque's famous *La Parisienne*. A play perfectly simple, but exquisitely constructed. Only one important character – played really with genius by Mme Devoyod. Yes, genius. The play is well entitled. This *is the* Parisienne, even *the* woman. And it is human nature with all its sins presented without the slightest ethical or didactic tendency – with an absolute detachment from morals. It is certainly one of the great plays of the period. I learnt a lot from it, not only in technique, but in the matter of fundamental attitude towards life.

I hate, now, having any evening quite free, with no society. It is on these evenings, although I amuse myself with writing letters and reading, that I feel 'out of it'. And that phrase expresses the whole thing. 'Out of *it*.' What *it* is I don't exactly know.

Thursday, December 3rd. – I had a fine example this morning of the instinctive opposition of the industrial intelligence to any new machine which it doesn't understand. My grand new stove had extinguished itself early this morning, and the *domestique* had to light it. She had been expecting me to buy another sort of stove, simpler. In about five minutes she had almost lost her head. After a few days she will have settled down to the novelty, and will praise it to her friends.

Friday, December 4th. – The day before yesterday, or a bit earlier, two children were born in the streets of Paris the same day. C. explained to me that the thing occurred not infrequently. Accouchement in a 'maison' was an expensive affair, comparatively. Hence women, at the very last moment, went to the *poste de police* and demanded the assistance which the law binds itself to give.

It is extraordinary how the leading cafés of Montmartre are absolutely crammed at midnight. Till a day or two ago I had scarcely known of the existence of the Café Graff. I was in there last night and at 12.15 there was not a seat empty. I came home and found my stove gone out. I lighted it, at 1 p.m., but it would not 'take'. This trifling thing annoyed me wonderfully. It got on my nerves. I could not sleep and was extremely depressed about everything.

Saturday, December 5th. – Dined at Mrs Devereux's last night. Frank Hurd, Mrs Richard Le Gallienne, and a Maurice F— (I forget the name – son of one of Napoleon III's generals and an English mother); also Blanche Devereux. Hurd, who seemed to know Italy very well, gave a lot of interesting details about the 'keeping up of appearances' there by the reduced aristocracy, which he said far surpassed anything in the same line of effort in England. He told how in Naples a number of families will join in a carriage, and each have their own emblazoned doors, for fitting on to the carriage on their day for using it. But the most curious thing he related was the story of a carriage accident in Rome (I think) where a lady occupying one of the carriages concerned absolutely declined to get out, although the wheels were inextricably locked. Eventually she was pulled out, and it appeared that though she was magnificently dressed as far down as the carriage-rug, below that she wore a ragged old skirt and a pair of bedroom slippers.

The young Maurice F—, whose father was in the very middle of the Boulangist movement, told us how he himself drove the cab containing the general on a famous occasion and how the populace insisted on getting on the roof of the cab. And he gave particulars of the General's *liaison* with Mme Bonnemain, and how his father predicted the ruin of the 'cause' from the moment Madame went into the General's *appartement*, and how she telegraphed to him to leave Paris when he certainly ought to have stayed and how generally she ruined a thing which might have succeeded.

Monday, December 7th. – *From Casanova I. 147.*

'The artifice which I employed was to recount the thing simply, and just as it was, without omitting even any circumstances which might be hurtful to me. It is a secret which every man is not able to employ, because the greater part of the human race is composed of poltroons and to be always true needs courage. I have learnt by experience, that truth is a talisman of which the charm never fails, provided that one does not squander it on rascals.' What a motto for my *Truth About an Author*!

Tuesday, December 8th. – I succeeded far beyond my hopes in planning out *A Great Man* yesterday, and in making a detailed sketch of the first chapter. I was, however, and I remain, extremely dissatisfied and discontented with my general condition. I suppose I shall always be more or less like this. I cannot think of any device or policy by which I could change my condition with any prospect of improvement. I want to be free and fettered at the same time, and it can't be done.

I read the first act of *Othello* last night, and it did me good.

Sunday, December 13th. – After buying papers and tea yesterday I lunched at the little creamery in the Place de la Trinité. Then I came home and read various papers and periodicals and *Casanova*, and fell asleep, sleeping uncomfortably. Then I tried seriously to find the ideas for Chapter II of new novel; I had been more or less asking for them all morning; no success. Then I went out for a walk, and felt tired even in starting. I walked through the St Lazare quarter to the Madeleine and turned along the Grand Boulevard to the Grand Café. I like the interior of this café. It is as much like the respectable ugliness of an English club as anything in Paris. I ordered a cup of chocolate because I felt empty.

I thought steadily for one hour over this chocolate and I seemed to leave the café with one or two germs of ideas. I walked home, cogitating. When I arrived, there was a telegram from Whitten requiring my weekly article two days earlier than usual. This upset my plans somewhat. I felt so tired – I had taken a chill – that I lay down under the eiderdown on the bed and went to sleep again, reading *Casanova*.

When I awoke it was dark. I made tea and felt better. A leading notion for the chapter had now formed itself. I went to the Comédie Mondaine to book a seat for Brieux's *Berceau*, and then to the Duval to dine, where I read *Le Temps* all through. Then I bought a cigar and had coffee in the Place Clichy. I cogitated at the café for an hour, and then I had the whole chapter clearly outlined in my head. This is a fair specimen of one of my cogitating days.

Friday, December 18th. – The most singular thing that I have heard from C. about Paris is that in the night (? after 12) one cannot legitimately ring up a doctor without the presence of a gendarme. You get the gendarme to go with you to the doctor's, then the doctor is bound to come. The gendarme enters with the doctor, remains in an adjoining room, and afterwards the doctor fills up the gendarme's 'feuille'.

Wednesday, December 23rd. – I had a smooth passage over on Monday.

Yesterday I saw Pinker twice, and after some hesitation on his part, arranged that he should pay me £50 a month certain during 1904.

Pinker, Barry Pain, and I lunched together. But Pain hadn't many new stories. I heard that Mrs Humphry Ward had £10,000 from Harpers for serial rights of *Lady Rose's Daughter*, and that the book sold 400,000 in America alone.

Woke up this morning at 4.30. Read de Maupassant, myself, and the *Telegraph*; but couldn't sleep again till 8.30.

Thursday, December 24th. – I came to Burslem yesterday evening with Tertia and William and a headache. Went out this morning and saw numbers of people. Walking to Hanley this afternoon I was struck by the orange-apple *cold* Christmas smell of the greengrocers' shops.

Saturday, December 26th. – Yesterday, Christmas Day, I was reading 'Falk' in Conrad's *Typhoon*, and then several stories by Wells. Also Mérimée's famous *Mateo Falcone*, which is nothing special except in the extraordinary cruelty of the plot.

I went to bed at 1.30 and was kept awake till 4.30 by a barking dog. Then at 7.15 Mater knocked on the wall. She was in the middle of a bilious crisis caused by overnight hare and bilberries. She stays in bed. Hence the whole atmosphere of the house becomes special, and 'sick roomy', and I can't proceed with my novel to-day, as I had meant.

·1904·

Sunday, January 3rd. – I came to Paris yesterday, and wrote letters all the way over on the boat.

Wednesday, January 6th. – All yesterday I was ill – probably owing to mussel-soup at Sylvain's on Monday night, but I do not feel sure. Rawson called for his lunch and I was obliged to send him away again. C. came in the evening and stayed till midnight. I had slept nearly all day. As curiously illustrating the customs of costume – she cannot go out to do household shopping in a hat. She must go *nu-tête*. I couldn't read anything yesterday but newspapers. I read Stead's new paper *The Daily Paper*, first number, all through. It made me admire the man, but if the paper succeeds I shall be surprised.

Although feeble I did a good day's work.

Friday, January 8th. – I forgot to set down, on the 1st, the brief record of last year. I wrote five-sixths of *Leonora*, and twelve short stories. Four books of mine were published, *The Gates of Wrath*, *The Truth about an Author*, *How to become an Author* and *Leonora*. The great fact illustrating my commercial progress was that the *Windsor Magazine* gave me a commission for six short stories. I did nothing in the way of drama except the sketch of the play which I am now about to write with Phillpotts. I did practically no work between January 15th and March 15th, when I was travelling in Algeria, etc. I returned from Algeria Mch. 1. and spent a fortnight or so in England preparatory to settling in Paris. Then between April 1st and June 30th I wrote nearly all *Leonora*.

On June 29th I went to England, and messed about England till Sept. 18th, doing scarcely any work – a summer cut to pieces and wasted and therefore not a pleasant one. I came to Paris about Sep. 18th, spent 10 days in taking and furnishing a flat; then I started to work and I have worked ever since. I propose to work almost without intermission at any rate till July 30th.

I bought the *Gates of Wrath* (Tauchnitz edition) and read some of it. Its smartness and clarity prevent me from being quite honestly ashamed of it.

Thursday, January 14th. – I left the rue de Calais yesterday, depressed, at 5 p.m. after having lunched with C. The drive to the Gare de Lyon along the interminable length of the rue de Rivoli got on my nerves. And I was decidedly excited and 'wrought up' when the *train de grand luxe* came up and I saw Phillpotts. Much talking and mutual satisfaction. (I have a sore throat now.) The train left sharp at 6 p.m. and arrived here at Menton sharp at 9.56 a.m. this morning. On the whole a really good sound train. It would be almost perfect if it had a drawing-room car, as it certainly ought to have. The ceaseless noise and jolting did not noticeably affect me much. I took a sedative and slept very well, though mostly conscious of the action and the din. Coming along the coast, I had my first glimpse of Monte Carlo and the salons thereof. I was duly impressed by the beauty of the coast, and of Menton in particular. But my thoughts were chiefly occupied with the idea of the train, that luxurious complete entity – running through a country and ignoring it. I seldom had the least idea where the train was. Space, as a notion, had vanished for me. I might have been in the void.

[Menton], Friday, January 15th. – I woke up this morning just before dawn, and there was a red streak of light along the horizon, and the sea smoke-colour, and the lamps and the riding lights of the vessels just beginning to be ghostly. On either side the hills with their bare rocky tops. Then, when I woke up again, the strong sun was shining brilliantly on to my balcony and almost into my face. There must be a fairly strong off-shore wind blowing, but this place is very sheltered and the sea seems quite calm. However, one can *hear* the wind. The beauty of the landscape and of the old Italianate town to the right, with its red flat-square conical roofs, and the delicate softness of the air, make a deep impression on one.

I took my tea and *croissant* out on the balcony in the 8.30

a.m. sun, wrapped in my largest overcoat, and in the sunshine. It was tremendous, after the bed breakfasts of a Paris flat.

Night. The beauty of this place even grows on one. The afternoon and dusk were simply miraculous for colour. Before lunch I went for a walk up on the hill and then down again and along the coast. I walked into Italy in about a quarter of an hour.

Sunday, January 17th. – Hanbury, of Allen and Hanbury's foods, and the great botanist, editor of the *London Catalogue*, came to lunch. He is staying with his cousin Sir Thomas Hanbury, the Lord God of these parts. Sir Thomas has the finest private garden in the world, 100 acres, 5,000 species (some absolutely unique) and 46 gardeners. Speaking of Monte Carlo, he told us how he was at the tables 30 years ago and saw two Russian Princesses there losing heavily, but keeping stoical silence, the tears streaming down their cheeks. He is emphatically not a man of the world, and his Russian Princesses were probably French whores, but nevertheless his picture of the women playing and losing, in silent, irrepressible, hopeful-despairing tears, was an effective one.

Monday, January 18th. – Breakfast again on the balcony, while the fishing boats went out one by one straight into the dazzle of the sun, with an extraordinary *sentimental* effect. A highly dandiacal yacht, with fittings all brass and mahogany apparently, had been at anchor since we came: she was moored by two ropes to the jetty, and by two anchors from the stern. I noticed a detail of actualness which might be brought into a scene with great effect. The yacht swung from side to side on the jetty ropes, lifting first the starboard and then the port rope clear of the water, and as each rope came clear of the still water, the drops from it fell into the water in hundreds for a few seconds making a wonderfully pretty pattering sound. On first catching this sound I did not perceive how it was caused.

Monte Carlo, Tuesday, January 26th. – On the whole I was disappointed by the exterior aspects of the town. It lacks spaciousness, and since it is in the absolute control of one autocratic authority, spaciousness is what it ought not to have lacked. Some of the villas, however, with their white paint and general air of being toys, are *excessivement chic*. The casino is all right in its florid, heavy way – but what a chance for an architect, on that site over the sea! The whole town had an air of being Parisian, but not quite Parisian enough.

Inside the gaming-saloons (4 o'clock) I found a large crowd and many tables in full work. The crowd not so distinguished in appearance as I had (foolishly) expected. I saw few signs at the tables of suppressed or *ex*pressed excitement, though quite a large proportion of the people seemed to be gambling seriously. I had no intention of betting, but after I had watched several tables and grasped the details of roulette (30 and 40 I didn't attempt to grasp) I remained at one table, as if hypnotized; without knowing it I began to finger a 5-franc piece in my pocket, and then I became aware that I was going to bet. I knew I should bet some seconds before I formally decided to. I staked a 5-franc piece on an even chance and won. Like a provincial up from the country, who has heard tales of metropolitan rascality, I stood close to a croupier and kept a careful eye on my coin, and picked up the winnings without an instant's delay. I kept on playing, carefully, and always on even chances, for some time, and stopped when I had made a little money and went and had some tea. I didn't play again.

The idea of gambling quite absorbed all my thoughts; obsessed me; and I had schemes – such as that it would be experimentally worth while to go there with say 5,000 francs, and deliberately become a regular system-using gambler for a time. There is no doubt that the human spectacle of the gaming saloons is tremendous; unequalled; the interest of it could not easily fail for an observer. To a stranger, of course, one of the most curious things is the sight of large sums of money in notes and gold constantly being flung about the tables. I am told that the Casino employs 1,800 people altogether. The croupiers work 6 hours a day each, so I estimate there must be about 200 croupiers altogether. I just missed a tram in coming home and had half an hour to wait; all that time I thought of gaming, gaming. And I look forward to going again on Friday.

[*Paris*] *February 15th.* – I was influenza-ish all day yesterday and on Saturday evening – until last night, when it passed off. We dined on Saturday and yesterday at Sylvain's, and last night went into the Casino de Paris for an hour or so.

I heard again the story of the life, death and burial of the mysterious pretty Englishwoman from Liverpool who gave lessons in English to a constant stream of *messieurs chics*, and expired alone at 7 rue Bréda after being robbed by a Spanish male friend. The arrival of the English relatives and all that! It seemed to me I might use up a lot of the stuff in *The History of Two Old Women*, which it seems more and more likely will be my next serious book. I went out this afternoon (Mardi gras) towards the Grand Boulevard. The crowd got thicker and thicker and confetti more and more plentiful. I left the rue Montmartre for the 'passages', and became blocked in the Passage Jouffroy and so returned. The carnival was nothing but an excuse for stupidity and horseplay. It began to rain, and soon rained heavily, and kept on till 8.30. I was morosely glad to see the carnival thus ruined. It may break out again to-night, though I had promised myself a concert of old music to-night, but after trudging in the wet to the hall in the rue d'Athénès, I found the place shut up.

Wednesday, February 17th. – I really enjoyed working on my novel to-day, and this although I had a headache most of the time.

Friday, February 19th. – I paid a call in the afternoon. Something depressed me afterwards, either I had caught a chill or it was something else, and I had the greatest difficulty in forcing myself to recommence work. However, I dined at the Place Blanche and sat down to write at 9 p.m. It is a good thing I never write down here my moods and things.

Sunday, February 21st. – This afternoon, Lamoreux concert, to hear, chiefly, Richard Strauss's *Life of a Hero*. It came at the end of an exhausting programme, but I was much impressed by its beauty. I heard it under difficulties, for the audience grew restive, talked, and protested. One old man insisted on going out. There is a rule about not entering or leaving during a piece, but this old man cried so loud and shook the doors so that the *pompiers* were obliged to let him through. Applause and hisses at the end, from a full audience. One more exhibition of the *bêtise* of an audience when confronted by something fresh, extravagant and powerful. It would be absurd to condemn this or any other particular audience, for all audiences are alike. The sarcastic and bitter opposition must be taken as a tribute to the power of the art. Was not *Tannhäuser* simply laughed off the stage at the first performance? I liked the piece better than I thought I should – a great deal. The first thing of Richard Strauss that I have heard.

Twelve thousand five hundred words written this week.

Sunday, February 28th. – I finished another section of *A Great Man* yesterday at 3.30 p.m., having written nearly 10,000 words in a week. I ought easily to complete the book by March 20. It seems amusing enough, and very good in places. But if I treated this as a draft, and really thought out types and made the book fuller, I could make it much better. However, I have a mania for producing a lot just now. And further, this sort of book, though I can do it, is scarcely my natural *genre*. I do not take quite the same terrific interest in it as I take in a serious book, nor do I get quite the same satisfaction out of a passage which I know to be well done. And often I have the greatest difficulty in starting my day's work. I am all right when I have started. But the starting is *pénible*.

Monday, February 29th. – Last night seemed to be one of the bitterest we have had in the present cold spell; yet I noticed a number of people sitting out quite unconcernedly on the *terrasses* of the cafés on the Grand Boulevard. Some cafés had thick mats spread over the terrasse, and one had a coke brazier, red and smoky, set among the tables.

When a youngish horse is just starting out fresh from the stable in the morning, up a hill, with a light trap behind him, he brings his nose down under his neck, so that the line of the head is parallel with the foreleg before it takes a step; his hind feet slip a little perhaps on the stones, and he pulls bravely. That is a beautiful sight. It was the first thing I saw, going out yesterday morning.

Tuesday, March 1st. – I bought a new copy of *La Grande Encyclopédie*, bound in cloth, 31 vols, for 290 francs, yesterday morning. It can be bought through *Le Journal* for about 400 francs. It seems a good thing, and I read 'in' it yesterday. I found, however, nothing under the head of 'Cotgrave'; I wanted the date of the first edition of his dictionary. Schwob, on whom I called yesterday afternoon, praised it highly. He mentioned specially such articles as 'Aristotle' by Boutroux, as being the very finest of their kind. I looked up this, and it certainly impressed me. Brunetière's article on 'Style' is admirable; also Rémy de Gourmont's on 'Aretino'. Schwob was in bed, and had been there for a month. We discussed the war, and Dickens. He stood up for Dickens, and said that, for style, the opening of *Hard Times* is one of the finest things in English. Of course I disagreed. He said that Dickens's ghost story *The Signalman* was 'plagiarized' from something in Defoe's essay on apparitions, but much improved. He told me about the dinner to Edmund Gosse. Said Gosse was charming, but pedantic.

Wednesday, March 2nd. – I walked a good deal yesterday: extremely cold. I called in at the Petit Palais and saw some good things that I had not noticed before. I was in search of ideas for the continental part of *A Great Man*. But I could not keep my mind off the serious novel which is to make a third to *Anna* and *Leonora*. I thought of a fine name for the title: *Carlotta*. About six o'clock, after useless efforts all day, I got the leading idea which I wanted for *A Great Man*. In the evening, concert. Quartets of Brahms and Beethoven, and songs by Brahms, Schumann, and Schubert. Full house. The affair was most inspiriting. Again I could not keep my thoughts off *Carlotta* (as I shall now call it), and it seems that after all I may do this book before I do *The History of Two Old Women*. ... This morning, snow.

Monday, March 7th. – The Davrays dined with me last night at the Hippodrome, and afterwards we went to the Grand Café. He gave me sundry particulars about the French dinner to Edmund Gosse, and said that Gosse's speech (which he, Davray, translated into French for him) was simply admirable and was continually interrupted, at every sentence, by applause. Schwob's speech in English was also very good, he said.

Gosse received the offer of his appointment to the Librarianship of the House of Lords on the very morning of the banquet. So, Davray said, Gosse told him. Davray saw the letter offering the appointment, from Sir Henry Loundes Graham, and said it was extraordinarily flattering.

Davray gave me a new instance of politeness. At some English house a foreigner called (nationality obscure, I forget, something small) wearing what looked like an overcoat. The hostess urged him to take it off; said it was the custom etc. He took it off, and appeared in his shirt-sleeves. Consternation of the hostess, especially as other guests were expected. Presently Laurence Housman came in and was advised privately of the situation. Housman took off his own coat, and sat down also in his shirt-sleeves; then complained of the cold, and demanded from his hostess permission to resume his coat; the foreigner followed his example.

'C'était très fin,' commented Davray.

Wednesday, March 9th. – I finished *Le Crépuscule des Dieux* yesterday, and was very much disappointed in the book. When we were discussing it on Sunday night Davray admitted that it 'lacked life'. It also lacks construction. The author thought the theme was big, and it isn't. It is only royal. The meant-to-be-big scenes, such as the attempt to poison the Duc, are absolute failures. Further, the symbolism of the title, borrowed from Wagner, and the use made of Wagner's opera at the beginning and at the end – these things are too facile. A really great artist would not have employed them.

Two curious things I have noticed lately. The Société Protectrice des Animaux keeps spare tip-horses all day at the foot of the principal inclines in Paris (e.g. rue Notre Dame de Lorette), and carmen can employ them for the ascent for one penny. Another thing is that, just about now, there is an eruption of women in the street selling all sorts of veils. They carry their light gauzy stock in an open umbrella held downwards.

Thursday, March 10th. – I can see at once that *Les Liaisons Dangereuses* is a great work. It has the classic truthfulness and sobriety on every page. Letter XVIII in which Cécile describes the covert love scene between herself and the Chevalier Danceny is a most perfect and marvellous rendering of a young girl's feelings. It seemed to me to be one of the most beautiful things of the kind I had ever read.

Sunday, March 13th. – I finished *A Great Man* at 11.30 this morning, having written about ten thousand words in the last five days. I am more satisfied with it than I thought I should be. I began it with an intention merely humorous, but the thing has developed into a rather profound satire. I began the book about the 10th December; during two weeks of the time between then and now (Xmas) I put it aside, and during three other weeks I put it aside in order to write the play with Eden. So that I have been engaged on it nine weeks altogether. It is 60,000 words in length, and my eighth novel of one sort or another.

On Friday and Saturday I had an extremely severe cold in the head, but nothing could prevent me from finishing that novel. I was in the exact mood for writing, and had all the ideas arranged in my head.

Wednesday, March 16th. – I meant to go and see *L'Étrangère* at the Français on Monday night, but was too unwell – a mysterious lassitude. So I bought *La Petite Roque* of de Maupassant instead, and came home. Yesterday I bought Taine's *Graindorge*. This book brought to a head the ideas which I have had for writing 'impressions' of Paris. I find I must write something. I can't lie quite fallow. Moreover I have now been in Paris exactly a year, and my ideas are becoming defined. So this morning I started a book of impressions, with an account of, and reflexions upon, the opening of the Concerts-Berlioz, which I went to last night.

Friday, March 18th. – Yesterday morning I received a letter from Whitten asking me to discontinue my 'Log Book' in *T.P.'s Weekly* in six weeks' time from now. This rather depressed me. I enjoy doing these articles, and I shall have to make up the £165 a year by other work – probably fiction. So all my work will be fiction.

Wednesday, March 23rd. – On Friday night last *Le Dédale*, play in 5 acts, by Paul Hervieu. I thought this one of the greatest modern plays I have ever seen, especially as to the three middle acts. Constant spiritual action of the piece, and constant drama, conflict of emotions etc. rising at times to great heights. The famous catastrophe of the precipice in the fifth act did not convince me; nor was I convinced of the necessity for any such fatal tragedy at all. On the other hand the catastrophe may have seemed ineffective because I demanded a scenic effect which the stage-manager could not realize, or had failed to realize: the sense of a dizzy height etc. . . . When one has been extremely pleased with a work one always tries to reason away what one fears may be faults.

On Saturday morning I went down to Les Sablons to stay with the Davrays. We went for a walk in the forest of Fontainebleau in the afternoon. I noticed on entering this vast forest, intersected with glorious roads, a characteristically French signboard: 'General instructions for reading the signposts in the forest.' The system of signposts seemed to me to be absolutely complete. I found the forest quite up to my expectation, but bigger.

On Sunday Dr Vallée took us to Nemours, a delicious old

town with a castle, ramparts, moats, and the Loing; full of wonderful views. Mme and I went to buy cakes and we all had tea on the pavement in front of an inn; while the landlady and another woman sat and sewed near by. Seeking the *garçon* to pay the bill I got into a vast kitchen full of all kinds of curious domestics and copper pans. Passing along the street we saw a tailor, old, in black, white hair, and a strangely shaped head, standing at the door of his shop. Davray and I both exclaimed at once: 'Balzacian'. *Ursule Mirouet* is laid in Nemours, and the extraordinary veracity of Balzac's descriptions strikes one everywhere. His descriptions were not exaggerated. I was enchanted with Nemours. We came back to Les Sablons on the great Paris-Antibes road, passing from that to the great Paris-Marseilles road, stupendous highways both, straight, interminable, with double rows of trees on either side.

At night music, and that freedom of speech which is one of the joys of France.

Friday, March 25th. – I have gradually seen that my sensational yarn must be something remarkably out of the common, and that therefore I must take the greatest care over the conception. I had the idea for the 'scene' of the book. Then I thought I would buy and read Gaboriau's *Le Crime d'Orcival*, of which I have heard so much, and see whether that would conduce to a 'flow' in me, as Balzac always does. It did, at once. It is, I think, the best elaborate long detective story that I have read. It contains much solid and serious stuff, is extremely ingenious and well planned, and has real imagination. My sensational work does not and would not in the least resemble Gaboriau's, and yet Gaboriau has filled me with big, epic ideas for fundamental plot – exactly what I wanted. The central theme must be big, and it will be; all the rest is mere ingenuity, wit, and skill.

Thursday, April 7th. – Thinking about my new serial to-day, and got one or two ideas after several hours; but I had a cold all over me, and the weather was too wet to walk much.

Moréno sent me an urgent note to go and dine with them.

Schwob dined in his bed and we dined at a table at the foot thereof, while the Chinaman waited. Herz, the impresario, had asked Moréno and Coquelin Cadet to do a season in London together, but he wanted a short play, half in French and half in English, to begin the bill, and he wanted it written specially for her and C.C. She asked me whether I would write it if Herz arranged terms with me. I said I would. Both Moréno and Schwob, with their curious sanguine temperaments, seemed to regard the affair as an absolute certainty, but I think it is far from that. Herz hasn't even got a theatre in London yet. However, I drove with her to her theatre, and left her there, and at that moment she seemed certain that all was smooth. She was to telephone to Herz this morning and Herz was to see me, and I was to write the play, and they were to play it, and it was to make a great splash, and the season was to be an enormous success, and much money was to flow into all pockets.

Saturday, April 9th. – I went to Schwob's yesterday, and then took Moréno and her precious 'griffon belge', Flip, in a cab to the Gaîté Theatre, where we saw Henri Herz, and discussed the proposed play for Coquelin Cadet's and Moréno's proposed English season. The matter seemed to be arranged subject to Herz getting a London theatre. Herz and Moréno were evidently old friends. It was all 'tu' and 'toi'. She called him 'mon petit chéri', and he called her 'ma belle créature'. Very theatrical. I liked him. She told me I should. He seemed straight, and rather English in affairs of business. The two united to curse M. B., for whom they couldn't find adjectives sufficiently bad. It seems he takes all his mother's money, with the result that the underlings at her theatre are not paid. Moréno gave me a very funny account of how Sarah Bernhardt fooled, and amused herself with, an American female versifier whom we both knew, who wanted to read to Sarah a drama in verse on the subject of Delilah.

A heavy thunderstorm broke over Paris yesterday and lasted from 4 to 10 p.m. I was in the Parc Monceau when it began with a slight shower only.

It is extraordinary the terrific upset made by a shower of rain in a placid park peopled by nursemaids, children, mothers, and old people. Great excitement over perambulators, mothers searching for cabs and driving off with the kid, leaving the poor nurse to trudge home in the rain with the empty perambulator; crowding under inadequate shelters and so on. 'Maternal solicitude' is all over the place.

Tuesday, April 19th. – I went to the Concert-Berlioz on Sunday morning. I was struck by the wonderful cleverness of Saint-Saëns. It was the Algerian Suite, which I knew thoroughly, and yet it seemed to appear to me in a new light. I don't think it is first-class music by any means, but it is wonderful music.

The Salon seems to give a perspective of French life every year. I once thought it was on the average no better than the R.A.; but it is – a great deal. There is a good deal of English work in it, very distinguished. The virginal simplicity of Lavery's English girls strikes a curious note there, so different from anything else.

Wednesday, April 20th. – Yesterday I started my new romantic book, *Hugo*, with great fervour, and much enjoyed the day's work. I have announced to Pinker that it will be infinitely better than the *Grand Babylon Hotel*; so it will have to be.

Thursday, April 21st. – I went down to Montparnasse and had tea with Mrs Stapley, who had hunted up an Empire secrétaire for me, in fact several. Afterwards we went to view them. The best one had a mirror at the back, above the small drawers. I said to the shopwoman that I objected to a mirror. 'Ah!' she said. 'But when Madame leans over your shoulder while you are writing – !' I bought the secrétaire and also a clock for 140 francs.

Wednesday, April 27th. – Yesterday when I was in Paillard's, it occurred to me that the difference between the most excessively *chic* restaurant and an ordinary good one is very slight.

Paillard's has the reputation of being the best, or one of the three best in Paris, and therefore in the world. Yet it is small, and not in the least luxurious, and the waiting is no better than it is elsewhere. The *monde* has no special appearance of smartness. The food was very good, and so was the wine. But scarcely appreciably better than at Sylvain's, Maire's, or Noel and Peters. And the prices were about 25 per cent dearer than at those other places – not more. In the evening, at a Boulant, I had for 6*d.* a bifteck and soufflé potatoes better than which could not possibly be obtained anywhere, at no matter what price. When you have thoroughly good, well-flavoured, tender meat, perfectly cooked, – you cannot surpass that.

Friday, May 6th. Dinner at the notorious Bohemian Restaurant Garnier in the Boul. Raspail, last night. Crowded, chiefly with Americans. We dined out in the street, fenced about by trees in tubs; and I was introduced to about a million girls. The food was mediocre – not so villainous as I had heard; the wine was bad, and this morning I had a headache. Afterwards at Miss Thomasson's studio, I met Hubert Bland and his Liberty-clad young daughter Rosamund. Mrs Bland [E. Nesbit] was too indisposed to come. I also met Sep's friend and champion, Berta Ruck, and some other people. Late, an artist named K— came in; a loud, gross man. He had been dining with 'Johnny Lavery', and he was full of Johnny Lavery's wonderful new German model whose portrait is in this year's Salon. Told us how she was aged 19, and the rage of Berlin, asked to lunch at the Embassies, received 5 proposals in 3 months; how Lavery looked after her, sent her to bed at 9.30 every night; how she refused to sit for anyone but Lavery, and would only sit even for him 2 hours a day, and he had to hire a woman to play to her or talk to her the while.

Sunday, May 8th. – I drafted the whole of the second instalment of *Hugo* yesterday, finishing a little after six, and working with difficulty through the inception of a liver attack (which culminated this morning). In the evening, Concert-

Berlioz, rather interesting. A duet for two flutes with piano, and 3 little pieces for wood-wind sextet, both by Berlioz. I meant to have heard a Schubert Mass at St Augustin this morning; but too liverish.

Monday, May 9th. – [Lewis] Hind told me that Max Beerbohm lived on the £5 a week he got from the *Saturday Review*. Strange, if true. After a great deal of talk about journalism I felt an inclination to go in more for journalism. But, as I told Hind, I had contracted an almost invincible *dis*inclination either to asking for work or to do any work that was not directly commissioned beforehand.

Tuesday, May 10th. – There was a phrase in the newspaper yesterday about the 'great and continual accumulation of unemployed capital in Paris'. Here is an instance, which I know of, of how some people can save even in a city where wages are generally low and living is generally dear. A widow, aged 56, lives alone in a single large room in Montrouge, for which she pays 200 francs a year. She is a sempstress, and goes out by the day. She is fully employed and has often to 'refuse' days. Her wages are 3 francs or 3½ francs and *all* food. If she does not take dinner in the house she gets an extra half franc. In order to net this extra half franc she often dines with one of her grown-up daughters. All her clothes she manages to 'make' out of the sempstress's 'perks', lawful or unlawful. She has therefore an income of about 100 francs a month (for she works Sundays), and practically no expenses. I am told she is always buying City of Paris stock etc. etc. The thing is typically French. One of her daughters, a *lorette* in quite a small way, has saved 8,000 francs in 3 years. A son, a picture-restorer, is also continually saving money. On the other hand the eldest daughter, a dressmaker, with a staff under her, is spendthrift and so is the youngest son, just finishing his military term. There must be many families like that in Paris, quietly and really prosperous.

Thursday, May 12th. – I got down, via the quays, as far as the Luxembourg, and saw the temporary exhibition there of

Manet's, Monet's, and that school. Manet's 'Nana' was the chief thing. I thought how much more it had aged than the book. As a matter of fact I think Manet's conception of 'Nana' rather narrow – the idea of a man who had not 'knocked about' enough. The picture would be masterly had he not entitled it 'Nana'.

Saturday, May 14th. – I may now be said to be in the thick of *Hugo.* I worked at him an hour in the morning yesterday, an hour in the afternoon, and two hours at night, finishing at 12.30. And he has the air of being very good. The rest of the time I chiefly wasted, but I read a lot of Balzac and [Horace] Walpole, and contemplated my future.

The noises of Paris become more and more exasperating as summer approaches. A chair-mender who cries every morning at 10.30, I should like to destroy; also the parrot who exists on a window-sill on the first floor of the next house. The rattle of cabs I have grown quite accustomed to.

Wednesday, May 18th. – I finished *La Cousine Bette* again this morning. It is magnificent, but there is a wild creative rush about it that is rather too wild. The trick of leaving out is pushed to its farthest, perhaps too far, and though the book is long it contains nothing but fundamental stuff. Often, it seems to me, Balzac has not given sufficient care to the manufacture of convincing detail. He must have been decidedly in a very frenzy of creative impulse when he wrote it. The scene which remains most clearly in my memory is that in which old Hulot comes to Josepha for shelter and aid; her part in that has a tremendous *brio. Brio* is the word for the entire book.

Thursday, May 19th. – To-day *A Great Man* is published, my sixth published novel, and my eighth written novel. My copies of it arrived yesterday. I read through most of it in the evening. I thought one or two parts were too technical in detail; but on the whole it amused me well enough. I was struck by the ease and virtuosity of the writing (on that plane of writing) and by the sound construction. I don't fancy holes can be picked in these aspects of the book. But humour is often a matter of opinion.

Whit-Monday, May 23rd. – I have suffered heavily from liver for 4 days. The attack went off last night, suddenly, as all such attacks do. I continued to work on *Hugo* except on Friday, when I could do nothing. I finished Part I of him last night about 11 p.m. I heard disturbingly from Pinker on Friday night that Chatto wanted after all to publish *Teresa* and *Love and Life*, and had bought the illustrations for the former. For about an hour I was nearly telegraphing to Wells that I would go over on Saturday to consult him. I couldn't think of anyone else whose opinion in a matter so involved between business and art I really cared twopence for. However, I decided to wait till the next morning. And by the next morning I had thought of a compromise which satisfied me and ought to satisfy Chatto. This compromise would involve the re-writing of *Love and Life*, and I rather think I should enjoy doing that, because the fundamental plot of it is so good.

Tuesday, May 24th. – Mrs Devereux said she was at a dinner party the other night at which were also W. S. Gilbert and Douglas Straight. Straight was talking about peculiarities of memory, loss of it, etc. He said he could remember incidents when he was in Naples at the age of two. But if he was asked where he dined last week he couldn't remember. 'No,' said Gilbert. 'And if you could, probably you wouldn't be able to tell us.'

Mrs Laye maintained (not *apropos* of the above) that men didn't like being made fun of whereas women didn't mind; she said she had been astonished at some men. She told a good thing of a very old man on his dying bed giving advice to a youngster: 'I've had a long life, and it's been a merry one. Take my advice. Make love to every pretty woman you meet. And remember, if you get 5 per cent on your outlay it's a good return.'

Friday, May 27th. – To-day I am 37. I have lived longer than I shall live. My new series begins to appear to-day in the

Windsor. My name is not on the cover. Anthony Hope's stands there alone. And I am 37. Comment is needless.

I have now warned both the Mater and Tertia that I shall get married before I am 40.

Tuesday, May 31st. – I went down to Moret on Saturday morning and nearly missed the train owing to my servant. I was astonished how, during the journey on the Métro, the apprehension of missing the train at the Gare de Lyon got on my nerves, though it was a matter of no importance as there are plenty of trains. My nerves were all raw when I arrived at the Gare, and I was physically exhausted through urging the Métro train to accelerate its movements.

In the afternoon I saw the ceremony of the annual *Revision des chevaux* which takes place all over France about this time, every horse in France, except certain mares, being at the call of the Government for military purposes. It occurred under a tree in the open space between the Mairie, the church, and Davray's garden. A captain was seated at a small table, and by his side the mayor's secretary (the schoolmaster – exactly like all village schoolmasters, whether in England or France), and a soldier. A military vet., another soldier, two gendarmes, and two men that looked like *gardes champêtres* were also in the show; also a dog that lay under the table. The vet. and another man could have done the whole thing easily. Quantities of sheets of paper, minutely ruled with millions of lines for statistics, filled the table. As each horse of the commune was brought up, the vet. looked it over and described it very briefly for the captain to write down, and the captain asked questions as to ownership etc. At the last moment a young man galloped up on a black draught horse, and in answer to some query replied as he slipped off the horse: 'C'est un étalon, comme moi.'

Friday, June 3rd. – Some time ago a man named Martin had relations, *comme maquereau*, with a courtesan. She found a rich protector, and told Martin frankly that she could only see him on the quiet in future, as the rich protector would be jealous.

Martin got into her apartment, stood behind the door, and struck her dead with one blow of a knife in the heart as she entered one night. She was only a *fille*, and the affair was considered as a *crime passionel*, and Martin was acquitted (*Doux Pays!*). I was told yesterday that Martin, handsome and well dressed, frequents the Folies-Bergère and other places, and has relations with other women. There are a number of women who are proud to shake hands with, to drink with, and to be the mistress of an assassin. 'He killed a woman at one stroke!' In certain circles, Martin is the vogue! This is one of the most curious, and yet natural, things I have heard about Paris.

Tuesday, June 14th. – I wrote to Sir Douglas Straight the other day to complain of a review of *A Great Man* in the *Pall Mall Gazette*. It had grossly misrepresented the plot, and so I explained my conception of the negative duties of a reviewer who did not read a book.

Straight's answer is to review the book again, very favourably, under the title 'Second Impressions'. At the end of the review he says, after stating that he has read it twice: 'We say this the more readily because in first acknowledging the book, we recorded what was, after all, a superficial impression, and in making amends now we have said no more than any fair-minded reader will admit it deserves.' This is decidedly handsome. But many people will think I am a friend of Straight's and that the first review slipped in without his knowledge.

Sunday, June 19th. – I was thinking the other day, while reading a very sensual love-scene in *Le Lys Rouge*, that a novelist never describes the dishabille of the male in such scenes; I can't remember an instance where he even hints at it. This shows how incomplete 'realism' is. I see no reason why the appearance of the male should not be described in a manner to assist the charm of the scene. But tradition is decidedly against the practice.

Ullman brought out a theory that Wagner, though a great man, was essentially vulgar. He characterized as vulgar all the stage settings on which Wagner set so much store. I would agree as to the *Ring*, but not as to the other operas. *Tannhauser* may be, and is, lovely. So is *Tristan*. He said that with the same talent Wagner would have been a much finer artist had he been English or French; he was influenced by the fundamental German vulgarity. I could see what Ullman meant, but I thought he was chiefly wrong. However, he argued very well.

Later Rickards and I went to the Moulin de la Galette, and saw some good dancing. He leaves this afternoon for London. Reading *Le Lys Rouge* to-night. The love-scene (Chap. 23) in which Thérèse tries to rid Decharte of his *idées noires* concerning her absolute fidelity to him, is extremely fine in its sensual way. It is just the sort of thing that A. France can do, and it atones for much of the 'invertebrate' quality of the book. If I can accomplish anything as good in *Carlotta* I ought to be satisfied.

I had *idées noires* myself to-night. There are certainly times when the fact that existence is a choice of evils presents itself too clearly.

Monday, June 27th. – I see at the beginning of this volume I noted an instance of the *sans-gêne* – of Montmartre. Here is another. On Thursday last, at the Restaurant Boulant, a young *cocotte* came in with two young men and her '*bonne à tout faire*'. The *bonne* was not neat or clean, and was in her working dress. They dined all together and laughed and talked much. Perhaps it was because the domestic cuisine had gone wrong. But more probably the *cocotte* had only just arrived at the dignity of a *bonne* and was bound to show her off.

Paris, Monday, June 27th. – I had a letter from M. Berquand asking me to go and see him at the Hotel Terminus [about a cure for stammering]. His room was No. 465. I found it with the aid of a boy. M. Berquand is getting old. He struck me as a man of sincere character, and trustworthy. He said he had been mute till the age of 8, and thence till the age of 26 had stammered so badly that he was practically incapable of speech, and entirely incapable of earning a living. He had to be kept by his family. He then studied all the systems, maintained a strict silence for 6 months and cured himself in a year. He has travelled all over Europe on tours of curing, and has 'orders' from most European sovereigns. I arranged to go to Aberdeen on 1st August. He asked me a lot of questions, and said he was quite certain of success in a month or five weeks. In spite of the interview with him I felt rather depressed than otherwise.

I went down to Kelly's studio, a very large one, and he showed me a lot of his work which interested me very much. He made some good remarks about the present condition of painting. He said painters were afraid of making mistakes, afraid of being vulgar, and that they never used their eyes in search of material. They all painted the same things. He said some artist had said to him: 'We paint like governesses.' I certainly thought Kelly was doing good and original work, both in landscape and portraiture. Afterwards he took me to dine at the Chat Blanc. Stanlaws, the 'creator' of the 'Stanlaws girl', was there, a terrible American, and also a girl I had previously seen at Kelly's. The girl and Stanlaws and the man who was the girl's host threw bread at each other, and sang American songs very loudly. It was terrible at times. I could not stand such manners and customs for long. It is these things that spoil Montparnasse.

Thursday, June 30th. — Mrs. Le Gallienne talked to me with much freedom about her husband. She said she had found she could do nothing more for him, and, as they differed as to the desirability of life in New York, she had left him, and they corresponded, and so on. She described how charming he was when he *was* charming, and how diverting it was to live with such a wayward artistic temperament. There was one thing she could say – he had never bored her. However she had had enough of the artistic temperament.

Thursday, July 7th. – I took a turn through the Parc Monceau to the Étoile and back through the Champs Élysées last night between 9.30 and 11 in order to clear off a headache. Honest lovemaking in the Parc Monceau. In the Champs Élysées I saw four girls, aged 14 or less – one didn't seem more than 11 or 12 – being taken about by older women for the excitement of senile appetites. Some day soon there will be a tremendous outcry concerning this procuring of children. The police will become suddenly active in arrests – and then things will settle down again.

There were many pretty and well-dressed women in the Champs Élysées sitting patiently on chairs under the trees awaiting some masculine advance. I was astonished how distinguished some of them were. It was a lovely night, warm and starlit. Paris at its most Parisian. The lights of the al fresco music-halls, and the occasional bursts of music and applause that came from them, produced an extraordinary effect.

A fair is preparing on the Boulevard de Clichy. I wandered in and out among the half-built constructions this morning, watching the life of this dirty and gypsy-like population which wanders from fair to fair. But some of the big roundabouts have waggons, vans, and electrical machinery which are truly awe-inspiring, and which show how scientific methods and scientifically-directed enterprise have changed everything except the *spirit* of these undertakings.

Saturday, July 9th. – I went to the Bois yesterday afternoon and had tea at the Pavillon Royal. I was finding ideas for *Hugo*, but a party of women came to the next table and ordered tea – well-dressed, mature, *rusées* – and stopped me. It is extraordinary how much more critical such women are than men. The *garçon* was *agaçant* (I had not found him so); the tea was bad, the cakes were bad. But the women, by dint of not sparing the *garçon*, got the best that was to be got out of the place. And they gossiped all the time in their cold, pretty, rapid, hard tones. When I left the place was beginning to be full of such parties, with a few men here and there. Middle-aged women, well-dressed, had appointments to meet each other there. The day was torrid and superb. The lake glistened, and the park-men were watering everywhere, so that there was constantly the sight and sound of spirted water. A few motors dashing about, and many carriages. Everything characteristic of July and the end of the season. I walked slowly all the way home, stopping now and then to make notes of my ideas as they occurred to me. Before I went to bed I had finished *Hugo* in my head.

Monday, July 11th. – Last night I went through the July fair at Montmartre with Miss Thomasson. We shot at a shooting gallery. The attendant girls were brightly dressed in new pink fluffy frocks, uniformly. It seemed as if this detail signified the completion of the preparations for the fair. I have watched its development each day for a week – the gradual arrival of shapeless caravans, dirty men, and draggled women; the erection of the *baraques*, the emergence of finery, luxurious detail. And last night everything was accomplished, and our guns were served to us by damsels in marvellous pink. We spent $4\frac{1}{2}$ francs in ten minutes.

Wednesday, July 13th. – I have written 12,500 words of *Hugo* in three days. On Monday I utterly exhausted myself in writing between 3 and 4,000. Yesterday, between 10 a.m. and 12.30 p.m. I wrote over 6,000 without much exhaustion. The secret is to take a little 'recess' every 2 hours at most. To-day I wrote 2,500 words between lunch and dinner, and am tired.

The July Fair has been in full swing since Sunday, and I have examined it in detail. Last night I saw a gingerbread stall take fire. I was within a yard of it, but I watched other people put out the flames. The woman in charge behaved very well until the thing was quite finished, and then she nearly fainted while waiting for a glass of *eau-de-vie*. A stout, heavy, clumsy, and not-easily-moved woman, shabby – not in the least Parisian. The entire fair might have been burnt down. But of course one gets used to carrying one's life in one's hands – especially in Paris.

Thursday morning, July 14th. – Although I rested well last night, I heard the music of the *fête* each time I wakened, so at

4 a.m. I persuaded myself to get up and take a look at it. There was one roundabout going in the Place Blanche. Everything else was closed. A bright, hot morning. All the great *restaurants de nuit* were shut; but one *café*, the Coquet, next to the Cyrano, was open and had tables in the street. The stout lady in the cash-desk seemed just as usual. The 'place' was thick with *serpentins*. A few cabs waiting about, and a few idlers like myself. The women on the roundabout screamed just as they always do. They did not look very tired. There were four on one pig.

I then went down towards the Opéra. I saw that the foot-paths were swept by women in blue – with magnificent carriage and figures. I suppose that is due to the magnificent gesture of the broom. On the Boulevard des Italiens, three of them abreast were sweeping the broad *trottoir*. It was a fine sight. At the Opéra a large crowd for the *matinée gratuite* had already gathered – some hundreds; policemen to keep order.

This was the *real* people – dirty, stinking, brutal, importunate; the scum! Nearly all men, but just a few women. Some persons were lying asleep on the pavement. I noticed many other early-morning items, and fête-day items: such as omnibuses passing, full of policemen in spotless white trousers; a cavalry officer in full splendour walking to his rendezvous; many people beginning the day's enjoyment on their way to railway stations etc., the women dozing in the newspaper kiosks awaiting the morning papers; a youth walking along the middle of the road smoking a pipe a yard long; a drunken man trying to get up a fight with a barman concerning a small tricolour which he carried. Many bars were open. I returned home at 5.5 and wrote this at once.

Sandgate, Saturday, July 30th. – I came here by the 4 o'clock express from Paris on Friday. Wells and I walked the whole of to-day out in the country and lunched off bread and cheese at the second highest inn in Kent. We talked shop and women most of the day. He told me he had written a little humorous novel on the lines of 'The Wheels of Chance', and had been trying to persuade Halkett to take it for the *Pall Mall Magazine*.

Halkett protested he was delighted with it personally, but as to his public – well, the 'range of the story was rather narrow'. Wells defended it, and instanced Jacobs as a proof that the public did not object to narrow range. 'Yes,' said Halkett solemnly, 'but Jacobs is a humourist.' Wells was evidently very dissatisfied with his position. He talked seriously of gambling with six months of his time in order to try to do a couple or so of plays that would possibly bring in a fortune. He said he wanted £20,000 as a capital basis.

Sunday, July 31st. – I had a lot of curious sensations on returning to England after an absence of seven months – especially on waking up in an English house – shaking off France, and readjusting my perspective of England and finding how fine England was and how I was full of sympathy for it, and all that sort of thing. But I was too tired and too idle and too busy with Wells to bother about putting them down. Nearly all Wells's conversation would make good table-talk and one has a notion that it ought not to be wasted; it is so full of ideas and of intellectual radicalism. It seems a pity that it should not be gathered up. But after all there is a constant supply of it. You might as well be afraid of wasting the water from a brook. I read the proofs of *The Food of the Gods* these last two days, and gave him my views on it. He was very keen and restless and nervous to hear them.

Talking of education he said there was a particular time in human growth when each particular thing should be taught – before which it would be too soon and after which it would be too late.

The Rationalist Press Association would have liked to issue a 6*d.* edition of *Anticipations*. However, Watts broke it gently to Wells that 'God' was mentioned several times in the book and their subscribers would not like it. 'Of course,' said Watts, 'I know you only use the word figuratively.' 'Not so figuratively as all that,' said Wells.

Mr and Mrs Wells gave me between them a history of Gissing's tragedies. Gissing lived connubially with a French woman. Wells gave me an account, full of queer details, of how he went over to St Jean de Luz when Gissing was dying. Gissing's mouth had to be wiped out with lemon water, and his body sponged over with absolute alcohol. Wells did this. The woman was incompetent and stupid. The alcohol gave out, and he had to use methylated spirits. There was only one towel. One corner had to be used for the mouth-washing, another for the methylated spirits business. The corners got mixed up. Gissing, delirious, resisted. Then Wells had to *insist*, the woman objecting, on handkerchiefs being used; she said the handkerchiefs would get dirty at once – etc. etc. similar incredible stupidities.

Paris, Sunday, September 25th. – Ever since I left Paris I have wanted to come back. I came back on Friday and I am satisfied. I think I have never enjoyed the return to any place so much before. I could not keep my journal in England; there was no calm. And I was too busy with the Berquand treatment, which has yet to prove whether it will ultimately be a success.

Monday, September 26th. – My absence has had the effect of showing me how well I am established in Paris. Wherever I go, in restaurants and shops, I am recognized and greeted with the warmest cordiality. In three places to-day I have been the subject of an ovation. You would not get the same treatment in London under any circumstances. My books and my pictures (a few of each) have safely arrived, and I have bought a new bookcase and some other things, and I feel much more at home in Paris than ever.

Wednesday, October 5th. – My flat is repapered, my books shelved and pictures hung, and to-day I resumed my normal daily existence. I wrote about 3,000 words of the second story in the comic 'Jack Stout' series. I am just getting over influenza and colds. To-day also I received my fox-terrier pup Fly, and took it to the restaurant for dinner.

I am now certainly settled down in Paris. I was reading in the first two volumes of my *Journal* to-night, and found to my astonishment that I began it eight years ago. Some of it is very 'young'. But it was all enormously interesting, and some of it remarkably good.

I continue with *L'Assommoir*. It is not on the level of *Nana*. It seems all very earnest and meticulous. Yet in the scene where Gervaise is brought to bed of Nana, described with the fullest detail, no mention is made of the presence of Gervaise's elder child. But the presence of that child in such a small *appartement* must surely have been a considerable item in the affair. Also the scene in which Coupeau falls off the roof is distressingly forced and clumsy, with its artificial 'preparation'.

My hand trembles as I write; it has trembled all day. And I seem to remember noticing the same tremor very frequently this last few weeks. I certainly cannot write my old fine 'hand'.

Sunday, October 9th. – To-night I revised all the stuff for my book of stories, *Tales of the Five Towns*, to be published in January. In reading over 'A Letter Home,' which I must have written about 1893, I was a little surprised at the technical skill of it, seeing that it was the first story of any real decency that I ever wrote, and I was not in the least surprised to find it sentimental and conventional here and there. However, I only altered one word in it.

Friday, November 4th. – I saw Liane de Pougy last night for the first time, in a little ballet at the Casino de Paris. She still looked young, and, though she was too thin, like Cléo de Mérode, I thought her better than most Parisians will allow. I mentioned her name to Davray and Vallée to-day, and they both guffawed.

To-day I came down to my new lodgings at Les Sablons. The rooms face south and the weather is cold and lovely. I went for a walk in the forest, which was magnificent, but I felt suddenly tired and came back and fell asleep over Butler's *The Way of all Flesh* in an armchair which at first I had thought to be extremely comfortable.

The Way of all Flesh is exceedingly good in parts. Whenever the author is satirical he is excellent. And now and then he gets a sudden sharp effect of pathos. He is very careless in details of construction, writes without dignity, and has a tendency to moralize at length. But I read the book with real zest, which is rare. There is a vast amount of naked truth in the book.

Saturday, November 5th. – I walked into the forest [of Fontainebleau] this morning. There was a foggy mist everywhere, and on all sides could be heard the dropping of water from the drenched trees. And looking into the depths of the forest one could conjure up the magic of *As You Like It* and *A Midsummer Night's Dream*. At intervals cavalry trotted past towards Fontainebleau. One officer read a newspaper as he trotted along. For the second time in eight days the Government was in danger of falling yesterday.

Davray told me this morning that when a French newspaper was unable to live on its own it was bought up by a syndicate that exists specially for the purpose of buying moribund dailies. This syndicate prints every day one newspaper under various titles. Thus the *Rappel* and the *Radical* are the same thing under two titles. This is done for the sake of keeping the subscribers for a time. 5,000 or 500 subscribers may not be sufficient for a paper standing alone, but the syndicate can make such a number pay. And they get free passes for everything (and sell them). And when an enterprising person wants to start a paper he may buy a well-known title, and a list of subscribers more or less long, from this syndicate.

I was thinking this morning that the United States Republic has substituted an aristocracy of commercial cleverness for the old forms of aristocracy. It is said that every man has an equal chance in the U.S., and he has. But commercial aptitude, with as little honesty as possible, is the only thing that will be of use to him. And everything is so arranged that the 'risen' can trample on those who have not risen.

Friday, November 11th. – Davray told me a curious history about Héran the artist. When the latter first came to Paris from Germany he could not speak much French and was incapable of inventing the legends for his drawings. He did a drawing of a woman and two niggers (something he had seen in a café) for a small comic weekly, and the editor added a legend which led to a prosecution for indecency. Héran, the editor, and the proprietor were collectively fined 2,000 francs. That is, each was liable for the whole sum. Héran was told that it would be all right and that of course the paper would pay.

Between two and three years afterwards, Héran was summoned out of bed one morning by two police officers and taken to prison. The hour was 7 a.m. He had had no warning of any sort. The fine had not been paid. He wired for Davray. Davray went to see the 'Receiver of Fines', who was sympathetic but said he could do nothing. At length he said he would order Héran's release on payment of 666 fr. 66 centimes, and that Héran must then petition the President of the Republic to be freed personally from the remainder of the liability. Davray spent several days in collecting the money by means of subscriptions from his own friends. He told me how when he went to Anatole France, Anatole France, after hearing that an artist was in prison, would wait to hear no more, but immediately gave him some money and sent him off to the next place. At length, after very great difficulty, the money was collected, and Héran set free. Afterwards, the necessary petition was signed by Anatole France, de Hérédia, Berthelot, etc. and instantly granted.

Friday, November 18th. – Émile Martin explained to me pretty fully the financial working of his club, the Cercle de la rue Volnay. It has 1,800 members who pay 150 francs each. But the expenses are 600,000 francs a year; the rent is 100,000. The deficit is chiefly made up by the club's profits on baccarat. He seemed to be *au courant* of everything.

Sunday, November 20th. – On Friday night Mrs Devereux told me a fine retort of a pressing lover to a refusing mistress. 'Bah!' she said. 'With people like you, love only means one thing.' 'No,' he replied. 'It means twenty things, but it doesn't mean nineteen.'

Wednesday, November 23rd. – I noticed in the forest yesterday afternoon that the noise of the wind in the branches was indeed like the noise of the sea; but always distant – the noise never seemed to be near me. I got lost once, and took one path after another aimlessly until it occurred to me to steer by the sun. The moonrise was magnificent and the weather became frosty. After leaving Davray's at 10 o'clock I went as far as the forest, but the diverging avenues of trees did not produce the effect I had hoped for; there was too much gloom.

Monday, November 28th. – I went to tea at Cornillier's yesterday and met *inter alios*, Mrs Le Gallienne and Mrs James Welch. So I asked these two to dinner. We dined at the Place Blanche and then went to the Bal du Moulin de la Galette, which was certainly more wonderful than ever as a manifestation of the French spirit. The fair was proceeding on the boulevard. When we went up to the Moulin the music of the hobby-horses was deafening. But when we came down the legal hour for music had passed, and we were all three struck by the ghostly feeling of these merry-go-rounds revolving, brilliantly lighted, but quite silent.

I tried to find a leading idea for the concert scene in *Sacred and Profane Love*, but could not. I read late, and dreamed about the scene all night, and got it all mixed up, and generally wasted a vast amount of energy with no result at all.

Tuesday, November 29th. – Schwob talked a good deal about Meredith, and showed an extraordinary knowledge of the byways of English literature. He said Meredith was certainly the son of a tailor, and quoted a passage from *Peter Simple* where two characters go to 'Meredith the tailor', and he said this was George's father. It appears that Meredith now talks in a loud voice, but continually interrupts the conversation by talking to himself, mere senility of course. He has 'ataxy' or something of one leg and limps and always tells any visitor that he had the misfortune to hurt his ankle that very morning. Schwob heard this from Oscar Wilde and didn't believe it. However when Schwob called on Meredith, sure enough he had hurt his leg that very morning.

I searched after that idea for the concert chapter of *S. and P.L.* all day with no success. I stayed late at Mrs Devereux's, and then read a lot afterwards, and I didn't go to bed till nearly 2. I dreamed of the chapter all night and woke up at 6.30 after which I didn't go to sleep again. To-day, I received the *Fantasia* of Chopin from Tertia. This is the *clou* of the chapter, if only I can make it so.

Sunday, December 4th. – Schwob said at Mrs Devereux's: 'You English care about the end of a play. I mean your cultivated opinion. It may end sadly or happily, but the end must be good, logical, and strong, if the play is to satisfy you. We French are not particular about that. A weak close does not annoy us if there has been sufficient good stuff in the play.' I recognize the truth of this. But how strange that the French, so preoccupied with form, should be like that!

Saturday, December 10th. – X— described the general sensations of being well drunk as magnificent, splendid. 'But,' he says, 'you mustn't set out to get drunk. It must take you unawares.' He told me that when sober he frequently lost umbrellas, but when drunk never. He made a special point of retaining his umbrella then in his hand; it became his chief concern in life. Once he got badly drunk at Maxim's. He just had sense enough to take a cab to the rooms of a mistress he had then. She received him and undressed him and put him to bed. But he would not 'leave go' of his umbrella during the process. He passed it from hand to hand as she divested him of his coat, waistcoat and shirt, and he took it to bed. And he said: 'She became very angry with that umbrella.'

I was extremely pleased with what I did yesterday of *S. and P.L.* but when I read part of it this morning my enthusiasm was a little damped.

Wednesday, December 14th. – I worked at *S. and P. Love* till 11.30 Monday night; beginning at 3.30 in the afternoon, and I recommenced early on Tuesday and had got to the end of the first part by midday. I slept a long time after lunch and woke up with the first headache I have had for months. I went down to Rachilde's reception at the *Mercure de France* to meet Davray. He took me to an old bookseller's named Lehec, in the rue St André des Arts. We could scarcely get into the shop for books. Lehec told us he had a hundred thousand; the place smelt of damp paper. He was an oldish thin man, wearing a hat and a black smock like a French child's pinafore.

I wanted a good edition of *The Memoirs of Fanny Hill*. He had a copy upstairs in his flat. He took us up, in the dark, to the third story, and having opened the door made us enter quickly lest his cat should escape. When he had struck a light we saw the cat – a superb Persian. A curiously arranged flat, small, very clean and bourgeois. It reminded me of what Sister Glegg's might have been – in *The Mill on the Floss*. Here again all was books. He at last, after searching through several portmanteaus full of bawdy English books, found a fine edition of *Fanny Hill* in two volumes. I have since read this work. It is certainly a masterpiece of pornographic *literature*.

Davray and I went back to the *Mercure* and met the usual crowd. But Henri de Regnier, tall, thin, grey, severe, and looking quite the Norman aristocrat that he is, was there – talking to Georgette Leblanc. The latter is decidedly very beautiful. Davray told me that to have de Regnier dangling his legs from the corner of a table and talking obscenities in his calm exquisitely polished way, was a delightful experience. We dined at the Restaurant Italien in the Passage des Panoramas: a plain-looking place, with a bad atmosphere but a magnificent cuisine and good Chianti.

Afterwards we didn't quite know what to do, and Martin suggested that we should go down to the Porte Maillot and see the *cafés* frequented by chauffeurs and their mistresses. *Ça nous changera un peu*. We went, wandering down through the Palais Royal and then taking the Métro. We got a good café but it was empty, and we saw only one chauffeur and *he* hadn't a mistress.

December 30th. – I left Paris last Wednesday week, and stayed two nights with Wells. I read the typescript of the first part of his new novel [*In the Days of*] *the Comet*. He said that his financial position was becoming more and more secure. I came to Burslem on Friday

Walking through the town yesterday I saw two child's funerals exactly of the same kind; a procession of 5 or 6 pairs of women in black with white trimmings; two pairs carried the small oak coffin which was covered with wreaths and which they held by white cords over their shoulders. Immediately behind the coffin, the chief mourners, in one case a man and a woman. The coffin occurred about the middle of the procession. These little forlorn smug processions ambling towards the cemetery were very curious.

·1905·

England, Tuesday, January 2nd. – Last year I wrote 282,100 words, exclusive of re-writing. This comprises two plays with Eden Phillpotts, *Christina* and *An Angel Unawares*, the greater part of *A Great Man*, the whole of *Hugo*, and one-third of *Sacred and Profane Love*; also a series of facetious short stories entitled 'The Adventures of Jack Stout' and one other short story. I don't think I ever did anything like so much creative work in one year. I made no particular advance commercially. I had several grave disappointments including the result of my visit to Scotland, and the result of *Christina*, the loss of a dog and a pocket-book, and the commercial failure of *A Great Man*. On the other hand the artistic success of *A Great Man* was a genuine surprise to me. I firmly decided to marry.

I came down to Torquay last Friday. Eden and I have worked on *An Angel Unawares*, and to-morrow it will be completely finished.

Tuesday, January 3rd. – To-day we put the last touches to the play. I am frankly rather optimistic about it. Eden is too, but not frankly. It is the most saleable thing I have ever done, either alone or in collaboration.

Thursday, January 5th. – I went with Mrs Phillpotts to tea at the Findlaters. A spinsterish house. A mother aged over 80, rather fine, keen on liberal politics and the Scottish Church crisis. I liked her. Then the three daughters. Mora the oldest is the housekeeper, non-literary, aged about 43; a sort of Cinderella, certainly made use of and squashed by the other two. The other two are Jane Helen and Mary, aged from 36 to 40, better dressed than Mora, positive in their opinions, quiet, refined, and above all things canny. A nice Scotch tea with good old silver spoons and admirable scones; literature discussed rather from the business side.

Wednesday, January 11th. – On Wells's recommendation I have been reading Henry James's *The Ambassadors*. I have read 150 pages out of 450, and I have given it up. It certainly does contain, as Wells said, some wonderful little pictures of Paris, and the Anglo-Saxon colonies there. The writing, though difficult, is amazingly adequate. It is merely perfect. But I found the plot clumsily managed, and a very considerable absence of passionate feeling. I came to the conclusion that the book was not *quite* worth the great trouble of reading it.

Friday, January 27th. – I have recovered from a bad attack of influenza – three days in bed. All my work upset. I find I can't recommence writing without a change and I am going to London a week earlier than I meant. I have read a great deal in Mark Twain's *Life on the Mississippi*, a fine amusing, interesting work quite new to me. Also Balzac's *Rivalités* with much gusto.

I went through Frank Beardmore's works yesterday. The throwing was the most interesting. The thrower, a man thick and grey with clay, working in a filthy mess, proved to be a Town Councillor of Longton.

Saturday, February 11th. – Schwob told me that when he ardently wanted a book his voice always went hoarse in asking the price of the bookseller. A bookseller sufficiently acquainted with human nature, he said, could take advantage of such a symptom; and some did. He instanced Rahir of the Passage des Panoramas whom he called one of the three greatest booksellers, if not the greatest, in Europe. The other two would be Rosenthal of Munich, and Quaritch. He said that he was dining with M. L. of the Français the other night. She has a wealthy lover and keeps a considerable state. Though very ignorant of literature, she has just 'taken to' collecting books, and she described to him her feelings when looking at a fine book. They were the same as those of a woman tempted by lace, jewels, or a man. The desire was imperious and must be satisfied. ... And this in an ignorant woman!

Monday night, February 13th. – To-day I really recommenced work and I worked all day. Idleness is a very bad thing indeed for me in every way.

Tuesday, February 14th. – I went to the new Bal Tabarin last night. I think it is the only ball in Paris that is open every night. I saw the famous 'La Goulue' there perched on a high chair at the bar; a round vulgar, rather merry face, looking more like a *bonne* than a dancer and a *dompteuse des lions*. With an expenditure of 7 francs on drinks with another ex-dancer, I learned something about the life of the paid dancers in public balls. They get four francs a night, *'et elles peuvent trouver de bons amis'*, said the ex-dancer, whose younger sister, a fine big girl with a clear complexion, was dancing the *quadrille réaliste* on the floor. This sister I was told made 5,000 francs besides her pay as a dancer during the short season at the Jardin de Paris last year.

Thursday, February 16th. – *Tristan and Isolde* at the Opéra last night with Mrs. Devereux. Everybody and everything thoroughly bad, except Alvarez, and even he frequently sang through his nose.

When I told Mrs D. how surprised I was to learn from the newspaper that A. B. Walkley was married, she said that his marriage was one of the cardinal facts of his life.

Mrs D. said that perhaps I should not at first care very much for Walkley; that he united a very broad mind with a good deal of superficial conventionality, was prim, precise, very difficult to please, and ferociously ironic etc.

Tuesday, February 28th. – While I was lying in bed yesterday morning I read in the *Figaro* that Marcel Schwob had died on Sunday. He dined with me on the 16th and seemed vivacious enough. Since then I had heard nothing. I lunched with the Davrays yesterday, and Davray cried in talking about it. He had just been to the house and seen Maurice Schwob. In the evening I received from Maurice Schwob, via Philippe Champion, a request that I should communicate with Marcel's

English friends. Moréno is only supposed to arrive in Paris this morning.

Thursday, March 2nd. – Raphael told me a good story about Tree. Tree came to Paris and went down to the Français to demand free tickets. He was knocked about from one official to another till he found the right one. 'A quel titre, monsieur?' asked the official.

'Je suis M. Tree,' said Tree.

'Mais à quel titre demandez-vous des billets?'

'Je suis M. Tree, l'acteur de Londres.'

'Ah, vous savez, si nous donnions des billets a tous les acteurs de Londres ... !'

Friday, March 3rd. – Somerset Maugham came up for tea. He has a very calm almost lethargic demeanour. He took two cups of tea with pleasure and absolutely refused a third; one knew instantly from his tone that nothing would induce him to take a third. He ate biscuits and *gaufrettes* very quickly, almost greedily, one after the other without a pause, and then suddenly stopped. He smoked two cigarettes furiously, in less time than I smoked one, and solidly declined a third. I liked him. He said he had sold a play to Liebler through Fred Kerr, on the terms of £300 down, and £100 every quarter until they produced it – in advance of royalties. I asked him if he liked the Quartier Montparnasse and he said, 'Yes; the atmosphere of it is rather like Oxford.' He said that as soon as he could he should spend three years in travel.

Saturday, March 4th. – Raphael and Co. dined with me at the Place Blanche and then we went to the Alhambra, and I was introduced to the manager, a young and extremely English man who could scarcely speak any French. Houdini (an American) the 'handcuff king', was the principal attraction. It appears that this man really *has* a gift for getting out of handcuffs and picking locks. He certainly did some extraordinary things last night – including one in which Raphael's overcoat took a share. Raphael told me that Houdini 'had got out of all the principal prisons in the world'. In Germany he challenged the police to put him in a cell that he couldn't escape from. They took the challenge and he won. But they denied that he had won (from motives of policy). He brought an action against them which lasted three years (costs £1,000) and ultimately gained the day.

Monday, March 13th. – I brought Kelly down to Les Sablons on Friday. Davray told him, in talking about Meredith, that Meredith had told *him* that the preface to the *Egoist* is merely a series of imitations of various authors that Meredith knew, one after the other. Meredith read aloud this preface to Davray, vocally imitating each author, and Davray said the effect was astounding.

Saturday, March 18th. – Kelly gave me a notion for a dramatic situation the other day: two people married who find themselves brother and sister. I saw I could turn it into a good unprintable short story. While I was talking to Davray on Thursday at tea, the thing suddenly presented itself to me as a play for the Grand Guignol, and changing the conversation abruptly, I told him I had a subject for a play for the Grand Guignol. I saw the whole play, in two acts, like a flash, and I described it to him. He said: 'We ought to do that together.' At 6.30 I began to write the first act. I worked from 10.30 to 11.30 p.m., and yesterday for 25 minutes, and I had finished a full draft of the first act. I read it to Davray last night at the Nouvelle Athènes in the Place Pigalle, and he was much struck by it. I propose to write the second act to-day. Davray will re-write it in French. I have written it part in French and part in English.

Tuesday, March 21st. – I went to see Docteur L. yesterday. He has a flat on the entresol in the rue Marbœuf, *en plein quartier chic*. The door was opened by a rather agreeable, but not *excessivement chic*, girl, who politely picked up a pencil which I dropped. She showed me into a fairly spacious waiting-room horribly and characteristically furnished. A crimson plushy carpet all over the floor, a set of chairs and a sofa all in their *housses*; a modern Louis XVI table richly gilt and fairly well made, bearing old copies of *L'Illustration* and *La vie en plein air*. A huge lamp-standard in a corner; a piano with draped back; a column surmounted by a specimen of *art-nouveau* statuary; to wit a withered tree, with a huge rock near it, the rock cut in the form of a face, as big as the tree – this in bronze. Two pairs of double doors heavily draped. Odd statuettes and signed photographs of men.

The doctor surprised me by appearing through doors where I had not expected him. A man about 30, *hérissé*, hair and beard sticking out; slightly stiff in manner, but improving later. Beyond muttering the word 'Vallée' he made no reference to the extremely *empressé* introduction which I had to him. He evidently sprang from the lower middle-class and was unable to rely on his manners.

He took me into his consulting-room, a room more frankly and awfully *art-nouveau* than the waiting-room, but less distressing, because it was all in one scheme and showed some sense of design. I soon found that he knew his business; but with that he proved to be somewhat vain and self-important. He wrote out his *ordonnance* at excessive length, with *première-ment*, *deuxièmement*, *troisièmement*, and so on. He drew me the design of a *canule*, and he couldn't help referring to that design twice afterwards, as it were fishing for praise of his ability to draw at all. However, he was extremely practical. I should say he would be a brute in a hospital, and a brute with women. He looked a brute. But in some ways I did not dislike him. He is an *arriviste*, and quite young.

Friday, March 31st. – I went around with Vallée last night to see some of his patients. One was at Champagne – what is called a Cité Jardin, built for the employés of the Creusot Steel Company. The population must certainly be over a thousand, and is probably much more. We arrived when it was nearly dark. Vast blocks of houses four or five stories high, of dark stone, and fearfully ugly and forbidding. A *place* here and there and plenty of vacant plots. It was extraordinary how a four-or-five-storied block struck one as being out of place in the country, where land is plentiful. The houses were a cheap imitation of Parisian houses. No lights on the stairs, no lights in the streets, but windows lighted here and there, giving hints of mean interiors. He stopped in a narrow street (why narrow I cannot imagine), quite short, containing, however, three cafés – all pitchpine and zinc and a too cheap simplicity. It was Mi-Carême and the air was full of the sounds of uncouth instruments. A little troupe of masquers arrived from the outskirts, where the large residences of the Creusot managers are, and passed into a café. The whole impression was terribly forlorn, ugly, and dispiriting. It was a beautiful evening, with a warm, caressing wind, and flashes of lightning.

Sunday, April 9th. – Cornillier called yesterday morning, and I was telling him about a good early picture by Tissot that Ullman had bought for 200 francs. He said that a long time ago Tissot had a mistress, with whom he had continued relations for a considerable period. He decided to break the *liaison,* and he wrote one letter to his mistress, giving her the gentlest possible hint that the affair must ultimately come to an end, and another letter to an intimate friend, a man, saying brutally that he was sick of the thing and wanted to marry. He mixed the letters up, and the mistress received the wrong one. She committed suicide. Tissot was deeply affected, regarded himself as her murderer, and became *dévot.* This was really the origin of his journeys to Palestine, and the ruin of his art.

In the evening I went with Ullman to Antoine, and saw *Les Avariés,* which is an extremely good sermon, and an extremely bad play; and *La Parisienne.* I was more enthusiastic than ever about the latter. I can recall no portrait of a woman which is at once so true and so brilliant. But what a storm it would raise in England! I enjoyed myself. And as I walked home, I thought how fine Paris was, and that in old age, or even earlier, if I quitted it, I should look back on these days and perceive that I had been happy.

Tuesday, April 18th. – It is extraordinary how enthusiastic and graphic Davray always becomes when he talks of Oscar Wilde. This afternoon he finished an article on him, and at tea began to talk. He recounted lots of things. Here is one. After coming out of prison Oscar became friendly with Esterhazy, very friendly. Davray protested, and said Esterhazy was a *crapule* and all sorts of things. Oscar agreed. 'But,' he said, 'I must make my society of thieves and assassins now.' (This is a translation of the French phrase.) 'If Esterhazy had been innocent I should have had nothing to do with him.'

Saturday, May 13th. – I was telling Martin on Wednesday night at the Folies-Marigny how depressed I was on Sunday and how to cap all I suffered horribly from jealousy in the evening, and he said: 'Mais qu'est-ce que vous voulez? Ça, c'est la vie! Mieux ça qu'une vide? Moi, je n'ai jamais été plus heureux que quand je me trouvais malheureux!'

Thursday, May 18th. – Miss Thomasson said last night one of those picturesque things that only Americans do say. Of a Frenchman whom we know: 'He learnt to dance much more slowly than you do. He's nervous. If you look at him he fancies you are counting his legs and I'm sure he thinks he's got about six.'

Friday, May 26th. – At Hélène Berthelot's yesterday. A perfect museum of Chinese art. I saw some stereoscopic photos of Chinese tortures. They made me feel queer. Mme Berthelot told me a curious thing about them. When he took them the young photographer was so occupied with his work that he thought nothing of the scenes he was witnessing. But when he developed the negatives and printed them and saw what he had witnessed, he fainted.

Monday, July 17th. – I came down to spend the summer at Les Sablons. I still had 5,000 words of *Sacred and Profane Love* to write, and I finished the book yesterday morning before lunch. I wrote the third part with less verve than the other two parts, and was doubtful of it several times, but, when the thing was quite done, it seemed to me all right. During the last week or two I was unable to think seriously about anything else.

Tuesday, September 19th. – Mrs Devereux told me about Frank Harris. She said he was 43 when she first met him in 1895. He then had a fixed idea that he should die at 44. He had a marvellous voice. Lamperte offered him 5 years' tuition if he would only study, free, and said he would be the greatest bass that ever had been. His eloquence was astounding. He made a political speech, and was adopted as Conservative candidate for one of the Ridings. No dinner party was complete without him. Carlyle had thought very highly of him, and this opinion was echoed by a later generation. Lord R. Churchill thought him the greatest man he had ever met. John Walter of *The Times* believed in him long after most others had ceased to do so.

He bought the *Saturday Review* for £5,000 and sold it for £30,000. He was never mean. He was the sort of man who would stab a person in the back and rob him of all he possessed, and then give the entire proceeds to another person. He was easily influenced, and easily intoxicated by his own eloquence. During the Boer War, he was at a luncheon party, and began to talk about the sufferings of the Boers in such a manner that the entire party, including a general returned from South Africa, and anti-Boers to a man, was literally reduced to tears. Finally he burst into tears himself, jumped up and left the house.

Wilde offered him the leading idea of *Mr and Mrs Daventry* and he bought it for £100, and afterwards gave Wilde two further sums of £50. Harris wrote the play, got it produced, and made £4,000 out of it.

Friday, October 13th. – During the last week I have thought persistently over *Whom God Hath Joined*, and have had very good luck in finding ideas. So much so that on Tuesday night even, I was able to relate the whole plot to Madame Jane. Since then I have begun to sketch an outline of the first 30,000 words.

Saturday, October 21st. – I wrote the fourth of a series of Five Towns short stories complete on Wednesday; nearly 5,000 words. With the result that I had a violent colic after dinner, and a bilious attack yesterday.

Sunday, October 22nd. – I dined with Raphael and Madame last night. Went to bed ill and got up ill. This morning I went to Mrs Devereux's by appointment and was told we had to lunch with Ochs at Chevillard's at the Rond Point. Ochs was waiting for us. Francis de Croisset came in, kissed Mrs Devereux's hand twice in about 3 minutes and left: a young dandy, very young, and not quite quietly dressed. We then, after lunch, went to the Autumn Salon just for a quarter of an hour to look at the Rodins. It was the first time in my life that Rodin's work has appealed to me. Then to the Colonne concert, which was crowded and bad. But the No. 2 Brahms symphony pleased me very much. After the concert Ochs and I went for a walk along the quays, and then he came up here to have tea with me.

Thursday, November 2nd. – Yesterday was All Saints' Day, and I walked in the Montmartre Cemetery. It *was* rather like a City of the Dead. Certainly as much a relic of barbarism as anything one is likely to see in Paris, with its tons of flowers and ugly wreaths ornamenting the most deplorable monuments and houses of corpses. Vast crowds of people, many in black, but not all; many, if not most, out for an airing: moonstruck crowds before certain monstrous mementos of surpassing vulgarity. A very few women here and there with moist eyes. A file of soldiers (seasoned) at the gates, made to supply the absence of an iron railing to separate incoming from outgoing crowds – and naturally looking stupid. Also policemen and officials. In the street flowershops and stalls, and wreath shops and stalls and quantities of cabs.

At night I went to Calvocoressi's, and met Vignès the

pianist, an extraordinary enthusiast for Russian music and an exceedingly fine player. The two first played a duet, and then Vignès had the piano to himself. What struck me was the fine pure quality of the pleasure we obtained, all of us, the simplicity of the enthusiasm; and yet what years of cultivation had gone to provide it, in all of us. Calvocoressi's mother sat upright, on an ordinary cane chair, half blind with cataract, and encouraged our enthusiasm. I expressed my pleasure. 'Mais croyez-vous que nous ne sommes pas heureux comme tout, tous les quatre!' said Calvocoressi, his face beaming.

Vignès, having played a piece, would usually turn back the pages to find some particular passage and would end by playing the whole thing again. When explaining the beauties of passages while he played them he became quite incomprehensible to me, what with his bad accent and his rapidity. Yes, what struck me as I came away was the singular 'purity' of it all, the absence of sex, of anything in the nature of an aftertaste. It reminded me of fine musical evenings in London.

Tuesday, November 7th. – I have just finished reading *L'Œuvre*. It has taken me a long time, because I left it in the middle to read Wells's *Kipps*. What a colossal affair it seems by the side of *Kipps*, so serious, tremendous, and imposing. The middle parts seem rather carelessly done; the detail piled up without sufficient attention to the form. But the final scene between Claude and Christine – the fight between love and art – is simply magnificent; it moved me; it is one of the finest things in Zola. It is overdone, it goes farther than the truth; but purposely; Zola has stepped into the heroic in this scene, as he does now and then. All the close of the book is most affecting.

Thursday, November 9th. – Yesterday I formally began to write *Whom God Hath Joined*, and at 11 p.m. to-night I had written a thousand words. To-day I lunched with J. B. Atkins and his wife at their flat in the rue des Belles Feuilles. A large flat, but with a strange mixture of furniture, and the rent, 7,000 francs, seemed to me to be very high. There were no fires. Both of them very 'English' in the finest English way. I liked them much. Atkins said that Dilke never forgave Stevenson for his character's celebrated remark about the *Athenaeum*: 'Golly! What a paper!' and that herein was the explanation of the *Athenaeum's* persistent hostility to Stevenson. The story is at any rate *ben trovato*.

Tuesday, November 16th. – Calvocoressi brought Vignès the pianist here last night, and he played a good bit. He is a little man with red eyes, short sighted, and the first thing he did was to go peering at all the pictures. He has an extraordinary enthusiasm for all kinds of beauty. A thoroughly single-hearted artist, reminding me of Sharpe in some ways; but, being Spanish, his temperament is much warmer and less restrained.

I finished the first chapter of *Whom God Hath Joined* yesterday at 7 p.m. Ten thousand words odd. And it seemed to me rather original and rather good, and quite unlike anything I had done before.

La Rafale, by Bernstein, in 3 acts. At the Gymnase. I had heard a good deal of the play, which is a success, and of Simone Le Bargy in it. Crowded house on Tuesday. The play was clever but factitious, very showy in treatment. Simone was better than the play, but not a great deal better. She is much above the average 'leading lady'; there is not, however, a great deal of truth to life in her performance. Her talent seems more imitative than original. On the whole my opinion of the Paris stage is certainly declining. The number of things really first class is excessively small, and the success of such a show as *La Rafale* does not make for righteousness either artistic or moral. Deceit and swindling and gaming are the three things held up to one's sympathy in it. A house full of fine frocks, and much sniffling in lace handkerchiefs during the scenes held to be poignant. A wretched, uncomfortable, dangerous theatre, like all the rest.

During 1905 I published three books. *Tales of the Five Towns*, *The Loot of Cities*, and *Sacred and Profane Love*. The latter went slowly into a second edition and was also published by

Tauchnitz. It appeared serially in *To-day*, and the second serial rights were bought by Tillotsons.

I wrote:

1. The 2nd and 3rd parts of *Sacred and Profane Love*.
2. 'The City of Pleasure', a 60,000 serial for Tillotsons.
3. The first 30,000 words of *Whom God Hath Joined*.
4. Eight or ten short stories, all about the Five Towns.
5. A new series of 'Savoir Vivre' articles for *T.P.'s Weekly*, which began on December 1st. Also some articles for the *New Tribune*.
6. A little French play in two acts, translated by Davray. Title: *Que Faire?*

My total of words was slightly over 200,000, much less than usual, but then I took two months clear holiday in the summer. On the whole not a satisfactory year. Genuine success seemed as usual to delay and postpone itself. But I find that I am much less interested in money than Phillpotts and Wells.

·1906·

Thursday, January 18th. – To-day a contract was definitely fixed up with *T.P.'s Weekly* for a serial by Phillpotts and me at the price of £450. The first 3 instalments to be delivered by 20th February.

I bought three books this afternoon, having gone out in very bad weather to get theatre seats, and it seemed as if I had begun book-collecting again. I certainly wanted to have some books bound, and the idea of fine simple severe bindings seized hold of me. But one cannot buy bookcases and bibelots, and sterilized plants, and cigars, and jewellery, as I have been doing lately – and indulge in bookbinding too.

Saturday, January 20th. – After having dined with Raphael on Thursday night, I called at the *bureau de tabac* opposite the Opéra under the Grand Hotel to buy cigars and cigarettes. The *patronne*, a stoutish powdered agreeable woman of 50 or so, was in charge, with a young girl apparently her daughter. There is also a *patron*; quite a family affair. 'J'aime beaucoup mes clients,' said the *patronne*, and one could see that she *did* love not only her regular clients but the whole business. I told her that I called in nearly every night to buy a Mexican cigar, and yet she had not recognized me. 'That's because I'm not here at the time you call,' she said, which was true. 'But I'll come down earlier to see you. I shall know you in future.' There was a charming air of intimateness about the whole place, despite its extremely central position and fluctuating cosmopolitan *clientèle*, and this air I noticed for the first time. I also noticed for the first time the immense variety of stock which the French Government offers to its customers. It appeared that the manufacture of the flat Jupiter matches had recommenced, and I bought some for my flat matchbox. 'We have ordered ten thousand,' said the *patronne*.

Monday, January 29th. – After having written my *T.P.'s W.* article to-day I went out for a stroll through Paris, meaning to reach a bookshop on the Quai des Grands Augustins. I went down the Rue Notre Dame de Lorette, which I think is the street that pleases me most in Paris – and I bought Arsène Houssaye's *Souvenirs de Jeunesse* which I have been reading to-night. In the Passage Jouffray where I frequently find a book, I found nothing, and when I got to the Grands Augustins the *étalage* of the shop was already taken inside, it being 6.30.

I do enjoy these slow walks through Paris on fine winter afternoons: crowded pavements, little curiosity shops, and the continual interest of women. I walked back to the Châtelet station of the Métro and went to the Concorde and thence walked to the Place de l'Opéra, stopping at the Trois Quartiers shop, where there are some very nice things. Then I went to the *Standard* office, and Raphael came out and dined with me. I got home at 10. I have had several days of regular unhurried work lately, interspersed with such strolls. I have come to the conclusion that this is as near a regular happiness as I am ever likely to get.

Thursday, February 8th. – I half expected O'Connor to-night – kept the evening free for him – but he did not come. So after some hesitation I determined to spend it by myself, just to see how I got through with it. The restaurant was too full, and the service slow, and I didn't enjoy my dinner, and I ate too much, and read the *Tribune* all through. I came home at 9.30, and read a little of Voltaire's *Candide* – I bought a nice edition of his *Contes* yesterday, half bound, for two francs – and enjoyed it very much.

Then I meditated on the serial and got one or two notions. I was very gloomy at first, but got cheerful about eleven. I think I could accustom myself to reading in longer spells, and to spending evenings alone fairly comfortably if I tried.

I am reading George Moore's *The Lake*. It is so smoothly written, and so calm and beautiful that I can enjoy reading it without even taking in the sense. Frequently I have read half a page without grasping the meaning at all, or trying to grasp it. It is a most curious novel, perhaps not really good, but certainly distinguished in a Yeats-y way.

Sunday, February 11th. – Calvocoressi told me the other day, as an illustration of how journalism in France does not pay, that a friend of his had just started a theatrical and musical review, and had asked him to write for it. All the other contributors, except Calvocoressi, *paid* 25, 30, or 40 francs to have their articles printed. The editor said to him: 'Of course I shan't ask *you* to pay,' and Calvocoressi rather wittily replied, 'Well then, in those circumstances I shan't ask *you* to pay.'

Monday, February 12th. – I called at a *bureau de tabac* this morning to buy a box of Mexican cigars, and was told that the State was out of stock of them, and would not have any more ready till next month. A good example of State management. The same thing happened with Jupiter matches a few months ago.

I have been having difficulties with the tenants overhead, through the medium of the *concierge, apropos* of pattering about in boots on uncarpeted floors. I asked what the monsieur was by profession, and was told that he was manager of a large business office, and that he sang at the Opéra (presumably in the chorus) three times a week. This seemed to me very Parisian.

Tuesday, February 20th. – Opéra masked ball on Saturday night. The Atkinses supped with me at the Place Blanche. We got to the restaurant too soon, and found all the waiters asleep in odd corners, and the room darkened. It was like going into an enchanted palace. We woke it up, and lighted it up, in an instant. By the time we left, 12.30, there was a noisy band playing, and a crowd of guests.

We got to the ball at 12.45. Already an enormous crowd. Great cohorts of men in silk hats. I should say the men outnumbered the women by 5 to 1. The people who looked really well were the chorus girls etc. from the opéra who were thoroughly used to fancy dress and knew how to walk and how to dine. Outside these, and a few professional men, there was almost no fancy dress; but plenty of dominoes. The *coup d'œil* in the *salle* was superb, and the orchestras (3) fine and deafening, as they ought to be.

There was, relatively, very little dancing. Not a single well-bred Frenchwoman there, so far as I could see, and very few *toilettes* worth a damn. But the general effect was dazzlingly immense. And the cohorts of men, all on the look-out for something nice, seemed to lurch from time to time in one direction or another, as crowds do, bodily, and sometimes even to stampede. There was something undignified in these masses of masculinity. The waiters and *ouvreuses* seemed politer and gayer than usual. We left at 3.15. Many people had preceded us.

I was a wreck on Sunday, and the noises of people overhead got on my nerves. However I wrote a brief account of the ball for the *Standard*, rather sardonic, and took it down to the office.

O'Connor dined with me last night. He still slanged Sargent, and he said that Renoir was a master. In literature, with his usual charming violence, he cursed Conrad's style (very cleverly) and was enthusiastic about Thackeray. We came back here and went through a lot of my books. He proved himself at once a fairly accomplished bookman. But late in the evening, when we were talking about religion, Malthusianism, etc. I discovered that in some matters his ideas were a strange mixture of crudity and fineness.

Thursday, March 1st. – To-day I finished one half of the serial 'The Sinews of War', and to-morrow it begins to run in *T.P.'s Weekly*. I have kept my contract with myself, and the stuff is good of its kind; but I am slightly overworking. I sleep badly and digest not well.

Wednesday, March 28th. – I finished the 17th instalment of 'The Sinews of War' to-day, which leaves three to do, and this evening, on my return to Paris from Moret, I received in a letter from Phillpotts an adumbration of the plot for our next serial in collaboration.

Lately, besides having the influenza, I have been occupied in putting my Moret flat into an artistically habitable condition. Yesterday morning in a second-hand shop in Moret I found a Louis XV commode in carved oak in excellent condition, and bought it for 45 fr. without bargaining. I also bought a rather worn Empire bookcase for 20 fr. Impossible to keep my journal while I am so preoccupied with the serial and with questions of cretonnes, carpets, and the arrangement of old furniture and purchasing of fresh.

Thursday, May 3rd. – A week last Friday night I went to England, reached Waterloo on Saturday morning and Burslem on Saturday afternoon.

I left the mater's on Thursday in a snowstorm and went to London. I hurried off to the St James's Theatre to see *His House in Order*, and found a theatre organized and worked with the perfection of a battleship. An air of solidity, richness, cleanliness, decorum; punctuality, short entr'actes; general care for the public. Such a difference from Parisian theatres. The only things that were bad at the St James's were the play and the acting. The play, which is a great success, and has been seen three times and written about three times by Wm. Archer, and praised by Walkley and Jo Knight, is most certainly a thoroughly pretentious, sentimental, and dull play. It never convinces. It is badly conceived in its very essence, and in execution the skilfulness is only episodic. Some trifling passages of dialogue are absolutely true to life, startlingly so. And I can only account for them by the supposition that Pinero has overheard them and dragged them bodily into the play. Five-sixths of the acting was mediocre and worse. And I was struck by the funeral gait at which English plays are 'taken'.

However, I enjoyed the whole evening because it was so English and I was observing so interestedly the whole time.

Saturday, May 5th. – To-night, at Antoine's, *The Wild Duck.* An interesting experience, to see how one's ideas have developed! There was something, after all, in the old cry

against Ibsen that he was parochial. The play still seems
clever; it is sometimes brilliant. But it never strikes one as
beautiful. And it *does* seem fearfully Norwegian. The symbolism is simply deplorable, even in its ingenuity. If anyone
had hinted such ideas to me about Ibsen 15 years ago, I should
have accused them disdainfully of an inability to appreciate
masterpieces. Yet now I am pretty well convinced that Ibsen
is not a writer of masterpieces. And he is stagey! He who was
supposed to have rejuvenated the entire technique of the
stage, has become stagey in 15 years! I was several times
bored by the play, but nevertheless, a most interesting evening
of historical retrospect.

Sunday, May 6th. – And yet I was thinking this morning in
bed that perhaps I was too hard on Ibsen last night. We owe
him a great deal after all. He made one of those steps towards
realism which alone constitute the progress of art. He is very
able; he is in no sense an amateur, but a thorough expert; and
if he doesn't find actually much beauty, he shows us where
to find it.

At the Cornilliers' to-day, some talk of Rodin. Henri Havet
stated definitely that he was going mad, was in fact mad. Of
erotomania. He said also that he did pieces of sculpture and
then deliberately broke them.

Someone remarked that an artist had the right after all to
break up a piece that did not please him.

'Yes,' Havet explained, 'but not to send it broken to an
exhibition, in imitation of the Venus de Milo, etc.' A Madame
N., a very pretty woman, who knew Rodin personally, gave a
curious experience of his peculiarities. He is in the habit of
showing little erotic pieces to lady-visitors. He took her to one
such, a woman seated or bending down, in the middle of a
plate. 'Le sujet était assez clair,' she indicated.

He asked her what she would call that, by way of a title for
it. She said politely 'La source de volupté.' 'Splendid!' said
Rodin, and scratched the title on the plate. The very next day
her sister was at the studio, and was shown the same piece.
'What would you call that?' Rodin asked her. 'The Water

Fairy,' suggested the sister. 'Splendid!' said Rodin, and wrote the title on the other side of the plate. Someone said that he got his titles like that, by asking everyone and then choosing the best.

Cornillier said he once sat next to Rodin at lunch, and happened to say that a certain woman was not pretty. 'What!' cried Rodin solemnly. 'It has happened to you sometimes to meet a woman who was not beautiful? I have never met a woman who was not beautiful.'

I remembered, then, Rodin's dictum, published somewhere, that everything on earth is beautiful. With this, in a way, I agree.

Thursday, May 10th. – On Monday night, when I was at *L'Enfant Chérie*, by Romain Coolus, with Miss Green, I had most distinctly the sensation of being shocked. It was in the last act. An old man has been abandoned by his mistress, who has found another lover. The old man's daughter tries to get the mistress back for her father, as he is mortally struck by grief. There is a scene between the two women, in which the daughter urges her father's mistress to return to him. 'Look here,' she says, in effect, 'even if you can't go to him altogether, you could surely see him one or two afternoons a week.' I suddenly felt myself shocked; other people were in the same case. I can't at the moment remember ever having been shocked before. The experience gave me an idea of how pious Philistines must often feel, and was therefore useful. My being shocked was absurd. At the same time the scene was clumsy and bad artistically. Had it been good, should I have been shocked?

Sunday, May 13th. – A month ago the French inland postage was altered from $1\frac{1}{2}d.$ to $1d.$ I happened to see the notice of the change received as instructions to the postmistress at the local post-office at Les Sablons. I don't know how many post-offices there are in France, but there must be 50,000 at least. This notice was not printed. It had been written in violet ink in rather cramped irregular calligraphy, and then multiplied on one of the old-fashioned 'hektograph' machines, as we used to call them. At the same time as the change of postage, a new *carte-lettre* at 1d. was introduced. I asked for one of these *cartes-lettres* yesterday at Les Sablons, but none had yet been received.

I came down to Les Sablons yesterday. It is summer. The garden full of sun and flowers; the roads humming with insects. The chestnuts in front of the house 'snowing' all the time. Bright blue sky, with a border of 'capricious towering' white clouds. I walked up to the 'grand entrance' to the forest this morning, and it was so beautiful and so imposing that even Henry Ward Beecher's silly remark about a tree being finer than a cathedral seemed for the moment to be not so idiotic and meaningless after all.

Thursday, May 24th. – I finished another section (of 10,000 words) of the divorce novel on Monday night, having written it in 8 days.

I spent this afternoon with Eléanora Green. She told me a saying of her little brother who was taken by his mother to see the central meat markets: 'Maman, il doit y avoir pas mal d'accidents ici.' As an unconsciously horrible remark of a child's, it wants beating.

We went to the exhibition of Gustave Moreau's paintings. An artist, but not a great painter. Magnificent conceptions of literary subjects, well but not adequately treated. His preoccupation with the story of Salome is singular. We noticed one small painting where Salome was holding the head on a charger high up out of the way of a little dog who was yapping and leaping after it.

Friday, June 15th. – At 5 p.m. on this day in the forest of Fontainebleau I became engaged to marry Eléanora.

Friday, August 3rd. – At 11 a.m. on this day, at Caniel, my engagement to Eléanora was broken off.

In the meantime I had, with the utmost difficulty, finished my novel: *Whom God Hath Joined.*

Les Sablons, Friday, July 19th. – I only noticed yesterday that the mark of the aged female peasant in this village is a cap (I suppose it would be called a mob-cap – but I don't know what a mob-cap is at all), which is drawn very tightly over the head, very tightly indeed. It is apparently formed out of a cotton handkerchief, for there are the ends of bows to be seen at the top-back of the head and also below. These aged creatures are almost without exception deformed, chiefly by vast deposits of fat. They wear very short skirts (always some shade of blue much washed out); and, like the majority of peasant women of no matter what age in this district, they have exceedingly unpleasant voices.

But an even more extraordinary specimen of the sex passed along the high road last night while we were dining. This was an old woman harnessed to a small cart containing merchandise that I could not distinguish. On either side of the old woman was harnessed a dog about as big as a pointer. An old man stalked majestically behind at a distance of several yards, carrying a very long staff, and uttering at regular intervals a mournful cry of a few syllables which doubtless referred to his wares. The woman was, in the accepted phrase, 'little more than a brute', and there was no doubt about, no concealment of it. They did not belong to the district. Probably they toured like that through a whole department, or several departments, and as Madame Bergeret suggested, might be in easy circumstances.

Talking about eating, Madame Bergeret said that in the Midi (neighbourhood of Toulouse specially) there used to be men who prided themselves on enormous powers of eating. They did not usually eat a great deal, but on occasions, when put to it, they would perform terrible feats such as consuming a whole turkey. The result sometimes was that they were very ill. The method of curing them was to dig a hole in the muck-heap, strip the sufferer naked, put him in the hole, and pack him tightly with manure up to his neck. The people who did this did it with gusto, telling the sufferer what an odious glutton he was. The heat generated promoted digestion in a manner almost miraculous, and next day the sufferer was perfectly restored.

Saturday, July 20th. – There was a repercussion on me last night of the Lever *v.* Associated Press libel case. After all, even in an ultraplutocratic newspaper office like Harmsworth's a verdict of £50,000 damages must cause some friction, and probably a good deal of moral suffering on the part of the personnel. The spectacle of Lord Northcliffe in a rage is quite human and touching. In my present series of articles for the *Evening News* on buying a library, there were two articles praising and blaming in detail various cheap reprints. The first was printed without the least comment. Then (the next day) came the Lever verdict against the *Daily Mail* and the *Evening News*, and last night I received a very apologetic letter giving every reason but the right one why the second article should be shortened and modified. One phrase in the letter (which was impeccably polite and in good taste) struck me as very naïve and funny: 'It is almost impossible for one who is outside a newspaper office at the moment quite to judge the relative position of affairs.' *Je te crois!* I wrote at once and gave them a free hand.

Yesterday and the day before, in two walks in the forest and by the Seine, I constructed completely the first three acts (four scenes) of the play which I am taking from *Anna* for the Stage Society.

Monday, July 22nd. – On Saturday morning I walked for two hours in the forest, and completely finished the construction of the Five Towns play. I saw a big, strong deer that crashed fiercely through thick bushes like a stag out of Sir Walter Scott, stood watching me some time, and then crashed and crackled off again. Once I sat down to rest on a felled tree, and a squirrel appeared. It bounded to within a few yards of me, then sprang up a tree, hung to the bark like a fly for several seconds, and finally ran higher very rapidly, at the same time taking to the side opposite to me so that I could not see it. The tree was not a large one nor had it either many branches or much foliage, but I could not find the squirrel, though I walked round and round it and searched most carefully.

One might well call it a solitude, the forest! Yet at the end of a very long avenue one suddenly sees a puff of vapour arise and slowly disappear. It is the dust of an automobile flying down the Route Nationale which cuts through the centre of the forest.

In pursuance of my new invention of Sunday, I did no work of any kind yesterday. I trifled with the art of illumination, and read the greater portion of Jeanne Marni's *Pierre Tisserand* – chiefly to please Madame B., who is aunt of the author. Some of the dialogue in it is truly admirable. But all these novels of sexual sentimentality are altogether too narrow in outlook: they lack nobility: they do not arouse a single really fine emotion. This is what there has got to be in *The Old Wives' Tale* – a lofty nobility. I got it now and then in *Whom God Hath Joined*, but in the next book I must immensely increase the dose.

During the last day or two both Marguerite [Mrs Arnold Bennett] and I have definitely decided that we prefer living in the country. I had settled that we wanted a small *château*, in this district if possible, where there is forest and river and heaps of other scenery. And we were to have an auto and a small yacht on the river, and to give up the Paris flat: this change was to occur in about two years' time when my lease of No. 3 rue d'Aumale would expire. Before dinner we went for a walk to St Mammès where the water was busy with great barges. And I had suddenly the great idea of abandoning my deep ambition for a sea-going yacht, and having a barge as big as their barges, fitted up as a luxurious houseboat, with a small motor attached. This would serve as a complete moving home in summer, and we could go all over France in it. (We should keep the flat.) Indeed we could go all over Europe in it. This scheme took hold of me so strongly that I thought of nothing else all the evening, and became quite moody.

July 23rd. – I began to see yesterday how my 'fine writing' and illuminating must develop. I saw that I could only advance with any hope of continuing by uniting utility with beauty; that I must not therefore make fine manuscripts for the sake of making them, but rather in connexion with my own work; also that I must form a natural hand that could be written quickly. These principles having been arrived at, I began to practise a little.

M. and I went for a short walk in the forest last night. The moon was nearly full and very bright. But the effect was disappointing. I have noticed this before. To be at its best moonlight wants to be seen over a large flat landscape or on water. There is very little in the tree-tracery business – silhouetted against the moon, etc.

Wednesday, July 31st. – I seemed suddenly yesterday afternoon to wake up from the industrious calm of my honeymoon. The need came over me all of a sudden to leave my desk and go out for a walk. Although I had not really been working very hard, the top of my head felt as it feels when I *have* been working too hard at a serious book. M. came with me. We walked to the other end of Moret. Gradually I began to feel better. I said that I must have an excursion, a movement right out of Les Sablons. She said she perfectly understood that it would do me good to get away from here for a bit. So we at once arranged with the Marriotts that the males should cycle to Nemours and the women go there by train for the day, to-day. At night I read to the Marriotts four of my poems.

Thursday, August 1st. – At night Marriott was talking of the greed of certain famous painters. He said that at a pension table d'hôte on the continent, when the fish came round, F— would help himself to two whole soles, of course quite regardless of the rest of the company. Similar tales of B— who must be an inconceivable boor. When the round did not begin with B—, and he saw the dish travelling from person to person, he would cry out aloud his fears that not sufficient would be left for himself. On the other hand when the round began with him he would take so much that the waiters, perceiving his greed, would next time begin so as to serve him last. Marriott has also told (and Mrs M too) numerous almost incredible stories of B—'s tyranny over his wife – under the guise of being utterly devoted to her. That is to say, he passes his life in forbidding her to do, to eat, to enjoy things that he considers dangerous for her. The attitude has become a mania; it springs of course from a purely selfish fear of losing her. Without knowing B—, I have acquired quite a violent distaste for him: and each fresh tale that I hear of his monstrous egoism gives me a sort of morbid pleasure. I thought I might use him up as the husband of the stay-at-home sister in *The Old Wives' Tale*.

Friday, August 2nd. – I went out for a walk yesterday afternoon and stayed out two hours and a half. It rained about half the time. I meant to try to finish my poem 'A Love Affair', and by good luck I finished it. Nearly all the time I was walking very slowly in the forest. I was so tired in the evening that I could scarcely keep awake. Marguerite also was tired, through the strain of listening all day to English as it is mumbled by the English. Afterwards I wakened up, when I wanted to go to sleep, and explained to Marguerite the inadvisability of being jealous of my verse.

A LOVE AFFAIR

Down flew the shaft of the god,
Barbed with miraculous change.
Struck – and a woman emerged from a clod.
This was strange.

Eyes and a mouth it had owned,
Movable head that would nod,
Waist and a bosom agreeably zoned –
But a clod.

Now when her eyes met the male's,
Flame from them wrapped him in fire;
Breath of that bosom o'erwhelmed him in gales
Of desire.

Stung by the flattering wave,
Proudly his manhood he spent.
Rare was the gift of her soul – for she gave,
But he lent.

Wit she had none to amuse,
Knew not the trade of a wife,
Heard not the voice of the muse. Now the muse
Was his life.

Weary, he called on his God:
'Quench me this woman I've kissed!'
Lo! In due time she returned to the clod.
She was missed.

Saturday, August 3rd. – Yesterday I finished the full draft of
the second act of the play, being thus one day in advance
of my programme. I have not yet spent on it, in any one
morning, more than an hour and a half. The fact is that all
the imaginative work in it seemed to be, and really was, done
before I started.

Last night I had a letter from Pinker enclosing for signature
a most unsatisfactory contract for *The Statue*. I flatter myself
that this almost certain loss of money, at a time when I particularly want it, did not disturb me for more than a few
minutes. Thanks partially to my diligence in daily absorbing
Epictetus.

Saturday, August 10th. – At last I think I have got into a
fairly 'formed' formal hand for 'fine writing', and for the
writing of my next novel in particular. I wrote a letter in it
yesterday and gave it to Marriott to criticize. He found no
fault with it at all. Indeed he was very enthusiastic about it
and sent his wife up to look at it. He said it would puzzle
Johnston, the author of the text-book on writing and illuminating, to produce anything as good in the way of ordinary
quick calligraphy. Also that if I wrote a whole book keeping
up to the standard, it would be unique in the world. When I
lamented that one could not get a really *black* ink that would

run through a fountain-pen, he said he preferred the slightly greyish tint of common ink. He dissuaded me from doing the novel in double columns.

Yesterday I seemed to pass an entirely satisfactory day: Italian, piano, my play, writing finely, excursion with my wife, good meals, and reading my own stories at night in the garden to the Marriotts, who laughed continually as people ought to laugh at such stories. I also had news of the sale of *The Ghost* in Germany – not that the sale of *that* book gave me much pleasure.

Wednesday, August 14th. – After two days' work on the final writing of the play I now perceive that it will be a great strain to finish it at the rate of two acts a week. I gave nearly four hours of concentrated desk-work to it yesterday, and over three hours to-day, rising to-day before six o'clock. Some months ago, at intervals, I seemed to detect a very slight temporary deterioration of my eyesight. Then I noticed nothing. To-day I was conscious of a certain uneasiness in the organs. Several times there was a mist before my eyes, as there is now – a mist which I can dispel by a strong effort of the will, but which returns. I wonder whether this is the end of my hitherto magnificent eyesight, or whether it is merely due to my having got up too early this morning.

August 20th, 21st, and 22nd. – Martin lent me the recently published 4th volume of Taine's Letters. These letters are full of prejudice, of praise of the past, of distrust of the present and of the future; of distrust of the people. He seldom loses an opportunity of dispraising the present, of showing his profound pessimism. It is difficult to read *Graindorge* without thinking that the author was a first-class man, and it is just as difficult to think that the writer of these letters was a first-class man. As for his literary judgement, what can be said of a critic who enthusiastically places Macaulay's speeches above Pascal?

Sunday, August 25th. – The village is now 'full' for the season. And in the morning out of the windows of cottages comes the sound of women singing to cheap pianos. Bad songs, false sentiments, false notes, out of tune. It has a 'shocking' effect on the ear in the midst of a beautiful landscape. All the painful, artificial, idle, vicious mediocrity of Paris seems to surge out of the windows.

I had the idea to-day of introducing a French public execution scene into the second part of *The Old Wives' Tale*.

August 26th. – We bicycled yesterday through Montigny, Grez, Villiers-sous-Grez, Larchant, and Nemours. And I exhausted myself in pushing Marguerite about ten miles altogether against a head wind. We had tea at Villiers, just a straggling village without any attraction except that of its own life. During our meal the drone of a steam-thresher was heard rising and falling continually.

Tea in the street; they brought out and pitched for us a table, also vast thick basins, which we got changed for small coffee-cups. But we could not prevent the fat neat clean landlady from serving the milk in a two-quart jug which would have filled about a million coffee-cups. We sat in the wind on yellow iron chairs, and we had bread and perhaps a pound of butter, and a plate of sweet biscuits which drew scores of flies. Over the houses we could just see the very high weathercock of the church. Everything was beaten by wind and sunshine. From the inside of the little inn came hoarse argumentative voices. Curious to see in this extremely unsophisticated village a Parisian *cocotte* of the lower ranks. She was apparently staying at the inn. With her dog, and her dyed hair (too well arranged), and her short skirt, and her *matinée* (at 4.30 p.m.), and her hard eyes, she could not keep from exhibiting herself in the road. The instinct of 'exposition' was too strong in her to be resisted. She found fifty excuses for popping into the house and out again.

Wednesday, August 28th. – I am so tired to-day as to be depressed.

On Monday I finished my poem 'Town and Country'.

TOWN AND COUNTRY

GOD made the country and man made the town
And so man made the doctor, God the down.
God made the mountain, and the ants their hill,
Where grinding servitudes each day fulfil.
God doubtless made the flowers, while in the hive
Unnatural bees against their passions strive.
God made the jackass and the bounding flea;
I render thanks to God that man made me.

LET those who recognize God's shaping power
Here but not there, in tree but not in tower,
In lane and field, but not in street and square,
And in man's work see nothing that is fair,
Bestir their feeble fancy to the odd
Conception of a 'country' ruled by God;
Where birds perceive the wickedness of strife
Against the winds, and lead the simple life
Nestless on God's own twigs; and squirrels, free
From carking care, exist through February
On nuts that God has stored. Pray let them give
The fields to God's kind hand for just a year,
And then of God's own harvest make good cheer.

THIS cant of God and man would turn me sick,
Did I not deeply know the age was quick
With large conception of a prouder creed
Whereon we shall not feel the craven need
To count ourselves less noble than a weed.

FOR me a rural pond is not more pure
Nor more spontaneous than my city sewer.

Friday, August 30th. – Before tea yesterday I finished the play, and called it *Cupid and Commonsense*. It seems to me to be one of the best things I have ever done; quite as good as most of my novels. The title is merely *ad captandum*.

Friday, September 13th. – Three days' attack of influenza, or chill, by which I was incapacitated from any reasonable work.

I recovered to-day, and resumed *The Sole Survivors*, with hatred of it. I also went out into the forest and found some pretty good ideas for my novel.

I finished the fourth volume of Taine's letters. I have now changed my opinion about Taine being prejudiced. But the only dignified reason I can discover for his pessimism is his state of health. He was undoubtedly a great and an austere man, with very high principles. He thought only of his work, which was the ascertainment of historical truth. Not a single reference in all this volume to his money affairs, and scarcely a reference to physical comforts.

The portrait of the man gradually grew clear to me, and inspired me with ideals similar to his own: the doing simply of the work which one believes to be best, and the neglect of all gross and vain considerations. Why should I worry after fame and money, knowing as I do that these will not increase my happiness?

As I could not write I had leisure to think about myself. I saw that even now my life was not fully planned out; that I was not giving even an hour a day to scientific reading, to genuine systematic education; and that the central inspiration of my novel was not fine enough.

To-day I began to rectify this, resuming my Spencer. I came across something good in Spencer, in the essay on 'Progress': 'the profoundest of all infidelity – the fear lest the truth be bad'. Even such acquaintance as I have with Spencer has enabled me to perceive the inconceivability of at least two newspaper interpretations of the new theory of matter in Gustave Le Bon's new book; viz., that matter is quickness, a form of movement. In my pre-Spencer days I might have been capable of accepting such rot as at any rate suggestive. (I don't know if Le Bon is as silly as his critics.)

I bought Taine's *Voyage en Italie*, and was once again fired to make fuller notes of the impressions of the moment, of *choses vues*. Several good books by him consist of nothing else. I must surely by this time be a trained philosophic observer – fairly exact, and controlled by scientific principles. At the time one can scarcely judge what may be valuable later on. At the present moment I wish, for instance, that some schoolmistress had written down simply her impression of her years of training; I want them for my novel. The whole of life ought to be covered thus by 'impressionists', and a vast mass of new material of facts and sensations collected for use by historians, sociologists and novelists. I really must try to do my share of it more completely than I do.

Monday, September 16th. – We went out in the morning with a bottle of wine and a pasty, etc., attached to our bicycles and lunched ten miles off in the woods of Champagne, on the roadside, near to a large-ish property, preserved for game but arranged with a lack of taste and of dignity impossible in England. A ridiculous ornamental water, of irregular shape, in front of the house. This water passed by a tunnel under the road and terminated in a pool of disgusting filth. In the centre of the water was an island rockery, and on this rockery a large vase, about 3 feet high, gilded all over, with a plant on the top of it bearing pink flowers. The effect was lacerating.

Lunching modestly thus by the roadside, shut in by these two estates of wealthy people, it was impossible to crush altogether the snobbish feeling that one ought to despise one's self for the crime of being simple and unwealthy. I certainly have a liking for domestic display and largeness for their own sake.

I could not sleep well last night, nor the night before; and not all Epictetus and Marcus Aurelius could ensure cheerfulness and perfect equanimity. However I worked as much as usual, and now after tea, as I write this in the garden, with my feet chilled and the first breath of Autumn blowing on me, I am recovering command of the forces.

Thursday, September 19th. – I recovered this morning from a mysterious malady which resembled influenza in the intestines. It did not prevent me from working every day. In reading Smollett's *Travels* it has occurred to me that I go about very blind, wrapped up in myself.

To-day I finished the construction of the first part of *The*

Old Wives' Tale. I also conducted a sort of preliminary treaty with the Leberts and their architect for getting this house altered and taking it on a lease.

Monday, September 23rd. – Young men marched about the village yesterday to the accompaniment of one grotesquely-sounding brass instrument – difficult to imagine anything uglier or less dignified than this music, to which even portly, grave firemen in uniform will consent to parade themselves. I asked the barber what the noise was about, and he explained that it was the young conscripts who had on the previous day received their marching orders (*feuilles de route*) and were being merry (no doubt factitiously) previous to their departure a fortnight hence. Immediately afterwards entered another customer, a middle-aged man, who put the same question as I had put. 'C'est qu'ils ont reçu leurs feuilles,' replied the barber; these were his exact words, I think. The enquirer's eyes questioned for a second or so, and then he understood. Several middle-aged men began talking about the shortness of service nowadays. They were all agreed: 'Deux ans – c'est rien.'

Lately I have several times seen grown men and women holding cows on a rope in a field while the cows pastured. This morning I saw a man and a woman and a boy entirely occupied with five grazing cows. Economically justified, this means, must mean, that any device for tethering the cows (granted the absence of hedges and of trees suitably placed for tethering) would cost more than the value of the labour of these three persons. Smollett would enquire as to this. On the opposite side of the road were several cows tethered in an orchard. The absence of hedges in France has certain inconveniences.

Thursday, September 26th. – All day the drone of a threshing machine near by, rising and falling, with an occasional high shriek of a whistle to signal a stopping or a starting. A hot heavy day, with undecided hints of a storm. For several days the fine weather has shown a disposition to be capricious. Yesterday afternoon there was a boisterous wind, with a few drops of rain to threaten my beautiful white hat. Night fell to its howling. But later it died away, and this morning the sky was as pure as ever. It grew hotter, and I had to change, first into a white waistcoat, and then into a different suit. The temperature in my room was 22°. Then cloud came, full and dark and ragged, only to disappear completely and leave the sky without a mark.

After lunch I stood at my open window and watched two bees visit every flower on a bush, entering completely hidden into each blossom and emerging after a few seconds. I was surprised at the certainty, rapidity, and thoroughness with which they exhausted the bush of perhaps a hundred flowers.

Saturday, September 28th. – Madame Lebert has ascertained for me that a threshing machine, with 12 men, will thresh 60 sacks of wheat in a day at 30 frs. the sack; that the men get 5 frs. each and their food, and that the machine costs 50 francs; that altogether the work runs to 2 frs. a sack.

Saturday, October 5th. – Curious example of wit in Wordsworth; I should imagine it to be rather rare: The description of the old pack of cards in the first book of *The Prelude*, pp. 17–18 of the Temple Classics edition. I am now reading *The Prelude* with intense pleasure. I have abandoned several other books in order to read it. – *Travels of Wilhelm Meister*, Taine's *Voyage en Italie*, and Lessing's *Laocoon*. I have just read half of Proctor's *Primer of Astronomy*, and now for the first time understand how not only the varying lengths of days, but the seasons, are caused by the plane of the equator not being the same as the plane of the ecliptic. Simple enough! Perhaps one day I may comprehend the precession of the equinoxes.

I had a headache for three days, but I did my daily portion of *The Sole Survivors* and finished the thing, which I have damned a hundred times, yesterday morning. This is the last play I will ever touch, until I have a play produced.

On Tuesday I begin my novel.

Recently I have taken to long walks in the forest. On Wednesday I discovered the Malmontagne, with wide views of the forest. In nature it is large spaces, bleak, with simple outlines and little noticeable detail, that appeal to me most strongly. I am more 'sympathetic' to Dartmoor than to any other spot on earth. Next to that, the sea. Here, what chiefly appeals to me is the forest seen in the mass from a height, and the long smooth stretches of the Seine between St Mammès and Montereau. With such things I class in my memory the panorama of the Apennines, spotted with hill-towns as seen from the first range behind San Remo.

Paris, Tuesday, October 8th. – Lunch at the Davrays in their luminous new flat in the narrow Rue Servandoni. Victor Tissot was of the party. Editor of Hachette's *Almanac*, of *Mon Dimanche*, etc. What I call a typical Frenchman. Grey, aged between 50 and 60. In neat mourning. Low voice, with an air of quiet, resigned, amused, ironic philosophy. Talked well. Talked apparently on a system. He would go from subject to subject, and was careful to 'play fair' between your subjects and his. Travelled a good bit. Spoke of the most awful hotels as mere regrettable incidents in travel, but not worth making a fuss about. The queerest thing he told us was about a hotel at Pau, where, he being a *monsieur seul*, he had been refused a room on the ground that the hotel was a *hôtel des familles* and *messieurs seuls* were dangerous. He naturally told the landlady that if that was all he could easily find a woman and return with her in a short time.

Wednesday, October 9th. – I have often thought, during the last year, upon the uselessness of trying to describe faces in literature. No vision is raised by particularization in words. I now find this minutely explained in Lessing's *Laocoon*, which is certainly a most useful and illuminating treatise for the writer. Homer, it seems, never described Helen. He merely said she was beautiful, and kept insisting on the fact, and showing the influence of her beauty – as on the elders. This is the way to follow. Lessing's theory of the propriety of describing ugliness is ingenious, and perhaps good. The choice in subjects of a painter like Delacroix will not justify itself under Lessing's philosophy, and Lessing is undoubtedly right.

Delacroix was great in spite of his choice of subjects. *Laocoon* has clarified and confirmed my ideas very much.

Yesterday I began *The Old Wives' Tale*. I wrote 350 words yesterday afternoon and 900 this morning. I felt less self-conscious than I usually do in beginning a novel. In order to find a clear 3 hours for it every morning I have had to make a time-table, getting out of bed earlier and lunching later. This morning I calculated that I could just walk to the Croix de Montmorin and back in an hour. I nearly did it this morning without trying, in heavy rain. To-morrow I may do it. A landscape of soaked leaves and thick clouds and rain – nothing else. But I like it.

Monday, October 14th. – A young man named F— came to spend the week-end with us. I found him very enthusiastic about poetry, music, clothes, furniture, and architecture. He had a number of tales to tell of the stage in London. He said that the Court Theatre had really made a lot of money, but that at one time everybody believed it to be Shaw's own venture, that is to say, financially. He said that the best pieces had been the greatest failures, e.g. *Pan and the Young Shepherd*, and a piece of Hauptmann's, which played altogether to £13. He said that the season at the Adelphi of Hall Caine's plays was Hall Caine's own, that the profits on *The Bondman* averaged £75 a week, and the losses on *The Prodigal Son* £75 a night.

Wednesday, October 16th. – I have now written 7,000 words of the first chapter of the novel, and am still far from the end of it. Regarding it objectively, I do not see that it is very good, but from the pleasure I take in doing it, it must be.

Nothing but rain. I walked 4 miles in 59 minutes this morning in the rain. And this afternoon I went with Marguerite to Moret in pouring rain. A promenade on a thoroughly bad day in autumn is the next best thing to a promenade on a fine late spring morning. I enjoy it immensely. I enjoy splashing waterproof boots into deep puddles. Now it is dark and I write this by my desk-lamp (after only 1½ pages my eyes feel fatigue) and it is still raining on the window.

Friday, October 18th. – Calvocoressi said that you can call a man anything in Marseilles except 'mobile'. Call a coachman a 'mobile' and he will get down from his box and try to kill you. The majority of the Marseillaise have of course no notion why they object to being called 'mobile'. The explanation is that during the Franco-German war Marseilles enrolled a regiment to go to the rescue of Paris. This *garde mobile* got as far as Avignon where, someone shouting 'Prussians', it threw down its arms and ran back home. Calvocoressi is a native of Marseilles.

Sunday, October 20th. – A curious instance of avarice from Calvocoressi. An old lady living in a 9,000 fr. apartment in the Avenue de la Grande Armée, who pays two servants 150 fr. per month each in order to induce them to stand her avaricious ways. There is a story in this. If a piece of mutton was bought that was too much for one day and not enough for two, she would say to the servant: 'Supposing I don't eat any to-day will there be enough for to-morrow?' 'Yes, madame!' And she would starve. If her son was reading the paper in the evening she would say: 'Anything interesting in the paper?' 'No, nothing special.' 'Then let us turn off the light, and sit in the dark and talk.' When alone in the evening, in order to save the electric light, she would spend her time in promenading on the staircase.

Monday, October 21st. – To-day I finished the second chapter of my novel. I seem to be rather uneasy as to its excellence. The date of the first part worries me, as my own recollections don't begin till ten years later than 1862. However, the effect of the novel will be a cumulative one.

Lately I have been overworking, in spite of all resolutions to the contrary. I rise at 6.30 or so, and after reading Italian, one hour's walking etc. I begin on the novel at 9.30 and work till 12.30. Then my afternoons are often taken up with articles. I had meant to keep my afternoons quite free of composition. Nevertheless, my health, thanks to walking 4 miles in an hour each morning, is simply admirable, and I sleep well. But my eyesight is weakening.

Saturday, October 26th. – The forest is now, for me, at nearly its most beautiful. Another fortnight and the spectacle will be complete. But it is really too close to our doors for us to appreciate it properly. If we had to walk 5 miles instead of 500 yards in order to get into one of these marvellously picturesque glades, we should think we were exceedingly lucky in being only 5 miles off and not 50. On the whole a very wet month with, on days free from rain, heavy persistent fogs lasting till afternoon. The sound of voices is very clear in the forest in this mushroom weather. I have learnt a little about mushrooms. I have tremendously enjoyed my morning exercise in the mist or rain. But mushrooming only interests me when the sport is good.

In general, slightly too much work. 18,000 words of *Old Wives' Tale* in 2 weeks 4 days.

Much tempted to throw up my Italian and my piano, on account of stress of work, but I still stick to both of them.

Thursday, October 31st. – Apropos of the agitation for abolishing the Censor in England, it occurred to me that not even the advocates of freedom seek to justify the free treatment of sexual matters in any other than a high moral-pointing vein. The notion that sexual themes might allowably be treated in the mere aim of amusement does not seem to have occurred to anybody at all.

Monday, November 4th. – F— came on Saturday. I got him on to theatrical gossip. He regarded Waller as a mere irresponsible boy, always shirking business, always losing money to his backers. As an instance of business methods of running a theatre: dress rehearsal of some 'Waller play' was simply awful. Waller stopped it and drove off to Comedy Theatre to get hold of Louis Calvert. L.C. wouldn't come. L.W. begged and prayed, and at last L.C. yielded, giving orders that the waiting company should go out and eat or rest, and be back sharp at midnight. He began sharp at midnight, made the company first of all play the piece through as it stood, and refused to allow even Waller to comment on it. This took 6 hours. Then 1 hour's rest. Then he started over again, and began to cut heavily. People complained that he had left out all the first half of the first act, that everyone was lost etc., but he carried through the autocratic rôle, got the parts re-typewritten etc., and finished about 11 a.m. There was no other rehearsal. F— said L.C. ought to get £100 for the work. He said Alexander persistently used the same scenery over and over again. He said Alexander was a good business-like manager, but very 'near'.

I finished 1st half of 1st part of *Old Wives' Tale*. 8.30 to 11 walk by Seine and in forest. Thinking about next chapter of *Old Wives' Tale*.

Leberts and Siege of Paris, November 19th. – The Leberts in the little shut-off room in kitchen. Just room for 3. Fire burning in corner. Lebert with newspaper that he glanced at mechanically, with his cap on. Mdme half seated on corner of something. Cat.

I ask them details of siege of Paris.

It seems to have left no particular mark on their minds. They thought more of accident just before, and they had a lot of potatoes. They had 3 children (went to school as usual). At first meal 125 grammes each per day (but only 30 grammes later). Had 3 *bons de pains* every other day (1 lb. each person per day). As employé of railway, he was requisitioned for ambulance work when necessary. On field of battle when a horse fell the man leapt on it, and cut it up and carried it off. He was in Garde Nationale (1 fr. 50 per day). Exercise every day. The different companies of G. N'aux usually traversed Paris with their *musique*.

Personne ne travaillait.

The cold. The waiting on the greens.

Rice requisitioned specially for soldiers.

Convinced that Govt. did tricks with food towards the end, so as to induce the people to acquiesce in capitulation. Description, *exprès*, of food.

When capitulation announced, Garde Nationale (300,000) *faisait des potins*. Govt. accused of treachery.

Black bread, horse-chestnuts and *avoine*. During 10 or 15

days this bread quite uneatable. It destroyed stomach unless cooked over fire.

He bought wood at 5 frs. the 100 kilos.

When the Germans entered by Ch. Elysées, only Bonapartists and Royalists (among Frenchmen) were there. Republicans kept away. Cafés closed. One alone was kept open, and was afterwards sacked by the mob.

Prussians confined to C. Elysées, Cours la Reine and Place de la Concorde. Those who tried to *'forcer la consigne'* were roughly handled. One killed. This pride of Parisians in keeping away during 24 hours of German occupation seemed to strike the Leberts more than anything else. Otherwise they seemed *only to attach importance to the siege because I did. Like inhabitants of picturesque town or curious village.*

During the commune they lived in a cellar for a fortnight. Baker next door, and they got bread over wall. When this (for some reason) could no longer be done, they called out to passers-by to order bread for them, or something of that kind. Their cool tone in saying 'Yes, we slept in cellar and kept shutters closed because there were always shooting bands in the streets.'

Wednesday, November 20th. – I still hanker to write a book (and publish it) of personal impressions. Had several ideas lately for articles. One: 'The Individualism of Socialism'; dealing with what socialists such as I ought to do in the way of personal living, and dealing also with the fact that all political questions, such as those which agitate socialists, are simply questions of machinery – and do not directly touch the question of living (interiorly).

Mme Lebert withdrew from her offer to let this house (Les Sablons) with vegetables and fruit for 1,000 frs. a year. She shied at the vegetables and fruit. I would not give way, so we most amicably and affectionately agreed to part. I find myself, on the eve of going to England, without a programme, which is rather disconcerting. However, we are free to live where we like: by the sea, e.g. I feel I want to live by the sea, in Holland, at Fontainebleau, and on the S. coast of England all at once.

I am getting rather tired of the confinement of this little flat; but one day I shall look back to the evenings here, in the room where I work and sleep, with M. sewing or trying things on her mannequin, and the constant preoccupation of the fire and the temperature and my cold – with regret as a perfect time.

Regularly I have been doing 2,000 words a day at least. 12 to 1500 words of my novel in the morning, and pieces of articles in the afternoon. I am now almost sure to do 365,000 words in the year.

Tuesday, November 26th. – Yesterday I walked to Fontaine-bleau in the pouring rain, and walked in and about the town for over 2 hours with a house-agent looking at possible houses. I saw one small one, surrounded by a walled garden that might suit. Distinct pleasure in examining these houses. I fell in love with the one I liked, and at once, in my mind, arranged it as it ought to be. I lunched at the Cygne, had coffee at a café, and walked all the way home – and it never stopped raining! Then after tea I wrote 1,300 words of the novel. This morning, while the whole place was being upset with preparations for our departure, I wrote 2 to 300 words more of the novel, and this afternoon I packed my large trunk and arranged my papers. That I should have worked so easily at my novel in all this mess shows how it has got hold of me, or I of it.

Tuesday, December 3rd. – I finished the first part of *The Old Wives' Tale* here in Paris on Friday afternoon.

Wednesday, December 4th. – Came to England. Impressed again by the extraordinary self-consciousness of travellers. On the platform at the Nord, another man and I tramping up and down the platform got half-smothered in a cloud of malodorous steam. He could not help turning to me as we emerged, to share his sensations with me by means of a gesture. Had he not been on a journey he would have ignored my existence. The English side of the journey has improved.

Better carriages: electric light, contrasted with oil in French train. (Strangely medieval – oil lighting, requiring men, ladders, and very heavy lamps.) Permanent way much better in England than in France. Carriages quieter. Porters better and more agreeably man-like.

Friday, December 6th. – Dinner to Pinker last night. I sat between W. W. Jacobs and H. C. Marillier.

Pett Ridge told one good story about the little boy who said there were only nine Commandments, and when his father said that at any rate when he went away there had been ten, replied: 'Yes, but mother broke one last week.' Jacobs said it was disgusting getting older, and that he hated that young men should raise their hats to him out of respect for his superior age.

Daily Despatch offered me 6 guineas a column for articles, 50 per cent above my previous highest price. I had the idea of doing a series of impressions of the New London for them. A little in the G. W. Steevens' style. One notion for an article was the underground foreign population of waiters in London.

Tuesday, December 10th. – We went looking at private hotels to-day. Quite horrified by a decent one in Queen's Gate. Pail on stairs. Yet comfortable. But too horribly ugly and boarding-house-y. I had begun by putting cost at £40 a month. I then dropped it to £25, under M's influence. It must now go up to £30 or £35. Lunched at Harrods Stores, crammed; had to wait a minute for a table. Home in petrole-ous omnibus. This morning I walked 5 or 6 miles through Roehampton and Barnes. Impressed by the cleanliness, order, and sober luxury of all the dwellings I saw.

Tuesday, December 17th. – Dined with Pett Ridge at the Garrick. Pett Ridge said Arthur Morrison had sold his Japanese pictures to the British Museum for £4,000, and bought a motor-car. Also that B. Pain had bought a car off W. S. Gilbert and sold it again. We finished about ten. I had a fairly clear idea of P. Ridge's bachelor life. I liked much of his taste, and all his quiet 'fundamental decency'. Witty enough. Tales about old Hy. Kemble. E.g. speaking to young Bancroft (aged, kind, trembling voice), 'Your mother was a beautiful actress, a most delightful actress, but as for your poor bloody old father – well, there it is – it's no use talking.'

Sunday, December 22nd. – We came down to the Potteries yesterday afternoon. Seemed to have better ideas as to the scientific causes of provincialism.

I went for a walk this morning up Sneyd Green ['Toft End' in the Five Towns novels]. Untidiness; things left at loose end. Broken walls, deserted entrances to what had been spacious gardens. Everything very misty. Curious enclosed 'ash-court' place, with an iron device in the middle. Pit shafts – one only fenced in, another with a wall 12 or 15 feet high, and a low wooden door in it. Men in bright neckties sallying forth, rather suspicious, defiant, meanly-shrewd look. Mean stunted boy crouching along smoking a pipe which he hid in his hand while holding it in his mouth. Complete waste of Sunday: deserted goal posts in gloomy mist. Mild wind. Cold, chilling, clammy. Idea: public baths never bring in great profits to relief of rates, like gas. ... I was forgetting to note the sound of hymns from chapels and schools. People going into Catholic chapel. Kids waiting outside school-room door (Sneyd Green), evidently while first prayer was being said.

Tuesday, December 31st. – I spent just over 23,000 frs. this year, and earned about 32,000 frs. I wrote *The Statue* (with E.P.) and *Sole Survivors* (with E.P.), *Love and Riches, Death of Simon Fuge*. Five other short stories. First part of *The Old Wives' Tale*. About 46 newspaper articles. And my journal. Also my play *Cupid and Commonsense*, and scenario of a new humorous novel, *The Case of Leek* [*Buried Alive*]. Grand total: 375,000 words. This constitutes a record year.

·1908·

Thursday, January 2nd. – The most horrible east wind, which incapacitates me from arranging my thoughts in the streets. I began *The Case of Leek* [*Buried Alive*] yesterday, according to programme, and continued it to-day. But yesterday I was cold and to-day I had a headache. 1,600 words in 2 days. Chief observation in London: that it is a city of very rich and very poor. The vastness of this rich quarter is astonishing. In Bond St this morning the main thing to be seen was the well-groomed, physically fit, male animal: a sort of physical arrogance with it.

I continue to walk about and to have the richness of London forced into my head. It is almost disconcerting to think that all this vast idle class has to 'go' one day. The idlers in this hotel make an imposing array. Offensive many of them.

Curious example to-night of unconscious and honest sexuality by a decent woman. A Scotchwoman (age about 45) sitting by the fire in the lounge describing to another woman her sensations on seeing a regiment of Highlanders (with music) pass along Princes St, Edinburgh. 'I couldn't bear to look at them – made me cry – my heart was so full. Nothing moves me so much as a regiment of Highlanders. Their costume ... And so tall ... Such fine men ... Such white skins ... But I shouldn't like to be in the same room with them. I shouldn't like to know them.' She was quite unaware that phrase after phrase which she used was an expression of sexual feeling.

Finished 1st chap. of *Case of Leek*, and must write it again, damn it.

January 5th. – Frost and fog to-day. Curious romantic scenes around the Round Pond, its centre lost in fog, and exotic birds wheeling in and out of the unseen, and slipping on the ice when grabbing at food thrown to them. Sparrows hopping amongst them. Chatted with a policeman at the corner this morning. Evidently very young. So young and fresh that the only really policemanish thing about him was his uniform. A sort of man dressed up as a policeman. I have noticed this before in young policemen, but have never defined it so well.

Friday, January 10th. – I finished the first chapter of *The Case of Leek* on Wednesday – 5,400 words in three days – despite worry. But it was a sort of second-writing, as I had to begin it all again on Monday.

To-day I went to a rehearsal of *Cupid and Commonsense*. Not *quite* so depressing as I had anticipated. But bad enough. I was struck by the immensity and the wearisomeness of the producer's task.

January 17th. – Another rehearsal yesterday at Terry's Theatre. I saw all the play. It exhausted and depressed me very much. Nothing seemed to get over the footlights. The players now played too quickly instead of too slowly. Local accent all wrong, and certainly incurable. But the other people seemed to be quite cheerful and optimistic. All the surroundings – the manufactory of amusement repelled me. Women cleaning and whispering, etc. Cold. Oil lamps to warm. Smallness of theatre.

Proceeding regularly with the *Case of Leek*. To-day I re-wrote what I wrote yesterday. To-morrow I shall have finished a quarter of the whole. I am deliberately losing sight of the serial, and writing it solely as a book.

Sunday, January 19th. – Mist yesterday morning; fog this morning. Both days I noticed 'the gigantic ghosts of omni-buses' in the gloom. It is a phrase to use.

I called and saw Vedrenne at the Queen's Theatre yesterday afternoon. Seemed a decent sort of chap, more sincere than the run of them; also he kept his appointment to the minute. He said that in the theatre he thought that 'the author was every-thing'. I of course agreed. Said he had been paying G. B. Shaw £4,000 a year for four years past. And that he took £1,300 in Dublin in a week with a Shaw play. Also said, speaking generally, that he lost a lot of money last year. Said he had taken on Waller for 5 years, and had bought a 'morality' play by Conan Doyle.

Thursday, January 23rd. – I had tea with Lena Ashwell on Tuesday, her elder sister was there. Beautiful old house, arranged with taste. Flashes of common sense and of insight, but a little embittered. This would doubtless pass as intimacy was gained. She told me how Frohman had refused *Leah Kleschna*. Reason: because he thought the public would not be interested in a thief. When it had succeeded he paid a premium of £1,000 to get control of it, and then went about buying every play that had a thief in it. This anecdote has the same elements as nearly all the other anecdotes she related.

Rehearsals of *Cupid and Commonsense* now going much better. I began yesterday to get quite enthusiastic.

Friday, January 24th. – Lunch at G. B. Shaw's yesterday. Mrs Shaw, a very agreeable, sympathetic, and earnest woman. She looked just like the mother of a large family. Shaw came in just as lunch was served. Naturally self-conscious and egotistic; but he evidently made a decent effort against this. Talked most of the time during lunch; has a marked accent, and a habit of rubbing his hands constantly while talking. He related a tale about Estelle Burney and the Shelley Society much as a practised talker in literary circles might have related it. St John Hankin, who was there, would have related it much better.

Saturday, February 1st. – Dress rehearsal of *Cupid and Commonsense* began at 12.45 on Friday, 24th, and finished about 4 o'clock. This was the copyright performance. A bill outside announced that admission was one guinea. Performance extremely depressing. Lucy Wilson was got up more like a Spanish dancer than anything else. There was a sort of half rehearsal on Saturday. The first performance on Sunday night was much better. It held the audience. Lee Mathews said I must respond to the call, and I did; besides, I wanted to.

The performance on Monday afternoon was better, and though there was less applause, I think the play had a greater success. Wells was delighted, impressed rather deeply I thought. Some of the newspaper notices disgusted me. Especially *The Times* and the *Manchester Guardian*. But as they begin to come in, now, I perceive that on the whole they are favourable, and that the public is getting ripe for such a play as I wrote. I was ready to begin work on Thursday, but was stopped by a headache. Yesterday I wrote 2,700 words of the novel.

I made up our accounts to-night for the first month of the year, and found that we had exceeded our allotted sum of £50 per month for everything, by £8 17s. 7d. or £2 a week. This did not surprise me, but it disquieted me. The sum includes the monthly share of all rents, etc. I do not think we can live here at this hotel on £50 inclusive of everything; but we shall certainly do February on less; for one thing it is 3 days shorter.

To-day I finished one third of *The Case of Leek.*

Friday, February 14th. – We have seen two plays by G. B. Shaw: *Arms and the Man,* and *Captain Brassbound's Conversion.* I have been impressed by the moral power of both of them. The latter is frequently dull, but *good* except in its melodramatic skeleton, which is unblushingly absurd. On the whole, my opinion of Shaw is going up. The most surprising thing about his plays is that they should find a public at all. They must have immensely educated the public.

Difficult to live properly here. I seem to have no time and yet I waste time. I am reading nothing but Francis Newman's *Phases of Faith*. It is amazing in its ridiculous seriousness about dogmatic questions, for instance as to the relations between Christ and God, but it is thoroughly sincere and well done, and therefore, interesting.

Saturday, February 29th. – I finished the humorous novel: *Buried Alive* on Thursday morning. Except one chapter, which

I thought would be the best in the book, it is all pretty good. I handed the complete MS. over to Pinker yesterday.

We have certainly been living at a great pace; at least I have. Out almost every night. Yesterday I went over the *Evening News* office, and much wanted to use it up for a story. Whitten came to lunch on Tuesday, and ordered 16 articles. Pett Ridge came on Wednesday for lunch, and told us a funny story about a page at a ladies' club who made an income by cutting politenesses out of telegrams which he was entrusted with for despatch.

We have been to the Exhibition of Fair Women at the New Gallery. The *clous* of the show were three Sargents, all of which I should have greatly admired six years ago – and now I did not care for them at all. Ugly colouring and much mannerism. And I used to think he was a great man! We went to the British Museum. Elgin marbles the greatest sensation I have had for a long time. I used to think them cold. Now I see how passionately they were done. The illuminated MS. also made an entirely new appeal to me. And I was more than ever determined to do some decent illumination.

Thursday, March 5th. – Orage, editor and proprietor *New Age*, came on Monday night, and I sold him 'How to live on 24 hours a day' for his new series, and promised to give him an article on Wells, or an interview if Wells would agree. Went down to Wells on Tuesday, dine and sleep. He wouldn't agree. Said interviews must 'occur', with which I agreed.

Found him harder – yet politer and more reasonable in argument and posture than ever before. Seemed discontented about money, while admitting that he was making £3,000 out of *War in the Air*, which he wrote easily in 4 months. We had not enough time really to come to grips about things. He was extremely witty and fine about the attitude of Keir Hardie and so on (but not sufficiently sympathetic). He told a really astounding tale of a dinner given by Cust to about 20 men, including Balfour and himself, when the house got on fire over their heads. Talk so interesting that dinner went on, though Cust was obliged to absent himself for a few minutes.

Perfection of menservants who offered bath-towels with the port to protect from firemen's water coming through ceiling. Talk to accompaniment of engine throbs, swishing, tramping etc. Guests obliged to move table further up room out of puddles. Dinner lasted till midnight in dining-room, when they went to drawing-room to view the place gutted. One of the finest social recitals I have ever heard.

Monday, March 9th. – Calvocoressi, upon my saying that *La Terre qui meurt* though mediocre was sincere, replied that Bazin had not struck him as a sincere man but rather as a *sinistre fumiste.* He instanced that at Rodocanachi's when the hostess said to him: 'Prenez donc ce fauteuil,' he had responded: 'Non – merci, j'en ai un ailleurs.' A trifle, but it does seem rather bad.

To-day I began to prepare for taking up again *The Old Wives' Tale.* It seemed to come quite easily. Two hours at it in the forest.

Thursday, March 12th. – I have read through first part of *Old Wives' Tale,* and am deeply persuaded of its excellence. *Aussi ai-je pris mes dispositions pour commencer la deuxième partie samedi.* The ideas have come quite easily.

To-day I had a notion for a more or less regular column of Literary notes – title 'Books and Persons' – for the *New Age,* and I wrote and sent off the first column at once.

Wednesday, March 18th. – Marguerite came back last night from 2 days in Paris, and brought 2 books – new, French, fresh as fruit. Astonishing the pleasure of merely contemplating them as they lay on the table. I must really, once settled in Fontainebleau, resume the good habit of buying a book a day.

Worried about the finances of Fontainebleau lately. Still I kept myself in hand very well until the moment arrived last night for me to receive a crucial letter from Pinker. It was handed to me in the dark street. I had some difficulty in not stopping to read it under a gas lamp. I read it at the station. All right. No mistake, the constant practice of M. Aurelius and

Epictetus has had its gradual effect on me. Have never worked better than these last days. Immense pleasure, pretty nearly ecstatic sometimes, in looking at the country, in being *in* it, particularly by the Seine and in the forest.

Last week I began a column of book gossip for the *New Age*. Pleasure in making it *rosse*. Writing under a pseudonym, I seemed to think that as a matter of fact it must be *rosse*. Strange! This week's was better than last.

Thursday, March 19th. – I thought this evening that if only I was installed definitely at Fontainebleau I should be perfectly happy. Difficult to realize that even there something (undiscoverable) would still be lacking, and that I cannot ever be happier than I am now and here – in perfect working order and in good health and with my wits.

I have never been in better creative form than I am to-day. A complete scene of the novel (1,700 words) this morning in $2\frac{1}{2}$ hours, and 1,000 words of an article on the theatre before dinner. Beautiful cold weather. Four miles in the forest this morning; two miles' stroll this afternoon. I want more books here, not to read, but merely to see them around me. I read an extract from Brunetière's criticism in the *Deux Mondes* of *Une Vie* – cold, unappreciative, very niggard in even modified praise. This made me more content with some of the reviews of my 'big' books. I suppose that some day a collected edition of *my* novels will be issued – similar to that of de Maupassant's now appearing. I hope that when it does I shall be neither dead nor in a mad-house.

Monday, March 23rd. – Been reading *Une Vie*, after I suppose about 10 or 12 years at least. Rather disappointed, though it held me. I don't think, e.g. that Tante Lison is very good, and the avarice of Julien is not managed with much originality. Also a general air *terne*, as though lacking in liveliness, as though the book were rather self-conscious. However, I am only half-way through it. I don't like 'L'humble vérité' on the title page. Seems a bit affected. This never struck me before.

Change of weather last night. To-day, first day of Spring.

12 kilometres in forest. Through too much work I slept badly for several nights, which upset my digestion. Still my output is enormous. Pleasure in being in the country increases. Yet a certain dissatisfaction, an expectancy, behind the content. Probably this will always be there, wherever I am and whatever I am doing.

Wednesday, March 25th. – The news of the triumph of beer in the Peckham election this morning really did depress me. I understood, momentarily, the feelings of the men who give up politics in disgust; and I also understood the immense obstinate faith of those who fight for Liberalism all their lives. It is the insincerity and the deliberate lying of the other side that staggers me. I read in the *Daily Mail* this morning that when the news of the triumph of beer got into the music-halls last night there were scenes of wild enthusiasm, and perfect strangers shook hands with one another.

However, I worked well all day.

Saturday, March 28th. – Finished *Une Vie*. Disappointed. No novel affected me as much as this did when I first read it about ten or twelve years ago. It made me sad for days. Now I find it *bâclé* in parts. Too much left out – and not left out on one guiding principle but on several. The stuff not sufficiently gathered up into dramatic groupings. Recital often too ambling. Rosalie at the close rather conventional; overdrawn into a *deus ex machina*. The book too short. Sometimes too full, sometimes too hasty. But of course good. The best thing in it is the sea excursion of Baron, Julien, and Jeanne before her marriage. Paul's letters home are invariably admirably done.

Received to-day copies of *The Statue*. I hope I have now done with sensational work.

Monday, March 30th. – Curious affair in the village yesterday. Owners of land bordering the forest have the right to catch such deer as they find on their land. Now is the season when deer stray, in search of young shoots. They stray about dawn.

Villagers organize a sort of surprise for the deer. They arise before dawn and lie in wait. Yesterday morning sixty people caught six deer. The deer were killed in an open yard close to this house, and blood ran in gallons into and down the road. The 60 people drew lots for the best cuts, and one hears the monotonous calling of the numbers. One-tenth of a deer for each person. This morning I saw 4 *biches* and 3 *cerfs* slowly cross the road in the forest, about 100 yards behind me.

Yesterday I finished the 5,000 word supplementary instalment for *Helen with the High Hand*, begun on Saturday afternoon, and I posted it to Pinker this morning. Very proud of my extraordinary industry and efficiency at the present moment. Over 100,000 good words written in the first quarter of this year.

I tried yesterday and to-day to comprehend a résumé of the metaphysics of Prof. Bergson, in the current *Mercure de France*, and simply couldn't. Not the first time I have failed to interest myself in metaphysics. History and general philosophy much more in my line.

Friday, April 3rd. – Easily influenced! In reading Léautaud's preface to the 'Plus Belles' pages of Stendhal, I found him defending Stendhal's hastinesses of style; never going back etc., 'getting the stuff down' (as I say) without affectations or pose; reading a few pages of the Code to get himself into the 'tone' of plain straightforward writing. Now I could quite see the weakness of the argument, and I knew the clumsiness of Paul Léautaud's own style. Yet so influenced by what he says that I at once began to do my novel more *currente calamo*! Sentences without verbs, etc.

To-day received Tauchnitz' *Swinburne*. I came across 'England: an Ode'. I would not write a thing called 'England: an Ode'. This patriotism seems so cheap and conceited. I would as soon write 'Burslem: an Ode' or 'The Bennetts: an Ode'. I would treat such a theme ironically, or realistically. But loud, sounding praise, ecstasy – No.

Every morning just now I say to myself: *To-day*, not to-morrow, is the day you have to live, to be happy in. Just as complete materials for being happy to-day as you ever will have. Live as though this day your last of joy. 'How obvious, if thought about' – yet it is just what we forget. Sheer M. Aurelius, of course.

Each day, thrice, I expect romantically interesting, fate-making letters. Always disappointed. Astonishing how I have kept this up for years.

Eyesight going wrong again. Ought to go to an optician at once. But can't put myself out to go to Paris, hate the idea of explaining to an optician, etc. Yet I know I run risks. Yesterday I decided to go, and felt easier; to-day my eyes are better and I put it off.

Sunday, April 5th. – Habit of work is growing on me. I could get into the way of going to my desk as a man goes to whisky, or rather to chloral. Now that I have finished all my odd jobs and have nothing to do but 10,000 words of novel a week and two articles a week, I feel quite lost, and at once begin to think, without effort, of ideas for a new novel. My instinct is to multiply books and articles and plays. I constantly gloat over the number of words I have written in a given period.

All I want now is about 5,000 francs extra to fix us in the Fontainebleau house.

Sunday, April 12th. – Ill Friday and Saturday. Migraine. Recovering to-day, and this evening began to think of Part III of Book II of *Old Wives' Tale*. Last night I had news of settlement of all questions which might lead to financial worry. Therefore quite free in mind as to this for a long time to come. I *felt* free.

Yet to-day, somewhat depressed, entirely without cause, save physical fatigue after indisposition. This shows how 'the state of mild worry' is a habit, even with professed philosophers.

Wednesday, April 29th. – Ullman came down yesterday, fresh from U.S.A. I said: 'What is your general impression? Is the U.S. a good place to get away from?' He said: 'On the whole, yes. But for a visit, I am sure it would interest you enormously.' He said that I could form no idea of the amount of drinking that went on there. I said I could, as I had already heard a good deal about it. He said: 'No, you can't.' He stuck to it, though I tried to treat the statement as an exaggeration, that in the principal clubs everybody got fuddled every night.

Noticed in myself: A distinct feeling of jealousy on reading yesterday and to-day accounts of another very successful production of a play by Somerset Maugham – the third now running. Also, in reading an enthusiastic account of a new novelist in the *Daily News* to-day, I looked eagerly for any sign to show that he was not after all a really first class artist. It relieved me to find that his principal character was somewhat conventional, etc., etc. Curious!

Saturday, May 2nd. – To-day I finished the death of Samuel Povey in *The Old Wives' Tale*. Thought it perhaps a shade too stiff, too severe, as a narrative; no little dodges to divert the reader on his way. The fact is: I have been influenced by Beyle's scorn of ornament and device.

I haven't yet arranged my days here. I am doing no reading, no fine writing, no disciplinary thought of any kind. It is true that I still spend about two hours a day in working at the arrangement of the house, but then I get up at 6.30, and before 8 I have had my tea and read newspapers and correspondence. I am still hoping to keep this journal more fully; but I shall never do it in this format, which is too small. I dream of a folio double-column page, and I will realize that as soon as I have finished the present volume, if I can find a good paper that is not too opaque. That is the sole difficulty.

We both enjoy ourselves tremendously here. I take a pleasure that may be positively called 'keen' in walking across the park, getting a shave in a picturesque talkative barber's shop, and then strolling about the town. Our surroundings are certainly almost ideal; and the weather now is ditto. The fruit trees are in blossom. Lilac and peonies are coming. I startled a lizard yesterday in the forest. And there is a general cloak of thin green on the branches. We have tea in the kiosk, and eat our other meals with the door open. To-day I had to close the *persiennes* of my study against sun and heat. And this month I shall be 41!

Monday, May 4th. – These are the things that give me the liveliest pleasure among the little things of weekly life: opening and glancing through the *Athenaeum* and the *Nation* on Monday mornings, especially the advertisements of new books; walking in the park and in the town in the morning when everything is fresh; eating my lunch; drinking tea; and reading after I am in bed. The mischief as regards the last is that I always get sleepy too soon.

Monday, May 11th. – Since Tuesday last I have written an average of over 2,000 words a day, including 12,500 words of novel. I finished the second part this afternoon at 6.15, and was *assez ému*. This makes half of the book, exactly 100,000 words done. I had a subdued bilious attack practically all the time since Tuesday, but just managed to keep it within bounds. With all this I naturally shirked journalizing. I must not forget that I also corrected, in this time, more than 250 printed pp. of proofs. I had 3 books to correct at once: *Buried Alive, How to live on 24 hours a day*, and *Helen with the High Hand*.

Paris. Thursday, May 14th. – We went to Paris on Tuesday morn. I couldn't get used to the town. Felt as if I had been dragged out of my groove and resented it. But of course the weather was awful. Yesterday morning had *petit déjeuner* at the Café de la Régence, as ten years ago when I first came to Paris. And I enjoyed it just as much, perhaps more, except the newspapers, which had lost their old romance. I should think so indeed, seeing what I know of them!

Sunday, May 17th. – At last I have begun to receive catalogues from second-hand booksellers in Paris. I ordered three cheap books this afternoon, to make a commencement. This afternoon M., Emily and I went for a walk in the forest. Many people. A too sophisticated air. At the Caverne d'Augas a man with candles, on the make. Beautiful paths and glimpses and set panoramas, but unpleasing because part of a set show. Then sudden arrival on the Route Nationale 5 bis. Autos struggling up it, noisily, all the time, in a faint cloud of dust. Bicyclists chiefly walking. General Sundayish something that rouses always the exclusive aristocrat in one. M. getting tired, and more tired, and assuring herself by questions that I am taking the nearest way home. Then the arrival, amidst forced cheerfulness, and a realization that one's feet ache. I ran upstairs to read catalogues. The first languors of summer sunsets. House overrun with ants. Slight disquiet on account of this plague of ants. New carpets arrived this morning, re-arousing our pride in our toy house. I forewent my afternoon sleep in order finally to arrange the second spare bedroom.

Monday, May 18th. – For some weeks I have been occupied with the proofs of 3 books: *Helen with the High Hand* (*The Miser's Niece*), *How to live on 24 hours a day*, and *Buried Alive*. To-night I finished the last of these damnable nuisances. To-day I began seriously to construct Part III – Paris – of *The Old Wives' Tale*, and got on pretty well, in spite of a headache.

Saturday, May 23rd. – In the afternoon I continued reading Lewes's *History of Philosophy*, which I have undertaken in all its bigness.

While reading it I was seized again with the idea of learning Latin decently; it was so strong that I could scarcely keep my attention on the book. Another example of the indiscipline of the brain.

Yet I have gradually got my brain far better under control than most people. Always haunted by dissatisfaction at the discrepancy between reason and conduct! No reason why conduct should not conform to the ideas of reason, except inefficient control of the brain. This that I am always preaching, and with a success of popular interest too, I cannot perfectly practise. It is the clumsiness of my living that disgusts me. The rough carpentry instead of fine cabinetry. The unnecessary friction. The constant slight inattention to my own rules. I could be a marvel to others and to myself if only I practised more sincerely. Half an hour in the morning in complete concentration on the living-through of the day, and I should work wonders! But this all-important concentration is continually interrupted – interruptions which weaken it; sometimes deliberately abandoned for concentration on matters of admittedly inferior importance! Strange! One can only stick to it.

It is humiliating that I cannot get through one single day without wounding or lightly abrading the sensibility of others, without wasting time and brain-power on thoughts that I do not desire to think, without yielding to appetites that I despise! I am so wrapped up in myself that I, if anyone, ought to succeed in a relative self-perfection. I aim as much from love of perfection and scorn of inefficiency as for my own happiness. I honestly think I care quite as much for other people's happiness as for my own; and that is not saying much for my love of my own happiness. Love of justice, more than outraged sensibility at the spectacle of suffering and cruelty, prompts me to support social reforms. I can and do look at suffering with scientific (artistic) coldness. I do not care. I am above it. But I want to hasten justice, for its own sake. I think this is fairly sincere; perhaps not quite. I don't think I scorn people; I have none of that scorn of inferior people (i.e. of the vast majority of people) which is seen in many great men. I think my view is greater than theirs. Clumsiness in living is what I scorn: systems, not people. And even systems I can excuse and justify to myself.

Monday, May 25th. – I see that at bottom, I have an intellectual scorn, or the scorn of an intellectual man, for all sexual-physical manifestations. They seem childish to me, unnecessary symptoms and symbols of a spiritual phenomenon. (Yet few Englishmen could be more perversely curious and adventurous than I am in just those manifestations.) I can feel myself despising them at the very moment of deriving satisfaction from them, as if I were playing at being a child. And even as regards spiritual affection, I do not like to think that I am dependent spiritually, to even a slight degree, on anyone. I do not like to think that I am not absolutely complete and sufficient in myself to myself. I could not ask for a caress, except as a matter of form, and to save the *amour-propre* of her who I knew was anxious to confer it.

Tuesday, May 26th. – It must be very difficult, I think, to be really generous, i.e. to give something which you need. I doubt whether in this strict sense I have ever been really generous in all my life. I felt it this afternoon, in talking with E., when it was a question of giving £20 before I had heard definitely from my architect that the landlord at Paris had undertaken to refund my deposit. I might really want that £20, and though I decided at once to give it I gave it, not from a spontaneous instinct of generosity, but unwillingly (within myself), and in obedience to my ideas of rightness and propriety. Something forced me to give it. This is not generosity.

Friday, May 29th. – Just to note what the Bal des Quat'z Arts was in 1908. Calvocoressi went to this year's ball, being officially invited as a director of the Russian opera. He said that there were a large number of women there absolutely naked, and many men who wore nothing better than a ceinture of bones which concealed nothing. Calvo said that on leaving at 4 a.m. he saw a naked woman calmly standing outside in the street, smoking a cigarette, surrounded by a crowd of about 200 people. He said he had heard that afterwards a procession of nudities was formed and went down the Champs Elysées. The ball was held at the 'Bowling Palace' (or some such hall) at Neuilly, so as to be 'out of bounds' of the City.

He took me yesterday afternoon to make the acquaintance of the Godebskis, at Valvin. Husband, wife, 2 small kids. Poles. Among the most charming people I have ever met. Purely artistic. Godebski once owned and edited a little review. Looks like a Jew but is not one. I saw on a table a copy of Mallarmé's *Divagations*, with the *envoi* from the author 'À son vieil ami, Godebski'. Not interested in anything but artistic manifestations. I said I had gas and they hadn't. Godebski said he didn't like gas-lamps. I said: 'For cooking.' 'Yes,' he said, carelessly, 'but with alcohol and oil they can manage.' Didn't care a damn about inconveniences. A whole crowd of artistic youth there; various French accents. A picturesque, inconvenient house, full of good and bad furniture in various styles. A large attic, with rafters, formed the salon; a good grand piano in it. Déodat de Séverac played his new suite. He seemed a very simple sincere person, especially in his ingenuous explanations of his music: 'J'ai voulu évoquer. J'ai voulu évoquer,' again and again. Curious: Everybody was enthusiastic about the inventive fancy shown in knockabout turns on English music-halls. By chance this was all they found on this occasion to praise about England. But Mme Godebski said to me, 'I love the English language and everything English.'

I worked well at *Old Wives' Tale* yesterday, but indifferently to-day. I lack male society. A monotonous effect. Also the gardener spent too much money on stocking the garden. So that to-night I felt as if I wanted a change rather acutely.

Tuesday, June 2nd. – Gradually got involved in one of my periodic crises of work, from which I emerged last night, having written the first chapter of Part III of *Old Wives' Tale*, a 4,300 word story ('Cat and Cupid') and two articles. Considerable inconvenience from sleeplessness.

Wednesday, June 3rd. – Paris yesterday, upon Calvo's invitation to see *Boris Godounoff* at the opera. Very fine. Especially chorus and general completeness of production. Impression left of the barbaric quality of Russia; and its intense earnestness in art also. As to the composition, assuredly great. No close construction in it, its construction must certainly have been a matter of haphazard – I don't care what anyone says to the contrary; made one feel the unimportance of great skill in construction. Look at the haphazard way in which all Goethe's things were constructed. Uncanny effect of seeing suddenly a masterpiece of which one had scarcely heard and of which one knew nothing, and yet which was written in 1874 or published then.

I went 'behind' afterwards with Calvo. After all, the romance of the organization of these affairs interests me quite as much as the art work. Vast stage. Not well *agencé*. I went to see the *foyer de la danse*; got it lighted up specially for me. Most disappointing. Quite small with the end wall one vast mirror. Piffling, compared to its traditions. I should say not more than 30 feet long. Sloping floor: Curious the effect of the rail put in front of the seats, against the walls. Of course it is for the *danseuses* to hold on to while they practise their postures. But it seems as if it was to keep the *abonné* admirers from touching the girls. Similar effect to that of the *grilles* behind which sit Arabs' whores in Algeria. Eminently suitable to the character of the room.

Chaliapine was great and profound. Calvo introduced us afterwards, on the stage. I hate these introductions, but I was glad to go through the tedium of this one. A very tall man, with a noble bearing and a fine face. He is undoubtedly a sublime artist.

Much wandering about behind scenes after the performance. Inexpressibly tedious. The Calvos and we had drinks on the *terrasse* of Julien's. I was too exhausted to be intelligent. Bedroom in the hotel where every noise could be heard. Impossible to sleep. When I heard an alarm-clock go off in the midst of these multitudinous sounds, that struck me as that rare thing, a really *humorous phenomenon*.

I was out at 8 a.m. to-day. Certainly what interests me is organization. Outside the Magasins du Louvre, the despatch of thousands of parcels in dozens of vans was in full swing. A great effect. When I returned, in less than an hour, everything had gone. At 8.25 the interior of the shop was in going order, and well sprinkled with customers. The employés had a strange *un*-tired air.

June 26th. – In my 15th Human Machine article in *T.P.'s Weekly*, I wrote 'Meat may go up in price – it has done – but books won't. Admission to picture galleries and concerts and so forth will remain quite low. The views from Richmond Hill or Hindhead, or along Pall Mall at sunset, the smell of the earth, the taste of fruit and of kisses – these things are unaffected by the machinations of trusts and the hysteria of Stock Exchanges.' The *Westminster Gazette* quoted this, and more, but it left out the words '*and of kisses*'. Characteristic of the English newspaper!

Seriously disturbed by my novel. It is an immensely complicated undertaking. I took a day off yesterday and went to Paris chiefly for the Gaston La Touche exhibition. Rotten. He is always occupied with the feeblest symbolistic satire upon sensualism. Apes for men. Women dreaming of satyrs etc. But you see he really enjoys and admires the sensual spectacle.

Sunday, July 19th. – I finished the third part of *The Old Wives' Tale* on Tuesday last. Everything else gave way before it, and I simply did nothing but that book. It meant the utter defeat of all other plans. I spent Wednesday in reading through the second part.

To-morrow I shall begin to think about the fourth part of the novel. Reviews of *Buried Alive* and *24 hours a day* have been simply excellent. But I have heard nothing encouraging about the sales of either book.

Sunday, August 30th. – Finished *The Old Wives' Tale* at 11.30 a.m. to-day. 200,000 words.

Tuesday, October 6th. – At 2 a.m. on Thursday the 1st Oct. we arrived in Paris. We had 2½ days of fever in Paris. Though we did almost nothing I was excessively fatigued. The chief thing that interested me was the organization of the Magasins du Louvre, just close to the hotel. In the way of a descriptive background there is a great deal to be done there. It is the early hours, from 7 to 9, say, that are the most interesting. I went to the Galeries Lafayette with Marguerite and had a few large, synthetic impressions about that. I was more than ever convinced of the unhappiness of the vast majority of the inhabitants of a large town – owing to overwork, too long work, and too little pay and leisure. I had more than ever the notion of a vast mass of stupidity and incompetence being exploited by a very small mass of cleverness, unjustly exploited. The glimpses of the advanced and mad luxury floating on that uneasy sea of dissatisfied labour grew more and more significant to me. I could have become obsessed by the essential wrongness of everything, had I not determined not to be so. These phenomena must be regarded in a scientific spirit, they must be regarded comparatively, or a complete dislocation of the mind might ensue.

We reached home on Saturday at 5.30, I in an advanced state of exhaustion, and depressed by fatigue (also by the defection of a servant – not that that caused me any inconvenience). I went out into the forest on Sunday morning to find ideas for an article, and except that the odour was much finer, it was just like the height of summer. Crowds of people, some movement of pleasure-traffic, burning sunshine. This morning I walked for two hours in the park in search of my play, and I found a fairly complete scheme for the whole of it. Title to be, provisionally: *What the Public Wants: a tragedy in five Acts* – really, of course, a satiric farce. I think I can now go ahead with it.

Monday, December 14th. – We left Fontainebleau and arrived at Dijon for dinner. Hotel de Bourgogne. Excellent steam-heated room 7 francs. Otherwise hotel not too well kept. It rained from the time of our advent till nearly 9 a.m. the next morning. I walked out at night, and saw a chemist make me a cachet of pyramidon. Mystery of cachets, for me, is now for ever gone. Genuine effect, in the main street, of a town consisting chiefly of confectioners and gingerbread makers. Trams floating about rumblingly and ramblingly all the time. Witnessed an encounter between a young and attractive *grue* and a young man. They knew each other. After standing for a time under the glass marquise of the principal drapery shop, she shut up her own umbrella, and they went off together under his.

It is only at night, when there is little of it, comparatively, that you appreciate how much light there is when there is supposed to be none. At 3 a.m. you can discover traces of it everywhere, and it has a very beautiful quality.

Our train for Switzerland was the Paris-Simplon day express. Very English. Chiefly Englishwomen. Their lack of charm was astounding, absolutely astounding. And their aristocratic, self-absorbed voices made me laugh. The English consciousness of superiority is sublime in its profound instructiveness.

Vevey (quite dry – rain everywhere else). A different climate. Mild, *sec*. I bought a Swiss cigar, and we got into a tiny Swiss tram. Had the Swiss feeling. Feeling much intensified when, in the waiting room of the funicular, we found a vast musical box, which I caused to play for 10 centimes. Really rather a good device, especially when you have 45 minutes to wait.

I was so anxious to see the panorama this morning (*Wednesday 16th Decr*) that I slept badly. I thought it wonderful, but I was disappointed because it seemed so small. I had expected something much bigger. Well, it has been 'growing on' me all day. I thought the highest mountains on the opposite side of the lake were about 3,000 or 4,000 ft. high. I found the Dent du Midi was about 10,000 ft. high. I thought this Dent was 8 or 10 miles off. I found it was 24 miles off (38 kilometres). My opinion of the panorama is going up every minute. I can understand that it is one of the finest in *Suisse*. Sloppy snow everywhere under foot. Not cold enough, they say. Below us, cloud effects on lake continually changing. Really the scene is enchantingly beautiful. We see Vevey as though from a balloon. At night its lights are fairy-like – I wish there was another word. Can't find one instantly.

Thursday, December 17th. – In the basement of this hotel, very dark with windows that look on a wall that supports the earth, is the laundry, where human beings work all day at washing linen. We live on the top of all that, admiring fine literature, and the marvellous scenery. And to-day the cloud scenery, floating above the lake and below us, was especially marvellous.

December 31st. – I have never worked so hard as this year, and I have not earned less for several years. But I have done fewer sillier things than usual.

I wrote *Buried Alive*, ¾ of *The Old Wives' Tale*, *What the public wants*, *The Human Machine*, *Literary Taste: How to form it*; about half a dozen short stories, including 'A Matador in the Five Towns'; over sixty newspaper articles.

Total words, 423,500.

Friday, January 8th. – I wrote the first chapter of new humorous novel [*The Card*] (5,200 words) on Sunday and Monday. Spent Tuesday and Wednesday in bed with a consequent migraine. Was very feeble on Thursday, and managed to write a *New Age* article and a lot of correspondence, and to do a drawing for an illustrated article to-day.

After my row with 'Claudius Clear' I find in to-day's *British Weekly* an apology from him, and a signed review by Prof. John Adams of *The Human Machine* – I think the first regular review of a book of mine that has ever appeared in the *B.W.* C. C. once based an article on *Fame and Fiction*, but it was not a review. It was merely an insolence.

Miss Sains told me that she had known Rhoda Broughton, who had had sisters who didn't treat her properly, and that the ill-used sister in her early books was herself. Miss Sains had also met Mrs Humphry Ward. 'A charming woman. So nice. Always took two years over a novel. So particular. Always began by making a *lot* of extracts from other books, which she used in her own books. Her own books were *largely* made up of ideas collected from other books.' In short the usual clumsy crude account of a writer by a person ignorant of composition, and yet giving a rough notion of the truth, unconsciously.

Saturday, January 9th. – Maiden, aged about 30. Self-conscious. Big nose and eyes, and big features generally. Badly dressed. What is characteristic about her is her pose in an arm chair at night, needle-working. One arm always on chair arm. Looks intently at her work, with virginal expression, while others are talking. Then at intervals looks up suddenly; you can't see her eyes for the white gleam of her spectacles, and she seems to embrace the whole room, or perhaps the talker alone, in a wide, candid, ingenuous glance as of surprise, as if saying slowly: 'What the hell *are* you talking about?'

A honeymoon pair came the other night. Across the dining-room they looked immensely distinguished. He might have been a brother of Rostand. Fine nose. White hands. She seemed mysterious in a da Vinci way. I made sure he was some sort of an artist. No. He proved to be in business. When we saw them close to in the little reading-room – intense vulgarity of gesture, movement, etc. He seemed more like a barber's assistant and she a *vendeuse mal élevée*. Long time since I have been so taken in. Interesting to watch how gestures effective at a distance (theatrical) grew vulgar close at hand.

Sunday, January 10th. – Miss Sains related stories of a young woman well known to her who had charge of a crèche of 30 infants, and amused herself one day by changing all their clothes so that at night they could not be identified, 'and many of them never *were* identified,' said Miss Sains. 'I knew all her brothers and sisters too. She wanted to go into a sisterhood, and she did, for a month. The only thing she did there was one day she went into the laundry and taught all the laundry-maids to polka. She was *such* a merry girl.' Said Miss Sains simply.

Monday, January 11th. – Madame Posfay was in the court-yard of the palace at the time of the murder of the King and Queen of Servia, but knew nothing. 'What are they throwing bolsters out of the windows for?' she asked. It was the bodies.

Sunday, January 24th. – Thursday – goose. Friday evening bilious attack. But it did not stop me from working. Yesterday I finished the first third of *Denry the Audacious* [serial and U.S. title of *The Card*]. And ideas still coming freely!

Arranged with Tauchnitz to abridge the *Old Wives' Tale* so that he can get it into 2 vols. A damned nuisance, yet I secretly consider myself fortunate to get it in. I had begun to think the thing was off.

Letter from Waugh to-day to say that the book still selling, and their town traveller anxious that no new book should appear till this has run its course. All very healthy. A fourth edition is now quite possible. I had not in the least hoped for this success. It alters the value of all my future books. Yet I was depressed all afternoon because I could not make a sketch. Another proof that public success is no guarantee whatever of happiness or even content.

In becoming acquainted with people you uncover layer after layer. Using the word in my sense, one person may be the most *distinguished* of a crowd on the first layer, another on the second, and so on. Until after uncovering several layers, you may ultimately come to a person who, down below, is the most distinguished of all – on *that layer*. The final result may be quite unexpected. I suppose that the inmost layer is the most important, but each has its importance.

Wednesday, January 27th. – Finished to-day the fifth 'deed' of *Denry the Audacious*. It is pretty good. Probably too good for a serial. Also received a copy of the third edition of *The Old Wives' Tale*, and began to cut passages of it so as to make it short enough for Tauchnitz. Not so difficult as I expected it to be, but nevertheless a desolating and unsatisfactory business. Arthur Waugh wrote me that it was 'a sacrilege'.

Although I now do more work, more regularly than ever I did, I feel tired more definitely and more consciously than I did four or five years ago. I remember when I was writing *Leonora* at the Hotel du Quai Voltaire, I used to go out into the Rue de Rivoli (towards the end of the book) with a sensation as if the top of my head would come off. But I did not recognize it as fatigue, simply as the result of worry, a nuisance. I can now work hard all morning and I feel tired, and I know that if I kept on after lunch I should probably be ill. But by consciously refusing to think of my work, by vegetating, I can be sure that by tea-time I shall be restored, and can work again for a bit without letting myself in for a bilious attack.

On Monday and yesterday afternoons I wrote the first chapter of a book about novel-writing and the fiction-reading public, which will appear in pieces over Jacob Tonson's name. I was most enthusiastic over it. I calculate that in twenty weeks it will be done, and a striking book ready to be published. This is an extra. The notion probably came to me from my instinctive hatred of wasting newspaper articles. I hate to think that anything I write is bad enough, or fragmentary enough, to be lost for ever in the files of a paper.

I am writing a pretty good lot, but I am not doing much else. Not yet at the end of the second volume of *Les Origines* – in two months. No other reading, except newspapers as usual, and bits of Poe. Rather startled by the 1st classness of some of Poe's lyrics, such as the 'Haunted Palace'.

In weather, the season continues bad. Two days of fog or mist, then one day of splendid sunshine. And so on. No snow on the south face of the mountain. *In* the mountain, in the protected folds, large quantities of snow. I go walks there, and follow tracks made by an animal alone – I don't know what animal. When there is the least danger of slipping, I think: 'If I fell and sprained my ankle it would probably mean my death.' This is quite exciting, half pleasant, half unpleasant. When venturing up a steep slope to find a possible path, I think: 'I ought not to do this.' The great danger is certainly that of exposure after an accident.

I am always meaning to write character sketches of people in the hotel – as exercise – but I never do. The fact is that to write a 65,000 word book, full of novel incident, in two months, and a showy *travaillée* article once a week, leaves one with not much energy. The time-table has to be followed with exactitude, and it is *assez juste*.

A middle-aged Dutchman instructs me in billiards most evenings.

Tuesday, February 9th. – Keen frost and bright sunshine. I went to toboggan down a steep slope, but when it came to the point I was afraid and started half-way down, and rolled over. Afterwards I would not try from the top, though twice I climbed to the top meaning to do it. Curious. No danger as snow thick. But I had the '*trac*'.

Friday, February 12th. – Girl with voluptuous laugh, short and frequent. Half Scotch, half English. Age 24. Very ener-

getic, obstinate, and 'slow in the uptake'. Red cheeks. Good
looking. Athletic. Shy – or, rather, coy. Always the voluptuous
laugh being heard, all over the hotel. A wanton laugh, most
curious. Her voice also has a strange voluptuous quality.
They say the Scotch women are *femmes de tempérament*. This
one must be, extremely so. And her athleticism must be an
instinctive *remède contre l'amour*. Manners and deportment
quite irreproachable, save for this eternal, rippling, startling
laugh. It becomes more and more an obsession. One waits to
hear it.

Tuesday, February 16th. – Up in the woods. Long snow path.
Greenish-brown-black colour of wood cut and uncut coming
often in the distance, or rather flaming out with a spark or
spot of ochreish raw wood – the end of a fresh-cut log.
Immense amount of wood-cutting on the mountain-side. All
the upward paths lead up to and stop at either a farm or a
wood-cutting place. The paths seldom join each other. They
are nearly all blind. But this morning in a snowstorm I found
a path that led clear over the top of the mountain to the
southern slope; a long way. It stopped at a wood-cutting, or
diminished rather to a track of a dog's feet, which went under
a hedge and reappeared on the other side. But the slope was
too steep for me to follow. I could see Attalens. So I had to
turn back. Clouds broke, and strong sunshine.

Yesterday I finished three-quarters of *Denry the Audacious*.
I think that in book form I shall call it *The Card*. Good honest
everyday work, vitiated by my constant thought of a magazine
public.

Friday, February 26th. – Marguerite and Pauline Smith came
back from Vevey to-day with particulars of a *maniaque* shop
there, where, when you had bought an article, it was taken
from you and a number given in exchange. You then, after
purchasing all you wanted, paid at the desk, and then went to
another part of the shop, where were a number of pigeon-
holes numbered. Your articles were then taken out of the
pigeon-holes corresponding to your numbers and wrapped

up. The wrapping up could not begin till you had paid. At the wrapping-up place were a number of little brown paper bags containing pieces of string. Each bag had a different length of string. The packer chose a suitable length from the bag containing pieces only of that length. One can imagine the fussiness, indeed mania, of the proprietor, and hell of a time that the girls employed in it must have.

More and more struck by Tchekoff, and more and more inclined to write a lot of very short stories in the same technique. As a fact, *The Death of Simon Fuge*, written long before I had read Tchekoff, is in the same technique, and about as good. Though to say anything is as good as 'Ward No. 6' in *The Black Monk*, wants a bit of nerve.

Tuesday, March 2nd. – I finished *Denry* or *The Card* yesterday at 11 a.m. Began it on Jan. 1, I think. 64,000 words. Stodgy, no real distinction of any sort, but well invented, and done up to the knocker, technically, right through.

Monday, March 8th. – Dined with the D—s on Thursday. D. had had some business with the *commissaire de police du quartier*, with whom he is on very good terms, and in the well-furnished bureau of the commissaire he saw a picture by Harpignies. 'A gift,' said the commissaire. 'The old man and I had a little business together not long since ... Il avait houspillé une petite fille.' And the old man is about 80. Thus these things can be arranged in Paris.

England. – We left Paris on Saturday, Mch. 6 at 8.25. Traversing hundreds of miles of snow.

Gestures and style of people walking down to work past the Mater's window in the morning ought to be noticed. There are young men who seem so absorbed in a pipe as to be smoking it with their whole bodies. General deliberation and heaviness.

Thursday, March 11th. – Went to meeting of Tunstall Town Council in the afternoon (of which notes elsewhere). On the way there, down Scotia Rd, I saw a knot of girls here and there who had obviously left their work on a bank to come out and watch. Heads wrapped up in cotton against powdery workshops. Standing still in raw cold, very ill-clad. They were waiting for a funeral to pass. I saw this funeral just starting from a cottage lower down. The hearse just moving from the side of the road to the middle, and the procession hopping over snow heaps to join in. Two women, noses in handkerchiefs, immediately behind hearse. They seemed to place their hkfs. in position and to begin to cry just as procession started. About 15 or 20 men behind. Quite half without overcoats. You thought of the waiting hatless at the grave etc. Extremely foul and muddy road, and a raw day. Crowd blocking the pavement in front of the house. Burly Podmore elbowing his way through it to get in. As I forced my way past, smell, and sound of crying came from the house.

Sunday, March 14th. – Hawtrey, after accepting *What the Public Wants* on his own – that is, so far as he was concerned – found himself obliged to refuse it because his syndicate funked it. He said he thought he could ultimately have persuaded them, but we would not give him time. This is yet another instance of the way in which plays are chosen.

Tuesday, April 6th. – Expected first [Stage Society] rehearsal of *What the Public Wants* yesterday, but of course it was postponed.

Good Friday, April 9th. – Wednesday. Dinner at Ford Madox Hueffer's. John Galsworthy and wife there. Slight *gêne* on my part on first encounter with Galsworthy, seeing my recent articles on him. However, we did well together, and he asked me to dinner. Hueffer said that Henry James dictated so slowly that he insisted on his amanuensis having a novel open before her to read while he dictated. He said that Conrad was still as late as ever with his copy.

Thursday, April 29th. – On Wednesday 21st we went to spend the night at H. G. Wells's. After that I got more and more absorbed in rehearsals [of *What the Public Wants*]. Couldn't think of anything else.

Whelen had tea with me on Thursday. He said Tree was coming to the performance on Sunday, and that he would provide *W.T.P.W.* at Afternoon Theatre if no one took it for an evening bill. I also promised to do him a translation of *La Parisienne* which he promised to produce, somewhere.

I saw Pinker on Tuesday, who had got an offer from Methuen of £300, £350, and £400, on account of next three books.

Wednesday, May 5th. – First performance of *What the Public Wants* at Aldwych, 2nd May 1909. 2nd performance Monday afternoon May 3.

Thursday, May 13th. – Curious difference between the evident enjoyment of the critics both on Sunday and on Monday, and the cold, carping tone of most of their articles. There were only a few really enthusiastic notices. Particularly good ones in the *D. Chronicle*, the *Saturday Review*, and the *Westminster Gazette*. But all the others however cussed recognized that they had something striking to deal with.

Lunched with Frank Vernon Wednesday 5th. He had produced *Cupid and Commonsense* in Glasgow on the previous Thursday and told me of its striking success on the first night. I heard later that it played to £188 during the week. This seemed to me small, but the theatre people regarded it as very good.

On Monday terms were definitely arranged with Hawtrey's Syndicate, headed by Tom B. Davis, for production of *What the Public Wants* at Royalty. I was at theatre and Hawtrey presented to me various members of the cast he had engaged, including a young woman named Cleaver for principal part, who impressed me.

On Tuesday the contract was signed and Tom B. Davis paid over a cheque for £100. No sooner was this done than I met Hawtrey by chance in the street, and he was very angry with Davis, who would not agree to estimate for scenery etc. Hawtrey had cancelled rehearsal for that afternoon, for (as he said) diplomatic reasons – so as to force the hand of the Syndicate by making them think he would chuck it all up if he could not have his way. He said Syndicate were hard up. This worried me. I was glad to be leaving London the next day, with a postal strike in France.

We arrived at Fontainebleau at 9.30 Wednesday night, the 12th, having been absent 5 months. Now my ordinary life is to recommence.

Tuesday, September 14th. – Parot, the carpenter, came to-day, for a job. I once shook hands with him in a burst of fellow-ship, and always since he makes a point of this ceremony. He shook hands to-day. I left him with Marguerite. I was standing at the top of the garden when I heard him coming down stairs to depart. I walked hurriedly round between the kiosk so that he should not see me and I should not have to shake hands with him. I did this almost before I thought what I was doing. Why? A decent, independent chap, vigorous and energetic. Young. What is at the back of my mind is probably that I resent his insisting on the 'privilege' which I once granted him. Funny.

Sunday, September 19th. – At the week-end I had neuralgia for 40 hours. I read about half of *La Duchesse de Châteauroux et ses sœurs*. Daintily done, but unimportant. Taine would have done it differently. As a fact I only read it for the scandalous passages, and I often skipped in order to come to them.

Monday, September 20th. – Bazar de l'hôtel de ville, Fontaine-bleau.

I wonder how a description of this shop, the largest in the town, would sound 50 years hence. You go through a rather narrow vestibule, where soap, notepaper, and pins, studs, etc., are displayed, into a large hall, height of two storeys, a wide staircase at back, wide galleries round, and a roof of which the middle square is glazed. Cheap goods everywhere. Drapery, silks, ribbons, nails, ironmongery, glass and earthenware, leather goods, stationery on the ground floor; arranged on stalls and counters in between which are spaces for walking.

In the basement *articles de ménage*. The staircase lined at either rail with lighter articles of furniture. In the galleries, chiefly light furniture; extended on the walls, showy carpets, flowered etc., at such prices as 49 frs. We went to buy a screen. They had only one, four-fold, and we wanted three-fold. Ranged below it were several toy-screens. The price of the sole screen was 19 frs. Near by were about a dozen cheap marble-top washstands. Wicker chairs and flimsy tables about. Still, you *could* buy there nearly everything (non-edible) that goes to the making of an ordinary house. The frontage of the shop is of course an ordinary house-frontage. The shop itself must be a courtyard roofed over. It is in charge mainly of women. Sitting high at the cash desk near the entrance are two controlling women – one sharp and imperative in manner; with the table of electric switches at their right hand. They look up from books to direct entering customers and when they know what customers want they call out a warning to the assistants within. Very smiling, with a mechanical saccharine smile.

The bulk of the assistants are youngish girls; some pretty, all dressed in black, with black aprons, scissors etc. and blackish hands. They do not seem keen, but rather bored. Certainly the wages must be low. Hours about 12 or 13 per day – that is to say, hours during which shop is open. Besides these, there are a few men, who wear blue smocks, and attend to furniture, ironmongery and similar departments. One of these, with one girl, is always at the *étalage* at the front, where trinkets and souvenirs and postcards are exposed. Men seem even more discontented than the girls. I never saw anyone there who looked like a proprietor or supreme boss. The whole shop is modelled on the big general shops in Paris. There are similar shops now in most provincial towns. In Toulouse there were half a dozen splendid ones.

In all, the conditions of labour are disgusting to the social conscience, though probably better than in *ateliers*. There is a feeling of cutting down expenditure, especially wages, in order to sell cheaply, while making a good profit. A feeling that everybody concerned is secretly at the beginning of a revolt, and that the organizers of the whole organism are keeping out of the way. Yes, there is certainly this feeling! I am always uneasy when in such shops, as if I too were guilty for what is wrong in them. Of course nearly all shops are on the same basis of sweating, but in some it is masked in magnificence, so that one has to search for it.

A handful of customers always in, and a continuous movement near the entrance.

At closing time the *étalage* has to be carried in, and there is left a prodigious litter of bits of paper which has to be swept up. Then early in the morning (less than 12 hours after the closing) there is the refixing and arrangement of the *étalage*, and the gradual recommencement of the day.

Some of the women have a certain coquetterie. But not the young ones; the controlling women of 40 or so. These have the air of being always equal to the situation, but they are not. I remember once half the staff (it seemed) was worsted in an attempt to make a bicycle pump work that I had bought. They all conspired to convince me that it was quite in order, but I beat them, and they had to take the pump back. One of the controlling women began on a note of expert omniscient condescension to me, but she gradually lost her assurance, and fled. A man would not so easily have done that.

Friday, September 24th. – Lee Matthews said that he had got Tree to come to his flat, and his wife read to Tree the scenario of my *Don Juan*, and Tree said he was afraid he hadn't enough dash to carry it off. He took the MS. away with him, and Lee M. has heard nothing since.

In the afternoon he and I went to Moret by train, and walked down to St Mammès and up the Loing to Moret town. Beautiful hot day, with sailing architectural clouds. A great population of barges. We saw a Flemish barge, with white sculpture work on the doors of its cabin, all painted very nattily, with little imitations of the deck of a ship; very clean; a few plants in pots, including a peach tree in full fruit, loaded, in fact; also embroidered lace curtains at the little cabin windows. A delightful object. You never see a French barge like this.

On getting home I found a letter saying that Pinker had sold *What the Public Wants* as a serial to McClures for £100. The U.S.A. is certainly a very strange market indeed.

Yesterday I finished a story 'The Heroism of Thomas Chadwick'. This makes the third in about a fortnight. One of them, 'Hot Potatoes', is just twice too long for the amount of material in it.

Saturday, September 25th. – I went to Moret again this afternoon with the others. Exactly the same weather and conditions as on Thursday. I searched all the river from St Mammès to Moret for a subject, and couldn't settle on a good one. Then I began to sketch an old man in a punt fishing, but I was taken away from it and made to go and have tea at 'Robinson'. Blackish brown rats (not very big) kept coming up out of the bank to drag away at a large crust of bread that someone had tied by a string to a chain. Half-tame. Not being able to carry off the bread they would nibble and eat off it *in situ*. We saw a wedding procession, preceded by three musicians – a fiddler, a silver instrument, and another. Working people. Men in silk hats and short semi-frock-coats. The men had obviously drunk about as much as they could manage. Only one or two girls in white, – the bride and another. Perhaps 30 people altogether, including quite young ones, aged 15 or so. Bride about 25 or 26, certainly not a virgin. Procession came up from St Mammès, crossed the Loing Canal and disappeared towards Moret. As it approached the town the musicians began to play, and some of the people danced along. One couple stayed lingering behind, the man ran behind a tree while his girl waited for him; then he rejoined her and they walked on slowly after the procession. Nearly all the people had a brutish and very stupid look. In towns only as big as Fontainebleau, these marriage processions have ceased to occur, but they continue in villages. Our cook Maria had two days off not long since for her brother's wedding. The festivities lasted two whole days.

Bad sleeping for a week or two. I waste 2 or 3 hours of every night in useless bed. So I am trying to stay up later. This morning I didn't sleep after 4.30. I got up at 6.15. I went out at 8 to think about my play, and returned at 10, having done 2 hours' walking in hot sunshine and two hours' thinking. And I was exhausted for the day. I could easily have gone to sleep before lunch.

Our late servant Jeanne, who had only been with *commerçants*, was much exercised by our finicking and ritualistic methods of eating – spoons laid to right and at back, forks differently, certain particular plates, etc. etc. She must have thought it all very ridiculous, but of course she said nothing. One day Marguerite was offering some food to the dog, who refused it, and as he was ill she tried to put it down him with a spoon. Jeanne said: 'Il fait des manières, lui aussi!'

Thursday, September 30th. – After much rain, an exquisite morning. The views of the Seine as I came up to Paris were exceedingly romantic. I came without sketchbook, and my first desire was to sketch. So I had to buy a book. M. and I then went to the Aviation Exposition at the Grand Palais. Startled by the completeness of the trade organization of aviation; even to suits for aviators, and rolls of stuffs for 'planes. We first remarked the Farman aeroplane. Vast, and as beautiful as a yacht. Same kind of beauty. Yet a new creation of form, a new 'style'; that is newly stylistic. I had been reading Wilbur Wright's accounts of his earlier experiments as I came up in the train, and I wanted to write a story of an aviator, giving the sensations of flight. I left M. and went to the Salon d'Automne. But I found it was the *vernissage* and so I didn't enter. Crowds entering.

My first vague impression was here at last defined, of Paris. Namely, the perversity and corruption of the faces. The numbers of women more or less chic also impressed me. A few, marvellous. It was ideal Paris weather. I saw what a beautiful city it is, again. The beauty of this city existence and its environment appealed to me strongly. Yet the journey from the Gare de Lyon on the Métro. had seemed horrible. Also, I had waited outside the *bureau de location* of the Français, for it to open, and had watched the faces there, which made me melancholy. Particularly a woman of 60 or so, and her virgin daughter 30 or 33. The latter with a complexion spoilt, and a tremendously bored expression, which changed into a mannered, infantile, school-girlish, self-conscious, uneasy smile, when a punctilious old gentleman came up and saluted and chatted. The fading girl's gums all showed. She was a sad sight. I would have preferred to see her initiated and corrupt. She was being worn out by time, not by experience. The ritual and sterility and futility of her life had devitalized her. The mother was making a great fuss about changing some tickets. This ticket-changing had a most genuine importance for her. The oldish girl, mutely listening, kept her mouth at the mannered smile for long periods. But I think she was not essentially a fool.

Friday, October 1st. – We dined at the Bœuf à la Mode. A dull, good, nice restaurant. I gave the waiter my usual 10%, which happened to be 70 centimes. He was apparently not content, but politely thanked me. As he carried the plate out with the change on it, he held it the least bit in the world at arm's length, exposing it with scorn to the inspection of the *chasseur* as he passed him. It was a fine, subtle gesture, and pleased me as much as it annoyed me.

Sunday, October 3rd. – Row with the landlady of the Hôtel de Liège about price of room. When she had no other resource of argument left she said: 'Vous êtes plus riche que moi. Je travaille du matin jusqu'au soir,' etc. It seemed curious to hear this kind of thing in a hotel in the middle of Paris. In her anger she also accused me of sleeping all day in my bedroom, doubtless because I retired there to rest at intervals. It is simply astounding how I can get tired when in Paris or London on a holiday. A nervous fatigue that is positively acute. Half an hour's rest will drive it away for a time. But it will begin quite early in the morning. Salon d'Automne yesterday afternoon. I enjoyed it greatly. It was certainly an education to me, far more interesting than the Spring Salons. Except in a few wilful jokes, you could see a real idea in everything if you searched for it. I got several more notions for *'natures mortes'*. Also I got my eyes opened a little wider.

Tuesday, October 5th. – At eight o'clock this morning I began to write the first scene of *The Honeymoon*. I worked at it at full tension till 10.30, and then stopped. I don't think I am quite satisfied with it. I doubt if I have got the right tone. I may begin it again.

The finally corrected proofs of Harris's book on Shakspere reached me. I have read a quarter of the book since dinner. My previous impression of it is deepened. The thing is masterful and masterly.

Wednesday, October 6th. – Not quite satisfied with the 'key' of the opening of *The Honeymoon*, I decided to begin it again. But I had a headache and a creative malaise this morning, and couldn't work easily. An extremely enthusiastic letter from George H. Doran, the American publisher of *The Old Wives' Tale*, expressing deep admiration etc. and asking the 'honour' etc. of publishing other books. He said he had sold 2 editions of 1,000 each and was now ordering plates (of his own I suppose) for another edition. This produced a disturbance in me.

Monday, October 11th. – Last night I began talking to Pauline Smith [author of *The Little Karoo*] about her work, though I had some difficulty in getting *her* to talk. She gave me a notion of a half-formed scheme for a novel – nothing really but a dim idea. I enlarged it and straightened it out for her, and by my enthusiasm lighted hers a little, indeed much. I poured practical advice into her for an hour, such as I don't think she could have got from any other living man, and such as I would have given my head for 15 years ago. I told her exactly what to think about to-day and it was arranged that she should report to me to-night how far she had proceeded and that we should go further with the plot. After dinner to-night she began to read. It is true it was one of my books. I gave her a chance and waited for her to put the book down. Then after about half an hour I said: 'I shan't let Pauline read any more of my books. She doesn't do anything else.' She smiled, and murmured: 'Just let me finish this.' I then played a sonata, and then ostentatiously waited. No sign. She kept on reading till 9.30, and then went straight to bed. I now feel that the next word spoken between us as to her novel will have to come from her.

I received *Ann Veronica* to-day with the inscription 'The Young Mistresses' Tale, to Arnold B. with love from his nephew H.G.'

Wednesday, October 13th. – In the evening I got Pauline Smith to talk about her novel, but I think I mentioned it first. Sheer magnanimity and obstinacy mingled.

Thursday, October 14th. – Headache, began yesterday. The camel's backbreaking straw was probably a Dutch cigar that Godebski gave me. I nearly cured the headache twice to-day and then brought it on again by working.

I finished *Ann Veronica* yesterday. The last 30 pages are the best. But still, a minor work. Seems to me much too short; incidents not described in sufficient detail. Mere writing impudently careless of dissonant effects, and full of extreme colloquialisms.

Tuesday, October 19th. – This morning I had that excessive consciousness of one's self which comes from being a little over-tired, or (I have been told) after a 'drink', and which is favourable to creative work. I finished my first act easily. I may enlarge it a bit. This afternoon, we went to the Rocher d'Avon.

Wednesday, October 20th. – I got up exhausted. Misty. I was drawn towards the Place d'Armes instead of the forest, in order to see the dismantling of the circus. I saw it, half down: all the male performers were working as skilled labourers. This afternoon the trucks were loaded for entrainment at the station.

Then I went on up the Rue de France – a highly typical provincial residential street – to the Fourche, where a lot of soldiers were being drilled in squads of 16, 8, 6, 4, and even 1. I saw one man spend at least a quarter of an hour drilling a single awkward recruit, giving him the most minute instructions how to stop, start, and turn, with repetitions endless. He would say: 'Non, la patte droite est trop tournée,' mingling such phrases with stiff, shouted, conventional martial commands. Here one got down to the very unit of French army manoeuvres. I don't know what they teach privates inside barracks, but outside they teach them nothing except to be machines capable of executing only the most rudimentary tricks: scarcely even the beginning of even the A B C of military skill. One sees nothing but drilling, and hears nothing but the monotonous practice of drum-beating and crude brass instruments. All brutalizing. All the men were in fatigue whitish cotton or linen, except two officers in red trousers. The general tone was kindly, even friendly. All this in a pale autumn mist.

Thursday, October 21st. – I find that if I am to begin my new novel [*Clayhanger*] on 1st Jan. 1910, I must make a series of small preliminary enquiries. I do this perhaps at the rate of half an hour or an hour a day. I have read *When I was a Child*, and all I need of Shaw's *North Staffordshire Potteries*, and to-night I re-read the 'Social and Industrial' Section of the Victoria History, which contains a few juicy items that I can use. I work on the plot itself about once a week when I have an hour and feel like it.

Nothing at all occurred to-day, except that I began the actual transcription for my projected Dictionary of the Literary Ideas of W. S. Landor. I found this rather amusing and not in the least fatiguing. It is the sort of thing one could do while recovering from influenza.

Monday, October 25th. – After two days' dyspepsia; I began at a quarter to eight this morning, and at 11 o'clock I had been out for a walk in the rain and read the newspapers and written a complete draft of Act II [of *The Honeymoon*]. I hated doing it. This afternoon, after painting I walked to Les

Plâtreries and arranged the whole scheme, and most of the characters, of my next novel – the first of the trilogy. Assuredly a great day. After that I did a bit at my Landor dictionary and then it was dinner time.

Wednesday, October 27th. – I came to the conclusion yesterday afternoon that I had been shirking the play somewhat. And so I determined that this morning I would do three hours' genuine hard labour on it, – no messing about and wasting time. Which I did, rising up to that intent, fortunately in good form. 7.45 to 9.30, and 10.15 to noon. I wrote a good 1,000 words and was exhausted. Yesterday evening I read, very badly, the first act to Pauline Smith and Marguerite, and with Pauline, who alone could follow it, it certainly had a *succès très vif*. I was quite hoarse after reading it. I saw a few things in it to modify. I have never read a play aloud before. It is a very severe and excellent test, especially when the reading is inefficient.

To-day I heard from Pinker that Duttons had offered £250 down and a good royalty on each of my three next novels for U.S.A. This shows how enormously one's prospects can change there in a year. A year ago no American publisher would publish my work on any terms, and the copyright of *The Old Wives' Tale* was lost there from this cause. I am now sure of at least £600 each on my next three novels. By the afternoon post I had another letter from Pinker indicative of still further offers and hesitating about accepting Duttons'.

Sunday, October 31st. – Last night we went to see *Le Roi* in the Cinematograph *salle* of the town. Full house. *Quel monde province!* My little doctor – I forget his name – sat behind me, and was anxious for us to walk in the forest together in the evening. Unhappily he seems entirely uninteresting. My plumber, my house painter, my bicycle dealer, and my house-agent, were there with their wives. This seemed to be practically the only 'world' – that of *commerçants*. It seemed much more *province* than Burslem for instance. It is from such an audience that one may see how small Fontainebleau is.

Doubtless the society which considers itself *haute* kept away. And the theatre is in their minds designated for the tradesmen. A plain interior, with a too low-arching roof, ugly with pitch-pine, green hangings, and very badly disposed electric lights. Hard seats, with an appearance of chic. Very hard seats, after two hours.

Saturday, November 6th. – I was obliged by my conscience to go to the barber's. Happily it is a stately barber's, where hair-cutting and friction are treated with adequate solemnity. In the half-light, with its mirrors and rococo woodwork and complicated apparatus, it had '*du style*' tradition behind it. A little framed notice was hung up, as always on hunt days. '*Rendezvous de chasse. Croix de Toulouse.*' All this kind of thing will belong to a past generation probably before I'm dead. I shall recount it as something antique, quaint, and scarcely conceivable. The entire atmosphere was old-world.

Tuesday, November 9th. – To-day I rose in excellent health, began my last act, and at 5.30 had written one-third of it. I received a complete bound set of my Tauchnitz works from the Baron. Though ugly, the format was not too ugly to please me. I put the row of twelve volumes in Marguerite's secrétaire. Pauline seized *A Great Man* out of the lot, and has been reading it at every spare moment and smiling to herself the whole time. Not to be outdone, I began to read *Buried Alive*, and also smiled the whole time. I don't think I have ever read a funnier book than this.

Friday, November 12th. – Taine's long essay (over 100 pp.) on Balzac is really very good reading, especially when he comes to describe the big characters, such as Joseph Bridau, Grandet, and the Baron Hulot. Lying awake last night, after a fearful crash caused by the faience suspension falling out of the ceiling in the hall, I had a desire to do likewise for one or two English novelists. It is Taine's method that appeals to me, and the intoxicating effect of a vast number of short sentences or clauses hurled down one after another.

Sunday, November 14th. – I finished *The Honeymoon* at noon yesterday. I read the last act after dinner. It was a considerable success with Pauline Smith, but not with Marguerite as she could not follow it.

The dog woke me up last night after I had had 3 hours' sleep. After that my nerves were too tightened for me to try even to sleep (as I had just finished my play). I lay awake and listened, rather frightened, to the various noises, all very faint, that I could hear. (I had quietened the dog with a slipper.) Marguerite, the clocks, another noise, regular, that I couldn't and don't understand, and still others beneath these. About 5 I went on with Taine on Balzac, and came across some magnificent pages of generalizations about the art of observation.

Friday, November 19th. – Yesterday I finished making a list of all social, political, and artistic events, which I thought possibly useful for my novel between 1872 and 1882. Tedious bore, for a trifling ultimate result in the book. But necessary. To-day in the forest I practically arranged most of the construction of the first part of the novel. Still lacking a title for it. If I thought an ironic title would do, I would call it 'A thoughtful young man'. But the public is so damned slow in the uptake.

I am now getting to the end of my year's work. In a week, I shall have nothing to do except collection of information on the spot for the novel.

To-day I finished and mounted another water-colour, of Arbonne, – one of my least rotten.

Tuesday, November 23rd. – I have now written for rooms to hotels in Paris and London. First preparations beginning for our departure on Saturday. I am completely sick of all literary work, and could not possibly find energy to keep a journal *convenablement*. Very cold weather also. I began a chill yesterday, and to-day, as I was walking down from the Point de Vue de Calvaire, I had a stab of lumbago, and had to stand still for a few seconds in order to collect myself sufficiently to go on. But I have had worse lumbago than that in my time.

Friday, November 26th. – Exhausted. Especially with putting away books, dismantling the house, selecting all the necessary literary apparatus for our absence, packing it and my clothes, and smoking too much. After tea I went up into the town, to see the Foire de Ste Catherine. Too idle and bored to note features. Except these: Men singing songs – in set fashion – in order to sell the music. One man sang and accompanied himself on a sort of little organ. Another – an oldish man – had an orchestra of two behind him: rather an elaborate apparatus for so small a *'commerce'*. Secondly, a female quack, in mourning, stumping it from the box-seat of a large gaudily painted and gilded chariot. She spoke well and clearly in a quiet, carrying voice. Just as I paused in front of her for a moment, she said, holding up a bottle: 'Nous avons ici un ver solitaire sorti d'un homme de 42 ans, qui a quinze mètres de longueur.'

H. W. Massingham wrote me yesterday inviting me to contribute to the *Nation*. No editorial invitation has ever flattered me as much as this. He said he considered *The Old Wives' Tale* to be one of the one or two really great novels of the last thirty years.

Saturday, December 4th. – Yesterday morning I came to Manchester (where I write this, before leaving it again). Midland Hotel. Large Bible in the room.

I was entertained to lunch by Haslam Mills and G. H. Mair. The second, Scotch, educated at Edinburgh, Oxford, Grenoble and Paris. Evidently considered to be one of the stars of the future. Slight, delicate man, with a face retreating at the bottom. Scotch accent. The renowned C. E. Montague was present; also A. N. Monkhouse. Montague, though a Londoner born and bred, looks the typical provincial – rather like an intelligent S.S. superintendent; quite grey hair, low collar and queer necktie. A rather tight, prim way of speaking; when he disagrees or is not convinced, he is sometimes silent, with a slight working of the muscles of the face; probably due to sloth. They told me afterwards that he lived in a shell; but yesterday he came out, and people were surprised. Monkhouse a large grave man, slow-speaking, with an extraordinary sedate and sincere charm.

The lunch was very agreeable indeed. Mills has a good manner, which he has conventionalized and hardened, of telling yarns. All the talk was 'shop'. Lunch lasted till 4. I then went with Mair and Mills to the file-room of the *Guardian*. And when I had done there I was told that a tea-fight was awaiting me. We came back to the Midland. A man named Agate (not quite on the staff) and another man now joined us. Younger than the others, but still very fine. Even the satellites on the *Guardian* have their precise notions about De Goncourt. We took tea till 6.15, when I went to the Gaiety Theatre to meet Iden Payne. He took me out to dine at the Brazenose Club, where the food was excellent. He looks like a little original wild member of the Fabian Society. Cape instead of overcoat, held on by bands crossing the chest. Mair said he had seen him in sandals in his office. Highly intelligent. Self-centred. He then took me to the dress-circle. Performance of *Every Man in his Humour*. We missed most of the first act, so I didn't follow it, and found a lot of it confusing. But I thought the performance extremely artistic, and it provided me with a whole series of new sensations. Yesterday was one of the most agreeable days I have ever spent in my life. The fact is that *this* sort of thing is the real reward for having written a few decent books.

Sunday, December 5th. – I happened to see Conrad and Hueffer's *Romance* at Frank's at lunch to-day, and I took it to read. I read about 20 pp. after lunch, before the gas stove in the bedroom, but I doubt if I shall get much further in it. Also I doubt if I shall read much more of J. S. Mill's *Autobiography* here. I cannot read in Burslem. All I can do is to go about and take notes. My mind is in a whirl all the time. I have only been here 5 days, and yet all Paris and Avon seems years off; I scarcely ever even think of these places and my life there. Sometimes by accident I speak to myself or to one of the children in French.

Wednesday, December 8th. – After dinner I went to the Grand Theatre, 9.15 p.m. I was profoundly struck by all sorts of things. In particular by the significance of clog-dancing, which had never occurred to me before. Towards the end I came across Warwick Savage and walked home with him. This was a pity because I had got into an extraordinary vein of 'second sight'. I perceived whole chapters.

Thursday, December 16th. – Yesterday morning I did part of the walk that Clayhanger must do as he comes finally home from school in the first chapter of *Clayhanger*.

Sunday, December 19th. – We reached London prompt at 4 p.m. and found the Strand Palace Hotel very well organized, and strangely cheap. What makes this hotel unique among English hotels is such things as, hot and cold water lavatory in every room, free baths, no tips, second serving of any dish without extra charge. I think there is no other hotel that offers these things. I would stay in it, were it only for the lavatory and the bath. The difference to the comfort of the client is tremendous. Odd that in 1909 such elementary conveniences and commonsenses should be unique. You can live completely and keep yourself clean in the Strand Palace for

Room, bath, bkfast.	. . .	6	0
Lunch .	. . . .	1	6
Tea	. . . .	0	6
Dinner .	. . . .	2	6
Per day, absolutely inclusive	. .	10	6

Tuesday, December 21st. – Dined at Wells's, Lowes Dickinson, the Rothensteins and T. Seccombe. Rothenstein a good talker. Richard Whiteing, Mrs Nevinson, and a whole family of Radfords came in after. The whole family was exceedingly typical. The worn bright mother, the pure, downright, clever daughters, all young, and the elegantish young son. Also a doctor who could do excellent Cockney imitations. Mrs Nevinson was agreeably disagreeable of demeanour at first.

I soon broke down her barriers by talking about H.W.N.'s
Neighbours of Ours. Richard Whiteing was old, deafish, a good
quiet talker, and he had a sort of startled enthusiasm for *The
O.W.T.* He was half-way through it, and it appeared to have
knocked him over quite. But Lowes Dickinson was my man.

Thursday, December 23rd. – To lunch at Wells's. He and I
talked his scandal from 12.15 to lunch-time. Robert Ross, the
Sidney Lows, Mrs Garnett, Archer, and the young Nesbit girl
who was mad on the stage. I liked Ross at once. I got on fairly
well with Archer. He bluntly asked me why I had said in
print that he and Walkley were the upas-trees of the modern
drama. So I told him, less bluntly. I consider that he has no
real original ideas of his own. I mean to cultivate Ross.

Tuesday, December 28th. – Yesterday morning I went over
the Wesleyan Westminster building with Rickards. He is now
gradually getting hold of me again as a great artist. With
regard to the building – cornices, showing horizontally
through scaffolding. Huge upright girder half-way through a
doorway. Huge tripod of derricks going up through rein-
forced concrete floors, and so on. Iron tufted bars for rein-
forced concrete. Pools of water. Going up and down ladders.
Cement-y dirt and mud. Sticky feeling on hands afterwards.
Vibration of talking in crypt-like basement. Sound of people
in street talking as if in building. Sounds of water and mysterious sounds actually in building. Whole structure penetrated by ventilation flues – looked like Oriental places for
chucking down women into underground rivers. Con-
tractors' and architects' offices on entering. Clothes and boot
brushes. Effect of grand staircases sketched out in stone and
brick. The centre of the building was only a vast emptiness,
with a long iron girder poised on either side – supporting,
ultimately, the galleries. Blue light, distinctly blue, coming
down into basement through holes.

Wednesday, December 29th. – Bournemouth yesterday. I shall
never forget the appalling sensation of turmoil and jolly,

rough manners I had during lunch at the Hydro. A huge place. Crammed dining-room. Strident orchestra (women), rushing waiters of both sexes. Heaps of food but no service. *Patron et patronne* very good-natured. The whole crowd out for a lark, and enjoying the infernal vulgar din. A grand fancy dress ball the night before. What must it have been like? After seing this and the town I decided absolutely against Bournemouth. It was symbolic that I couldn't even get China tea there. Six hours in train. I got back to the hotel at 7.30. I had spent a day and a pound in discovering that Bournemouth was impossible.

Friday, December 31st. – Hueffer was genuinely pessimistic about commercial chances of the artistic novelist. He said that Conrad was in indigence. He gave a lot of interesting particulars about Conrad.

When I saw the acting and *mise en scène* of [Besier's] *Don*, I positively shrank from the prospect of the fight which I must necessarily have for years and years, if I am to get any sort of a decent production with such intractable material. It seemed to be all hopelessly wrong and conventional. But it wasn't. The play contained a fine central comic idea, clumsily and inadequately handled, nevertheless with fine moments.

Trench is supposed to be the artistic manager. Still, on first page of programme, his own name and Wyndham's name, and name of piece, but no name of author!

Sunday, January 2nd. – On Friday night, our last night in London, we went to the Tivoli. There were no seats except in the pit, so we went in the pit. Little Tich was very good, and George Formby, the Lancashire comedian, was perhaps even better. Gus Elen I did not care for. And I couldn't see the legendary cleverness of the vulgarity of Marie Lloyd. She was very young and spry for a grandmother. All her songs were variations on the same theme of sexual naughtiness. No censor would ever pass them, and especially he wouldn't pass her winks and her silences. To be noted also was the singular *naïveté* of the cinematograph explanation of what a vampire was and is, for the vampire dance. The stoutest and biggest attendants laughed at Little Tich and G. Formby. Fearful draughts half the time down exit staircases from the street. Fearful noise from the bar behind, made chiefly by officials. The bar-girls and their friends simply ignored the performance and the public. Public opinion keeps the seats of those who go to the bar at the interval for a drink.

We came down to Brighton by the 1.55 on Saturday, to the Royal York. Our first stroll along the front impressed me very favourably, yesterday afternoon. But I am obsessed by the thought that all this comfort, luxury, ostentation, snobbishness and correctness, is founded on a vast injustice to the artisan-class. I can never get away from this. The furs, autos, fine food, attendance, and diamond rings of this hotel only impress it on me more.

Monday, January 3rd. – I have read about a third of Edith Wharton's *The House of Mirth*. Not fine, but capable. No connection with literature; a certain fairly agreeable bitterness of satire now and then. It can just be read. Probably a somewhat superior Mrs Humphry Ward. I stopped reading it in favour of Marcus Clarke's *For the Term of His Natural Life*, which I picked up here at Brighton in a sixpenny edition. I am enjoying this, though in form and plot it is very *naïf*. I could drop it without tears.

To-day I wrote a *New Age* article, arranged the outline of an article for the *Nation*, and schemed out the first nine chapters of *Clayhanger* which I hope to begin to write on Wednesday. This afternoon we moved into our new room on the fourth floor, and I arranged everything for my work. We walked on the pier, and I saw subjects for water-colours and pastels.

The one advance which I made last year in worldliness was having a play put on at a West End Theatre for a run. That it failed is a detail. I bet it won't fail ultimately.

I wrote last year: *The Card*, novel; *The Glimpse*, novel; *The Honeymoon*, 3 act comedy; scenario for a play on the subject of 'Don Juan'; 'The Revolver', short story; 'The Tiger and the Baby'; 'Under the Clock'; 'Hot Potatoes'; 'The Heroism of Thos. Chadwick'; 'Why the Clock stopped'; 'The Boy, the Girl, and the blue suit'; seventy odd articles; my journal. Total 312,100 words. Much less than the year before.

Tuesday, January 4th. – When I came downstairs this morning full to the brim with the first chapters of *Clayhanger*, I found a letter from Herbert Trench asking me to alter tremendously the third act of *The Honeymoon*. My soul revolted, but of course I gradually gave way and then wrote him that I would.

I was occupied with letters till 11, and then I went out to recover myself for *Clayhanger* and I did do so. I worked till 1 o'clock, and again after lunch, and again after dinner. So that now I have got the opening of the book pretty ripe.

This afternoon we went to have tea with the Sidney Lows at the Metropole. Low told me how he discovered Kipling, and how his superiors on the Indian daily didn't think anything of him at all, but Low insisted on getting hold of his stuff. It seems he was very shy and young at the start. Low also insisted on Hall Caine's powers as a *raconteur*, as proved at Cairo, when he kept a dinner-party of casual strangers interested for 1½ hours by a full account of the secret history of the Druce case, which secret history he admitted afterwards was a sheer novelist's invention.

When H. C. was with S. L. in Egypt he saw everything as a background to *The White Prophet*, which was originally meant as a play for Tree. When S. L. showed him the famous staircases in the Ghezireh Palace he said, 'I can get three different entrances underneath that.' And when he saw the Pyramids, he said, 'Tree can do simply anything with those', etc. The S. Lows said he was the kindest nicest sort of man in private life (but S. L. told me behind his hand that he was apt to be tedious on the subject of himself, and *naïf*).

Wednesday, January 5th. – This morning at 9.45 I began to write *Clayhanger*. I felt less nervous and self-conscious than usual in beginning a book. And never before have I made one-quarter so many preliminary notes and investigations. I went out for a little recess, and at 1.30 I had done 1,000 words, which was very good for a first day.

We went to the Aquarium after tea, and heard mediocre music, and saw first-rate fishes, etc., living long under highly artificial conditions. The seals and alligators seemed to be intensely bored and sick of life, but perhaps they weren't.

Tuesday, January 11th. – Too excitingly busy just now to keep this journal every day. Hueffer telephoned me on Sunday at lunch-time asking me to do him a 3,000 word political article on the crisis for the 20th. In pursuance of my policy of never declining work that I am practically challenged to do, I accepted without a moment's reflection, though I knew that 12 guineas will be far from repaying me for my nervous expense on it. On Monday morning the *Sunday Chronicle* telegraphed accepting my price of 10 guineas for an 1,800 word article. I posted the article to them to-night. And in the last two days I have also written 2,700 words of my novel. In fact, terrific productiveness!

Grand rolling weather. Foamy sea, boisterous wind, sun, pageant of clouds, and Brighton full of wealthy imperative persons dashing about in furs and cars. I walked with joy to and fro on this unequalled promenade. And yet, at this election time, when all wealth and all snobbery is leagued together against the poor, I could spit in the face of arrogant and unmerciful Brighton, sporting its damned Tory colours.

I heard the door-keeper of this hotel politely expostulating with a guest: 'Surely, Mr —, you don't mean to say you're anything but a conservative!' Miserable parrot. After reading some pessimistic forecasts of the election I was really quite depressed at tea-time. But I went upstairs and worked like a brilliant nigger, and counted nearly 5,000 words done in two days, and I forgot my depression.

Certainly this morning as I looked at all the splendid solidity of Brighton, symbol of a system that is built on the grinding of the faces of the poor, I had to admit that it would take a lot of demolishing, that I couldn't expect to overset it with a single manifesto and a single election, or with fifty. So that even if the elections are lost, or are not won, I don't care. Besides things never turn out as badly as one fears. It is only when one does not fear that they go so surprisingly and bafflingly wrong, as with the Socialists at the last German general election.

Tuesday, January 18th. – Since Saturday night, when I stood out in the rain and wind 2¾ hours to see the election returns on the *Daily News* lantern screen in the Old Steyne, I have been perfectly obsessed by politics, perhaps to my harm artistically. To-day I finished my 3,000 word article on 'The Forces behind the Elections' for the next issue of the *English Review*. I don't think very much of it. It has a certain elegant quality – but is too vague. It lacks personality. The fact was I hadn't anything particular to say and anyhow wasn't in a state to say even what I had to say.

Frightful weather; wind, rain and gloom. And perhaps the chief origin of my existing dissatisfaction with things in general is that on Friday I had to consult an oculist, as I could only explain my headaches by the theory of a strain on my eyes. Yesterday I began to wear glasses. It is no light thing to begin suddenly to see the novel you have started with the naked eye, through a pair of eye-glasses.

Friday, January 21st. – I am gradually showing most of the symptoms of the average crass Tory. Merely to hear the opposite side discussing politics and agreeing with one another makes me furious and also coldly self-contemptuous. No doubt the elections are genuinely on my nerves. Depressed about them; preoccupied by them. After all, even allowing for Tory intimidation in villages, the nation will broadly get what it wants, anyhow. And I suppose that no politics, however idiotic, can make a great difference to the situation of middling, comfortable persons like me. Yet I continue to worry because the fools won't vote right, and I lie awake at night thinking about their foolishness.

I began a new chapter of *Clayhanger* at 5.15 to-day, after teasing the ideas for it since 7 this morning. I am trying to lift the whole thing up to a great height, but I feel sure that up to now it is nothing more than interesting in a nice quiet way.

Monday, January 24th. – I got so absorbed in my novel that the elections ceased to excite and disgust me. On Friday, Saturday and to-day, I must have written 6,000 words of it, and not bad.

I ought to do a brief account of my own psychological state during the elections. In some ways it had the faults shown by the Tory mentality.

Wednesday, January 26th. – I have done 2,000 words each day this week of *Clayhanger*, the stuff getting better, I think, each day.

Last night Orage sent me the first novel (I think) censured by the Libraries under their new scheme. I read 100 pp. of it.

Perfect weather to-day. Hard frost. Chilblains on all my extremities. Still reading *Le Rouge et le Noir* with humility.

Monday, January 31st. – I began *Clayhanger* on Jan. 5th and up to to-day have written 33,200 words of it. Total of over 45,000 words for the month. I had a letter from Hueffer this morning, in reference to my eulogy of the *English Review* in the *New Age*, saying I was the only one who had not tried to thwart him, etc. A characteristic letter.

Suggestion that I should do a weekly article for the *Daily Chronicle*. I said I would do it if I was free to be genuine and not merely bright, etc. I wrote to Tillotsons yesterday in reply to a demand for stuff, refusing to work any more at the old price.

Thursday, February 3rd. – On Tuesday we went in a taxi-cab to lunch with the [E. V.] Lucas's at Kingston Manor. *Un petit pays perdu.* I found Lucas slightly more Lucas than ever, and liked him more. His wife is like a nice Ibsen heroine. House slightly bare; a good staircase; plenty of colour; and some good little pictures.

The other morning I watched the sea-gulls helping the scavenger to scavenge the remains of the daily fish market on the beach. Rain. Strong wind. They could not alight. They had a lot of balancing and steering to do. They dived again and again for the same bit of offal, missing it, till they got it. Then each prize-winner sailed off against wind with difficulty towards Palace Pier, and out of my sight somewhere; but some seemed to swallow the piece *en route*. I was watching them alight in the water the other day; all did exactly the same; a planing descent, then, close on water, 2 or 3 half-flaps, a raising of the head, and they were afloat.

Wednesday, February 9th. – On Monday morning, in the bedroom and in the drawing-room, I finished the 1st part of *Clayhanger*, 42,000 words instead of 40,000. I wrote 2,000 words and was nearly going mad at lunch-time, but Webster and M. humoured me.

This morning I walked out and ordered a pair of spectacles, and began to get my ideas in order for the 2nd part of *Clayhanger* and did get them in order, rather well. On Monday I received a belated request from the *Manchester Guardian* to do a special telegraphic criticism of *Chantecler* for them. Of course I was here instead of in France, and it was too late. Nevertheless even had everything been favourable I doubt if I should have faced the unusualness and the worry of the task.

Hubert Bland having based his article in the *Sunday Chronicle* of 30 Jan. on statement that *The Glimpse* and other books were banned by the Libraries, I wrote to Smith's, Mudies, and The Times B.C. to ask if this was so, and if so why? They all replied that it was absolutely untrue. Smith's said they had 500 copies of *The Glimpse* in circulation at that moment.

Friday, February 11th. – Dinner at Chelsea Arts Club. Room long, low. Billiard-room. Rules and cues still hanging on walls. Some men in elegant evening-dress; some in fair ditto, some in smoking jackets, some in morning coats, some in lounge suits. Frampton in the last, with rough hair. Shannon, in chair, *très élégant.*

New ventilation put in roof for this banquet. Ventilation bad. Dinner sound. Service mediocre. Man on my right who grumbled at most things.

Caricatures, drawings and paintings round walls. Whitish walls. No elegance of furniture. The whole place rather like a studio.

Shannon's speech good. When replies began, *il commençait de se dégager* an atmosphere of brotherly love. You might have thought that success in an artistic career depended chiefly on help from fellow-artists. It grew almost maudlin. Enormous log-rolling, not principally as great artists, but as true friends, etc. Notoriously untrue, of course.

Note that the points of my speech that raised laughs were that I had bought pictures by members, that Orpen was a child, and that each member of the Club who was made A.R.A. was a hatchet buried in the ribs of the enemy.

Monday, February 14th. – To-day I began to get my second part of *Clayhanger* in order. I finished reading the first part, and found the penultimate chapter a bit dull, the last good and solid.

To-night I finished *Le Rouge et le Noir* for the second time. Nothing to beat it for solid truth anywhere, and nothing outside Russia to beat it as a special novel in the grand manner.

Thursday, February 17th. – Yesterday appeared the first of my series of articles in the *Chronicle*. In discussing the opinion of the young man of 1960 about *Chantecler* I said '*the young man of 1960, whose mother's parents probably met the night before last and were rather taken with each other*'! The editor cut this phrase out.

I began to write the second part of *Clayhanger* on Tuesday. I did 2,000 words, and a *New Age* article, and a lot of letters at night, and a description of *Clayhanger* for the publisher's Catalogue. I was very exhausted.

£12 odd is my share of result of nine performances of *What the Public Wants* at Glasgow recently.

I wrote to Trench on Tuesday telling him definitely I wouldn't alter the last act of *The Honeymoon*.

Two thousand words of *Clayhanger* to-day, and an evening of heavy correspondence. And I walked twice to Hove, and once to Black Rock, and once to the end of the Pier. We had tea with Mrs Granville Barker (Lillah McCarthy) who asked me to write a monologue for her. I said I thought I would.

February 20th. – All secure in the hotel. But terrific wind beating on S. windows and general shaking. Go out. You then see hotels from outside. Blocks of stone and yellow light, immensely secure. Very brilliant in lower stages. Aquarium a cluster of lights with its little absurd tower. Moon in cloudy sky. Little crowds at two points near pier. Vast sea of foam for about 200 yards out. Rows of little people in half-distance silhouetted like a long-toothed saw against this. I find the general look of these groups of people perhaps the most interesting. So small. Waves breaking over jetty and over Marine Drive. Waves coming between jetty and pier, running along wall of jetty in a line like the curves of a long rope shaken to imitate waves. Noise of naked shingles. Plenty of suffused light about. Sheet lightning from time to time.

There was a wonderful sunset the night before, salmon (and a salmon sea) in south, pink to east, and sapphire to west. In 15 minutes it was all grey. But while it lasted the sky was a composition in itself.

Wednesday, February 23rd. – M. and I went to see *The Merry Widow*. I felt I *had* to see it, in order to be *calé* on such things when it came to writing about London.

Same thing over again. Indeed I could notice no difference. Music even much less charming or superficially and temporarily attractive than I had expected. Troupe of about 40. Elaborate costumes, scenery, and appointments. Sylvia May, Kate May, and the other principals, all chosen for their looks. Not one could avoid the most elementary false emphasis. Thus Sylvia May looking at a man asleep on a sofa, 'But *he* may wake up' (when there was no question of another man asleep) instead of 'He make wake *up*.' This sort of thing all the time. Also such things as recogni*z*e. Three chief males much better. All about drinking and whoring and money. All popular operetta airs. Simply nothing else in the play at all, save references to patriotism. Names of tarts on the lips of characters all the time. Dances lascivious, especially one.

I couldn't stand more than 2 acts. Too appallingly bored.

Friday, February 25th. – Yesterday I signed contracts with Duttons of N.Y. for £1,000. Not much; but the most I have yet signed for in a day.

I wrote 2,300 words yesterday, and began feeling a wreck last night. Feeling complete this morning. Couldn't work. I walked about Brighton in cold showers till 12.30 and managed to get my first love scene into something like order.

Sunday, March 6th. – I got to work again yesterday, and wrote 2,000 words of *Clayhanger* which words I thought pretty good. In the afternoon we went out to the cliffs beyond Black Rock and I made a sketch. Marvellous fine weather, with east wind. In the evening the hotel was full of fair women and brave men.

Lately I have been reading Stephen Crane's *Bowery Tales* which was quite readable, and excellent even, in parts. Also Sturge Moore's *Art and Life* (about Flaubert and Blake) which in spite of its careful second-rate quality, I found enormously stimulating, if only on account of the extracts from Flaubert's correspondence and from French criticism. It certainly bucked up my novel quite appreciably. Also a bit of F. M. Hueffer's *A Call*. Slick work, but not, I fear, really interesting. He doesn't get down to the real stuff.

Tuesday, March 8th. – Last evening at 7.30 I received a letter from Trench accepting *The Honeymoon* definitely. (And to-day I heard from Lee Matthews who had received the second £100.) I had a great fit of triumph, as I thought about all that this Haymarket play *might* mean. But it soon passed. I had been looking for this Haymarket acceptance for weeks as a sort of goal, but it meant nothing to me, really. In fact this morning I soon found a new source of worry, as my *Chronicle* article did not appear as it ought to have done.

I wrote 1,200 words yesterday, though not making a start till nearly 5 o'clock. And 2,300 words to-day. But it will take me all my time to finish the second part of *Clayhanger* by next Thursday. Yesterday morning, being not fit enough for work, I walked to Rottingdean and back along the cliffs. The sight of sea and downs did me a sort of vague spiritual good.

Man bearing a card: Blind, through boy throwing mortar. Discharged by 4 hospitals. Incurable.

He evidently had been a street beggar for a long time. He had the continual stamping movement of such beggars. What a tragedy! It wouldn't bear much thinking about.

Thursday, March 10th. – Neuralgia all these days. Still averaging over 2,000 words a day of novel. Neuralgia only in gums, etc. Probably due to cold.

To-night Gounod's *Gallia* (rot) and Walford Davies's *Everyman* at Dome, by Brighton Sacred Harmonic Society (est. 1827). Rather good, this last.

Sunday, March 13th. – For several days much bored with neuralgia and indigestion. Still, I stick to it. But on Saturday I began to feel that I shouldn't finish the second part here. I collected ideas well on Saturday. M. went to London on Friday, and I worked so much, after a bad night, that I was painfully tired and kept showing it nervously to myself when I went for a walk at 6.30. On Saturday morning I wrote *New Age* article, and *Chronicle* article this morning.

Thursday, March 17th. – Impossible to finish the second part of *Clayhanger*. If I had finished it I should have spoilt it. I got up to within a few hundred words of 80,000 but the 2nd part will exceed the advertised length by 5 or 6,000. Moreover I was frightened by a lot of extraordinary praise of *The Old Wives' Tale* that I have recently had. I was afraid *Clayhanger* was miles inferior to it, and that by going on blindly I might lose a chance of bucking it up in Switzerland. ... Neuralgia gradually getting better. To-morrow we go to Paris via Newhaven. Our stay here on the whole has been a very great success. We have both enjoyed it. I have written over 100,000 words, and Marguerite three short stories. But I doubt if the climate suits us now that it has duly braced us up. Certainly I need less sleep; but smoking seems to affect me more and I have had neuralgia and headaches. Largely of course due to my book. But I have a feeling now against the climate.

Good Friday, March 25th. – Six days of perfect weather, with a N. and N.W. wind and nothing visible all day in the strong sunshine. I was able to begin the final chapters of the second part of *Clayhanger* without much difficulty on Tuesday, and I have averaged over 2,000 words a day of it. I finish to-morrow. The second part will be 50,000 instead of the estimated 40,000 words.

It is surprising that, a fortnight ago at Brighton, I could have thought it possible to finish the second part there. I had only allowed 2,000 words for the most important series of scenes – love scenes – in that part. On the whole I think it is fair. Anyhow it is honest and conscientious. I wrote 3,200 words yesterday, and pretty nearly killed myself, and was accordingly very depressed at night. This morning I went a long walk and wrote 1,000 words in an hour this afternoon.

Reviews of *Helen with the High Hand* strangely kind.

Wednesday, May 25th. – We returned home yesterday after three exhaustingly impressionful days in Paris. We unpacked all our trunks yesterday before dinner. Dined on the *terrasse* of Brunet's, and found the price of meals had gone up from 2 frs. 75 to 3 frs. Now they give coffee, worth about one *sou.*

Our waiter, who was in rather a hurry to dine himself, was cheerfully cynical about the continual rise of prices in Fontainebleau. When I said I couldn't drink the wine that was *compris*, and that I knew restaurants where they would give you mineral water instead, he said, with a singular intonation, 'Not in Fontainebleau, anyhow!' He said he had had 15 years of Fontainebleau, and implied that he had nothing to learn about the methods of the tradesmen here. I saw him dining afterwards. He was one of those waiters who have learned a whole philosophy in the practice of their vocation. Secretly scornful of human nature yet indulgent. Impassive, and supremely capable of keeping his end up.

M., after engaging a servant to-day, told me of the reply of the mothers, made to her on several occasions by different mothers when asked if the daughter could cook: '*Je crois bien qu'elle sait faire la cuisine. Quand je ne suis pas là elle fait la soupe. Et elle sait faire cuire un morceau de veau à la casserole.*' This seems to be the last word of cooking in that class. It throws light, the phrase does, on their habits.

I went out for an hour into *my* forest, and began to arrange ideas for the last part of *Clayhanger*. They came fairly well. I bought papers at station on way home and put on my eyeglasses to read them as I walked along. Then I thought, 'M. Porrier may be in the Avenue des Carrosses and would see me in my eye-glasses for the first time.' I didn't want him to see me in my eye-glasses for the first time. Although I laughed at myself, I had somehow taken the glasses off before I arrived at Av. des Carrosses.

Monday, May 30th. – Am just reading *The Man of Property*. Certainly I should say that the erotic parts – and there are plenty of them – were done under the influence of George Moore. If Galsworthy had never read and admired George Moore, the similarity is extremely remarkable.

Thursday, June 2nd. – I was in bed all day on Tuesday with a *migraine*; it sounds nicer than bilious attack. All due to eating a *fricot* on Monday night. By 7 p.m. I could read a little without making myself worse, and I began my new Stendhal,

L'Abbesse de Castro. It opens slowly and finely. The intrigue is exactly the same, in essence, as that of the *Chartreuse* and of *Le Rouge et le Noir*. Did he ever think of anything else except capturing the affection of women under the most difficult conceivable circumstances?

I began to work after tea yesterday, and wrote 1,400 words of the first chapter of the last book of the eternal *Clayhanger*. This morning (after supper of bread and milk) I arose in fine health at 5.30. I made tea and read a lot of my manual of tree-drawing that I bought a year ago and had scarcely looked at. And then I finished the first chapter of *Clayhanger* at 8.45, having written about 1,600 words in 2¾ hours. My day's work was thus done before breakfast.

Friday, June 3rd. – 3,000 words done of last part of *Clayhanger*. There is no doubt that when I finish my work at 8.30 or 8.45 a.m. I have a considerable leisure before me. At least it seems so. But then I haven't finished it then. After 10 I go out to arrange ideas for next day. That takes an hour. I may make a sketch *en route*. Anyhow I do nothing else but that and a letter or so before lunch. I must doze after lunch, and then read over my morning's work and occupy myself with the afternoon's post. Tea-time. Then I have 3 hours. Part of it must go in a walk. Yesterday I painted for 1½ hours of it. Then there is a lot of time after dinner (which for me now consists of a basin of bread and milk).

Last night I read André Chénier after playing the piano. Some of him amused me. I wish I could read miscellaneously like that every night. The *pharmacien* came in, late. I wanted him in my heart to leave at ten. He didn't leave till 10.30. I had so violently wanted him to go that when he did go, I couldn't sleep at first, and I had been thinking over my work at 4.30 that morning. *This* morning I got up tired at 5.45 and decided to put off my work, till after 9 o'clock breakfast. I read Tennyson's 'Palace of Art'. Some exceedingly brilliant suggestive impressionist landscapes in it, and pretty clever phrasing here and there. But the real basis of the poem seemed to me to be entirely banal, the notion of a fairly thoughtful clerk.

Saturday, June 4th. – Ravel and his mother came for tea yesterday; only both of them preferred water to tea.

Yesterday I finished *A Man of Property*. A really distinguished, passionate, truly romantic universal book. Many small faults, but the only large fault is that the end is not an end. The situation between Soames Forsyte and Irene his wife is not solved. But it is an impressive book, no mistake.

This morning I finished second chapter of last part of *Clayhanger*.

Monday, June 6th. – At Madame R's. I met Brunet Huart, the painter, aged 84. He wore light striped trousers, a waistcoat of black velvet, a rather large tie, rather large and striking gloves and generally was dandiacal.

He remembered Florence in 1858, and the anecdotes of King Victor Emmanuel's circus-like appearances in the *Cascine*. He liked Kipling, also Wells; but he thought Wells didn't explain enough. He remembered the fighting in the auditorium of the Theatre des Variétés on account of a play which made fun of shop assistants. The theatre was full of shop assistants and their sympathisers. When the noise grew unbearable, an actor came forward and thumped furiously on a table. Everybody was so staggered by this impudence of an actor to his public that silence ensued and the actor said: 'No! Never shall a counter jumper bring this curtain down.' The old gentleman was afraid of motor cars, and in particular of his young cousin's driving. He had just returned from a round of family visits, ending at Bourges. Then he curved off into a long story of an adventure in the Palazzo Orsini in Rome (when paper money as small as 5*d.* was issued – current in the city only), where he got enormous attention from a concierge by two payments of a franc each. 'The concierge would have given me a bed in the palace, I think,' said he. He had a curious and unusual knowledge of the relative sizes of things from St Peter's downwards. He was certain that a revolution would occur within six months, precipitated by losses due to inundations and bad harvests, and consequent labour unrest. He said that he had painted all his life, but had entered the studio of a celebrated master only at the age of 25. He now got his military friends, colonels and so on, to send him down a soldier with a horse for two or three hours daily. Here he explained in detail how he taught the soldier to lift up the horse's leg so that he could see how the light fell on the legs of a galloping horse. Even recently he had painted in the rain, enjoying the 'pretty colours', *'teints'* of barley, oats etc. He kindly offered to criticize my drawings. He was full of various energy, and affirmed that he had not begun to feel old until he was seventy. His chief subject was undoubtedly the Palais Royal.

'And, of course,' he said, 'the Palais Royal was in all its splendour in those days, and the plays given there were *really* witty.' (1850 to 1860.) But the samples which he offered of Palais Royal wit in those great days were feeble and flashy. He seemed to be able to remember in detail all the Palais Royal burlesques of popular tragedy, and he quoted miles of tirades in verse. He talked well, if too much.

Wednesday, June 8th. – Last night there was a concert in the Place Dancourt. We walked there, having missed a car, through the most beautifully coloured streets in Europe. Wonderful salmon-tints in the sky, also an extraordinary calm. We arrived late. The *terrasse* of the *grand café* was bulged out nearly to the newspaper kiosk, and crammed. Three or four waiters rushing about and sweating. We went into the café of which the glazing had been removed for the summer. Many officers of the 15th Regiment playing cards – chiefly bridge. I got two chairs and placed them close to the entrance, and stood waiting for M. who had disappeared. A young officer came forward to take one of them. I stopped him. As he persisted, I insisted. *'C'est à vous?'* 'Oui,' I said (No ceremonious titles). *'Vous l'avez prise?'* He asked me in such a tone suggesting that I had not, that in my excitement I replied *'Si'* instead of *'Oui'*! We glared at each other for an instant. I could have killed him. *'Eh bien, gardez-la'* he said roughly, and went off to get another chair. All the blustering *poltroonery* of the man came out in a flash. Afterwards I heard him saying something to another officer about 'Ce bonhomme-là', pointing to me.

I thought about this for a long time, forgetting the music, and constructed all sorts of versions of what would have happened if we had had a row. Colonels seemed to be thick upon the ground. I thought of all the wonderful apt, polished, polite cutting things I might have said.

Saturday, June 11th. – I began *Le Crime et le Châtiment*, which I have been wanting to read again for about a fortnight. The scene in the café and Marmeladoff's confession, seems even finer than it did when I read it at Hockliffe. It is certainly one of the very greatest things in fiction. Absolutely full of the most perfect detail. It really disgusted and depressed me about my own work, which seemed artificial and forced by the side of it. I expect that in most of my work there is too much forcing of the effect. An inability to do a thing and leave it alone.

Yesterday walking in the forest, I thought of all the life in it, humming, flying, crawling, jumping etc., the tiniest insects that you can scarcely see, the ants, all sorts of flies, worms, beetles, bees, snails, lizards, *and the gigantic birds*. As for the rabbits, squirrels, and deer, they are simply monstrously gigantic compared to the mass of the life in the forest.

I didn't seem to be getting near to the personality of Hilda in my novel. You scarcely ever do get near a personality. There is a tremendous lot to do in fiction that no one has yet done. When M. comes downstairs from the attic, in the midst of some house arrangement, and asks me if such and such a thing will do and runs up again excited – why? And the mood of the servant as, first thing in the morning, she goes placidly round the house opening the shutters! The fact is, the novelist seldom really *penetrates*.

Tuesday, June 14th. – I seem to be doing an average of 2,000 words a day now of my novel. Only 13,000 words remain to be done. But they are very much on my mind. When I am not working here, I am walking in the forest and worrying over the invention, 5 to 7 miles a day. I rise at 5.45 and go to bed about 9.30.

Wednesday, June 15th. – Juliette said the other night, '*Ça fait du bien de manger les asperges. Ça lave la vessie.*' She and Marguerite had a great banquet of snails yesterday. They and the servant ate 150. Marguerite said 'It's horribly cruel. I couldn't do it as Mother does. She puts them alive into cold water, and lets them boil up slowly, *à petit feu.* It's horribly cruel.' And she went on eating them. Last night they were again collecting snails in the garden, and Marguerite came across one of the other sort of snails, *limaces*, big things without shells. It had two tiny little ones with it. 'I can't bring myself to kill them,' she said, 'but they do a lot of harm. I wish you'd kill them.' I instantly put my foot on the three. She squirmed with horror and went off.

Thursday, June 23rd. – I have just (3 p.m.) finished *Clay-hanger* one week in advance of time. 160,800 words. For the last few days it has monopolised me. But quite contrary to my general practice towards the end of a novel, I have kept in magnificent health.

Monday, July 11th. – It seems that the *curés* in Brittany forbid dancing, except at wedding feasts. Nevertheless in this village there is dancing in the very shadow of the church every Sunday afternoon after vespers. We saw it yesterday afternoon. About 10 couples. The *charcutière* danced with another girl. Heavy girls. One couple obviously in love. A drum and a brass instrument.

Of the three men here, one is a *passementier*, and another, a commercial traveller, and the third a *fabricant* of something. They sit at a table and sing together. The luggage of one married pair arrived to-night, 36 hours late. The wife is of the odalisque sort, and she put on some more striking clothes at once. She lolls at her bedroom window for 30 to 60 minutes each morning. A beautiful young woman. *Elle se cambre tout le temps.* She would have made a good *courtisane*. Alcock says that she leaves a table at which an intellectual conversation is proceeding – about war or feminism for instance – with a gesture which says: 'What has all this got to do with IT?'

Tuesday, July 12th. – Alcock said that Werg had been playing a lot in *Electra*, and considered Strauss to be more of a mathematician than a musical composer. When rehearsing, if the players tried to put any musical feeling into their playing, Strauss stopped them and said: 'No, not like that. You are not musicians, you are wild beasts.' This is the most illuminating thing about Strauss's genius that I have heard.

Monday, July 18th. – Tertia said that the mater said, on seeing *Carmen* at Hanley Theatre: 'I don't like that woman at all.'

Sunday, July 24th. – Ile Callot yesterday morning. Strong smell of seaweed spread over the fields for manure. Just a few groups of cottages or hovels collected round the church. A church there since the 6th century. Primitive. Probably barbaric. The men working barefoot in the seaweed did not even look up as we passed. At night we saw from dining-room windows the islanders going home in their carts. A girl waiting to be taken up in a cart. Sun already set. Silhouette dark blue-black of horse, cart and people – no details in side outline.

Monday, July 25th. – Characteristic gesture of an old fisherman. He took off his cap, held it upside down under his mouth, dropped his plug (of tobacco) into it, and whipped it on his head again, all in the twinkling of an eye.

Godebski said that C. L. Philippe never saw the sea till 2 years before his death. Fargue took him to Havre. On meeting the sea, he lay down in a sort of ecstasy of hysteria, on his stomach, and lapped at each wave as it came in, as if determined to make up for lost time by the violence of his sensations.

Monday, August 1st. – Too short of sleep and sardonic to write anything yesterday. Baptism of a new pleasure boat, the *Blanche* yesterday. Three *curés* and three choir-boys with instruments, and a bottle of champagne to do it. Nearly upset in going out in dinghy.

Women minding cows. Fat, old, in many skirts. They just stand, moving slightly from time to time. Towards 5 or 6, they pull the cows home by rope, but on approaching stable the cow trots on in front. A sign of barbarism this. Very queer that even an old woman's time is not worth more than that of a cow, that she can't earn enough to keep a cow.

Monday, August 15th. – I have now taken, what nearly everybody said I was incapable of taking and never would take, a long holiday. From July 2nd to yesterday I did nothing whatever in the way of work except three short articles for the *New Age*, which I was obliged to do. Of course I had to attend to my correspondence; but I kept that as short as possible. I wrote an illustrated journal at Carantec, and I also did a number of paintings and sketches.

We came definitely home on Friday night, and found everything in order. To-day I resume my literary business. The three things that occupy me are; a good short story for *T.P.'s Magazine*, my 'Life in Paris' for the *English Review*, and a play founded on *Buried Alive*.

I have done no regular sustained reading now for something like ten months. So I shall resume Taine. I propose to do as I did in May and June here. Get up at 5.30, and begin creative writing at 6, and finish that on most days before breakfast at 9 a.m. I have now satisfied myself that it is my best time for working, particularly now that by means of milk dinners I have cured my biliousness. It is 3 months since I had a headache due to indigestion. After breakfast I can do my oddments and correspondence, etc., and arrange my ideas for the next day. And thus have the whole of my work finished at noon. Afternoons for reading and painting and crass idleness. I have openly sworn – openly, in order to make it impossible for me to forswear myself decently – never again to work as hard as I have done in the past.

Friday, August 19th. – All proofs of *Clayhanger* came on Wednesday morning, so that after 9 o'clock in the morning I did nothing on Wednesday and Thursday except correct them.

575 pages. I finished them on Thursday afternoon. Errors in the typescript made them very amazing. A great deal of it is as good as anything I've done. I noticed the far too frequent use of the word 'extraordinary', but I loathe altering a work once it is done – no mistake about that.

Wednesday, September 7th. – Being unable to get rid of influenza-ish inquietudes of the stomach, and having had several very bad nights *de suite* I stayed in bed to-day, and therein read and wrote. Yesterday I finished the third or the fourth perusal of *A Mummer's Wife*. This book really is original and fine and beautiful. The Islington scenes are superb. You have squalor and sordidness turned into poetry. And the painter-like effects of visualization are splendid throughout. Language a bit clumsy and coarse occasionally. 'Booze' and 'Boozed' are amazing words. There are others. But what an original and powerful work!

Last night I began Spencer's *Autobiography* and this morning, by dint of much wakefulness, I had arrived at p. 224. I found it very interesting and jolly well done. It is much better done and much more artistic than J. S. Mill's auto-biography. Nevertheless Spencer's little attempts at narrative in the manner of a novelist – beginning for example with a fragment of conversation, or with such a phrase as 'If on such a day anyone had been looking at such a spot they might have been surprised to see', etc., are funnier than he intended.

Tuesday, September 13th. – My old Gaveau piano went on Saturday. I sold it for 250 frs., the money to be spent on hiring. I got a Pleyel grand instead. I had to spend Friday night in altering the arrangement of the whole room for the reception of the grand. Naturally when it came I had to spend a great deal of time in playing.

On Sunday morning arrived the first copies of *Clayhanger*. It is the best-produced of all my novels, I think; but I could have spared the girl's portrait on the cover. I read a lot of it, and thought it pretty good. A few misprints. On reflection I think it does contain more sociology than *The O.W.T.* I had promised this in the prospectus of it, but I was afraid I had not fulfilled the promise. It was only when Marguerite began to read the book that I realized – without her asking any questions – how full of difficulties it must be for a stranger, and how unlike the ordinary good novel.

Wednesday, September 14th. – Beautiful promenades in the forest yesterday. In the morning I was astonished by the grandeur and multitude of the spider's webs. I broke two to see what they would do, but they did nothing, – just hung loose in the breeze.

Thursday, September 15th. – Says Herbert Spencer, speaking of Thackeray's insignificance at dinner (*Autobiography*, II, 91): 'I have heard that he could be a lively companion; but it seems possible that usually when in company he was occupied in observing traits of character and manner. A painter of human nature as variously manifested must ordinarily be more a listener than a talker.' Yes, perhaps. But unconsciously occupied. The painter of human nature is not consciously engaged in the act of observation.

The chapter of the *Autobiography* dealing with the finishing and publication of *First Principles* is unimposing, and disappointingly deficient in emotion. (Compare Gibbon in the finishing of *his* big work.) Nothing of real interest is recorded about the undertaking. This is a pity. But everywhere Spencer's narrative skill is very clumsy, and his little attempts to be dramatic are extraordinarily feeble. I am struck in reading by the stolid indifference with which his biggest books were received. It was appalling; it desolates. Yet this kind of reception is quite common. I am also struck throughout by a whole series of odd remarks – almost asides – which give you the disconcerting feeling that nearly all common valuations are relatively quite wrong. That is, that nearly everything – gifts, acquirements, possessions, achievements – is either under-valued or over-valued.

When I think how *First Principles*, by filling me up with the sense of causation everywhere, has altered my whole view of life, and undoubtedly immensely improved it, I am confirmed in my opinion of that book. You can see *First Principles* in nearly every line I write.

Friday, September 30th. – I began to foresee a comparative failure for *Clayhanger* in England, and then also in America. Useless for me to argue that my contracts in England and America assure me a reasonable income for three years, whether the publishers lose or not. Useless for me to argue that it is absurd for me to *expect* even a good circulation for books like *Clayhanger*, which arouse enthusiasm in just a few beings! This in spite of the fact that I cannot make less than £1,500 next year, and may make £2,000 or over, – and this by doing only the work that pleases me – my very best work. I was still gloomy this morning. I hated to go on with my play. But I did go on with it.

Sunday, October 2nd. – Yesterday I had a goodish large notion for the Hilda book – of portraying the droves of the whole sex, instead of whole masculine droves. I think I can do something with this, showing the multitudinous activities of the whole sex, the point of view of the whole sex, against a mere background of masculinity. I had a sudden vision of it. It has never been done.

Finished Gibbon's *Autobiography*. It is a distinguished book, but my feelings about the author are mixed.

Thursday, October 20th. – Now I am reading Ste Beuve almost for the first time. Except for a few of the 'Causeries du Lundi' – and that a long time ago – I have read nothing of him. I read the essay on Madame de Sévigné last night (and ordered a volume of her letters this afternoon). I read the essay on Bayle this afternoon (and read Bayle's preface to his Diction-naire to-night). There is no doubt that Ste Beuve is exces-sively *agréable à lire*. He flatters you into believing that your taste is as cultivated as his own. And, in the essay on Bayle, his remarks on the *esprit critique* are full of nutriment brilliantly served. It has seemed to me that these days I am living, as distinguished from preparing to live. In autumn weather; plenty of heavy continuous rain, which is pleasant to hear when you are safe in the house and busy in the house, and the ground floor and the bedroom floor are both warmed. Work in the morning, on the play, which goes pretty easily. Sleep and reading after lunch. 30 pp. of Taine per day, *comme devoir*. New books coming in every day. Grand piano. Discovery of playable Schubert. *Clayhanger* in its third English edition. Agreeable tension of anxiety of waiting for news of this book's reception in America. Journey to Paris now and then. Miscellaneous browsy reading in the evening. Good appetite. The drawbacks to this idyll are – no progress in drawing, fairly bad sleeping, and some neuralgia. But then it must never be forgotten that since the end of May last, thanks to evening break and milk, I have never had more than one hour's continuous stomachic headache. . . . It cannot be long before some infernal nuisance supervenes. Such a state of content will not be allowed by destiny to last much longer.

Friday, October 28th. – To-day I finished Act IV of play, which will be called *The Great Adventure*. Although never working very long at it together I haven't thought about much else.

Neil Munro in a letter yesterday pointed out to me that Aylmer Maude's *Biography of Tolstoy* (Vol. II) contains Tolstoy's admission of the justice of my criticism of 'The death of Ivan Ilyitch' in the *New Age*. The criticism was really Farrar's, and I gave it as that of a doctor.

Sunday, November 6th. – On Saturday, Oct. 29, M. and I went to Paris to look at furnished flats, and we took one at 39, Rue de Grenelle at 225 frs. per month. I should have made some notes on the hunting if I could have made them a week ago.

I had a fearful headache the next morning. It was the beginning of a slight influenza, from which I have not yet entirely recovered. The Davrays came for tea on the Sunday afternoon, and he told some good stories about General Galliffet.

On Monday, Tuesday, Wednesday and Thursday I was unfit for work. I tried to begin Act 4 of *The Great Adventure* on Wednesday, and simply wrote rot. On Thursday I decided to leave the play and write the next 'Paris Night' for the *English Review*, which I did on Friday and yesterday, doing altogether 5,000 words in the two days.

Friday, November 11th. – Still unwell all week. Nevertheless I finished *The Great Adventure* this afternoon at 4.30 p.m., four days in advance of time. Actual dialogue 20,300 words. I shall doubtless cut it to less than 20,000. There are now two complete plays of mine – this, and *The Honeymoon*, renounced by Trench – for sale.

The two American Reviews of *Clayhanger* to which I looked forward with the most interest, *Boston Evening Transcript* and *Chicago Evening Post*, are both absolutely satisfactory in their enthusiasm. Doran wrote me, in response to my query, that he had sold about 12,000 of *Old Wives' Tale* to date, and that the demand seemed like continuing indefinitely.

Sunday, November 20th. – On Friday Dr Otto (of Tauchnitz) came for tea, and stayed for about 2 hours, and produced a most favourable impression on both of us. Also he was exceedingly flattering in a very discreet way. Talking of relations between publishers and authors he said that Macmillans had published for Rhoda Broughton for 45 years, but she had never seen any member of the firm; apparently didn't want to.

Thursday, December 8th. – I have been working daily at construction of *Hilda Lessways*. As it was pouring with rain this afternoon, I went to the Gare d'Orsay, and had tea on the platform-*terrasse* of the café, and walked about for 2¾ hours, and really worked excellently at the first book, and was moreover all the time amused and diverted by the phenomena of the terminus. This is a most excellent dodge for wet days.

Saturday, December 17th. – I went into St Sulpice again this morning to look at Delacroix, and came across a great ordination service. Dozens of young priests in parti-coloured capes, etc. drinking the sacred wine with elaborate ceremonies, music, etc. They were all, or nearly all, tonsured. A startling mummery, right in the middle of Paris. Crowds of women.

December 31st. – This year I have written 355,900 words, including *Clayhanger*, *The Great Adventure*, 'Paris Nights', 'Night and Morning in Florence', and probably about 80 other articles. I think only one short story, 'Mimi'.

Paris, Friday, January 6th. – After several days' delay owing to indisposition, I began to write *Hilda Lessways* yesterday afternoon; only 400 words. To-day, 1,100 words. It seems to be a goodish beginning.

Wednesday, January 18th. – I finished third chapter of *Hilda Lessways*. Usual doubts as to whether the thing is any good.

Friday, January 20th. – I have written about 14,000 words of *Hilda* in 16 days. The stuff is slowly improving. I had not been able to even read, until I received H. G. Wells' *The New Machiavelli*. This book makes a deep impression on me, and even causes me to examine my own career, and to wonder whether I have not arrived at a parting-of-the-ways therein, and what I ought to decide to do after the book – after *Hilda* is finished. London or Paris?

Sunday, January 22nd. – Friday night, visit with Chateaubriant to Romain Rolland. Found him in a holland-covered room, disguised bed in one corner. Tea at 9.45. Sister, spinster aged 35. Bright, slightly masculine. Mother, an aged body, proud of children, shrewd, came in later. Romain Rolland, arm in sling; large face, pale, calm, kindly, thoughtful, rather taciturn. Giving a marked impression of an absolutely honest artist, and a fine soul. Considerable resemblance to Marcel Schwob; but bigger and more blond. No particular talk. But an impression of rightness, respectability in every sense, conscientiousness, and protestantism (intellectually).

January 31st. – I went to see the historic Durand Ruel collection. The furniture of the abode was startlingly different in quality and taste from the pictures. All the furniture might have been bought at the Bon Marché. The table in the dining-room was covered with the chequered cloth so prevalent in small French households. (In this room was a still-life of Monet.) The doors, however, were all beautifully painted in panels. Aged and young domestics moved about. There was a peculiar close smell – no, not peculiar, because it permeates thousands of Paris homes.

From the front windows was seen a fine view of St Lazare Station, with whiffs of steam transpiring from the vast edifice. The visitors while I was there included two Englishmen; one very well-dressed, though his socks were behind the times and he had rouged his nostrils; some Americans, and four doll-like Japanese. Certainly the chief languages spoken were American and Japanese. The 'great' Renoir (the man and woman in the H box of a theatre) hung in the study. It was rather thrilling to see this illustrious work for the first time, as it were, in the flesh. There were Monets of all periods and the latest period was not the best. A magnificent Cézanne landscape and a few other Cézannes; Manet, Dégas, Sisley, Boudin – all notable. Yes, a collection very limited in scope, but fully worthy of its reputation. Only it wants hanging. It simply hasn't a chance where it is. The place is far too small, and the contrast between the pictures and the furniture altogether too disconcerting. Still, the pictures exist, and they are proof that a man can possess marvellous taste in a fine art, while remaining quite insensitive in an applied art.

Afterwards I looked in on a painter in Montmartre, and learned to my astonishment that it was precisely he who had painted Durand Ruel's doors. 70 doors had been ordered.

The painter told me how Durand Ruel had bought Renoirs for 20 years without selling. The 'great' Renoir had been sold at Angers for 400 francs, after a commissioning amateur had refused to give Renoir 1,500 francs for it. The amateur had said: 'Yes, it's very good of course, but it isn't what I expected from you.' (They always talk like that – these commissioning amateurs.) Then Durand Ruel bought it. And now he has refused 125,000 francs for it. In my friend's studio I was told how dealers who specialize in modern pictures really make their money. A 'lord' wants to dispose of say a Rubens, on the quiet. It comes mysteriously to the dealer, who puts it in a private room, and shows it only to a very few favoured young painters, who pronounce upon it. Soon afterwards it disappears for an unknown destination. The dealer is vastly enriched, and he goes on specializing in modern pictures.

Wednesday, February 15th. – I got as far as the death of Mrs Lessways in *Hilda Lessways* on Sunday afternoon, and sent off the stuff as a specimen to Pinker yesterday. 33,000 words. During this time I haven't had sufficient courage to keep a journal. I suspect that I have been working too hard for 5 weeks regularly. I feel it like an uncomfortable physical sensation all over the top of my head. A very quick sweating walk of half an hour will clear it off, but this may lead, and does lead, to the neuralgia of fatigue and insomnia and so on, and I have to build myself up again with foods.

April 21st. – London. Palace Theatre. Pavlova dancing the dying swan. Feather falls off her dress. Two silent Englishmen. One says, 'Moulting'. That is all they say.

Thursday, May 25th. – *Mozart, Strauss Concert.* 3 p.m. Old man with St Vitus next to us. He stood some time at door with young girl in charge waiting for first piece to finish. She armed him with difficulty to seat. F. C. B. helped him to sit down. Long thin legs. Knees that stuck out to next seat. Both hands trembling violently nearly all the time. Kept his head down. Took him about a minute to lift up one hand to his face to move his specs. Peculiarly smooth reddish skin of hands. The girl put programme in his hands. He could read it, in spite of shaking. Handkerchief stuck in waistcoat. She wiped his moustache for him. She took his gloves off, and afterwards put them on. He never looked up the whole time. Once, not being comfortable, he had to be lifted and re-sat, and at intervals he stood up, holding on the front seat. All his movements very slow and trembling. Once when hand on knee it did not tremble. Lips, and especially upper lip with moustache trembling all the time. We left her arranging him for departure.

Wednesday, June 14th. – On Tuesday morning I finished *Hilda Lessways*, which is exactly 100,000 words – a curiously good forecast. I re-read *Hilda* and put in chapter headings after dinner.

Saturday, July 8th. – On Thursday I went to see the [T. B.] Wellses at Pont de l'Arche. I came back yesterday, and found myself in a railway accident at Mantes. 6 wounded.

There had already been a breakdown in a tunnel. Officials said that a *rotule* of an *attaché* had got broken. It was repaired, and we jolted onwards at, I should say, about 30 or 35 kilometres an hour. Then, just after we passed Mantes station, there was a really terrific jolting. I knew after four or five jolts that one coach at any rate had left the metals.

I was in a sort of large Pullmanesque compartment at the back of a first-class coach, two or three coaches from the engine. The windows broke. The corridor door sailed into the compartment. My stick flew out of the rack. The table smashed itself. I clung hard to the arms of my seat, and fell against an arm-chair in front of me. There was a noise of splintering, and there were various other noises. An old woman lay on the floor crying. I wondered: 'Shall I remain unharmed until the thing stops?' Immense tension of waiting for the final stoppage. Equilibrium at last, and I was unhurt.

I couldn't get out at first. Then someone opened the door. I soothed the old woman. I took my eyeglasses off and put them in their case. I found my hat (under some débris) and my stick. My bag had remained in the rack. I left the train with my belongings, but I had forgotten all about the book I was reading, *L'Éve future*. This book was all that I lost. Two wounded women were ahead lying out on the grass at the side of the track.

Up above, from street bordering the cutting, crowds of people were gazing curiously, as at a show. One woman asked if she could do anything, and someone said: 'A doctor.' I walked round to the other side of train and a minor official asked me and others to go back. '*Ce n'est pas pour vous commander, mais. . . .*' We obeyed. Two coaches lay on their sides.

One of them was unwheeled, and partly sticking in ground. No sound came from an overturned 2nd-class coach, though there were people in it.

Presently some men began lifting helpless passengers on to cushions which had been laid on the ground. I had no desire of any sort to help. I argued incompassionately that it was the incompetent railway company's affair. I held my bag and stick and I looked around. I didn't want to see any more wounded nor to be any more *impressionné* than I could help. My recollection of appearances quickly became vague. I remember the face of one wounded woman was all over coal dust. We had shaved a short goods train standing on the next line, and the tender of the train was against our coach. A young American said that it was sticking into our coach, but I don't think it was. He said that the front part of our coach was entirely telescoped, but it wasn't entirely telescoped. It was, however, all smashed up. My chief impression is of a total wreck brought about in a few seconds.

I walked off up line towards station and met various groups of employees running towards train. At last two came with a stretcher or ambulance. I passed out of the station into the *place*, and a collector feebly asked me for my ticket, which I didn't give. I went straight to a garage and demanded an auto for Paris. But all autos had been taken off to the scene of the accident. Having been promised one in due course, I waited some time and then had a wash and took tea. I couldn't help eating and drinking quickly. Then I was told that two Americans wanted an auto. I said that they might share the one promised to me. Agreed. At last my auto came. The price was 100 francs. A Frenchman came up who wanted to get to Paris quickly (he had not been in the accident), I gave him a place for 20 frs. making a mistake in thus dividing 100 by 4. This detail shows I really was upset under my superficial calmness.

Sunday, August 13th. – I began to write *The Family* (tentative title of play in collaboration with Edward Knoblock) on August 1st. I had finished the first act on August 6th. He revised it (but slightly) and on Friday the 11th he read it in our kiosk to the Mairs, Alice K. and her brother, Ed. Sheldon, and me.

I read the draft of what I had done of the 2nd act. *Succès très vif.* I shall finish the 2nd act on Wednesday, and count to have the whole play finished on the 29th. I write a scene of the play each morning and Knoblock comes in most afternoons for tea to go through what I have done. His revision consists chiefly of rearranging the dialogue here and there, and shortening. Whenever he adds a phrase of his own it is heavy and uncolloquial, and has to be altered. Still, he knows the stage, and his help is valuable. Also the original idea of the play was his, and the skeleton his.

Saturday, August 19th. – Finished 2nd act of *The Family* on Wednesday, and I began to write the third this morning. I have found two good titles for this play: *The Man with the Scythe*, and *The Milestones*, or *Milestones*. The latter will probably be used.

I have been reading *Tom Jones* for about a year. I finished it the other night. It is equal to its reputation; consistently interesting. There is no dull chapter. But he makes the hero too good. He seems to think that so long as Tom goes in for a little miscellaneous fornication he will be saved from priggishness. I doubt if this is so, especially at the end, where Tom's angelicalness upon the misfortunes of Blifil is a bit thick.

Wednesday, August 30th. – On Thursday, 24th, I finished the play which we finally decided to call *Milestones* (my title). Knoblock finished the revision of the last act on either Friday or Saturday, and it was sent to the typewriters on Monday.

I leave for London to-morrow morning and do not mean to live at Avon any more.

October 7th [*en route for U.S.A.*]. – 2nd class crowd afar off. Much waiting and crying for them. None for us.

We left at 5.40, landing-stage; then anchored in river to wait for tide.

Gent at dining-table: 'I wonder how many souls we have on board.'

Strong also on the indecency of the Russian ballets, which however he much admired.

At sea. Sunday, October 8th. – Strange noises through the night. Tappings. Waiting for the dawn to come, forgetting that there could be no dawn. The dawn was the turning on of the electric lights in the corridor.

Walk on navigating deck, where all the ventilators were secretly whirring, and two engineers arguing about a valve. Steering places hidden off. Top steering place deserted, so that it seemed as if the ship was steering herself. I looked down a shaft like a coalpit (into depths of ship) which is lighted at stages by electricity, and there is a great draught *up* it. What it was for I didn't know. Enormous amount of covered-in machinery on top deck, but I could actually *see* one fan whirring.

Lovely morning. Rippled sea as we leave Ireland. Dining saloon for breakfast. Size of it shown by sudden perceptions that features of people in opposite corner were blurred by distance.

Humility of people waiting till they are served. It would want some pluck to make a row in this place, the stewards are so self-respecting.

Going out on to starboard deck (on this floor) I am startled to see it crowded. Steerage passengers. This is their playground. I walked round the forward part of the ship and saw their dining-rooms, kitchens and broad staircases leading to different sections of berths, I had a glimpse of one berth; it seemed all right. All along deck here and there were entrances to paradises forbidden to them. Netting hung down from deck above gave sense of being cooped up. Certainly they were very close together. A certain natural brazenness about some of them – girls, who would not give and take to me in passing.

I discovered vast parts of the ship whose existence I had not imaginatively preconceived.

Monday, October 9th. 7 a.m.

Ragged sky. Black water all round horizon. Nothing in sight. Moon not set. Full moon.

Again, sense of unsuspected populations. This sense helped by a mysterious ringing of a bell in distant part of ship, calling some unknown population to its meal.

Inspection of ship with Mr A—, Chief Steward. 3rd Class. Inoculation for small-pox. Fares £7.

Men watching girls and girls then watching men. 'Having their sweet revenge,' said A. Another of his great phrases was 'No time like the present'.

1st Class. Kitchens. All this steerage was another world mysteriously opened. We went back into a still unknown part of our world.

Roasting ovens. Intense heat. Revolving spits.

Special orders written on a board with hours marked, then I heard a man call out 'Baked potatoes for four at 8 o'clock. Extra order.'

Fire. In 1st class kitchens, a table of posts for every man. I noticed a list of about 30 or 40 stewards 'To control passengers'.

52 cooks for 1st and 2nd class.

The baking goes on day and night, never stops.

Dough-mixing by electricity.

Potato-peeling machine.

Egg-boiling machine. 1 minute, 2, 3, etc. Automatically lifted out when done.

Firemen's kitchen. Special menu for leading firemen. 12 leading firemen. Meal served every 4 hours (goes down by lift) night and day. 110 firemen on each watch.

Every member of crew has a bunk.

In each store dept. (wine, grocery, etc.) in the depths of it, a quiet, generally nervous man, keeping accounts on a green cloth.

The second class was like 1st class on a small scale. Less

space. Many obviously well-to-do men in smoke-room. Fine view over stern of ship.

Had we not been in 1st class it would have seemed spacious and magnificent. Little difference in berths. Prices from £13. £20 for a whole room. But all this is over 4 propellers making 170 to 180 revolutions a minute.

Purser at dinner. He said he knew practically the whole of the professional gamblers. Once 2 got on unawares. At night when smoking-room full, he got carpenter in, who prominently took down all warning notices of gamblers and prominently put up new ones underlined with red ink. Still, they won 40 dollars off a man, who however refused to pay.

Forbes Robertson, Knoblock, Burton, and me in lounge after dinner. Got talking of theft of Mona Lisa, and then each told tales of thefts – marble mantelpieces out of Russell Square, etc. Italy; pictures rotting from damp through neglect in Venetian churches, and so on, until one had the idea that the whole art world was undermined and everything going or gone.

Bit of wind at 11 p.m. Looking through porthole of hall of E deck. Waves swishing by. Hopeless position of anyone overboard. Suddenly a wave bangs up against porthole with a smash, and you draw your face away startled.

Tuesday, October 10th. Visiting ship with Chief Officer. Chart Room. 'Holy of Holies.' Brass and mahogany effect. Dodge for detecting and putting out fires in inaccessible holes. Fan to draw out smoke and steam attachment to drown it. All same pipes. 4 or 500 feet of piping at least.

Sounding tubes? Wire draws out water from a tube. Even the wire so drawn in by an electric motor. It can be done at full speed.

Bridge. 75 ft above sea. The house was carried away and wheel carried away once by a wave – one wave. One dent, made by glass, left in wood, to commemorate the day.

Subterranean signalling. A bell sounds through it like tapping a pencil on wood. Nantucket bell heard *16 miles off*.

Down below, forward of steerage, capstan gear.

The cables will each break only at 265 tons. That is, they could hold in suspension 26 10-ton trucks of coal. The capstan gear is so strong that it will break the cable if it is overwound.

Imagine 265 tons of M.P.'s dropped into the sea.

Well may all this powerful machinery be encaged, just like wild beasts in a menagerie.

7 different steering gears. The last by a hand wheel almost direct. Auxiliary engines etc. We went down 2 or 3 stories from lowest passenger deck and saw the tremendous gear actually at work slowly and apparently capriciously moving to and fro at intervals in obedience to sailor on bridge 5 or 600 feet away and 70 feet higher up.

Up and down steel ladders. Climbing over moving chain (like a bike chain) of steering-gear, through stray jets of steam, in a forest of greasy machinery, guarded by steel rails, grease on floor: all apparently working alone under electric lights, but here and there a man in brown doing nothing in particular. Dials everywhere showing pressures, etc.

Up a flight to dynamo room.

Machines revolving 1,200 to the minute.

Then to stokehold. Vast. Terrible. 190 colossal furnaces, opened and fed every 10 minutes, and coal flung in. Mouths of furnaces seemed to me very high for coal to be flung into them. This effect was like that of a coal mine with the addition of hell.

This was the most impressive part of this ship. It stretched away with occasional electric lights into infinite distance. 1,000 tons of coal a day. Finest coal. Very hot. An inferno, theatrical. Above, confectioners making petits fours, and the lifts going for 1st class passengers.

The Englishman's reverence for his old institutions, of all kinds, and his secret sentimentality comes out all over the ship the whole time.

Marvellous after-sunset exactly ahead, as we came out. Sea like slightly uneasy oil.

·1912·

Hotel Californie [*Cannes*]*, January 6th.* – Georges d'Espagnat reported how Renoir's pictures 15 years ago were admitted by dealers to be unsaleable. Now the slightest sketch fetches 4 or 5,000 frcs. And pictures which formerly had a theoretical price of 5,000 frs. sell for 70 or 80,000. Dealers came down from Paris while d'Espagnat was at Renoir's, and bought and paid for everything that Renoir would let them take away. He has been a terrific worker, and in spite of very large sales, still has 2 or 300 pictures to be disposed of. He now lives luxuriously. Formerly *dans la dèche*, d'Espagnat had known him rent splendid houses in which he could not put furniture. He is 71, and scarcely able to move a limb. Cannot rise without help. Has to be carried about. Yet manages to paint, even large canvases. He said to d'Espagnat that were it not for ill-health, old age would be a very happy time, as it has all sorts of pleasures special to itself. Although so old, he has a son aged only about ten. This child came as a surprise, and Renoir was furious.

Tuesday, January 23rd. – The other day a *vendeuse* and an *essayeuse* came up from the Maison de Blanc, with a *robe d'intérieur* for M. and another for Mrs Selwyn. A porter of the Maison Blanc carried the box. The general tableau; – the two employées, young and agreeable, but certainly not *vierges*, with soft liquid persuasive voices, speaking chiefly English; the frothy garments lying all about on chairs and in the box, Selwyn, Alcock, and me lounging on chairs, and M. and Mrs S. playing the mannequin, and the porter waiting outside in the dark corridor – this tableau produced a great effect on me. Expensive garments rather – and I felt that for my own personal tastes, I would as soon earn money in order to have such a tableau at my disposition, as for a lot of other seemingly more important and amusing purposes. A fine sensuality about it. There was something in the spectacle of the two employées waiting passive and silent for a few moments from time to time while we talked.

Weather still very bad indeed. We did, however, yesterday make our *auto-canot* excursion to Les Îles Lérins without getting wet. Sea-ward tower on Île St Honorat, quite striking. On grass by this was an old shepherd tending brown sheep. One of these sheep had 3 tufts of old wool left on the back, making her look like a kind of miniature triple dromedary. Marguerite asked the shepherd what it was for. He replied: 'Oh, madame, c'est seulement un peu de vanité.' He was quite simple, and answered simply, but he was evidently a bit of a character.

Tuesday, February 6th. – On day of last writing I began an attack of *gastro-entérite*. Very decidedly ill on Wednesday afternoon. Full development of attack on Thursday. Doctor on Thursday and Friday. I got up for a few minutes yesterday morning and more in the afternoon. Not yet achieved complete disappearance of symptoms. While ill, I read Dostoievsky's *Le Sous-Sol*, which is great. [Valéry] Larbaud, who calls to see me nearly every day, prefers it to anything else of Dostoievsky's. Also Dostoievsky's unfinished *Le Crocodile*. Good.

I ought to have begun my humorous novel on Thursday last, and I have not yet begun it. But on Sunday night I decided on the title *The Regent*.

Friday, February 16th. – On Wednesday morning at 7 a.m. as 'programmed' a week ago, I began *The Regent*. By noon this morning I had written 4,500 words of it.

Yesterday afternoon Mrs Julia Frankau (Frank Danby) called to make my acquaintance, and produced a very agreeable impression indeed on us and on the Selwyns. A thorough London type; very chic, extremely capable and alert, of wide ideas, and of a sympathetic nature. She must have a full life, with a large family and her literary work, of which latter, by the way, she said about twenty times – really – that she was ashamed.

Tuesday, February 20th. – Yesterday the Frank Harrises called and took us to St Raphael for lunch. He said, 'God when he was young had a liking for the Jews. But when he was old he had a senile weakness for the English.'

Monday, March 4th. – Coal strike began last Friday.

Said Mrs Frankau, who came for tea yesterday: 'Of course I'm feudal. I'd batten them down. I'd make them work. They *should* work. I'd force them down.'

A man stopped me on the stairs the other noon, and asked me my opinion about Kipling's neologisms. He had been reading an article in *The Times*. I referred him to Wordsworth. He understood. Staggering, to find any Englishman in a cosmopolitan grand hotel with even a faint curiosity about the processes of literature. Such a thing never happened to me before.

Wednesday, March 6th. – *Milestones* by me and Knoblock produced at Royalty last night. I had four telegrams to-day all agreed as to its immense success, if only the coal-strike won't upset it.

Battle of Flowers yesterday. The most interesting people were the flower-vendors. 3 frs. the panier, without the panier! Seat-shower quarrelling and grumbling about ticket holders all the time, 'Vous avez le No. 1. Eh bien le No. 1 est pris. Vous pouvez vous mettre là. Qu'est-ce que ça fait?'

Larbaud brought André Gide in at 5.30. And we kept them to dinner and had a great evening that finished at 10 p.m.

I wasn't so well to-day.

Thursday, April 11th. – To-day at 3.30 I finished *The Regent*, 78,200 words, written in two months less three days. So far this year, I have written:

Four articles of 'Your American States' (two last year, 10,000) for *Harpers*	22,000
'Clay in the Hands of the Potter' for *Youth's Companion*	2,200
The Regent	78,200
	102,400

May 29th. – John Burns: National Liberal Club:

He did not smoke. The first thing he said was, 'We must talk about Federation,' then he immediately changed the subject to the [coal] strike. He talked most of the time leaning back in a chair and looking round sharply if he thought any other person in the smoking-room was observing him. Often he left out his 'h's' on purpose. When he had told me that he had read all that I had written (exaggeration), and I said that I could not understand how the busy public men had the time to do all they appeared to do, he said that public men soon began to cultivate a special faculty.

He said, socially speaking, England is the laboratory of the world. At the present time all the new movements are initiated here: untrue! He said, 'I get more letters about my town planning and housing scheme from the United States than I do from England.' He then, after quickly asking me about New York and Chicago, went on to describe his own adventures in New York, Chicago and Denver. He explained how the editor of the *Chicago Record & Herald* came out thirty miles from Chicago to obtain his impressions of the city before he had arrived, and when he declined became angry. Afterwards he saw this man in Chicago and made his celebrated epigram that Chicago was 'a pocket edition of Hell', or, if the newspaper-man preferred it, 'Hell was a pocket edition of Chicago'. This man worked up such an agitation against Burns that when the time came for him to speak on 'The Duties of Citizenship' at a very large meeting in Chicago, not a single member of his committee dared to appear on the platform. However, he came on alone, and, little by little, won the enthusiastic sympathy of the audience. As he did so he said that he could hear the members of the committee coming, one by one, behind him on to the platform. All this made a very good story, but he must have told it a great number of times, and have gradually arranged the details for his own glory. He said that his little epigram about Chicago had been appropriated by Choate, and that Choate had stolen more of his things than any other man in the world.

He then described how in the strike at the docks either last year or the year before, he was sent down by the Prime Minister to try to persuade the men to obey the leaders. He took a lot of matches out of the match stand and arranged them in two squares. He said:

'Well, there were 5,000 military in this square and 15,000 workmen in the square next door. And there was only a gravel path of about twenty feet between the two. The socialists were walking round the outksirts of the crowd pointing to the soldiers, who could plainly be seen, and the guns, and things looked very threatening indeed. I regard this as the greatest crisis that I have ever been through. I remembered my old cry, and in a voice of thunder I shouted out: "A gangway, lads," and they made enough room for me to go into the centre and stand on the cart. I talked to them and called for three cheers for the leaders, and so on, and so on, and I could see their old-time affection for me returning etc. etc.' These were the exact phrases he used. He was not exactly conceited, but vain in a rather ingenuous way. He spoke freely of the conceit of other people.

As we walked home, passing through Downing Street, a young boyish-faced man in evening dress, carrying a bag, came out of the Prime Minister's house. Burns called across the road and then went to meet him in the middle of the road and spoke to him for a minute or two. Practically all the illumination came from a small gas lamp over the Prime Minister's door. This was Mr Asquith's secretary. He seemed to me to be an exceedingly ordinary and good-natured young man.

As we passed along the front of Wellington Barracks, Burns began to explain how the moral conditions of the soldier had improved during the last twenty or twenty-five years. He said:

'There, in spite of all their faults, are 8,000 of the very finest infantry in the world.'

As one soldier after another came walking along in the gloom, he seemed to be able to tell at a glance from the medal strips, even in the dark, what campaigns they had been through. He remarked how they were all walking perfectly straight and how twenty-five years ago not one of them would have been able to walk straight, or, perhaps, even to walk at all. This is a specimen of his picturesque way of stating things.

Tuesday, October 1st. – Hospital for Incurables. West Hill. What must be feelings of patient as he drives into entrance of this Hospital, and sees the big sign: 'Hospital for Incurables'?

Thursday, October 3rd. – Granville Barker's *A Winter's Tale* at Savoy. Quite half the words incomprehensible. Esmé Beringer alone was clear. No music. Impossibility of seeing whole of stage from front row of dress circle, near middle, without leaning on the balustrade. Scarcely ever possible to distinguish blank verse. Revels in last act agreeable. Very little good acting – except Whitby's Autolycus and Esmé's Paulina. Lillah [McCarthy] fairish in last scene, when she could be statuesque. The text was given almost integrally, and one perceived portions of dullness which might have been cut with advantage. General impression of a simple, good, impossible plot with lofty emotion in it – delectable enough after *Bunty*. But the beauty of detail nearly all lost.

October 7th. – Beecham at rehearsal. A player said: 'You said you'd beat 4 in that bar, sir, but you're only beating two.' Beecham: 'You're thinking of another bar.' A voice: 'Four ale bar.' Roars of laughter.

When Henry Wood conducts, he changes three times a day. Perspiration. It drops out of the back of his flannel jacket, having penetrated it. Always takes his waistcoat off.

Cedric [Sharpe] spoke very highly of his extraordinary energy. Often stays up till 2 or 3 or all night, reading scores. On a Wednesday, in midst of Birmingham Festival rehearsals, he said: 'Energy! You shall see next Monday – I shall have some sleep on Sunday night. Wait and see me on Monday.'

October 8th. – 2nd Post-Impressionist Exhibition. Self-satisfied smiles of most people as they entered. One large woman of ruling classes with a large voice and *face-à-main*, in front of a mediocre picture: 'Now no one will ever persuade me that the man who painted that was serious. He was just pulling our legs.' Self-satisfied smiles all over the place all the time. One reason of the popularity of these shows is that they give the grossly inartistic leisured class an opportunity to feel artistically superior. A slight undercurrent of appreciation here and there. A woman to whom a young man pointed out a pencil drawing by Matisse said: 'That's what I call beautiful.' (It was.)

I met Frank Harris. He was prepared on principle to admire everything, though there was a large proportion of absolutely uninteresting work. When I said I had seen much better Picassos than there were there he hardened at once. 'I find it all interesting,' he said grimly. The photograph room, where photos of Gauguin, Van Gogh, etc. supposed to be on sale, was in charge of an ignorant young ass who had all the worst qualities, from the languishing drawl to the *non possumus* attitude, of the English salesman.

October 10th. – Dinner. Talking about women's suffrage, someone said that it would come when the majority wanted it, and George Moore said: 'The majority never *wants* anything. I don't think the majority even want to breathe.' He talked in this pseudo-effective strain nearly all the night – probably nervousness as usual. About half a dozen times he repeated that for *The Winter's Tale* Barker had made the stage 'look like a public lavatory'. He said he liked farces and preferred *Charley's Aunt* to Barker's *Winter's Tale*. And he thought *Lady Windermere's Fan* was 'a charming and fine comedy'. Which it is not. Not until somebody said that *The Importance of Being Earnest* is the finest farce of modern times (which it is) did he think at all of Wilde's only good play. He liked Becque, and he thought Ibsen's dialogue unequalled and that it would probably not be beaten by anybody hereafter. But he regarded the theatre generally as a clumsy and infantile art, in which he was quite right. 'You've made a very great deal of money,' he said to me politely. I told him that that wasn't my fault, and I couldn't help it. Whereupon he emerged from his *gaffe* with a certain grace by saying with a serious air that he wished *he* could do it.

October 12th. – Tate Gallery. Crowds. A class of girls. Many couples, who simply used the place as they would a park in summer. One couple stood right up against Steer's 'Music Room' (which I went specially to see) for about a minute, and then retired saying it looked queer. This picture still seems as good as I first thought it was. What's the difference between a lot of Post Impressionism and Turner's 'Interior at Petworth', a picture I never remarked before, but one of the finest pieces of rich colour in the world? Very little difference in method of seeing and treatment. Note the dinginess and dirtiness of Turner's paint-box in a glass case. Inconceivable almost that those pictures came out of it.

October 21st. – F[rank] H[arris] told me more fully than ever before the story of Oscar and *Mr and Mrs Daventry*. He said he gave Oscar £50 for the screen scene and £50 for the whole scenario. He never got the scenario, though he paid for it. Oscar was to have written the first act. Mrs Pat insisted on F. H. writing the first act. F. H. refused as it had been allotted to Oscar. Then Oscar refused. So F. H. did it. F. H. then found out that Oscar had sold the screen scene and the scenario to Leonard Smithers, and the latter showed him the whole MS. of scenario signed by Oscar. F. H., after saying to Smithers that he didn't want the scenario and that in any case he owed him nothing, promised £50 in any case and £100 if play succeeded well. He said he hadn't a cent at that time. Smithers got the money from F. H. in tens and twenties. F. H. gradually found out that Oscar had sold the screen scene and scenario to eleven different people. When taxed with this by F. H., Oscar didn't deny it. He merely said: 'The fact is, Frank, by writing this play and getting it produced you're taking away one of my sources of income!' Later Oscar asked for another £150. He badgered F. H. till he got it. He then said, 'Frank, you've paid me £250 for the screen scene from *The School for Scandal*; and you're a very poor man of business.' Thus F. H.'s version.

F. H. said that Oscar was most brilliant as a talker during his last days in Paris. He had listened to him for five or six hours together, saying nothing but 'Go on, Oscar. Go on.'

F. H. stuck me out that *Lady Windermere's Fan* was good. Indeed, he said it was one of the six best comedies in English!

Wednesday, November 6th. – Day before yesterday, after having written about 6,000 words of new novel, I decided to begin it again, in a somewhat different key, but with exactly the same construction. And I did begin it again, and at once felt easier in my mind. I also decided that I would not make a fine MS. of it. The regularity of the lines and handwriting does not seem to accord with style in which this novel is to be written. A freer style than before – a little more capricious and swinging.

Tuesday, November 19th. –

A Conductor's Phrases in taking a Rehearsal

Must be all dubious.
I want a savage staccato.
Nice and limpid.
Nice and stormy.
Nice and gusty.
Nice and manifold.
Weep, Mr Parker, weep. (Mr Parker weeps.) That's jolly.
Press that 'A' home.
Don't handicap the crescendo.
It's not a bee's wedding, it's something elemental.
Gentlemen of the first fiddles.
Try it slurred, a sort of dot and carry two.
Not a wind you can cut with a knife, you must come and die.
This echo is so teasing.
Sorry to tease you.
An intimate 'cello solo.
Sixth desk forward, please. (Somebody in the orchestra, 'Sign, please.')
Sigh and die.
Now, side-drum, assert yourself.

Everybody must be shadowy together.
I want it mostly music.
That regular rum-tum which you do so ideally.
Let the pizzicato act as a sort of springboard to the passage.
A freshness inside the piano.
A sudden exquisite hush.

December 31st. – A material year. Largely occupied with intestinal failure and worldly success. By Chetham Strode's direct treatment of massage and vibration I am now almost cured of intestinal caprices, but I shall ever be feeble in that quarter.

All my five later plays have been performed this year. About 1,155 pfces altogether. I received (less agents' commissions) about £16,000 during the year, which may be called success by any worldly-minded author. It is apparently about as much as I had earned during all the previous part of my life. And I bought a car and a yacht, and arranged to buy a house.

January 6th. – Henry James. At Pinkers. Very slow talker. Beautiful French. Expressed stupefaction when I said I knew nothing about the middle-class, and said the next time he saw me he would have recovered from the stupefaction, and the discussion might proceed. Said there was too much to say about everything – and that was the thing most felt by one such as he, not entirely without – er – er – er – er – perceptions. When I said I lay awake at nights sometimes thinking of the things I had left out of my novels, he said that all my stuff was crammed, and that when the stuff was crammed nothing more could be put in, and so it was all right. He spoke with feeling about his recent illness. 'I have been very ill.' Said he was now settled down in Cheyne Walk, and had one or two faithful dependable servants, and so on. An old man, waning, but with the persistent youthfulness that all old bachelors have.

January 28th. – Political Debate between G. B. Shaw and Hilaire Belloc as to Connection between Private Property and Servitude. At Queen's Hall. Went with Vaughan. Crammed, at concert prices. Not a seat unsold. Shaw very pale with white hair, and straight. His wife beside him. Effect too conjugal for a man at work. Sidney and Beatrice Webb next to them. Effect also too conjugal here. Maurice Baring supporting Belloc, both very shabby. Maurice with loose brown boots and creased socks. They spoke thus. Belloc 30 mins. Shaw 30. Belloc 20. Shaw 20. Belloc 10. Shaw 10. Time was kept to three minutes. Belloc's first was pretty good. Shaw's first was a first-class performance, couldn't have been better; the perfection of public speaking (not oratory); not a word wrong. But then afterwards the impression that it was a gladiatorial show or circus performance gained on one, and at the end was a sense of disappointment, as the affair degenerated into a mere rivalry in 'scoring'. Still I have never seen Shaw emotional before, as he was then. Curious trick of audience, as of all audiences, of applauding sentiments with which they were already familiar, and receiving anything relatively new in silence.

January 29th. – First Production of 'Rosenkavalier' in England. Covent Garden. Began at 8.20 (20 minutes late) and finished at midnight, with many cuts. Then 30 minutes' wait nearly, for motor in procession of motors. The thing was certainly not understood by stalls and grand circle. What its reception was in the amphitheatre and gallery I was too far off to judge. First act received quite coldly. Ovation as usual at end – and an explosive sort of shout when Thomas Beecham came to bow. The beauty and symmetry of the book came out even more clearly than on reading it. An entirely false idea of this opera so far in England. Not sensual, nor perverse, nor depraved. It is simply the story of a young man providing a tragedy for an ageing woman by ceasing to love her, and an ecstatic joy for a young woman by beginning to love her. All the main theme is treated with gravity and beauty. The horseplay, and the character of Ochs, and the 18th-century colour is incidental. It seemed to me to be a work of the first order.

January 30th. – Courting. To-night sheets of rain, strong wind. I put on over-shoes and mackintosh to go to the corner of the street to the post. Several times lately about 10 p.m. I have noticed a couple that stand under the big tree at the corner next to the pillar-box, shielded by the tree-trunk from the lamplight. They stand motionless, with hands nearly meeting round each other's backs, tightly clasped. They were there to-night. The man was holding an umbrella over them. Can't see what sort of people they are. In the first place I don't like to intrude and in the second place the shade is so dark.

Tuesday, April 1st. On Tuesday, February 25th, I came to live at Comarques, Thorpe-le-Soken.

On Monday, March 3rd, we went to London (Berkeley Hotel) for the dinner to celebrate Mrs Atkins's recovery, and for the anniversary of *Milestones*, and for rehearsals of *The Great*

Adventure. After being very lively at the Atkinses' dinner at the Café Royal on Monday, Marguerite fell ill. No sleep. No sleep for two nights. I had Farrar, and then two nurses. One of them, an Irish woman, lively, who broke most things she touched, came up with us to Comarques on Monday, March 10th, and stayed about a week. The *Milestones* anniversary supper was a great success except for the absence of Marguerite.

Great Adventure produced at Kingsway on Tuesday, March 25th. M. said it was the most successful 1st night of mine she had been at. But she's been to so few. It finished at 11.40 and thus made the critics cross.

Knoblock told me about a fortnight ago that in discussing terms of French contract for *Milestones* with Lucien Guitry, he said, to shelter himself behind me as regards certain conditions: 'M. Bennett est très autoritaire,' whereupon Guitry said: 'Quelle belle chose, l'autorité: mais – pourtant. . . . !'

We went to London on Saturday last, and I saw my first public performance of *The Great Adventure*. House held £125. Barrie with an adopted son on either side was there and he never laughed. C. K. Shorter in a box opposite roared nearly all the time. Wish Wynne a genius. I formed the opinion that there was a goodish run in the play.

Thursday, April 3rd. – Hugh de Sélincourt came in the afternoon, and left yesterday afternoon. His face is getting more and more strikingly bizarre in its line, and his hair much greyer. He said Coleridge's 'Ode to Dejection' was one of the supreme things. He was convinced that both Lord and Lady Northcliffe were 'dead keen' on his work, and that satellites in the *Mail* office were up against him. Anyhow he had received two autograph letters from Northcliffe, and Lady Northcliffe, in response to a long telegram from its parents, had been to see the baby Bridget. At present de S. gets £100 down and 15 per cent. royalty, and he has published seven books. These details will be precious in 50 years.

Unable to resume my novel yet, though I am now on the very edge of doing so.

Friday, April 4th. – Yesterday morning I wrote a complete 1,500 word article, 'Phenomena at Covent Garden', for the *New Statesman* – a gift to the Webbs, due to the skilful fascinations of Beatrice Webb. I was tired after it. I read Coleridge's 'Ode to Dejection', and liked it, but didn't think it one of the supreme things in the language. . . . Another of an intermittent series of bad nights, so that I couldn't resume novel this morning as I meant to do.

Receipts of *Great Adventure* at Kingsway mounting up. Which inspirited me somewhat.

Monday, April 7th. – Last week, being in need of an inspirational bucking-up, I dropped *War and Peace* and read Balzac's *Curé de Tours* and *Pierrette*. Latter better than Saintsbury says it is. Balzac was an ignorant and a crude man, often childish in his philosophizing. But if he had been properly educated and influenced he would have been a great social philosopher. His *aperçus* are often astounding. And his vitality is terrific. He is full of inspiring and agreeable ornament. Nothing of the kind in Tolstoy. All a flat recital. Often dull, unless you give yourself to it. But if you do, he is never dull. Some of Tolstoy's long descriptions (such as of the wolf-hunt on Count Ilza's estate) are extremely beautiful. Natasha is the most beautiful character – anyhow up to p. 700 or so, where I now am.

Monday, April 14th. – Advance of age. I now sit down to brush my hair and put my collar and tie on. I also take a decided pleasure in forming habits, and re-forming old ones connected with the furniture from Fontainebleau, whose little peculiarities of locks and knobs etc. I recognize again with positive satisfaction. The pleasure of doing a thing in the same way at the same time every day, and savouring it, should be noted.

I am now at close on p. 1000 of *War and Peace*. Curious, the episode of Lavrushka the valet, and Napoleon, in which he takes a historical incident, and feigns that as recounted in history it is all wrong, and gives you what he alleges to be the real truth. Even in this early book his theory of war is already fairly complete and obvious.

Monday, April 21st. – Exhibition of Max Beerbohm's cartoons at Leicester Galleries. Crowd. I was at once recognized – with a certain lack of politeness – by two men. I was ill all day. Probably liver – anyhow pains in back – very mysterious and disconcerting. Bad night. Same illness on Friday complicated by dyspepsia. I went to Leicester Galleries and bought my caricature. Then to Agnew Galleries to see alleged finest collection of water-colours by Turner ever got together. I thought both the Blue and the Red Righi rather overpraised, and I preferred the 'Scarborough' picture – marvellous microscope figures of women in foreground. A few loud-voiced English upper classes patronizingly present. This show superb, but still I left it with slight disappointment – a flat feeling, a suspicion of prettiness and academicism. Lunch alone at Reform. Ill.

Thursday, April 24th. – Finished *War and Peace* on Tuesday. The last part of the Epilogue is full of good ideas the johnny can't work out. And of course, in the phrase of critics, would have been better left out. So it would; only Tolstoy couldn't leave it out. It was what he wrote the book for. The first part of the Epilogue is as good as anything. All that domesticity is superbly rendered, with a natural and yet ruthless veracity. The battle of Borodino is fine. The Rostov family is fine. And many of the 'set' descriptions of Russian life – such as the wolf-hunting on the Rostov estate. Terrific book. I wanted to write one of the same dimensions, and the final thrills of it *did* inspire me to a good basic scheme for the foundations of the third *Clayhanger*.

Friday, April 25th. – Yesterday we went over to see the *Velsa* [his barge-built yacht] in Brightlingsea creek. She looked superb in every way, except inside the engine case. Entirely Dutch crew, of whom two cannot speak any English at all. I liked the aspect of the cook, but it was impossible to communicate any ideas to him direct.

Dreadful worry over third instalment of *Harper's* serial. It is an infernal nuisance writing scenes which you know all through are only sound instead of being fine. Health imperfect.

I now notice one or two devoted heads among critics who lose no opportunity of going for me both tooth-and-nail. And it is astonishing how this small minority of criticism, convinced though one may be that it is obviously wrong-headed, and perhaps malicious or prejudiced, has a capacity for annoying the successful person surfeited with money and laudation.

Tuesday, April 29th. – Ill for last 3 days. Perfectly laid aside by a sort of chill effect yesterday.

Began to read Flaubert's correspondence all through the other day. Much of it is as depressing as the rest is inspiring. The letters to Madame X are the most terrible, and must have been terrible to receive. This sentence (Vol. I, p. 107) shows the 'maladif' quality of Flaubert very well. 'Un amour normal, régulier, nourri et solide me sortirait trop hors de moi, me troublerait, je rentrerais dans la vie active, dans la vérité physique, dans le sens commun enfin, et c'est ce que m'a été nuisible toutes les fois que j'ai voulu le tenter.' Also his declared habit of cutting himself off absolutely from the world in order to have peace! What a mad scheme for a novelist! It is this kind of thing in Flaubert that stopped him from being in the first rank.

Wednesday, June 4th. – Still unable to do any work. *Une espèce de rechute.* Very bad headache on Monday. But I have amused myself with d'Aurévilly's *Une vieille Maîtresse* – admirable romanticism.

Thursday, June 19th. – Yesterday I finished the first half of the Harper novel. Wrote 1,400 words on Monday. But, exhausted by work, and by an excess of physical exercise (taken to cure liver) I took a *froid sur la digestion* on Monday night. Yesterday I wrote 1,900 words between 10.15 and 1 o'clock. Enormous. Went to bed immediately after dinner, feeling cold on shoulders and *ventre* (*cependant, temp. de 20° centigrade* in bedroom); had a hot water bottle, which so stimulated me that I had no desire for sleep till 3 o'clock, when it was light again.

I had 3 hours sleep at most. Nevertheless I feel fairly fit this morning. This is a fair sample of 'how I go on'. To-day I have no doubt I shall find all necessary ideas for the last article of the series, 'The Story-teller's Craft'.

Wednesday, July 30th. – I finished 75,000 words of *Harper* serial on Monday, having written over 12,000 words in 7 days. Health much better, and a great return of form, but during last 4 nights very little sleep. H. G. Wells and wife and Mrs Byng (future neighbour) came yesterday for lunch and tea. I beat H. G. at tennis; he played in bare feet.

August 31st. – Read through the third quarter of the *Harper* serial this morning. It seemed goodish. But there is no doubt in my mind now that I want to change to another sort of novel – much more autobiographical than I have yet written. The first and third part of *The Glimpse* contained a lot of essentially autobiographical stuff, and *Clayhanger* something of me as a boy. But I want to write more immediately autobiographical work. The third *Clayhanger* must be quite different from *Clayhanger* and *Hilda*. I think I am now beginning to be anxious to write the 3rd *Clayhanger* but there is a play, also two stories, to come in front of it.

Thursday, October 2nd. – Finished *Harper's* serial, *The Price of Love*, at noon fifteen on Monday last, in a state of some exhaustion.

Thursday, October 15th. – Last night we drove to Harwich, took G.E.R. steamer *Vienna* and arrived at Antwerp at 8.15 a.m. to-day. Grand Hotel. Room and bathroom, both large. 20 frs. Old fashioned and ugly; but seemingly good. Dreadful ride in hotel omnibus over cobbled roads from quay to hotel. We drove out at 10 a.m. in closed cab, round boulevards to Musée Plantin, where I searched for a particular room whose details I thought I had remembered for 16 years, and couldn't find – indeed was about convinced that such a room had never existed.

Friday, October 17th. – After lunch we visited port. Finest thing in Antwerp. We were first struck by little *brasseries* along good main street, each with a little *grue*, aproned and *nu-tête*, sitting outside sewing, to attract; they must be extraordinarily attractive to sailors. Scores of these places. Glimpses of streets *encore plus louches*. Immense impression of *travail*. 30 miles of quays. New basins still being constructed. Bridge from one road to another opened for passage of steamer. Much traffic held up on both sides. By the time it is closed again, hundreds of workmen collected, and dozens of heavy waggons. Some men chewing monstrous lumps of bread. Red Star Liner *Lapland* had arrived from U.S.A. Long processions of returned emigrants therefrom; some stupid, some full of character. One procession solely men (with a long *camion* in middle full of their handbags); another both of men and women; all had little round discs on breast.

I saw one steamer move out (scraping her side all the way) and a larger one come into a basin with 4 tugs. Immense area of port. Superb view of Antwerp with spires from one spot, over blue water. Magnificent sunset; all masts and derricks gradually became black and silhouetted. Drove back to town, passing through 2 streets full of café concerts. Same effect of silhouette against superb red and orange. Port full of grain and wood.

Brussels, Sunday, October 19th. – We came to Brussels yesterday. At Gare du Nord, scarcity of porters, and very bad and unwilling work because tips are put into a common fund. It takes one man's time to watch what the men receive. A non-porter said to me: 'Les porteurs sont trop fainéants pour venir ici' (i.e. to the far end of the platform where the train stopped).

I dined alone at Rest. du Helder, and it made much the same impression on me as 17 years ago. Good, but not good enough. Too dear. Still, a discreet place, with good service. A fat middle-aged man came in with a *grue*. *Grue* very vulgar. She turned her head away from the *grosse* brute most of the time, and sneered a lot. The efforts of the man to be gay and natural were rather good. She was just another of those who are content to take money which they are too careless to earn.

Paris, Thursday, October 23rd. – Arrived in Paris at 5.15 yesterday afternoon. We dined quickly and unpacked and dressed with marvellous haste, and were at the Théâtre du Vieux Colombier at 8.30 for dress rehearsal of *Une femme tuée par la douceur*; and *L'Amour Médecin*, with Copeau in charge. Crowded with first night public, and literary public. Many women trying to look young and only succeeding at a distance, with worn-out skins. Many very cheaply dressed. In fact nearly all the literary public had the air of being *dans la dèche*. Extraordinary muddle at *vestiaire*. A slight feeling of preciosity. But play well and sincerely done. A naïf thing, getting fairly strong towards the end.

Friday, November 21st. – Walking last night for exercise along the Station Road (6.30 p.m.) I saw the light of Clacton (not the lights – the light) and of Frinton, over the brows; a reflection in the sky ... Idea of a desolate coast (relatively) with the human settlements rather precariously here and there upon it. Darkness everywhere and just those lights on the clouds from below. Sense of the adventure of living on the earth at all; and of the essential similarity of all human existences. Idiocy of loathing or scorning a different kind of existence from your own; e.g. my attitude towards the primness of Frinton and its golf-club.

I am putting rather more work into draft of *Don Juan* than usually in my drafts of plays. The realistic idea has gone nearly altogether in this play. In its ignoring of realistic detail in order to get an effect required, it is rather impressionistic. This is the first time I have realised the possibility of a similarity between literature and art in impressionism. I expect that in looking for a parallelism to art in literature, I had been looking for the wrong thing, while the right thing was under my nose all the time.

Monday, November 24th. – As I was reading history this afternoon, I thought: 'I am 46. On the decline. Why fill my head with knowledge?' An absurd reflection, but it passed several times through my mind.

Friday, November 28th. – Deranged slightly all week with a chill on the colon. B. came yesterday for the day to discuss wills and leases. He told me with perfect seriousness a story of a commercial enterprise in which he was interested – a search for the Ark of the Covenant, Urim and Thummim, plate of the Temple etc. – based on a cypher discovered by a Finnish scholar in an early copy of the book of Ezekiel at St Petersburg. Over £3,000 already spent on the excavations, stopped by Turkish authorities who have now given permission again; but the affair is in suspense at present as the principal contributor of funds (who has already given £20,000 alone) is in a lunatic asylum. The singular irony of this did not seem to strike B.

Saturday, December 27th. – I am now re-reading *The Way of all Flesh*. It stands it. There is very little wrong with this book, even technically. But the trick of reading a piece of the narrative to the hero himself and then writing down what the hero's comment on it was, is a mistake – especially when it is repeated.

Wednesday, December 31st. – I finished *The Way of all Flesh* yesterday. All this book is good. I even suspect it may be better than I think it is.

I finished the first act of *Don Juan* yesterday. It seems *assez bien.*

According to Miss Nerney's calculations there have been over 2,700 performances of my plays during this year. I have published *The Regent, Paris Nights, The Plain Man and His Wife* and *The Great Adventure*. I have written most of *The Price of Love*, the whole of *The Story Teller's Craft*, sundry articles, 2 short stories, and one act of my new play. I did no work for

over a month when we moved in to Comarques; I took the
whole of August for a holiday in the Baltic, and 3 weeks in
Belgium and Paris in October and November.

Added later.

Net earnings received during 1913. *Books* £6,924 18s. 1d.
Plays £8,524 19s. 0d. Total £15,449 17s. 1d. The gross sum
(before paying agents' fees) was £17,166 10s. 1d. In addition,
interest on investments, £405 11s. 3d. All this handsomely
beats last year's record.

Friday, January 2nd. – I began 2nd act of *Don Juan* yesterday. Stopped by neuralgia from working to-day. I had it yesterday, but I worked.

January 3rd. – The [E. F.] Spences came over to dinner on Thursday night. Spence said that Mrs Maybrick was understood to be guilty, and that she had confessed to wardresses immediately after sentence. It was said that she had arsenic in pocket of her *peignoir* and administered it by means of a handkerchief pressed to Maybrick's mouth when he complained of dry lips or something of that kind. But Spence did not explain how Charles Russell remained always persuaded of her innocence.

Monday, January 12th. – More information as to the lower class holiday in August. A specimen of the co-operative holiday of the middle-class, where under the strain of idleness and new conditions, most of the manners (mediocre at best) of the middle-class go all to pieces at one moment or another. The secret provincialism of the whole crowd (except the younger generation) came out clearly. A set that frequents only itself.

Sunday, January 18th. – Barber's yesterday at Frinton. Behind tobacco shop. Long white curtains over window (clean) to hide back yard. Very small room. Very small fire. 3 marble basins with fitments.
No antiseptic arrangements so far as I could see. Room cold. Sturdy small boy who opened door for me, knickers, apron (not clean); 'Shall you operate on me?' 'No, sir,' with a grin. Man doing shaving. No greetings from barber. Dirty apron and coat hanging up on wall. Array of mugs with sponges. I stood with back to fire, and looked at *Daily Mirror*. Had not to wait long. Place looked clean but wasn't. Thick dust on

gas-shades and many cobwebs. Chair too high, a modern chair, which required footstool. I commented on height. Barber said: 'It's not high enough for me as it is. I always have to stoop.' I suggested footstool. He said, 'They do have them in some places.' I asked if business good. 'No, very short season.' A nice mild man, tall, badly shaven, baggy worn knees. But decent. No energy. Had to go out in middle to talk to a customer about mending a pipe – 'Excuse me, sir.' Parted my hair on wrong side and badly. Shoved his sleeve in my eye. Didn't show me the back of my head. Doubtful towels. Indiarubber sponge. Price 10d. Still a decent chap.

Conrad's *Chance* came yesterday. Read 150 pp. This is a discouraging book for a writer, because he damn well knows he can't write as well as this. The episode of the arrival of the news of de Barral's bankruptcy at his house in Hove where his daughter and her superb friend of a governess are living is simply sublime.

Saturday, January 24th. – I finished Conrad's *Chance* in the middle of the night. It is very fine. The best chapters are 'The Governess' and the last one. The Tea Party chapter, and 'On the Pavement' chapter are too long. The indirect narrative is successfully managed on the whole, even to fourth hand narrative, but here and there recounted dialogue and gesture is so minute as to be unconvincing.

In P. G. Hamerton's *Round my House* (p. 160) he says that rise in prices during 'last ten years' in France had been so great as to induce some French people to dispense with servants. No date on this book. No clue to its date. But I should put it in the seventies. I suppose this rise of price business recurs at intervals, and always makes the same upset and then adjusts itself.

London, January 31st. – I finished *Don Juan* on Sunday night, rather to my surprise. Lunch at Reform. Henry James joined us afterwards and reminisced excellently. Hy. James said of Reform: 'This is for me now a club of ghosts. There were special corners and chairs. It is fuller, too, now than it used to be.' He also said that the club was built before clubs were fully understood, and he objected to largeness of atrium or cortile, making all rooms round it seem small. He described in full James Payn's daily life: – drove down from Maida Vale or somewhere to Smith Elder's, and left there before 1 in order to be at club at 1. Numberless friends. Amusing companion. Played whist etc., every afternoon and got home (driving) about 7. Never walked. Never wanted other interests. No intellectual curiosity. Large family, but was not interested in it. I asked when he did his work. James said he certainly never worked either afternoon or night. He was continually politely sarcastic about Payn. He now lives on river at Chelsea. He likes pavements, shopfronts, and the convenient taxi. He said 'If I was rich, instead of being in grovelling poverty' – He made as if to go once, then asked if he might stay a little longer, and did so.

Monday, February 9th. – *Parsifal* at Covent Garden. Putrid performance. Bodauzky commonplace conductor. Poor orchestra. Appalling scenery, costumes, and scenic effects. Ugly. Some good singing. Rotten female chorus amazingly ugly and ill-dressed. Also long stretches of dull music. I never saw uglier scenery. I went to sleep in middle of each act. Over after 11. Great deal of music fine. Better than I expected. Friday, Vernon came. Details settled for production of *A Good Woman* [*Rivals for Rosamund*] ('Be sure your sins will find you out') at Palace Theatre on Monday 16th. At night, first night of *A Midsummer Night's Dream* at Savoy. Stylistic quality of much of this play is marvellous. But the two love stories and the love-philtre-ing tedious. Scenery not really good, but exquisite after Covent Garden.

Saturday, February 14th. – I finished the third of the *Velsa* articles for the *Century* on Thursday morning, and finished reading and correcting typescript of *Don Juan* on Thursday afternoon. Also I finished reading Jules Romains' *Mort de Quelqu'un*. This short novel, though often amateurish, and indeed sometimes puerile in technique, is a really original work. The collective feeling of groups of men, and the influence of thought on thought, are remarkably done. It could properly be called 'psychic'.

Wednesday, February 18th. – *Rivals for Rosamund* received with amiable indifference at Palace Theatre on Monday night. Last night I went to see it myself with J. Atkins. The first half was quite well received; the last half coldly. This was right. It is no real good, and if I had realized this earlier I would not have let it be done. Production and acting goodish.

Thursday, February 19th. – I bought *Autobiography of Mark Rutherford* and *Mark Rutherford's Deliverance* in 7*d.* editions at station. And in the night I had finished reading the latter. Very impressive and original. Fine style, no scheme of construction. As a continuous narrative extraordinarily amateurish. The man had no notion of fiction. But a work not easily forgotten. Full of wisdom and high things.

Middle-aged couple in our compartment yesterday. Well and quietly dressed. Upper class. Restrained. Extremely good natural and trained manners. The woman (35) especially was charming in her admirable breeding. Evidently wealthy. They talked in such a low tone that, although the articulation was perfectly clear, one did not hear unless one listened. After about an hour the woman, reading *Daily Mail*, said: 'What is a tympani solo?' The man made a gesture of non-comprehension. She passed him the paper. He read the passage, and made a scarcely perceptible sign of ignorance. 'Don't you know?' she asked quietly. He repeated the sign – would not speak (as they were not alone). Her glance seemed to say to him: 'Pardon me asking you such an outlandish impossible thing.' She took back the *Daily Mail*.

Saturday, February 21st. – Pianoforte recital by F. M. at Frinton Hall last night in aid of Tendring Parish funds. Hall centrally heated, but draughty. Uncomfortable chairs. Rush-bottomed chair (cost about 3*s.*) for pianist. Old Broadwood baby grand. Pedal creaked. Rotten tone. Ladies of Frinton and of Tendring parishes in evening dress. Two parsons, who felt they must speechify afterwards. Pianist a man about 40, agreeable slightly curt smile. Ferocious look when he was playing often. Beethoven, Rameau, Chopin, Scarlatti, Debussy, Liszt, etc. Piano impossible. Intense, almost tragic sadness of provincial musical affairs, second-rate or tenth-rate under bad conditions. A gentle snobbishness (artistically) among the women. One man (friend of pianist) called out 2 or 3 times after a piece, amid the applause, "Core, 'core', very loudly and staccato. And he had his encore. Audience determined to appreciate high-class music, and applauding the noisiest and most showy. Crass inertia and stupidity of sundry women around me, determined to understand and to enjoy nothing.

Orvieto, Tuesday, April 21st. – Rather windy. Dusty. Splendid sky-scapes. The Campagna full of purples and bright greens. Turned off high road to Viterbo in order to see Capricola and palace thereof. Lunch at Viterbo after a sharp descent from chilly hills. Old waiter at hotel said he had always been honest. Thus he was a Roman, and did not like to say that Viterbo water was better even than Roman water, but it was, though it was against the interest of the hotel trade in mineral water to say so.

Then to Montefiascone. Great view of purple and bright greens. Hundreds of sq. miles. Then descent to Lake of Bolsena and Bolsena town and then rise to hills, and sudden view of Orvieto in midst of amphitheatre of hills. Unsurpassed. Like a show mushroom grown there. Serrated outline of towers. Slept in a longish room of a palace with large paintings of Judith and Holofernes etc. Marble floor. Plenty of pre-renaissance architecture in this town. I walked to bottom end of Corso Cavour last night and heard voices and saw groups and lights of blinds. Everything was alive up the dark courts, lighted by one electric lamp.

Siena, Wednesday, April 22nd. – Too ill most of yesterday to sit up in the car and be intelligent. Before leaving Orvieto we went into cathedral. A fiendishly noisy office going on between 3 or 4 old priests with awful voices. No audience. Chapels good. Well pleased. Then round town. Went to find very early church. S. Giovanni, *très* primitive. After we had entered it and gone away, it occurred to me that we had not seen it at all, but another quite ordinary church. So much for one's artistic education. *On gobe tout.* Gorgeous and glorious drive over mountains from Orvieto. At first we couldn't see Orvieto Cathedral; then we saw its peaks, and then we couldn't see anything else; it was the one thing that stood out on Orvieto's hill. Lunch at Montepulciano. I couldn't see it; but I walked about a bit, after taking a room at Albergo Marzocco to sleep in. Fine palaces. A great deal of Garibaldi.

Then to Pienza, where the piazza is small but fine. At S. Quirico, Read wouldn't stop, and we had a lovely glimpse of a primitive carved church. Had I known the name of the place I should have stopped the car, but I didn't. As it is, the glimpse remains exquisitely in the memory. This is a good way of seeing things occasionally.

Arrived at Siena at 3.50. Surprised at liveliness and beauty of this town. Drove to Duomo. 7.15. Office going on. Crowds entering, large crowds. Priests at a large desk transacting business with the Faithful, in front of a large box marked *oblazioni*. Then a monk in a brown robe appeared in a high pulpit and began to preach. We had to leave.

Albenga, Saturday, April 25th. – Yesterday, Pisa to Massa, Spezia and Genoa. Vile, dusty, busy road to Massa and beyond. Flat. Marmoreal environs of Carrara. Over hills for a few miles into Spezia good. Fine hill road (1,700 ft) to Sestri di Levante. With snow peaks in very far distance. This was truly sublime. From Sestri to Rapallo, road follows coast. Got Max's [Sir Max Beerbohm] address at post office and went to Villino Chiaso for tea. Max in whites, no waistcoat, and a calico sort of jacket. Fine tiled terrace. He was engaged in altering a portrait of George Moore in *Century* in order to tease Moore. Fine tea. Good servant. Picked a lemon off tree for tea.

Toulouse, Thursday, April 30th. – Rain last night, the first appreciable for about a month or more. Drove aimlessly about in the afternoon. Lift-boy in this hotel, aged 13, works from 6.30 to 11 p.m. or later every day. He has been here a month and looks aged. He is very nicely and smartly dressed, and very small, and he spoils the hotel for 'thinking people'. The young man aged 17 or 18 who served our *petit déjeuner* this morning excused his delay with '*je suis seul*'. Certainly overworked. Last night in the rain, paper-sellers and tram-conductors in felt sandals that would sop up water like a sponge.

Tuesday, May 26th. – Two aquarelles on Sunday.

Yesterday at 5.55 a.m. I began to write the third *Clayhanger* and did 1,200 words in the morning.

Thursday, May 28th. – 47 yesterday. Very sleepless night. Many annoyances in the morning; chief, a summons to Chelmsford Jury for June 11th, the week I have made all arrangements for being in London. Fatigue, and this, put me right off the novel.

Tuesday, June 2nd. – Read Ransome's *Oscar Wilde*. Well-meant stuff. Curious that a man with such decent notions on style should have none. After reading Dostoievsky's *Les Précoces*, it suddenly occurred to me, a few pages from the end, that it was merely an episode lifted from *Les Frères Karamazov*. The name Karamazov does not occur in the first part of the book, and when it does occur the translators somehow transmogrify it into ' Chestamazoz'.

Clayhanger III proceeding pretty well. But bad nights continue, so that after writing 1,100 words yesterday morn. I was nearly prostrated at night.

Sunday, June 7th. – Edgar Selwyn told us about Alf. Woods, once a cheap-theatre manager, thence out of that by cinemas, and now one of the chief N.Y. producers. It was he who said after 1st Act of *Milestones*, 'Who is this guy Bennett?'; after second, 'No, you couldn't give it me!' and after 3rd, 'He's got

me. It'll never *stop* running in N.Y.' He says he *smells* a good
or a bad play. Showing MS. of an accepted play to Edgar he
said: 'Smell that. Smell it. Doesn't it smell good?' Once when
listening to an idea for a play, he sniffed all the time – sniff,
sniff, sniff – and at the end said: 'No, that don't seem to me to
smell very good.' Once Michael Morton intruded on him; he
refused to listen, but Michael made him. Michael said: 'My
idea is for a little Russian girl who wants to study, and she
can't get away unless she takes the prostitute's ticket – the
yellow ticket as it is called. That's what they have to do, you
know.' Said Woods, startled: 'It *is*? It *is*? I'll buy your play.'
Morton said it wasn't finished. 'Never mind. I'll buy,' and he
bought it on the spot.

Thorpe-le-Soken, Thursday, August 6th. – On arriving at
Brightlingsea on Monday afternoon, I was told that petrol
could not be got in the district; that it was fetching up to 10*s*.
a tin at Clacton; and that Baggaley, the regular hirer of motor-
cars at B'sea, had gone forth in an attempt to get petrol. At
Clacton yesterday the price was 2*s*. 3*d*. or 2*s*. 4*d*. a gallon. I
have 60 gallons in stock.

A great crowd of holiday makers at Clacton in the showers
yesterday. No difficulty about getting change for a £10 note
in gold and silver. At the fish shop, slight increases of price in
poultry and eggs. The man said there was no chance for him
to make money (in response to a friendly jibe of M's). He said
he expected to get no more fish after that day.

Yesterday we heard noise of explosions destroying inconvenient houses at Harwich. The sensations of Harwich people
must be poignant. Nevertheless the G.E.R. in yesterday evening's papers was advertising its Hook of Holland service (with
restaurant cars etc.) exactly as usual, and I believe the boat left
last night. We also heard thunder; and the children affirm that
they distinctly heard the noise of firing – not explosions.
(Report of action in North Sea in evening papers.) I saw one
warship in the offing at Clacton; but an ordinary steamer
coming to the pier, and a barge sailing northwards.

An officer came yesterday to complain of a fox terrier

(? ours) which flew at despatch-riders on motor bicycles. He said it would be shot if found loose. These despatch-riders are the most picturesque feature of the war here. They rush through the village at speeds estimated up to 50 miles an hour. I am willing to concede 40.

I agree that Russia is the real enemy, and not Germany; and that a *rapprochement* between England and Germany is a certainty. But I doubt whether it is wise, in the actual conduct of affairs, to try to see so far ahead. I think that the belligerency of England is a mistake – for England. Yet if I had had to choose, I believe my instinct would have forced me to make war.

Sir Edward Grey's astounding mistake, in his big speech, was the assertion that the making of war would not much increase our suffering. It will enormously increase it. The hope for us is in the honesty and efficiency of our administration. The fear for France springs from the fact that the majority of French politicians are notoriously rascals, out for plunder. The corruption of Russian administration is probably even worse. The seriousness of the average French private will atone for a lot, but it will not – for instance – create boots for him. The hope for France is that the German army, arrogant in its traditions etc., may be lower than its reputation.

After reading the diplomatic papers leading up to the rupture between England and Germany, this morning, one has to admit that Sir E. Grey did everything he could, once he had stated his position. The war is a mistake on our part, but other things leading to it were a mistake, and, these things approved or condoned, the war must be admitted to be inevitable. Judged by any current standard Sir E. Grey is a man of high common sense. He has not yet grasped the movement of social evolution; but then very few people have. And you cannot properly or fairly try to govern a country on a plane of common sense *too* high above its own general plane.

Apart from Germany two countries are pre-eminently suffering at the beginning of the war – France and Belgium. Both are quite innocent; Belgium touchingly so. I can imagine the Germans among them if they get the upper hand. The

Germans are evidently quite ruthless and brutal and savage in war. This is logical; but a large part of their conduct is due to the arrogant military tradition, which will one day be smashed. If Germany is smashed in this war, the man most imperilled will be the German Emperor. If she is not smashed the man most imperilled may be the Tsar.

Monday, August 31st. – The girls came home with a positive statement from the camp that 160,000 Russians were being landed in Britain, to be taken to France. The Colonel had brought the news from Colchester.

The statement was so positive that at first I almost believed it. But after about an hour I grew quite sceptical. Only the Archangel route could have been used. Think of the number of ships and the amount of convoying necessary. In the end I dismissed it, and yet could not help hoping ... The most curious embroidery on this rumour was from Mrs A. W., who told Mrs W. that the Russians were coming via us to France, where they would turn treacherous to France and join Germans in taking Paris. 'We could not trust the Russians.' This rumour I think took the cake.

Thursday, September 3rd. – London absolutely as usual in summer, except the 'call to arms' on the taxis. Conference at Wellington House of 'eminent authors'. Hall Caine, Zangwill, Parker, among them. Masterman in chair. Zangwill talked a great deal too much. The sense was talked by Wells and Chesterton. Rather disappointed in Gilbert Murray, but I liked the look of little R. H. Benson. Masterman directed pretty well, and Claud Schuster and the Foreign Office representative were not bad. Thomas Hardy was all right. Barrie introduced himself to me. Scotch accent; sardonic canniness.

Sunday, September 20th. – Yachts, dinghies and other small boats were moved inland from Brightlingsea creek last week, as part of a plan for defending Brightlingsea and the Colne in case of a German invasion. The notion seemed to be that the

G.'s might use them as pontoons. I said to old Capt. Brand that it was only done because a number of people had a desire to do something, and this strange proceeding could not do any harm. He said the same thought had occurred to him.

Wednesday, November 4th. – Pinker had seen Conrad that morning, just returned from Austrian Poland. C. had no opinion of Russian army, and had come to England to influence public opinion to get good terms for Austria! As if he could. Pinker had also seen Henry James, who often goes to see Page, American Ambassador, in afternoons. They have long, quiet talks together. First time H. J. opened his heart to Page, he stopped and said: 'But I oughtn't to talk like this to you, a neutral.' Said Page: 'My dear man, if you knew how it does me good to hear it!' Hy. James is strongly proEnglish, and comes to weeping-point sometimes.

Then tea at A.B.C. Shop opposite Charing Cross. Down into smoking-room. A few gloomy and rather nice men. One couple of men deliberately attacking dish of hot tea-cakes. Terrible. Familiar smell of hot tea. A.B.C. shops are still for me one of the most characteristic things in London.

After tea to N.L.C., but I saw nobody I knew. Then, through latest dusk, to Reform, where Rickards and I dined. London not so dark as I expected, owing to lamps in centre of roads throwing down a volume of light in the shape of a lamp-shade (they are blackened at top).

Sunday, November 8th. – *The Great Adventure* finished its London run last night (673 pfces.).

Yesterday Sale and Show at Frinton, organised by Marguerite for Belgian Refugees. Total gross receipts £82 6s. 7d. and about £3 more to come. Expenses under £5, I think. Opened by Marguerite, who during her speech kept jabbing a pair of scissors into green cloth of table. Hall full of exhibits, plants, flowers, jam, vegetables and sundries; and of visitors.

I walked out to sea. Lovely afternoon. I went home for tea and wrote most of a war article and returned at 8 p.m. for auction of things left. This auction, worked with difficulty by a good auctioneer, fetched over £8. Young housewives hesitated to buy astounding bargains in fruit etc. The affair as a whole was a very striking success.

Friday, November 20th. – On Wednesday afternoon I went to Burslem to see Mater, reported to be past hope. I saw her at 8 p.m. and remained alone with her for about half-an-hour. She looked very small, especially in the hollow of the pillows. The outlines of her face very sharp; hectic cheeks; breathed with her mouth open, and much rumour of breath in her body; her nose was more hooked, had in fact become hooked. Scanty hair. She had a very weak, self-pitying voice, but with sudden outbursts of strong voice, imperative, and flinging out of arms. She still had a great deal of strength. She forgot most times in the middle of a sentence, and it took her a long time to recall.

She was very glad to see me, and held my hand all the time under bedclothes. She spoke of the most trifling things as if tremendously important – as e.g. decisions as if they were momentous and dictated by profound sagacity. She was seldom fully conscious, and often dozed and woke up with a start. 'What do you say?' rather loud. She had no pain, but often muttered in anguish: 'What am I to do? What am I to do?' Amid tossed bedclothes you could see numbers on corners of blankets. On medicine table siphon, saucer, spoon, large soap-dish, brass flower-bowl (empty). The gas (very bad burner) screened by a contraption of Family Bible, some wooden thing, and a newspaper. It wasn't level. She had it altered. She said it annoyed her terribly. Gas stove burning. Temp. barely 60. Damp chill, penetrating my legs. The clock had a very light delicate striking sound. Trams and buses did not disturb her, though sometimes they made talking difficult.

Round-topped panels of wardrobe. She wanted to be satisfied that her purse was on a particular tray of the wardrobe. The mater has arterial sclerosis, and patchy congestion of the lungs. Her condition was very distressing (though less so than the Pater's), and it seemed strange that this should necessarily be the end of a life, that a life couldn't always end more easily.

Friday, November 27th. – The mater died about 1 p.m. on Monday.

I learnt from Jennings that the 'last journey' had to be 'the longest', i.e. corpse must always go longest way to cemetery. I asked why. He sniggered: 'So as to prolong the agony, I suppose.' Real reason nowadays and for long past must be ostentation. We naturally altered this.

Funeral. Too soon. Orange light through blinds in front of room. Coffin in centre on 2 chairs. Covered with flowers. Bad reading, and stumbling of parson. Clichés and halting prayer. Small thin book out of which parson read. In dim light, cheap new carving on oak of coffin seemed like fine oak carving. Sham brass handles on coffin. Horrible lettering. Had to wait after service for hearse to arrive. Men hung their hats on spikes of hearse before coming in. No trouble in carrying coffin. I kept Uncle J. L.'s arm most of the time as he is nearly blind. He told me he still managed 700 accounts. Long walk from cemetery gates to region of chapel. By the way, the lodge at gates is rented as an ordinary house to a schoolmaster. John Ford's vault next to Longson, with records of his young wives ('The flower fadeth' etc.). This could be exaggerated into a fine story. No sign of any other coffins of course in Longson vault.

Curious jacket and apron of first gravedigger. Second stood apart. Both with hats off. Parson put on a skull-cap. On return, carriages trotted down slope from cemetery, but walked as we got to houses near Cobridge station.

Tuesday, December 1st. – On Saturday ended the run of the first revival of *Milestones*. For nearly three years I had had a performance, and frequently two, every night without intermission in the West End of London.

Friday, December 4th. – Patriotic concert last night in village schoolroom. Full. All the toffs of the village were there. Rev. Mathews and family dined with us before it. Most of the programme was given by soldiers, except one pro. It was far more amusing than one could have expected. Corporal Snell, with a really superb bass voice, sang two very patriotic, sentimental songs, sound in sentiment but extremely bad in expression. They would have been excruciating in an ordinary voice; but he was thrilling in them. Our Lieutenant Michaelis was there, after mining the roads, together with a number of his men. The great joke which appealed to parsons and everyone was of a fat lady sitting on a man's hat in a bus. 'Madam, do you know what you're sitting on?' 'I ought to. I've been sitting on it for 54 years.'

This morning, with an endorsement by G. B. S. himself, I received a suggestion from Mark Judge that I should edit Shaw's Manifesto [*Common Sense about the War*] for volume publication.

Saturday, December 19th. – From Thursday in last week to last Thursday I did nothing on my novel. I was fairly free to go on with it on Wednesday, but I had neuralgia. I wrote 2,500 words of it yesterday.

·1915·

Thursday, January 7th. – Dr H. called this afternoon in a great state of excitement: 'I've called about a most unpleasant thing. But I thought I ought to tell you,' etc. His news was that the village was seething with the news that R. was a pro-German, and taking advantage of his position as chauffeur to the military representative to transmit secret information as to English plans through his sweetheart, a German girl, to the German authorities. H. believed it or half-believed it.

Friday, January 8th. – I wrote to the Police Inspector last night and he called to see me to-day. He said he was constantly having complaints about signalling etc., all absurd. I told him that R. was engaged to an English girl and that the whole thing was idiotic. He said he had received a letter about it (signed) and had to make a few inquiries, but expected of course no result. A very decent sort.

Tuesday, January 12th. – Captain Bath and Lieut. Way of Ammunition Column of W. Somersets billeted here yesterday. 40 horses in Dakins's yard. Bath told me a tale of a party of German officers who spent some time in his town, Glastonbury – I think last year – with a fleet of cars in which they went out every night. They had a field and pretended to be perfecting a process for getting petrol from peat. They showed some petrol stated to be so obtained. Then they departed suddenly and mysteriously. I asked: why all this? He said it was to reconnoitre the country. I asked why they should reconnoitre the country at night when they were free to do it in the daytime, but he had no answer. Anyhow, he was fully persuaded that it was a great case of 'intelligence'.

Danielsen came to see me yesterday as to the case of the postmaster at X., an alleged spy. The contents of a military telegram of no importance had been divulged. I knew that this had happened to civil telegrams up there in the past. I sent for the postmaster here, and questioned him, but fruitlessly. Speaking yesterday of the difficulty of dealing with spies, Maj. Danielsen said: 'It's this damned vote-catching government. They're out to get the vote of the alien.' He is a quite honest man, and seemed to believe this. That the spy business was the exclusive affair of the War Office, and that he was arraigning the beloved K. of K. did not seem to occur to him.

Saturday, January 16th. – London to see work of Queen's Fund. Lunch at Mrs McKenna's. Largeish house in Smith Sq. designed by Lutyens. Very bare, and lacking in furniture. But there was some good furniture. Present: Masterman full of good humour. Brock, Secretary of National Relief Fund; and Mary MacArthur, stoutish matron, with a marked Scotch accent. I met her on doorstep and introduced myself. I liked her. Mrs MacArthur had prepared a timed programme of our pilgrimage, with times in it for leaving like 2.48. We kept to it fairly well.

Thursday, February 4th. – A wealthy maltster called to tell me all he knew about spies and suspects. He said there was nothing of the sort, and all he could speak of were one or two people afflicted with 'cussedness' – people who *would* argue that the English were no good and that Germans must win, etc. He saw this cussedness in various forms all over the country. I agreed. But he said that it was all due to the abolition of flogging. He brought ingenious old arguments in support of flogging. The chief was that if you fined or imprisoned a man you punished his wife and children. Whereas if you flogged him you punished *him* and the thing was over at once. He got quite excited on this subject, and could scarcely leave. A quiet, nervous man – public school, etc.

Saturday, February 6th. – Yesterday Brig.-Gen. Hoare (called the Brig) came to inspect ammunition column's horses. He asked W. full details of every horse. W. only knew about 20. He invented the rest. He says you must never say 'I don't know' in the Army. Hoare asked him if horses were getting chaff. He said they were (it was true). When asked how, he was floored and ultimately said he bought the chaff himself. A lie! 'I must speak to you about that later.' Later Hoare took him on one side and said: 'It's very kind of you to pay for that chaff out of your own pocket. Don't do it in future. The proper thing to do is to exchange spare horse-rations with farmers for chaff.'

Saturday, February 13th. – I finished *These Twain* yesterday.

Monday, February 22nd. – Friday, Saturday and Sunday I corrected *These Twain* and cut it from 128,000 to 100,000 words.

Saturday, March 13th. – Pinker called after lunch. Harmsworths starting a new weekly (he didn't know what – afterwards disclosed as the *Sunday Pictorial*) – and they wanted some star contributions – 1,500 words. They came to him for advice and help. Their idea was Corelli and Haggard! He suggested me at £100, and said I was the greatest and most expensive star. They at once accepted. I wrote the article on Wednesday and it was advertised on Thursday. Pinker offered H. G. Wells, but when approached Wells said he had already written on the subject suggested, and moreover he was very busy with his novel. In the end the *Sunday Pictorial's* star trio was me, Horatio Bottomley, and Austin Harrison!

Wednesday, March 24th. – [G. H.] Mair and Sullivan came to lunch. As usual Mair was full of authentic information on things. Meeting of W.A.R.C. 4–5. Then I went to see [Clifford] Sharp and Squire at *New Statesman* office. Rumours as to its imminent death untrue. They asked me to qualify as a director. I said I would.

Thursday, March 25th. – Mrs Lowndes gave dinner at Sesame Club. Mrs Reg. McKenna, Lockwood (an American Rhodes scholar), us, and Sir George Riddell, who came very late. He said the Press Bureau had sent out a notice to newspapers asking them to stop being optimistic. On top of this came the interview (Havas Agency) with Sir J. French, predicting a short war.

Good Friday, April 2nd. – Having cleared up all my correspondence and found room for all accumulations of new books, I decided yesterday to get ideas into order and begin my new novel *The Lion's Share* to-day. I was rather disturbed by the prospect of going to the Front with G. H. Mair.

Saturday, April 10th. – I finished the first instalment of *The Lion's Share*, 12,500 words, to-day, having begun it on Good Friday, and written an article as well.

The novel is light, and of intent not deeply imagined, but it seems to me to be fairly good and interesting.

Monday, April 19th. – Owing to alleged existence of a German spy in British officer's clothing and in a car, in this district, order that no officer shall be out at night in a car unless on duty and with the password of the day. Personally, I don't see what good this will do. Highly inconvenient for officers. One officer coming through Chelmsford, got stopped on his way to this district. He did not know of order, and had no password. He telephoned for help. A despatch cyclist was sent from Great Bentley to give him the password. This cyclist, although on General Hoare's orders, was not allowed to go through Colchester, and in the end the officer had to get home by train.

Pinker told me that Hy. James had intimately conversed with two men sent on missions by Wilson through Germany. One, unofficial (the 'King of Texas', great friend of Wilson's), to ascertain state of Germany (? and Austria); the other, official, to try to arrange something as to complex social relations (Germans with American wives, etc.). These two men only met at the end of their work, and in London. They agreed in their observations.

1. German Government had no hope whatever of a victory.
2. German Government was in a 'state of *terror*' as to the British Navy, feeling themselves like men in a room from which the air was being slowly withdrawn.

3. Food question likely to be very troublesome before harvest.

4. No first-class leader in Germany.

Wednesday, April 28th. – I finished the 3rd instalment of *The Lion's Share* on Sunday; wrote an article on Monday, and went to London yesterday for Wounded Allies Committee Meeting, at which I was in the chair.

After lunch I had a talk with Spender, who told me that Italy had 'signed on' definitely in the Quadruple Alliance. He gave the war another 18 months. I asked him if he kept a diary. He said no. He said that at the beginning of his intimate friendship with Rosebery, Rosebery asked him if he kept a diary. 'I'm glad,' said Rosebery when he had the answer, 'now I can be free with you.'

Thursday, May 13th. – Lunch yesterday with Wells and Gardiner at Automobile Club. Wells said he knew that French (Sir J.) believed the war would be over in June. Afterwards with 'H. G.' to Royal Academy. I had no use for Sargents, Orpens, or Clausens. A fairish crowd there. Then to tea with him at Carlyle Club. First time I had been in this Club. Furnished in a horrible manner. The tea, however, was good.

Then to meeting of Executive Committee of Wounded Allies at Sardinia House. It lasted from 5 to 7.35, and Lord Swaythling kept re-lighting *one* cigar the whole time.

Dined with M. at Hotel. Then to reception at Charles Trevelyan's to meet the Managing Committee of the Union of Democratic Control. But the only member that I found there was Arthur Ponsonby; a pale, light, large-foreheaded man. Seemed surprised when I said that Germans would be beaten, and that Government would stand. All these chaps have twisted ideas.

Tuesday, May 18th. – Sir George Riddell sent a man and a car to conduct me to St Dunstan's, Regent's Park, where Arthur Pearson has established a home for blinded soldiers. Very large place; belongs to an American financier named Kahn. 15 acre garden etc.

Pearson very natty, and a constant and rapid talker. Practically *quite* blind. He may have vague sensations of dark and light. His wife came. He kissed her hand when she left. I liked her. Two blind officers; secretary of Blind Institute, Pearson's secretary; the Matron, a wounded soldier, and the Bishop of London for lunch. The last is certainly clever – for the *mot* particularly. He is, perhaps excusably, deeply impressed by the fact that he is Bishop of London, but he turns it off always into a joke. Thus: 'When I get into a car it always breaks down. People say the Bishop of London is a Jonah' etc. 'A strange thing for the Bishop of London.' Small thin sharp face, with small trembling eyes. Ordinary Tory ideas. He told us that every general had told him to impress upon the country that the army was very short of ammunition; and one general told him he was only allowed 2 rounds a day! He spoke agreeably, with simple well-worn forms of jokes, to the men after lunch about his experiences at the front.

Friday, May 21st. – Yesterday I lunched and dined at the McKennas, and learnt a lot about the crisis. Runciman fine. McKenna and Asquith and others extremely hurt and pained by the crisis. Kitchener not very good. Crisis made by Repington's article in *The Times*. Churchill with French at same time as Repington. Rep's article 'arranged'. Excellent War Office defence against charge of lack of shells, namely that French, knowing circumstances, demanded a certain quantity, and that this quantity was not only supplied but doubled. Fault therefore with leaders at front. French not now liked by Army, who want Robertson. Battle of Aubervilliers of Saturday, 8th, bloodiest of war. Not a defeat, because men could not be shifted, but we lost 28,000 men. Operation undertaken against advice of other generals.

Thursday, June 3rd. – Dance last night in aid of Blinded Soldiers and Sailors. About 40 people paid, and something over 30 came. Receipts about £11. Began at about 9.15 and finished about 1.30. Curious method of sitting out. Couples went to sit out in the motor cars waiting in the stable yard.

Coldish night. The earnest air of young couples, especially the girls, and the short-statured girls sitting about in my study, my bedroom, and M.'s rooms, also on the top stairs, was just as comic to me as ever it was. It is the small girls who seem to take the dalliance so seriously. I danced with six women, – a record.

Sunday, June 13th. – The *Strand Magazine* objected to my novel *The Lion's Share* on the ground that it contained suffragette scenes. They held a meeting of directors and solemnly decided that the *Strand* could not print a suffragette serial. However, I think that I have reassured them.

Wednesday, June 16th. – Still waiting for a telegram permitting me to go to the French front.

I was told positively on Monday that Dardanelles were forced. Last night Asquith said that there was no truth whatever in the rumour. This rumour has been very strong.

Sunday, June 20th. – London on Friday. I paid three visits to Godfrey, Mair's secretary, to get my passport for France and police pass, and in the end the police pass was wrongly filled up. The passport had been marked 'Havre' instead of 'Boulogne', although no passengers are allowed to land at Havre. Godfrey's calm under these provocations was remarkable.

Monday, June 21st. – Victoria Station 7.45. Given a form to fill up. Couldn't get a big bag through without registering. People coming off train. Shabby, respectable girls etc. Hot Summer's morning. Soldiers, officers. Staff officers on train.

A general: crossed sword and baton with star: 'What I should really like to know is, how they relieve those trenches at night.'

My police pass saved me a great deal of trouble of waiting at Folkestone, more at Boulogne. Channel covered with shipping. Boom for several miles outside Folkestone, buoyed at about every 100 yards.

Arrival of bevy of nurses, white starched muslin blue- and red-edged in car at 'Stationary Hospital'. Arrival of Army

Postal Van, with legends about Y.M.C.A. and Kaiser written with a finger in the white dust on the sides.

Étaples. Hospitals and Camp. As English as England. Hay in some places made and laid in cocks. Arrived Abbeville 4.15, having taken 3 hours to do 80 or 90 kil. The whole line, station and scene, make an impression like perpetual Sunday, except for soldiers and camps.

Amiens. Very old man in a new long blue blouse and swagger check trousers showing beneath, acting as porter and shoving a truck along. Probably had retired and been brought back again.

Paris. I had at first a rather false impression about streets; in big streets over half the shops were closed. Then I recollected that the hour was after 7. A peculiar feeling certainly all over Paris. No autobuses, but trams. Few taxis. I saw the horse bus, Madeleine-Bastille, with a woman in charge, bareheaded, and with a great black bag over her abdomen. About 40; on easy terms with the passengers.

Paris, Wednesday, June 23rd. – I learnt yesterday that it was impossible to leave yesterday for the Front. Gide, Godebski and Mair came to lunch. Gide intellectually more than ever like an orchid.

General Sketch of Impression of Paris. View from Hotel. Destruction of gardens and architecture; St Clotilde. Station. Trees. Young man and woman playing silly ball game in dust. Shops. No buses. Concierges sitting out at night on pavements. Very close and hot, and as it were expectant. Number of young men for various reasons left. Lack of chicory and salt. Sound of guns in distance. Variety of uniforms. Bad puttees. Women's heavy mourning.

Meaux, June 24th. – House by roadside, roof damaged, contents taken away by G.'s. Why? What they couldn't take they destroyed.

Trenches. Character of country: rolling upwards. Farms. Wheat, oats, *poppies*. Heavily wooded in places. High horizon of tree-lined roads.

Many tombs in wheat and hidden by wheat. Barbed wire on four stout posts (a bird on post), white wooden cross. Always a small white flag. Not always a name. On every side in these fields, the gleam of cross or flag, as far as you can see. Scores and scores. Dark green-purple of distant wooded hills against high green of fields.

Cemetery used for firing from. Holes in wall.

Wheat absolutely growing out of a German.

General impression. How little is left. How cultivation and civilization have covered the disaster over!

Paris, June 25th. – Mair and I dined at Meaux. Lord Esher came in, wearing a fancy military costume – perhaps that of Constable of Windsor Castle. A star was depending from his neck. As soon as he saw my eye on it he tucked it inside his double-breasted khaki coat.

Paris, June 30th. – Ravel came to lunch. He is a *second* in autos. He wanted to be in aviation, but his friends would not help him on account of danger.

Near Ablain, July 8th. – Young prisoner, 21, just caught. Trousers and coat pierced by bullet. Consumptive, enfeebled. Called up in Dec. 1914. Examined by officer, then went off with a soldier. Had work in paper factory. Infinitely pathetic. Scared little consumptive. Why military ambition?

After car came to road at Souchez Germans began to fire on road 78 high explosives. Searching road at 50 yards' distance or 100 up and down each shot. Almost every 2 minutes, and 1 minute sometimes. Tremendous waste of ammunition. The thing burst before sound of sizzling has finished reaching your ears.

Nearest shot 100 yards.

Ypres, July 12th. – Market-place full of people, up to April 22. Acacia tree still flourishing. St Martin's stands, but irreparable. Only walls left, and tower skeleton. Organ stands. Apse blown out. Vast heaps of bricks in meeting of transept and nave etc. All yellowed by picric acid.

Grande Place – except for one white building (convent) all the rest jagged needles of walls.

Sat in a shell-hole to do sketch in front of convent. Aeroplanes overhead.

High wind. English guns booming. Fitments in houses creaking and rattling and cracking.

On ramparts, dug-outs, birds lustily enjoying odour of gas from shell.

We never saw a Boche aeroplane.

Saturday, August 14th. – Clifford Sharp told me that Brooks had told him Brooks was in Northcliffe's room when N. himself dictated the *Daily Mail* article about Kitchener, and that it was very much stronger then than in print. It seems Northcliffe, having no sons, is very keen on his nephews. He has already lost two in the war, if not three, and he regards them as having been murdered by Lord K. When remonstrated with about his attitude to Lord K., he burst out: 'But he's murdered my nephews!'

Wednesday, September 15th. – Zeppelin excitements nightly. It was said in the village that a Zeppelin hung over the village church for an hour on Monday night, but I did not believe this. A station-porter, however, told me that they could see a Zeppelin on Sunday night, as it passed. He said that another Zeppelin or some Zeppelins had been signalled for that night (Monday). It was dark when I talked to him on the dark platform. (They had had instructions as to lights by telegraph.) The only lights were the reds of the signals, high up. I asked him as to Marguerite's train. He said that the train had 'asked' for the line and would arrive soon. This mysteriousness of unseen things known to be coming – such as Zeppelins and trains – was rather impressive. Then suddenly a red light changes to green in the air. Two engines attached to each other rumble through the station. Then M.'s train. And after a long delay Marguerite's silhouette very darkly far down the platform.

Saturday, October 2nd. – [To McKenna's for lunch.] [Reginald] McKenna was very strong against conscription. He said it would lose the war. He said the army was already too large for our resources, that the demands of the Allies were always growing, and that the financial strain was very great. John Burns was in great form. He gave most amusing and convincing pictures of artisan family life etc. He said that when he had been buying a book too many he would leave it at the club and then take it home last thing at night, after his wife was in bed, and hide it.

Saturday, October 9th. – Left home at 10 a.m. and drove over slippery roads in a Scotch mist to Little Easton. I walked with Wells in the park at dusk. Stag rutting season. All the bucks were roaring like lions, and we were somewhat intimidated. Two of them made a show of fighting, but funked it. Before this, original ball games in the arranged barn, in front of which a farmyard and cesspool had been turned into a very sightly sunk garden with bathing tank in the middle.

Immense park, belonging to Lady Warwick, and practically wasted for useful purposes. And there must be hundreds such.

'It ought to be taxed out,' said H. G.

Tuesday, October 12th. – I returned from Wells's yesterday morning. It is Wells's tremendous energy that makes the place so entertaining. If there is no real talking then he must instantly play at some game. I played at Badminton, hockey, his own pat-ball, etc. He has turned a barn and a farmyard into something very nice, and a great 'escape' from the house. He works in his bedroom at a very small table, and has a primus stove to make tea there. He sometimes gets up and works in the night. The house is partly steam-heated, and is fairly comfortable and very bright; but some of it is badly planned and arranged. It is like a large cottage made comfortable by people rich but capricious. H. G. drives a car very indifferent bad; but he enjoys driving.

Wednesday, November 17th. – Directors' meeting at noon of *New Statesman*, Shaw, Webb, Simon (large employer at Manchester) and Clifford Sharp. Shaw said we ought to attack Asquith. Said we ought to make Haldane P.M. Shaw had no conception of public opinion at all. Afterwards, in the street, he told me he had talked like that as a 'hygienic operation', and that it was necessary to exaggerate in such hygiene; he wanted to stir Sharp up. He said he went to Torquay sometimes for a holiday, and worked harder than ever. The fundamental decency and kindliness of Shaw was evident throughout.

Saturday, December 4th. – London, Thursday. Slept at R.T.Y.C. Very good. I finished *The Lion's Share* on Wednesday night and slept very ill, and was really too fatigued for London, but I took a tonic, which did me good. Max Beerbohm lunched with me at Reform, and I urged him to start on some cartoons.

December 30th. – I wrote 272,200 words this year, not counting journals. I had the best book and serial year I have ever had (though I didn't issue a single new novel), and by far the worst theatrical year since before *The Honeymoon*, I think.

I finished re-reading *Esther Waters* last night, after a bad bilious attack. It still vigorously lives.

·1916·

Saturday, January 22nd. – On Friday after a third sleepless night I lunched with Methuen at the Reform. He told me *These Twain* had sold 13,350 in the first week. Some rotten reviews. Apart from other things, the book is too jolly true for some people. They say it lacks the ideal, and mean that it refuses to be untruthful. Several of the best critics have noted this with satisfaction and laudation.

Monday, February 21st. – Haymarket concert in aid of W.A.R.C. at night. This went off without a hitch, and I was very glad when it was over. I had no particular trouble but I will never organize another. The theatrical element, Ainley and Nelson Keys, had a much greater success than the musical element. The latter was naturally jealous, but could not help peeping and hugely enjoying the former. One is more struck than ever by the forced cordiality of all greetings and all praise in this *monde*. Miss Ada Crossley, the oldest singer there, has very great charm, and she got the first encore. After Ainley, people began to go, and after Nelson Keys a lot went. These two had each more than one encore, and occupied a great deal of time, so that the concert was not over till 10.25. I had a rotten night.

Tuesday, February 29th. – As regards the great invasion scare. The two batteries 'stood by' yesterday morning from 4 a.m. till sunrise and to-day from 5.30 a.m. till sunrise, all ready to move off – except that bits weren't in harness. The reinforcement which came in a hurry from Colchester here consists of convalescent wounded gunners from the front, appointed only to light duty and to extreme emergency duty. In the fatigue of yesterday's field day (which was utterly useless) the wounds of two of the gunners were reopened. It is considered that the early morning standing by is connected with high water, and that some attempt at a landing is feared. Only the Ammunition

Column remains in Thorpe. The two batteries have taken with them 100 rounds per gun. The rest is stored in our out-buildings.

Saturday, March 11th. – Birthday dinner at Mrs McKenna's. Short dinner, but 3 man-servants. Birrell, very boyish, with much grey hair and short of a front tooth; decided, gay, wary. Edwin Montagu and wife, both very Jewish. Nothing seemed to be known about future of war and McKenna didn't seem to believe in a smashing of Germany; but Montagu did. Montagu rather diffident and quiet. It was stated that nobody *could* be worse at the War Office than Kitchener. He wasn't even a brute.

Friday, March 17th. – To Grafton Gallery where the most mixed show (Allied Artists' Assocn.) you ever saw. Good modern things and cubism, and the rottenest amateurishness of the worst old-fashioned kind. For instance a cat sitting on a polished floor, and necklace thereon, with the title 'Reflections'. No Strand picture dealer would have dared to put it in his window. The place was ready for a reception to Pachmann. I don't know how we managed to be let in. All the snobs began to arrive. We left then. Tea at Hatchetts. Then to Westminster Cathedral for evensong. Beautiful darkening empty building, very sad, and a sing-song by six priests and their leader. I dined at the Reform, alone, and alone to the Alhambra. Very empty. *Les grues* allowed to sit in back row of dress-circle. London very wet and dark and many *grues* mysteriously looming out at you in Coventry Street.

Thursday morning, to W. Nicholson's. He was in a black leather jacket, covered with paint. He gave me the portrait of Wish Wynne that was used in the production of *The Great Adventure*. He showed me some most ingenious 'still lifes', and Eric Kennington's biggest war picture – very striking.

Friday, May 5th. – Mair mysteriously telegraphed me to go to an 'important' luncheon at the Garrick to meet a Swedish author. The author was Brunius. Also present George Alexander, H. B. Irving, W. L. Courtney, another Swede living in England named Valentin, I think, and Mair's colleague Carnegie. I had to sit next to Brunius. He seemed a very nice, sound, provincial chap, with pretty bad English. But what the luncheon was for, and why such a strange gathering, I haven't the least idea. It was a Government luncheon, in a private room at the Savoy. Brunius specialises in Shakespeare, and he had come over for the celebrations. Alexander is very well preserved, and behaved with great restraint (especially for an actor or any sort of artiste); quiet voice. Tells a story lengthily and without a spark of originality, but with effect.

Monday, May 8th. – Reading Marcel Dupont's *La Campagne* last night and night before. There is no genius in it (40th Edition), but it gives a plain notion of what war is, and some things are moving. Curious sensation lying in bed reading this, nightingale singing violently across the road, and horses and motors passing at intervals, and the thought that exactly similar scenes might be occurring here at any time, and that *this* house might be a ruined chateau and that *our* furniture might be defiled by German officers. At any rate according to the theory of the War Office. A period of extreme vigilance now on.

Friday, May 26th. – Some weeks ago Davray, official Press agent of French Government, asked me to write an article on conscription in England. He laid down the lines, which he had taken from previous articles of mine in the *Daily News*. I wrote the article exactly on these lines and he was most enthusiastic about it. It was for *Le Temps*, which the Government now controls. The French Censor turned it down entirely, and Davray in a letter to me this week gives the Censor's actual words. He says the figures were not official (which they were) and might give rise to polemics. Moreover that conscription was now accomplished and no more to be said. But he had kept the article since before the final conscription bill was brought into Parliament. The Censor's reason for refusing the article was, of course, purely political. This article gave the arguments on both sides; it stated that conscription – certain to come – would not greatly increase the army – and spoke of the necessity of trade, munitions etc. The Censor didn't like that.

The article would have cleared up misunderstandings into which the French public have fallen. The Censor didn't like that either.

Thursday, June 8th. – Came to London Tuesday morning for the Wounded Allies 'War Fair' at the Caledonian Market. Heavy shower. Great success. I sold books at M.'s stall. After 5.30, crowds of young women came to look at books and some to buy. One well-dressed man had never heard of Balzac. Demand for Kipling, Chesterton, Conrad, and me. Difficulty of selling autographs. Enthusiasm for Jepson's *Pollyooly*. Met Pett Ridge and he looked just like an actor. Various estimates of profits of 2 days; but you can see that the men keep estimates lower than their hopes. Thus Mr Henry – £8,000 to £15,000. Selfridge estimated attendance first day at from 25 to 30,000. I agree. Yet one man in charge of a gate said that through that gate alone he estimated that 30,000 people had passed. And so on. There were not enough goods, nor stalls. The place looked nearly empty when I arrived, and remained so. It was too big. I did a very good trade in books, but I brought down prices at the end considerably, and autographed favourites were going for 3s. and even 2s. 6d. Habit of women of squealing out in ecstasy over name of a book, and then refusing even to consider the purchase of it. Perhaps they were so startled to find that they recognized a title.

Saturday, October 7th. – Yesterday lunch at McKenna's. I sat between Fisher and a girl. In two minutes he had referred to 'bloody experts'. Touching Falkland battle and Cradock's defeat, he said that a tortoise had been sent to catch a hare, and then two tortoises. He ordered the two fastest ships there were to go off at once. People protested. An admiral came up from Portsmouth and said that really they ought to be overhauled before leaving. 'Not at all,' said Fisher, 'they must leave to-night.' And he said to me: 'They only arrived ten minutes too soon. The only real victory we've had at sea yet. It doesn't want an expert to see that a tortoise can't catch a hare, and that a hare has never yet been wounded by a tortoise and won't be.' Then the phrase about bloody experts. He was evidently still feeling his shunt from the Admiralty. He said: 'I was the only one who objected to the Dardanelles Expedition. Kitchener was in favour of it. He's dead. Won't say anything about him. He got the Order of the Garter. I got the Order of the Boot.'

He said that in October, 1914, having *carte blanche* from Lloyd George, he ordered 612 new vessels for the Navy. He didn't think the German line would be broken in the West, and was in favour of an invasion of Pomerania, only 82 miles from Berlin. He said that this possibility was the only thing that had ever made Frederick the Great afraid. He seemed to have developed this scheme. He told some excellent stories with strong language. They say he is like a boy. He absolutely is. He said: 'I'm told I shall live till I'm 110. So I've plenty of time yet.' He gave me his favourable quotation:

> Not heaven itself upon the past has power,
> What has been, has been, and I have had my hour.

They also say that he smacks more of the forecastle than of the bridge. There is something in this, too.

Monday, October 9th. – Clegg brought a Capt. B. (of his Battery) to lunch. Had been out at Ypres ten months and then wounded in the head, in front of right ear. He carries a good scar. He talked well, and said he should like to write if he could. I told him he could.

He said the newspaper correspondents' descriptions of men eager to go up over the parapet made him laugh. They never were eager. He related how he had seen a whole company of men extremely pale with apprehension and shaking so that they could scarcely load their rifles. Then he said that men who nevertheless *did* go over in that state were really brave. He told us how his battery saw hundreds, thousands, of grey figures coming along only 1,000 yards off, and every man thought he would be a prisoner in ten minutes, when suddenly thousands of Canadians appeared from nowhere, and the Boches fled. The cheering was delirious. He told this very dramatically, but without any effort to be effective. He said he really wanted to be back with the battery. For a long time the fellows wrote to him regularly once a fortnight, and every letter ended with: 'When are you coming back?' He said they had had glorious times now and then, glorious. He said that to sit on a factory chimney and see the Boches going over was better than big game shooting. He said the Boches had any amount of pluck and grit. Both Clegg and B. facetiously contrasted the rough, anyhow, bumping treatment the wounded get on their way from the firing line (when they really *are* ill) with the hushed, tender, worshipping treatment they get on arriving in London when many of them are doing pretty well.

Friday, November 3rd. – I came to London on Wednesday and took possession of apartment 'C' at the R. Thames Y.C. which I have rented. Rather like celibate life in Paris again. I dined at the Club and read Macready's diary; extraordinary sensation of having resumed a closed chapter of existence.

Tuesday, November 14th. – I came home from town on Friday afternoon, with Swinnerton and Marguerite. Swinnerton was walking out on Sunday evening (dark) in the village looking for me, and not finding me, he asked a little boy whether he had seen a gentleman, Mr Bennett, with 4 dogs. The boy mumbled a negative. Swinnerton then proceeded to describe me, etc., and the boy said, 'I seen Mr Bennett with *one* dog.'

Friday, November 24th. – H. G. Wells told me his scheme for a whole series of new books, some being novels. He wants monarchy destroyed, of course, and to have a new religion (that there is one God – and apparently he can be what you like) without priests or churches. He thought very little of British high command at the front, had had difficulties with Censor about his articles on Front, and meant to say what he thought in a book to be issued in January.

I went up to the Omega workshops by appointment to see Roger Fry. Arrived as arranged at 2.30. I was told he was out. Then that he was at his studio, down Fitzroy Street. I went there and rang. He opened door.

'Come and have lunch,' he said. 'I've had lunch, it's 2.30,' I said. 'How strange!' he said. 'I thought it was only 1.15.' Then as he went upstairs he cried out to a girl above: 'Blank (her Xtian name), it's 2.30,' as a great item of news. Fry expounded his theories. He said there was no original industrial art in England till he started i.e., untraditional. He said lots of goodish things and was very persuasive and reasonable. Then he took me to the showrooms in Fitzroy Square, and I bought a few little things. I did not buy a fine still life by Duncan Grant. But I may, later. I gradually got to like a number of the things, especially the stuffs. He said manufacturing (English) firms roared with laughter at his suggestion that they should do business together. One firm quoted an impossible price when he asked them to make rugs to his design at his risks. But when a eulogistic article appeared in *The Times* they quoted a lower price, a reasonable one. He said that both French and German firms would take his stuff. I began to get more and more pleased with the stuff, and then I left with two parcels.

Thursday, December 7th. – In the afternoon read through what I have written of my new novel. Not so bad. Undoubtedly I have been refreshed and invigorated by reading Dreiser's *The Financier*, which absolutely held me. *The Titan*, which I am now reading, is not so good.

Wednesday, December 13th. – Lieut. R. of a mobile A. Aircraft unit stationed at Thorpe, came for tea. He said he carried £15,000 worth of stores. He said that after big raid at Hull end of last year about, when Mayor of Hull had been assured that Hull was one of the most heavily defended places, and a Zep dropped 15 bombs in the town, the population afterwards mobbed officers, and A.A. officers coming into the town had to put on Tommies' clothes. Also that Naval Unit was telegraphed for and that when it came with full authorized special lights, the population, angry at the lights, assaulted it with stones and bottles and put half of it in hospital, and had ultimately to be kept off by the military. He outlined complex administrative system of unit, and showed how utterly and needlessly idiotic it was. He told me how he had been sent to some golf links with a big mobile gun, and had put gun into a good spot where it interfered with play on first hole, the officially indicated position being a bad one. The affair was urgent as a raid expected that night. He successfully repulsed various complainants from golf club; but next morning an Infantry officer came specially down from War Office, with instructions (positive orders) that gun must be moved. R. gave reasons against. Infantry officer: 'I don't know anything about artillery, but that gun has got to be moved. It is my order to you.' In order to fix gun in inferior official position, R. indented for railway sleepers to the tune of £127, and got them. Meanwhile the golf club professional had told him that it would be quite easy to modify the course.

Thursday, December 21st. – Ill ever since last entry. I got up for lunch yesterday. To-day I was up for breakfast and have read through last finished chapter of new novel. But I can't yet write, except articles (for *Statesman*). During illness I have had excellent ideas for novel.

Sunday, December 31st. – I finished the first part of my London novel [*The Roll Call*] this afternoon. 35,000 words. I wrote only 127,600 during the year. The totals of later years, however, cannot be compared fairly with totals of earlier years as latterly I have not counted my journal.

London, January 4th. – [Robert] Ross told me, as regards inaccuracies in *Dict. National Biog.*, that he offered to look through the proofs of Wilde's biography, but proofs were never sent to him. He found 18 mistakes of fact in the biography.

After the immense public row between Lloyd George and [A. G.] Gardiner [editor of *The Daily News*], the following lately occurred. T. P. O'Connor came up to Gardiner and said: 'You may be interested in a piece of information which I have. It is not second-hand. I myself heard the words spoken. The other day Ll. George spoke of you in very friendly terms. He said you were not like the rest. Your difference of opinion was honest and he respected it. Yes, he spoke in the kindliest terms of you.' A few days later another henchman of Ll. G. came up to Gardiner at the N.L. Club and said: 'You may be interested to know that I heard Ll. George speak of you in the very friendliest terms the other day.' And so on as before. Thus is it sought to work the oracle.

Comarques, Saturday, January 14th. – Wednesday evening I went into Westminster Cathedral, and saw how to use it again in my novel. Very cold day. Nice warm cathedral. Ugly chapels, detail invisible. A non-R.C. parson or two squinting about. Noise of a charwoman washing floor. Exceedingly few people. Then at 10.10, either Prime or Tierce. A few performers came in, after a bell had rung; took their seats, and then the intoning begins; scarcely audible for a second or less. It 'steals out'. Words utterly incomprehensible. Outside, front of shop devoted to rosaries, crucifixes, etc.

Yacht Club, London, Thursday, February 8th. – Dined at Mdme Van der Velde's, and sat at a spiritualistic séance with a clairvoyant, named Peters, who brought his son, a youth in R.A.M.C., home for a few hours on leave. This son said there were 500 professed spiritualist soldiers at Aldershot. Theosophist. Peters (*père*), man of 45 or so. Short. Good forehead. Bald on top, dark hair at sides. Quick and nervous. Son of a barge owner. Present: Yeats, Mr and Mrs Jowitt (barrister – she very beautiful), Roger Fry, hostess and me. Peters handled objects brought by each of us. His greatest success, quite startling, was with the glass stopper of a bottle brought by Jowitt. He described a man throwing himself *out* of something, down, with machinery behind him, and a big hotel or big building behind him. Something to do with water, across water. He kept repeating these phrases with variations. The stopper had belonged to a baronet (I forget his name) who threw himself off a launch, in response to a challenge from X., at 3 a.m. into the Thames, after a party up river. He was drowned.

He succeeded, with my toothpick, in getting me to the Potteries, and into the office of the *Staffordshire Knot* or *Sentinel*, and described a man that might be either Goold or the editor of the *Sentinel*, and said that known or unknown to me, this man had greatly influenced me. He insisted on the word 'Zola'. 'Zola.' He said there was a message to tell me. I hadn't done my best work. I am morally sure he hadn't the least idea who I was. And even if he had, he didn't know the toothpick belonged to me, even if he knew it was I who had brought it, which he might conceivably have done as it was the last thing he picked up off the tray. I made full notes.

Friday, February 9th. – To-day George Moore and W. Sickert came to lunch. Sickert had swum that morning and skated. He had his skates with him – no overcoat. I said little. They talked. Moore was the man of letters. He said, of a Landor dialogue between Horne Tooke and Johnson, that it would not interest ordinary people, but that a man of letters might read it under his lamp at night with great amusement.

Sickert said that he cooked his own food, and cooked it very well. Formerly he used to read between spells of painting during the day. Now he cooked. He would go over to the stove and say 'Ça mijotte'. They both used a lot of French and spoke it very well. Moore recited a French ballad which he had written about a *maquereau*, which I thought rather good. Then he recited Villon. Moore evidently wants to get into the theatre again. Unfortunately I had no encouragement for him. He has an idea for dramatizing *The Brook Kerith*. He is naïvely and harmlessly vain, and very agreeable. I enjoyed these men very much. Moore seemed to have detached himself almost completely from the war. He said he didn't read newspapers now, as they only made him feel depressed and did him no good. He said several entirely foolish things, such as that he could not understand (very much emphasized) how anyone could read a *war book*. To read about new war devices he could understand, but how anyone could read a war book he could *not* understand. Sickert was much more reserved – he is much more normal.

Yacht Club, London, Wednesday, March 7th. – Massingham, Ross, and I dined together. I was thus between two pacifists.

Massingham told a good story of an Australian who was asked his opinion as to the end of the war. The Australian said: 'I think what my friend Fritz thinks. Fritz was my German prisoner – a very decent sort of chap. Fritz said: "You'll win, but you'll all come home on one steamer." '

This of course expressed Massingham's view beautifully, also Ross's.

Yacht Club, London, Thursday, March 15th. – H. L. Rothband, the Manchester manufacturer, lunched with me yesterday at Reform, about his scheme for employment of disabled soldiers. Curious mixture of ingenuousness and acuteness. I missed the beginnings of a shindy between Spender and Massingham. Masterman brought this safely to an end by leaving the smoking-room with Massingham and sitting in the gallery. Spender was with Buckmaster.

I wrote another 1,100 words of novel yesterday after another very bad night, and I was so exhausted in the afternoon that I could scarcely even walk.

Yacht Club, London, Saturday, March 24th. – Dined with Sir W. Weir (Director of Air Supply), Major Weir (Flying Staff, W.O.) and Richmond, at Savoy, after spending ½ hour in the Angelica Kauffman room at Weir's flat.

They began to try to startle me right off. Weir and Richmond said that the labour situation was acutely bad. Tyne strike not better. Men out at Barrow, and men out at 3 or 4 small factories that worked for Weir. The strikes were not officially countenanced by Trades Unions; the organization alien (U.S.A.) working through shop stewards, etc.

Talking about the Labour question they all agreed that the margin of labour was sufficient. That is, that the Government could draw all the men it needed for the Army out of essential occupations and that the men left in the essential occupations could do all the work provided they would *produce their maximum output*, which they don't and won't. All three were enthusiastic about the effort of France. W. Weir said that as regards aeroplane supply, the Germans got the best designs they could, and made a lot of it, telling the manufacturer meanwhile to use the field-experience of his machines in thinking out a new and better design, but sticking to the execution of the original order. We were always trying after improvements, and Weir said that you can't 'force' technical progress advantageously beyond a certain speed. The result was that while we always had easily the best machine in existence we never had enough. He intended that this should be remedied in May.

Yacht Club, London, Wednesday, April 11th. – Last week I had an immense burst of work. I did not go to London. I wrote about 5,000 words of my novel (including 2,500 in one day), and finished penultimate chapter of it. On Monday I wrote *Daily News* article, and more *Statesman* stuff. I slept badly the whole time, but a dinner at the Greys on Saturday, where we met the ultra-blonde Danish dancer Karina, and her husband Captain Janssen, did me good. Karina ran over Janssen in her auto and broke both his legs, and then married him. He looks after Karina so completely that he even cuts out leather for her shoes. She is very pretty and agreeable. I sat next to her and enjoyed it. Hard frost driving home.

Yacht Club, London, Tuesday, April 24th. – I lunched with Webbs. Webb told me that Lloyd George, contrary to the usual habit of Ministers, would not deal with papers. He preferred to be talked to. Webb said that most Ministers were followed about by despatch boxes full of papers which they had to approve and initial. Sometimes hundreds of papers. He said there were several grades of keys; the highest would open all despatch boxes. When he was at the Colonial Office he had a second-grade key, which would open some despatch boxes but not all.

He said that Ministers were still unable to get anything done as Ll. G. would not face the labour of deciding and giving authority. Mrs Webb, who had just returned from a meeting of Reconstruction Committee, said that at one meeting recently at 4 p.m. just before the meeting started, the Marquis of Salisbury went to the mantelpiece and prayed aloud. She was talking to somebody else and could not hear what he said, but he was certainly praying aloud.

Yacht Club, London, Wednesday, April 25th. – I wrote the last scene but one of *The Roll Call* to-day, and was exhausted. Lunched alone at crowded Reform Club.

I walked down past Buckingham Palace this morning. Two naval petty officers outside in full fig, and their women. A police superintendent (?) and a policeman at gates. Former said to latter: 'We'd better be getting 'em in,' and then to the sailors, 'You decorations? Come on. Come along. Come on,' curtly, as if they had done some deed suspicious, and not valorous. The sailors talked with their women for a few moments, and then went obediently within the precincts. They were two roughish, short, thick-set chaps.

Called at Reform Club, where I spent 40 minutes with Wells and an American journalist-lecturer-professor named Macdonald, over here for the New York *Nation*. Wells was talking about the after-war exacerbationary reaction on nerves, which would cause rows, quarrels etc. unless it was consciously kept well in hand, and Macdonald said that a year or so after the San Francisco earthquake prominent S.F. men would disappear; they were in sanatoria, etc. Also lifelong friends, such as business partners, would quarrel over some trifle, each go to his solicitor, and never speak to one another again.

Comarques, Monday, April 30th. – To-day, in accordance with time-table, I finished my novel *The Roll Call* at 4 p.m.

Yacht Club, London, Friday, May 4th. – I came to town on Tuesday meaning to take a few days' holiday after I had written my *Statesman* stuff. But Pinker had arranged for me to do the official War Savings article in 3 days for the *Strand* so that it could appear in their July number. So that I had to begin at once. And I had so much neuralgia yesterday that I couldn't do anything at all.

Thorpe-le-Soken, Sunday, May 6th. – Returned here on Friday and met Bertie Sullivan in the train. Carrying F.O. mails over to Holland in the *Copenhagen*, he had been torpedoed by a submarine. He said 6 subms. waited for the boat, in 3 pairs. He was shaving. He seems to have kept pretty calm, but he said he couldn't get his boots on. 'I was flurried,' he said. Of 17 bags, he saved 16, and sank one. Result, after several days, a sort of lack of feeling in fingers. (It was March and he was not in rowboat for long.)

Yesterday, for the first time, and at my suggestion, we had no bread on the table at dinner. People who want it must ask for it from the sideboard. Wells gave me this tip. The value of these dodges is chiefly disciplinary. If the whole of the well-to-do classes practised them, the wheat problem would be trifling.

Yacht Club, London, Wednesday, May 9th. – On Sunday I had an idea for a short novel about an episode in the life of a French cocotte. I thought I could tell practically everything about her existence without shocking the B.P.

I came to London Tuesday. Lunched at Webbs. Apropos of Squire's poem in current issue of *Statesman* the Webbs were both very funny. Mrs Webb especially. She said, 'Poetry means nothing to me. It confuses me. I always want to translate it back into prose.'

Yacht Club, London, Friday, May 11th. – After lunch it was funny to see H. G. Wells talking with an Indian Ruler (I didn't catch his name) whom he was entertaining to lunch. He brought him to us. The Ruler talked very sensibly, with a slight accent but extremely correctly. His burden was: 'England cannot now throw us over by abandoning the Monarchy. We need it.'

I met George Moore, and he said that he had never made money out of his books worth talking about. £1,500 or so out of *Esther Waters*, £1,000 out of his latest, and so on. It seems that before I asked them to lunch he and Sickert had had a frightful row, which began by a newspaper scrap and ended by Sickert inviting himself to dinner at George's and getting practically turned out. This was George's version. They had not met since till my luncheon. At that affair they were charming to each other.

Comarques, Thorpe-le-Soken, Sunday, May 13th. – Robert Ross gave a lunch at Automobile. Mr and Mrs Edmund Gosse, Eliz. Asquith, Mrs Colefax, Captain Miller and Dr Borenius. I sat between Eliz. A. and Mrs Colefax. Eliz. A. looks quite young. She seemed decent and hard, and socially extremely experienced. A tendency to phrase-making. Much deep ignorance of literature and even superficial ignorance, e.g. she didn't know that the French translations of Dostoievsky are incomplete and the English ones are complete, and read D. in French. She thought it easier to write a novel than a short story. She said she would send me a play of hers to read. It arrived to-day. I liked old Gosse again. He is, anyhow, educated.

Yacht Club, London, Friday, May 25th. – I returned to London Tuesday. Squire and Desmond MacCarthy lunched with

me at the Reform. At night, after writing the Sardonyx article
[for *The New Statesman*] I went to Russian concert at Russian
Exhibition, and it was very good. The pianissimos of the
Balalaika Orchestra were marvellous, especially with music
like Borodin's. On the other hand I had little use for Tchaikowsky's *Grand Trio* (A minor). Place pretty full.

But the chief thing yesterday was that I began on my novel
about the French cocotte, with gusto.

Thorpe-le-Soken, Friday, June 1st. – Last Sunday my 50th
birthday. Twelve people to dinner.

To-day lunch given by Davray to M. Helmer, an *avocat* of
Colmar, in England to give lectures about Alsace-Lorraine.
T. P. O'Connor, Massingham, Gardiner, Spender, and 4
Frenchmen. 'T. P.' began to Gardiner and me about his early
youth. He evidently has a fancy for this sort of reminiscence.
He said he had been the most trustful and easily deceived man
imaginable. It was all very well, he said, but the connexions
of a simple man with women were apt to have 'pecuniary
endings'.

Yacht Club, London, Friday, June 8th. – Walking about these
streets about 10 to 10.30 when dusk is nearly over, is a notable
sensation; especially through Soho, with little cafés and co-op
clubs and women and girls at shop doors. It is the heat that
makes these things fine.

Comarques, Saturday, June 9th. – Siegfried Sassoon lunched
with me at the Reform yesterday. He expected some decora-
tion for admittedly fine bombing work. Colonel had applied
for it three times, but was finally told that as that particular
push was a failure it could not be granted. Sassoon was uncertain about accepting a home billet if he got the offer of one.
I advised him to accept it. He is evidently one of the reckless
ones. He said his pals said he always gave the Germans every
chance to pot him. He said he would like to go out once
more and give them another chance to get him, and come
home unscathed. He seemed jealous for the military reputation

of poets. He said most of war was a tedious nuisance, but there were great moments and he would like them again.

Yacht Club, London, Thursday, June 14th. – I came to London Tuesday, unwell. On getting to Yacht Club from Richmond at 1.30 I had a telephone message from Marguerite to say that she and Anna were in the air raid at Liverpool Street and unhurt. To-day I found out that though the end of their train (11.38) was bombed, M. knew nothing of it, and Anna was only sure that she saw smoke 'by the side of the train' behind her. Neither heard cries of wounded, nor broken glass or anything. M. heard 4 bombs, or 5. Anna said she heard a noise and thought it was guns; then she saw a girl porter running and heard her cry 'Oh', and thought it was an accident. When she realized that it was bombs she remembered nothing more till she 'found herself' near underground lavatory, where people were taking refuge, with M. They were in different carriages and had lost each other. She saw people 'crouching down' (near base of girders, apparently).

Yacht Club, London, Wednesday, July 25th. – Went to dine at Barrie's with Thomas Hardy and wife. Barrie has an ugly little manservant, and the finest view of London I ever saw. Mrs Hardy a very nice woman, with a vibrating attractive voice. Hardy was very lively; talked like anything. Apropos of Tchekoff he started a theory that some of Tchekoff's tales were not justifiable because they told nothing unusual. He said a tale must be unusual and the people interesting. Of course he soon got involved in the meshes of applications and instances; but he kept his head and showed elasticity and common sense, and came out on the whole well. He has all his faculties, unimpaired. Quite modest and without the slightest pose. They both had very good and accurate appraisements of such different people as Shorter and Phillpotts.

Later in the evening Barrie brought along both Shaw and the Wellses by phone. Barrie was consistently very quiet, but told a few A1 stories. At dusk we viewed the view and the searchlights. Hardy, standing outside one of the windows, had to put a handkerchief on his head. I sneezed. Soon after Shaw and the Wellses came Hardy seemed to curl up. He had travelled to town that day and was evidently fatigued. He became quite silent. I then departed and told Barrie that Hardy ought to go to bed. He agreed. The spectacle of Wells and G. B. S. talking firmly and strongly about the war, in their comparative youth, in front of this aged, fatigued and silent man – incomparably their superior as a creative artist – was very striking.

Yacht Club, London, Thursday, July 26th. – [At Covent Garden] I met Ernest Newman, very estimable and sound as usual. We agreed in our estimate of Beecham. He astonished me by saying that he liked a great deal in *Louise*. Apropos of Ravel, he said 'No great man is ever idle'; which is very true. Apropos of Newman's liking *Louise*, Hardy said that he liked Lytton and that *Pelham* was a very able book. Both Hardy and Barrie expressed great admiration for Trollope, but they both expressed perhaps a little too much.

Thorpe-le-Soken, Friday, September 14th. – On Wednesday Shufflebotham carefully examined me at the Club, and decided that I must be X-rayed. He guaranteed that I had had appendicitis several times without knowing it. He also insisted on a new visit to the oculist. All these things added to my gloom due to the sudden and long attack of neuralgia.

Yacht Club, London, Wednesday, September 26th. – I wrote a chapter of novel in the morning and a Sardonyx article in the afternoon. Began the day feeling perfectly rotten, and ended it feeling quite well. A raid began precisely at the moment I left the Yacht Club. The buses seemed to quicken, the streets appreciably emptied. Most people hurried; I did; but a few strolled along. I was glad when I got to the Albany. Firing when there nearer, and everything was faintly lit up with flashes. I found that the Albany alley had been covered with thick glass thrown over from an explosion or a hit on the Academy on the previous night.

Yacht Club, London, Thursday, September 27th. – Dined with M. at Waldorf. To get there, strange journeys in Tube. Very wet. Very poor women and children sitting on stairs (fear of raid). Also travelling in lift and liftman grumbling at them because no fear of raid, and they answering him back, and middle class women saying to each other that if the poor couldn't keep to the regulations they ought to be forbidden the Tube as a shelter from raid.

S. said he had seen dreadful sights of very poor with babies in Tube on Monday. One young woman was in labour. He asked her if she was and she said she was, and that she had got up because she was told to go with the rest. He got her taken on a stretcher to a hospital. Proprietor of a Restaurant, where I lunched to-day with Swinnerton, said that although his place was always full at night, he only had four people on Monday night, and *not a single customer* on Tuesday night (fear of raids). He said also that at fish and vegetable markets he couldn't get what he wanted because supplies were not there, and that wholesalers had not taken supplies because they couldn't dispose of them, and that stuff was rotting. A raid was feared to-night, but evidently the German machines were turned back before reaching London.

Yacht Club, London, Wednesday, October 3rd. – Too unwell to go to Webbs for lunch. Moreover an air raid alarm was on (false). Piccadilly emptied very fast. All the people *ran* out of the Park. One old man remained walking about there.

Yacht Club, London, Wednesday, October 10th. – Wells came in, and slanged the Webbs as usual, and incidentally said: 'My boom is over. I've had my boom. I'm yesterday.' He said that in air raids he was afraid of going to pieces altogether, so if there was a balcony he stood on it. He had been through several raids at Southend. He said: 'I get huffy and cross just as if – ' but I can't remember his comparison.

Comarques, Tuesday, October 16th. – Went through all first two books of cocotte novel, and fairly well pleased with everything except last chapter or so. To-day I tabulated all my information and ideas afresh.

Thorpe, Sunday, November 18th. – I made the acquaintance of Lord Beaverbrook Thursday week. He and Ross lunched with me on Friday. At this second meeting he asked me to take him to Leicester Gallery where I had mentioned there was a good etching of Rops. I did so, with Ross. He asked which was the etching, bought it (20 guineas) and gave it me on the spot.

This was at only our 2nd meeting. *Un peu brusque.*

Comarques, Sunday, December 9th. – Better arrangements must be made for keeping this damned journal. On Thursday last I made my début at the Other Club, to which I was elected without my knowledge. I sat next to F. E. Smith, who is a live companion, inclined to recount his achievements, but interesting and informed. Duke of Marlborough in the chair – merely to propose the Royal health.

Sir Mark Sykes seemed the most interesting man there. He did a very original caricature of F. E. Smith and me. I heard he was the best amateur actor in England. He certainly has brains, and political brains. Lutyens amiably played the amusing fool. I greatly enjoyed the affair.

Yacht Club, London, Friday, December 14th. – Had some talk with [D. S.] MacColl who was rather professional in appearance but not at all in ideas. He made one more real expert to confirm me in my anti-Sargent views. I spoke to him about his own water-colours and he said that the one that I liked took him half an hour, but that all his water-colours were chances – at any rate the sketches, and that the percentage of successes was about five only.

During the evening F. E. Smith, Attorney-General, rang me up – how he got hold of me God knows – and said: 'Will you go to the United States with me on Saturday morning?' He then spoke, low, some confidential remarks about his mission. I didn't catch them all and didn't get him to repeat them as I hadn't the slightest intention of going – especially for 2 months. He said: 'Nominally you'll be my secretary, but only nominally, of course.'

Although I like him as a companion I didn't see myself going to U.S.A. as F. E.'s secretary and boon companion. Still, he has considerable points.

Fog and mist, and a most damnable romantic London.

Yacht Club, London, Sunday, December 16th. – I worked most of yesterday at *The Pretty Lady* and got to the end of another chapter. Saw Chalmers Mitchell, H. G. Wells, and Massingham at the Reform. Dined at flat with M. and Richard (who came home yesterday) and then to Barrie's *Dear Brutus*, where we had seats in the back row of the dress circle. A great success and deserved. For a fanciful play the idea is A1 and it is worked out with much invention. As soon as I saw the scheme of the play I feared for the last Act. However the last Act was very good. I enjoyed the play nearly throughout.

On coming away, vast jostling crowds in the streets, and the feel of a tremendous city in the dark.

Yacht Club, London, Tuesday, December 18th. – To lunch at the Reform Club, where I joined Robert Ross who had two young poets, Robert Graves and Philip — (I forget his name [probably Philip Heseltine, who used the pseudonym Peter Warlock] and am not even sure if he is a poet). I was very pleased with both these youths. Lately I am more and more struck by the certainty, strength, and unconscious self-confidence of young men, so different from my middle-aged uncertainty and also my lack of physical confidence in my own body.

Yacht Club, Wednesday, December 19th. – To Turkish Baths. I was wakened out of my after-bath sleep by news of impending air-raid. This news merely made me feel gloomy. I didn't mind missing dinner at flat, or anything – I was merely gloomy. As soon as I got out into Northumberland Avenue I heard guns. Motors and people rushing. Then guns very close. I began to run. I headed for Reform Club, and abandoned idea of reaching the flat. Everybody ran. Girls ran.

However, I found that after the Turkish bath I couldn't run much in a heavy overcoat. So I walked. It seemed a long way. Guns momentarily ceased. So I didn't hurry and felt relieved. But still prodigiously gloomy. I reached the Club. Hall in darkness. No girls in coffee room. The menservants manfully tackled the few diners. Nothing could be had out of kitchen as kitchen under glass and deserted.

Comarques, Wednesday, December 26th. – I read a lot, all I shall read, of Saintsbury's *History of the French Novel*. Very prolix, and bursting with subordinate sentences and clauses, but containing plenty of useful information; also it shows that he does understand something of the craft of novel-writing. His tracing of the development of the technique of the novel in the 17th cent. is interesting, and, to me, quite new. The amount of this old man's reading is staggering.

Comarques, Thursday, December 27th. – Dinner last night at 2/1st London R.G.A. at Bentley Huts. Caffery came and fetched us in a Ford car. About 30 people. Goodish dinner. I did nothing all the evening except sit in front of the stove. Solo whist and bridge partners, and much noisy dancing. After midnight the Ford car could not be started, and it never was started, though 6 men spent pretty nearly 2 hours on it, with blowpipes and things. M. and Olive slept at Steel and Caffery's lodgings. I came home in a G.S. waggon with 2 horses and 2 men, easy chair in waggon, rugs, eiderdown, and a rug like an extinguisher all over my head and face. Freezing hard, but I was quite warm. This journey took about 1½ hours. I made the two men happy, and then had a hot bath, and must have gone to sleep about 4.40. I slept till 8. I was thoroughly bored until it was discovered that the car wouldn't start. Thenceforward I was quite cheerful.

·1918·

Comarques, Tuesday, January 1st. – Much work on the novel these last two days. I wrote 2,600 words yesterday. Last year I wrote 255,000 words. Not bad, considering the circumstances.

Comarques, Monday, January 7th. – 2,000 words of novel Saturday. 2,000 word article for *Daily News* yesterday, and a bad night in between. Sundry officers, including Saunders, Jacob, and Cummings, dined on Saturday night, and the delight of these two last in singing more or less at sight good and bad songs from the *Scottish Students' Song Book*, to my bad accompaniment, was most extraordinary. Last night Richard was talking about being set to learn 40 lines of 'L'Allegro' in 45 minutes prep, and to write essays in ten minutes. What a fool of a master. I couldn't find my Milton, but on my offering a reward of 6d., Richard found it. I re-read some of 'Paradise Lost', and thought it very fine and interesting. The remarks of Adam and the Angel about the relations of man and wife have not yet been beaten for sense.

Comarques, Tuesday, January 8th. – Another chapter of *The Pretty Lady* yesterday. Too much smoking, ostensibly to provide Richard with tobacco ash for chemical experiments.

I have read 100 pages or so of Hammond's *Town Labourer*. There is undoubtedly a pleasure in reading recitals of horrible injustice and tyranny.

Comarques, Wednesday, January 9th. – I didn't like reading the child-labour chapter in Hammond's *Town Labourer*. It exceeded the limits, in its physicalness. I wish I had read it before I wrote the child-chapter in *Clayhanger* to which the Hammonds refer. I could have made that chapter even more appalling than it is. But at that date probably all the materials had not been collected, as the Hammonds have since collected them.

Comarques, Monday, January 21st. – M. has now joined a
Y.M.C.A. canteen for soldiers coming home on leave, near
Waterloo Station. The hours were from 10.30 to 3 p.m., no
interval for lunch. She came home and said that 'any fool
could do the work' and that it was 'easy and interesting'. She
was going to undertake 4 hours on Tuesdays, Thursdays, and
Saturdays, going to town on Monday afternoons, thus leaving
only Sundays for Comarques. However, I stopped this. She
really began as a formal helper on Saturday. She was put on
to washing-up. She had a nice girl of 15 as colleague, very
smart. It seems they had to work at really top speed all the
time, in order to cope with the demand. This was for 3½ hours
– 11 to 2.30 or so. No interval of any kind for lunch, even a
sandwich, not 5 minutes. A cup of coffee brought to them,
from which they snatched sips. (No breakfast before starting.
No dinner in the evening owing to concert.) Standing all the
time. There is no doubt that she and all the other women think
this rather fine, but still she admitted that it was thoroughly
bad organization. Women do like this exhausting kind of
work. It wears them out and then they think they have done
something grand.

Comarques, Monday, January 28th. – To-day at lunch-time I
finished my novel *The Pretty Lady* – about 80,000 words. The
close seemed to me to be rather ingenious, well-executed, and
effective. But for years past I have ceased to try to judge the
value of a novel until it has been published for a year or two –
I mean one of my own. I thought *The Old Wives' Tale* was dull
when I had finished it.

Yacht Club, London, Wednesday, January 30th. – The Galsworthys and a Mrs Bainbridge came to dinner at the flat.
Air-raid maroon warning at about 10 p.m. We went down
into the Bank basement, which is well heated, and stayed till
12.30 a.m. Marguerite and the cook knitting. I noticed that
John was just as chivalrous to the cook as to any of the other
women. He even gave her a chocolate. The time passed
quickly, even on hard chairs. From time to time I went out.

The red warning with 'Take cover' on it, shone steadily at the intersection of Oxford St and Tottenham Court Rd. But people were walking about. Infrequent guns. Then the G.'s ventured to depart.

Yacht Club, London, Monday, February 11th. – I came up a day earlier in order to meet Grey at Spender's, as one of the 'Writers' Group'. Grey looked younger than I had expected. Hair scarcely grey. Trousers too wide. He played with a pencil-case half the time. He looked well, and spoke easily, clearly and well. We all sat in chairs in Spender's study in Sloane Street, surrounded by Spender's water-colours, some of which were very good. Grey said that both Italy and Roumania had not been asked to come in. They suggested coming in, and gave their terms, which in the main we had to agree to, in order to prevent them being inimically neutral, or, as regards Roumania, going over to the other side. He said that agreement with Russia as regards giving her Constantinople, was result of Turkey, after promising to be neutral, wantonly attacking her ports. He explained why none of the principal Governments *dared* make peace – they could offer nothing to their peoples to show for the war.

Yacht Club, London, Wednesday, February 20th. – We now ask nearly everyone whom we ask to dinner to bring some food. On Saturday I finished off the proofs of *The Pretty Lady*. I can now see things that I have left out of that novel. Nevertheless the story well held me as I read it again – a good test.

Yacht Club, London, Thursday, February 21st. – I lunched with Rosher to meet Kennedy Jones at Thatched House Club. He is a Glasgow man, aged 52, with pale eyes, and when talking he screws them up a little and looks far away as if cogitating on the most difficult and interesting aspects of what he is discussing. During the lunch he said that *he* was really the parent of the new journalism, because he was the journalist – and it was he who had gone to Northcliffe with the idea of buying the *Evening News*. This I fairly believed. He also drew out of his pocket a cutting from a Bristol newspaper about 7 ins. long of a speech of his. He said this showed what attention his remarks had in the Press. He spoke humorously, but was serious behind the humour, or he would not have pulled the thing out of his pocket at all. I laughed and said it proved nothing, because he could do what he liked with any newspaper. He laughed and said I was cynical.

He related stories of how American newspaper owners stole 'men' from each other, and how Hearst had stolen X. from Pulitzer, and Northcliffe had stolen him from Hearst, in each case after being specially requested not to do so. He said Northcliffe had taken on Wells for the *Mail* because he felt that 'new ideas' were coming, and he wanted to be able to say when they did come that he had favoured them, etc.

K. J. struck me as a powerful and ruthless man, but I wouldn't have any of his ruthlessness. When he was firm, I was firmer. In spite of the superior knowledge of which he boasts he has already lost 2 bets to Rosher, about the war. I wouldn't like to be one of his 'men', but he was interesting enough to meet.

Yacht Club, London, Wednesday, March 13th. – The 'Writers' Group' entertained Asquith at the Reform last night, and there was a very good dinner and plenty of various wines. Twelve people. Asquith looked very well. He came in a smoking jacket and a good soft silk shirt, but his overcoat and soft hat were ridiculous. Only Spender of the hosts was in evening dress. Asquith ate and drank and laughed well. He has a good 'contained' laugh at implications. He showed no signs of decay. He was surrounded by first-class men, some very first-class, but easily held his place as chief man.

Apropos of taxation Spender told a funny story. He said a Frenchman (official) in England had recently asked him for details of our income and super-tax. Spender gave them, but the Frenchman would not believe them. He could not credit the high rates, and demanded documentary proofs. When he got them and was convinced he exclaimed: 'Mais c'est l'anarchie !'

Comarques, Sunday, March 24th. – The great German offensive began on Thursday and yesterday. After various delays due to exhaustion and neuralgia, I began my new play. I wrote the first scene from 5 to 7 p.m.

Comarques, Monday, March 25th. – Second scene of play yesterday, but whereas the first scene was practically in final form, the second was only a draft. I couldn't get the ideas right; but as soon as I had finished it and was changing for dinner, I saw quite clearly what was up with it.

Tuesday, March 26th. – Brothers McKenna at Reform Club on bad war news. They came in together. I said 'The Brothers' and they sat down with me, and asked if I'd been to any newspaper offices to get news. 'My god! It's awful,' said Ernest, in a quiet, disgusted, intensely pessimistic tone. I referred to Spender's 2 articles that day. Ernest said Spender was a good man, kept his nerve – but Reginald looked at the first article, saw one line and said: 'Now, I need read nothing but that. The man who will say that –' etc. Ernest said: 'There's only one thing to do. Call Parliament together at once and get more men.' Reginald repeated this after him. They had evidently been long talking together and had exactly the same ideas on everything. 'Robertson was right. Jellicoe was right,' said Reggie oracularly. 'Robertson is on the beach. Jellicoe is on the beach. In order to be on the beach you only have to be absolutely right.'

Yacht Club, London, Wednesday, March 27th. – [Sydney] Webb said his wife couldn't sleep on account of the war news, and he had to exaggerate his usual tranquil optimism in order to keep the household together. It was one of the rare human touches I have noticed in the said household. However, they were soon off on to the misdeeds of the Reconstruction Committee. I was told that certain of the staff of the 'Department of Information' had resigned when Beaverbrook was appointed Minister over them, refusing to serve under 'that ignorant man'. They won, and were transferred to the Foreign Office – one more instance of the hand-to-mouthism of Ll. George.

Sybil Colefax gave a very good description of the All Clear Signal in a few words at dinner. She said she was walking with her husband in the streets towards the end of a raid. Everything was quite silent. Then the searchlights began winking the 'All clear' all about the sky. Then the sound of the 'All clear' bugles was heard. Then the footsteps of a man. Then the footsteps of ten people, of twenty, of a hundred. The town was alive again.

April 4th. House of Commons. – Lloyd George's introduction of Man Power Bill, for conscripting Ireland and raising military age etc. Policeman looks at card outside. Then you go up in a lift. Through an outer room with one or two journalists, hat pegs, etc. Then an inner room, with two Morse instruments tapping, and then into Gallery, at entrance of which your ticket is looked at again by an official (very friendly with all reporters, and doing their little errands etc.) in evening dress with a large insignia on his breast.

Two rows of seats with narrow desk all round. A few standing at either corner, including Spender, Gardiner, and me. Reporters passing in and out all the time, crushing past; a horrible lack of space. No light in House of Commons except through glass roof. No repose in Press Gallery. Sharp corner of elaborate wood carving against which you knock your head if you sit or lean in corners. Cheap effects of Ll. G. looking round as if challenging; trick of dropping his voice for last, rather important word of sentence. Unpleasant Nonconformist voice.

He did not know his case, and having made a muddle deliberately left the muddle. Truisms about values and will-to-win cheered. Proposal to conscript Ireland loudly cheered a long time by Tories. No applause as he sat down. The whole thing a vast make-believe, with an audience of which a large part was obviously quite unintelligent and content with the usual hollow rot. Ll. G.'s oratorical effects very poor – like a Lyceum melodrama. Asquith with long hair very dignified, at home, and persuasive.

Yacht Club, London, Wednesday, April 10th. – Too much occupied and preoccupied with the British defeats, the Government proposals for increasing the army, the publication of *The Pretty Lady*, political journalism, the gardening and household difficulties, chill on the entrails, neuralgia, insomnia, Marguerite's illness, the nightly rehearsals in the small drawing-room of a play for a Red Cross performance at Clacton, and my new play – to be bothered with this journal or with notes of any kind. However, I did at last, in spite of all distractions, get my play going, and it *is* going.

Meeting of British War Memorial Committee this afternoon. Beaverbrook arrived. He told me that he liked *The Pretty Lady* better than any other book of mine, and better than any other modern book. As regards sales I hear that it is 'doing very nicely'.

Maurice Baring and F. Swinnerton dined with me to-night at Yacht Club. After F. S. had gone, Maurice grew communicative about the war. Knows Haig. Thinks him a real personality, with decision, grit, and power of command. Never rattled. A good soldier; but not a genius. Henry Wilson a wind-bag. He spoke in the *highest* terms of Trenchard, chief of Air Service; also very highly of Cox, chief of Intelligence. He said that Gough and others protested against having to take over extra front, as ordered by War Cabinet. Gough's front was under-manned and under-gunned. No reserves in France. Depots empty. Ll. G. always refused to look at facts, but liked ideas, grandiose, etc. for new stunt. Gave particulars of how Northcliffe had announced months ago that Robertson would be attacked and have to go; ditto in regard to Spring Rice. Cabinet did not believe in German offensive. Soldiers did.

Haig told Cabinet long ago facts as to inferiority in man-power, and expected them to be frightened out of their lives. They were not, as they did not believe in offensive. He expected an attack on Haig next. He didn't think we should lose war, – we could hold on and Germans would crack. He said that Haig had no desire to conceal the facts as to lack of troops, and spoke freely of them and permitted others to do so. Unfortunately of course one can't print the facts; although the Germans probably knew them pretty well.

Yacht Club, London, Thursday, April 11th. – I went to see Beaverbrook this morning to ascertain, in view of the fact that I am to write for *Lloyd's Weekly News*, whether he was going to buy the paper, and if so whether he meant to change the politics. He said he wasn't going to buy it. Before this Beaverbrook asked me to accept the directorship of British propaganda in France. After objecting, I said I would think it over and let him know. He said no one could know French psychology better than I do – this conclusion he drew from reading *The Pretty Lady*! Rothermere was in the room before we began business, walking about, sitting down, standing up. He wanted a holiday. I told him it would pay him to take one. He said he couldn't. 'Here's this great united Air Force of 170,000 men just come into existence. I can't leave the baby.'

Comarques, Tuesday, April 16th. – On Sunday I wrote to Beaverbrook agreeing to his request that I should enter Ministry of Information in order to direct British propaganda in France.

Yacht Club, London, Friday, April 19th. – Yesterday morning I drafted the whole of the second Act of the new play. Lunch at Reform, where Spender was exceedingly good and Davray exceedingly emotional. In the afternoon I wrote a preface for the Catalogue of Paul Nash's exhibition. I dined with the Nicholsons at the Café Royal grill. Lutyens and Mrs Stuart-Wortley were there. The latter nervous and quiet. The former full of puns and tiny jokes, but agreeable and ready to stand being teased. Then I saw Nicholson privately as to his proposed work for Memorials Committee and his situation in the army. Before going to bed I wrote a report on this for the Committee. A day! Last night the new Military Service Act became law, and I am now legally, at nearly 51 years, in the Army Reserve.

Comarques, Sunday, April 28th. – I read a lot of *A Dreary Story* of Tchekoff in the night. I had read it once or twice before. It now seems to me quite fresh, full of new powers and beauties, and one of the finest things I ever did read.

Yacht Club, London, Friday, May 10th. – I finished my play *The Title* on Wednesday, but in order to do so I had to knock myself up and also to inform people with whom I had appointments in London that I was laid aside with a chill. I wrote the last act in four days' actual work.

Yesterday I came to London to take up my duties as head of the French section of the Propaganda Department of the Ministry of Information. On the whole the first day was rather a lark. It began with a lunch to allied journalists, where I sat between *Le Journal* and *Le Petit Parisien*, and had the *Débats* opposite. I didn't like my room, nor my staff being on different floors from me.

Night: Dinner of the Other Club. I made the acquaintance of Smuts. He has a peculiar accent (foreign) and puts his hand on your knee constantly while talking to you. A man of principles, and a fine man; but I doubt if he is the great man some of us thought. He was quite serene about the approaching end of the war.

Yacht Club, London, Saturday, May 11th. – Dined at F. E. Smith's. An enormous house, considering it isn't a special house, but only at the corner of a row (32, Grosvenor Gardens). The library is even equal to his boastings about it, but he would continually refer to prices. What astonished me was that he does not keep even really valuable books (from £100 to £2,000 apiece) under glass. He was greatly amusing over incidents of his American trip, and especially as to how he and his brother Harold, in one of the dryest States, Nebraska, made the Professor of Rhetoric at some University drunk – although this Professor was the origin of the dryness. They drank to the great orators, and then to the stars of American literature. At the end the Professor said of F. E. 'The most brilliant man I ever met,' and later, to friends, he said of F. E. 'He is a *whale*.'

Yacht Club, London, Tuesday, May 14th. – Did 4 hours' hard work at the Ministry. I have now abandoned literature until either I am chucked out of the job, or the job ends, or I am called to a better one. But I do journalism, and a damned nuisance it is.

Yacht Club, London, Tuesday, June 4th. – In arranging for the King to attend Westminster Abbey on France's Day I thought I had set in motion a great thing to my credit. It was not so. I was misled. I took things for granted, made mistakes on them, and the whole affair had to be cancelled. Religion was at the bottom of the trouble. Hence the trouble.

Yacht Club, London, Tuesday, July 2nd. – Last night I dined with Beaverbrook, the Edwin Montagus and Diana Manners being of the party, at the Savoy. Dinner arranged for 9 p.m. At 9.15 Montagu and I having waited, began. The rest arrived at 9.20. When the conversation turned on Diana being the original of Queen in *The Pretty Lady* my attitude was apparently so harsh that Beaverbrook changed the subject. We afterwards went 5 in a taxi to B.'s rooms at Hyde Park Hotel. After a time Diana and I sat on window-sill of B.'s bedroom, looking at the really superb night view over the park. One small light burning in the bedroom. B.'s pyjamas second-rate. Some miscellaneous talk about life and women. After they had all gone but me B. asked me what I thought of Diana. I told him I thought she was unhappy, through idleness. He said he liked her greatly.

Yacht Club, London, Thursday, July 18th. – Minute from War Cabinet yesterday censuring me for my most successful pro-France article in the *Observer* on Sunday. It had been used on Monday by *Daily Mail* as an axe to hit the Government with about 'baleful secrecy'. Lord B. was furious, and asked me to write a pungent letter in reply, which he signed. By evening Ll. G. had apologized and promised to have a new minute of the Cabinet prepared.

Yacht Club, London, Tuesday, October 8th. – Nigel Playfair told me he was trying to get the Lyric Opera House at Hammersmith for what is wrongly called a Repertory Theatre. He had got the rent promised, but one of the London ring of managers had made a bid over his head, without even having seen the theatre, just in order to keep the ring closed. Playfair didn't know whether he would get the place after all. I told him if he did I might collect £2,000 for him.

Yacht Club, London, Tuesday, October 15th. – Reflection upon the German answer to Wilson's reply to their request for an armistice made me think the end of the war was getting very near, and that the whole policy of the M. of Information would have to be swung round. I drafted a Minute before catching train; Mair added to it a little, and when I showed it to Beaverbrook in the evening he said he would use it as a Minute to the Cabinet. For me there was already an air of unreality in the wish of the Ministry, and especially about our scheme for re-organising it.

Yacht Club, London, Saturday, October 19th. Rothermere gave a dinner in my honour at the Marlborough Club last night. He chose his company in the most extraordinary way. Australian Hughes, a good talker, sheer brass, but a good slashing talker; very deaf, with an apparatus looking like a rather large Kodak closed, on the table, and a flex from it to his ear. Henry Dalziel, a bluff person, not without a certain attractiveness. Hulton. Andrew Caird, manager of the *Daily Mail*, bluff and decent and crude, but clever. He told me everything I already knew about propaganda after dinner. Churchill. Blumenfeld, somewhat quiet. F. E. Smith came very late and said little. Churchill talked the best. I like Rothermere. He told me he wanted to sell all his papers except the *Sunday Pictorial*. He said he had worked hard since he was 14, and if a man had succeeded and chose to slave as hard as ever after 50, it merely proved that that man didn't understand life. He was turned 50.

Yacht Club, London, Sunday, October 27th. – The sensual appeal is now really very marked everywhere, in both speech and action, on the stage. Adultery everywhere pictured as desirable, and copulation generally ditto. Actresses play courtesan parts (small ones, often without words but with gestures) with gusto.

Yacht Club, London, Tuesday, October 29th. – News of Austrian separate demand for armistice yesterday afternoon. I heard a newsman in Oxford Street cry: '*Evenin' News.* Last edition. All abaht it. To-night's and to-morrow night's too. Only one German left.'

Committee meeting in the morning at which I preside. About 30 present. Masterman insisted on the dangerousness of our handling and spreading documentary peace terms which the Government had approved but would not publicly approve and certainly would not publish. Suppose these came out. He called them Trinitrotoluol. He didn't seem to see that this was one of the essential, primary risks that a Ministry of Information must take.

Yacht Club, London, Wednesday, October 30th. – I was summoned to Beaverbrook yesterday. He was in bed, bandaged, depressed, having been told by the doctor in the morning that he had septic poisoning. When Lady B. and Needham had left the room, he began to smoke and to talk intimately, and said: 'You know, Arnold, my life has been all crises. I was worth 5 millions when I was 27. And now this is a new crisis, and it's the worst.' However, he cheered up. Bonar Law came in and was very courteous and cautious to me. He said his sister had been a very great and constant admirer of mine, but since *The Pretty Lady* she had done with me.

Beaverbrook's resignation in the papers. I got instructions to carry on.

Yacht Club, London, Thursday, October 31st. – Dined at Barrie's and saw his Lutyens room. Good, short dinner. He told me that he didn't smoke till 23, and that he wrote *My Lady Nicotine* before he had ever smoked. He said when he first came to London, he dined on 2*d.* a day (four halfpenny buns or scones) for a year, eating them in the street, and ate little else. He wrote about two articles a day and sold about one in six. He found at the end of the year that he needn't have been so economical; but he was afraid of the rainy day. He said it took a long time for him to see that there was any material in Scotland. He wrote *An Auld Licht Wedding* and sold it, and thought he had exhausted Scotland. Next few articles he didn't sell, and then an editor said: 'We liked your Scotch stuff.' So he wrote *An Auld Licht Funeral*. And so on.

He told us that he had had Asquith and Birrell to dinner the other night and had arranged with Asquith's daughter-in-law and another female friend that they should dress up as house-maids and serve the dinner. They did so. The daughter-in-law wore a black wig. Neither Birrell nor Asquith recognized the women. But after dinner, in the drawing-room, Asquith said: 'One of those maids is extraordinarily like my daughter-in-law.' Barrie told this practical joke with great restraint and humour.

Yacht Club, London, Wednesday, November 6th. – On Monday at lunch at the Reform I learnt the details of the secret history of Northcliffe's encyclical to the newspapers of the world about the proper peace terms with Germany. According to C. M. [Charles Masterman] the idea of the letter was not N.'s at all, but C. M. got Campbell Stuart to persuade him to do it. Stuart took N. out to lunch for that purpose. The thing was written by C. M., but the style being too good, it was re-written down to some resemblance of Northcliffe's supposed style. Northcliffe then signed it and immediately went off to Paris (where, as Beaverbrook told me last night at dinner, Lloyd George took good care not to see him at all) to be near the scene of the armistice negotiations.

Yacht Club, London, Thursday, November 7th. – Yesterday afternoon I arranged with Alistair Tayler that he should join the Board (Playfair and I being the others) of the Hammer-smith Lyric Theatre Enterprise, and that I should be the Chairman.

Yacht Club, London, Friday, November 8th. – Yesterday afternoon my secretary was twice rung up by officials at the War Office to know if the war was over – that is, if the armistice was signed. The rumours were immense and numerous.

Yacht Club, London, Tuesday, November 12th. – In Sunday's papers we saw the Abdication of the Kaiser. Returned to town yesterday morning. In Lower Regent Street first news that armistice signed – a paper boy calling out in a subdued tone. 10.45. Maroons went off at 11, and excited the populace.

A large portion of the Ministry staff got very excited. Buchan came in to shake hands. Girls very excited. I had to calm them. Lunch at Wellington Club. We had driven through large crowds part way up the Mall, and were then turned off from Buckingham Palace.

Raining now. An excellent thing to damp hysteria and Bolshevism. Great struggling to cross Piccadilly Circus twice. No buses. (It was rumoured that Tubes stopped. I believe they were stopped for a time.) It stopped raining. Then cold mire in streets. Vehicles passed festooned with shouting human beings. Others, dark, with only one or two occupants. Much light in Piccadilly up to Ritz corner, and in Piccadilly Circus. It seemed most brilliant. Some theatres had lights on their façades too. The enterprising Trocadero had hung a row of temporary lights under one of its porticoes. Shouting. But nothing terrible or memorable. Yet this morning Brayley, my valet, said to me the usual phrases: 'You wondered where the people came from. You could walk on their heads at Charing Cross, and you couldn't cross Picc. Circus at all.' When he came in with my tea I said: 'Well, Brayley, it's all over.' He smiled and said something. That was all our conversation about the end of the war. Characteristic.

Last night I thought of lonely soldiers in that crowd. No one to talk to. But fear of death lifted from them.

Yacht Club, London, Thursday, November 14th. – I dined at flat on Tuesday night (Pinker there) and slept there, so I didn't see anything of the 'doings'. But there was a bonfire in Piccadilly

Circus, kept alive by theatre boards and boards off motor-buses. Girls are still very prominent in the 'doings'. Swinnerton told me that the staidest girl they had suddenly put on a soldier's hat and overcoat and went promenading in it.

Was told that the scene at the Carlton on Monday night was remarkable. Any quantity of broken glasses, tables over-turned, and people standing on tables, and fashionable females with their hair down. On Tuesday night I noticed that all the principal restaurants had commissionaires in front of doors scrutinizing people who wished to enter and keeping out (apparently) all who had not reserved tables. Last night a cabby told me he would go Westwards but not towards Picca-dilly Circus as he did not know what would happen to him.

The feature of last night was girls with bunches of streamers which they flicked in your face as you passed.

Yacht Club, London, Friday, November 15th. – My resignation from Ministry took effect yesterday. Buchan, the liquidator, came down to see me, and was very explanatory and apologetic. The behaviour of the Cabinet to me was of course scandalous. But they have treated many others similarly, so I was not surprised. The only notice I got was a Ronco'd copy of the War Cabinet Minute. I was never consulted in any way.

Yacht Club, London, Tuesday, November 19th. – I went to Wells's alone for the week-end. Second time I have gone away alone because M. could not leave her dogs.

Yacht Club, London, Tuesday, November 26th. – Week-end at Beaverbrook's, Cherkley Court. Good, except that not enough food, B. not being interested in food. The Hultons came over on Sunday afternoon and stayed to dinner. Hulton had been trained for the R.C. priesthood. An agreeable pair. He with a certain sense of decency, not a fool, a Lancashire accent and rather ignorant. For example, he had never heard of the Labour Party programme!

I read B.'s printed account of the conspiracy that overthrew Asquith in Dec. 1916. It was exceedingly well written, and showed great judgement of men and some sense of historical values. In fact it was remarkable and heightened my originally high opinion of Beaverbrook. The War Office and Ll. G. both came badly out of the account, especially the former. B.'s own share in the affair is kept very modestly in the background. He seemed almost inclined to publish it in the *Daily Express*. I advised him against this.

Yacht Club, London, Tuesday, December 10th. – Week-end at Dr F. Keeble's at Weybridge. Lillah McCarthy also there. In spite of my neuralgia we had a great week-end, full of good and not too serious conversation. I promised to write her a play on the subject of Judith, if a firm contract was made at once. In fact I constructed the play on the spot, after having read *Judith* myself and having heard it read by Keeble. (Some difficulty in getting an 'Apocrypha'.)

Yacht Club, London, Saturday, December 14th. – Interview with Lillah McCarthy and Drinkwater at Adelphi Terrace at 12.45. I promised to write *Judith* by the end of January, and they promised to produce *Don Juan* also. In the afternoon Captain Basil Dean came to see me about his London theatrical scheme. He said he could get and control £20,000. I definitely promised to write a play for *him*, too. This with Goodall's, Vedrenne's and Lillah's, makes 4 plays!

We dined at the Galsworthys, Grove Lodge, Hampstead, and the Masefields were there. Mrs M. and I got on excellently. Masefield gloomyish, and very precise in diction. Fine voice. Diction of a public speaker. Galsworthy very nice. Ada Galsworthy adorable.

Yacht Club, London, Thursday, December 19th. – I met a Captain Griffin (from Walsall) at Reform yesterday, with Shufflebotham. He had been wounded 9 times, I think, prisoner in Germany. Was reported dead. After he returned to life, his solicitor among other bills forwarded the following: 'To Memorial Service (fully choral) 3 guineas.'

·1919·

Comarques, Saturday, January 11th. – Having given up all the work except 'Observations' for the *New Statesman* I came to Comarques on Saturday last, 4th inst., with the intention of writing *Judith*, the play for Lillah McCarthy, and finishing it before 7th February. I began it on Sunday, 5th inst., and to-night, 11th, I finished the first act.

Last year, in spite of the fact that I was engaged officially at the M. of Information for 7 or 8 months, I wrote 165,700 words of my own stuff.

Comarques, Tuesday, January 28th. – I finished *Judith* yesterday at 7.30, having written it in twenty-three days. I had several very slight headaches, but no dyspepsia worth a damn. Nervous dyspepsia did give indications of attacking me, but the mysterious and expensive tablets which I got kept me in excellent order.

Comarques, Saturday, February 8th. – *Judith* was delivered yesterday week. On Tuesday Marguerite met Lillah McCarthy, who nearly fell on her neck in the street, from enthusiasm about the play. Eaton also wrote to me that he was 'violently enthusiastic' about it.

These two and old Drinkwater came to dinner at the new flat on Tuesday last. Drinkwater said nothing good or bad as to the play until late in the evening, when I asked him.

He then said indifferently that he liked it, but didn't care much for the last act, or words to that effect.

Comarques, Sunday, February 16th. – I am chiefly occupied with the stage. I give a considerable amount of time to the Lyric, Hammersmith, where money has been lost in my absence owing to the lavish expenditure. And I am also being drawn into the production part of *Judith*. Lillah McC., Drinkwater, Eaton and I, had a séance of nearly three hours on Tuesday about the cast.

Comarques, Monday, March 3rd. – On the 1st I began my book on women, but I only wrote about 100 words. I meant to go on with it yesterday, but couldn't. After muddling about nearly all day I began at 5 p.m. and wrote 600 good words before dinner. The book is now really begun.

Yacht Club, London, Wednesday, March 5th. – A. E. W. Mason told us some of his secret service adventures in Mexico. He was very good as a *raconteur*, and evidently has a great gift for secret service, though he said he began as an amateur.

Mason said that practically all the German spies and many of the Zeppelin men carried a packet of obscene photographs on their persons. I fully expected he would laugh at the reputation of the German Secret Service for efficiency, and he did. I felt sure the German temperament is not a good secret service temperament. Too gullible and talkative. Mason said their secret service was merely expensive. Money chucked away idiotically.

Comarques, Friday, April 11th. – To Eastbourne last Saturday for the first production of *Judith* (Devonshire Park Theatre).

Lillah McCarthy behaved well, considering her double anxiety of manager and star, – both as it were making a fresh start in life. Lillah had there Dr Keeble (her fiancé), her mother, her sister, and a niece and nephew offspring of another sister (or brother). All these were all over the theatre all the time. She protested that all the creative producing work had been done by me, M. and her. I had to put this right. Ernest Thesiger, the Bagoas, grew sterner as the hour of performance came nearer. I don't think he smiled on Monday at all. He is really an artist. He gave a magnificent performance. Esmé Hubbard (Haggith) remained light and merry throughout, and gave a magnificent performance. Fredk. Volpé (Ingur) behaved rather like Thesiger and was very fine.

Evidently Lillah is used to authors who will stand no damned nonsense. She got rather excited after both 2nd and 1st performances because Bagoas's rushing forth and killing a spying woman detracted from her kissing Holofernes, and she had to be soothed. Her tent costume frightened one of the lessees of the theatre. Above a line drawn about ½ inch or 1 inch above the '*mont de Vénus*' she wore nothing except a 4-in. band of black velvet round the body hiding the breasts and a similar perpendicular band of velvet starting from between the breasts and going down to the skirt and so hiding the navel. Two thin shoulder straps held this contrivance in position. Bracelets and rings of course. The skirt was slit everywhere and showed the legs up to the top of the thigh when she lay down there at Holofernes' feet. She looked a magnificent picture thus, but a police prosecution would not have surprised me at all. She gave an exceedingly fine performance – as good as could be wished for. The house was very full for the first night.

Comarques, Sunday, May 4th. – I never before took so much interest in the production of a play of mine. *Judith* was produced at the Kingsway Theatre, London, last Wednesday, 30th April. It certainly bewildered people. Numerous comic touches were quite lost in the 1st act. In the 2nd act Lillah McCarthy had put down her dress as low as it was at the first night at Eastbourne (after raising it for later performances at Eastbourne, and for dress rehearsals in London). The end of Act II might have been spoilt by an untimely descent of the curtain 10 seconds too soon. The performance as a whole was excellent. The disinterested applause was fair. The interested friendly applause was too insistent. House held over £150, the highest first night the Kingsway ever had, I think. The ordinary first night public was *dérouté*. Common people seemed thoroughly interested and well pleased.

The Press criticisms next day were without exception unfavourable. The Sunday criticisms that I have seen were not bad, though there was much exception taken to Lillah's nudity in Act II. In general the Press quite failed to comprehend the play, and said the most ridiculous things about it, showing immense stupidity.

Yacht Club, London, Thursday, May 8th. – Came to London on Tuesday after a week-end in which I did nothing but get up to date with my things. Saw *Judith* on Tuesday night. The news that Hardy was enthusiastic about the play gave me more satisfaction than anything that has happened to me for a long time.

Yacht Club, London, Wednesday, May 14th. – Constant insomnia. Doing nothing except the series of articles about women, which I shall be immensely relieved to finish. Then a year of plays. Seeing Rickards weekly.

The receipts of *Judith* were just under £900 last week, the first complete week. Marguerite began to be less sure about its success. I know that there is too much psychological realism in the play to please a large section of the public. On Monday night the receipts fell to £56. This was a bombshell, especially for Marguerite. We knew after this that the play must be regarded as a failure.

Yacht Club, London, Friday, May 30th. – H. G.'s *The Undying Fire* came along. The machinery of it is bad and unconvincing, but the stuff is good. I hope to finish my damnable, pedestrian, fair-minded, sagacious *Woman* book on Monday.

Comarques, Monday, June 2nd. – To-day at 4.30 I finished my book about women. I haven't yet come to any conclusion as to its value. I now have 3 plays to write in the next nine months, all commissioned; and fortunately I have nothing else.

Yacht Club, London, Thursday, June 5th. – Dined at Osbert Sitwell's. Good dinner. Fish before soup. Present, W. H. Davies, Lytton Strachey, Woolf, Nichols, S. Sassoon, Aldous Huxley, Atkin (a very young caricaturist), W. J. Turner, and Herbert Read (a very young poet). The faces of Woolf, Atkin, and Read, were particularly charming in their ingenuousness. Davies I liked. He had walked all the way from Tottenham Court Road to Swan Walk. A house with much better pictures and bric-à-brac than furniture. In fact there was scarcely any what I call furniture. But lots of very modern pictures, of which I liked a number. Bright walls and bright cloths and bright glass everywhere. A fine Rowlandson drawing. Osbert is young. He is already a very good host. I enjoyed this evening, though I knew I should have indigestion after the creamy sweet, and I have got it.

I dined with Garvin to-night at the Café Royal. Knoblock also there. Garvin said: 'I said to Ll. George, "The 19th century was the transfer of the vote. The 20th century will be the transfer of profit." He was rather struck by that. I'd given him something portable.'

A. told the greatest theatrical story I ever heard. He said that X., talking about why he had refused to play in a certain play, said to him: 'You may think I'm conceited, but I felt the public would never understand a girl preferring anybody else to me.'

Yacht Club, London, Wednesday, June 18th. – Basil Dean told a good rehearsal story. He said that they rehearsed Shaw's *Pygmalion* for 9 weeks at His Majesty's and that in the middle Mrs Pat Campbell went away for two weeks on her honeymoon. When she returned she merely said by way of explanation: 'George (her new husband) is a golden man.' There was some trouble about her rendering. When she had altered it she said to Shaw, 'Is that better?' Shaw said: 'No, it isn't. I don't want any of your flamboyant creatures, I want a simple human ordinary creation such as I have drawn.' He was getting shirty. Mrs P. C. was taken aback. She replied, however: 'You are a terrible man, Mr Shaw. One day you'll eat a beefsteak and then God help all women.' It is said that Shaw blushed.

Yacht Club, London, June 19th. – Masterman and I got Barrie to lunch at Reform Club. He remained very quiet for nearly 2 hours, and then began to talk about the cricket team that he used to organize. For about 10 minutes he was brilliant.

George St, Hanover Sq., Wednesday, July 9th. – Official religious celebrations took place last Sunday. Official pagan celebrations will take place on Saturday, 19th, but the chief interest of an enlightened public has been the lawn tennis championships, and the Transatlantic voyage of R. 34. My chief interest has been my new play, of which I started the actual writing on Thursday; and the process of getting fixed in this flat – interminable. However, the play is so interesting that I don't mind sleepless hours in the night, as I can think about it and see part of it.

Comarques, Tuesday, July 22nd. – Marguerite came home yesterday from the Peace Celebrations on Saturday. She said, '*Tu n'as pas idée.* The air was positively *warm* with the *frénésie* of the reception of the procession.' The only thing that happened at Thorpe was that the village mob threw an adulterer into the mill pond because he'd attacked the woman's husband. They would have lowered him into a well but they couldn't find a rope.

Dublin, August 30th. – Yesterday I went to see George Russell (Æ) in the morning at Plunkett House – 3rd floor, editorial offices of *The Homestead.* Susan Mitchell there as sub-editor. Russell very untidy. Longish beard. Gleaming glasses. He said he could not stand the dullness of the walls. So he had given 4 afternoons to painting the whole of them with figures and landscapes.

Russell said he had said to Yeats that Moore's *Hail and Farewell* was the finest biography Yeats would ever have.

Dublin, August 31st. – Yesterday morning with O'Connor and Bodkin to National Gallery, where James Stephens is Registrar. A little thin man, untidy, strange accent, with a continuous flow of ideas and fancies. He said '*The O.W. Tale* was "It", but *The Pretty Lady* was "itter",' and he put it at the top of all modern fiction. (On the other hand, a society journalist at the Races in the afternoon said to someone, who told me, that Elinor Glyn would have given the story 'a more human touch'.) Stephens seemed to me to be a stronger man than I had thought. He said that anybody who re-wrote Doyle's detective stories from the standpoint of psychoanalysis would make a vast fortune.

Liverpool, September 4th. – At 6 I went down to the Pier Head and witnessed the departure of a liner, the *Canada*. Boats of all sorts, rafts. Passengers all packed on starboard rails. Crows-nest. Going and coming over gangway seemed as if it would never cease. Absurd tiny fluttering of handkerchiefs. Then drawing in of hawsers. Bell ringing. Band: 'Auld Lang Syne'. She slipped away. No perceptible movement of propellers, but the helm moved. She just grazed floating outposts of landing-stage. A tug joined her and closed her. Many other steamers made much smoke obscuring her and the distance. She seemed to stop in mid-stream a few hundred yards down, the tug hugging her starboard bow. People said she would wait there till midnight. It was a moving sight.

Liverpool, September 6th. – W. G. Fay came to dine with me last night. He entered the hotel and then the restaurant with almost as much modesty and diffidence as if he had never had any experience at all. He said he was not interested in money and had kept all his simple habits. He told me how he and his brother had started a theatre in Liverpool with £5 capital each which they previously had to work for and save. They took a hall and made the seating themselves. He said his father was a civil servant and he was to have been one, but he failed at the preliminary and hated it. During his first theatrical enterprise he worked as an electrician in Dublin from 8 to 6. Then worked on his theatre from 8 to 11, and then would go and talk to Yeats or Martin or Russell till 2 or 3 a.m. He said the opposition to the *Playboy* was indirectly due to the opposition to *The Well of the Saints*. The opposition to the latter made Synge say: 'I'll write something that *will* make 'em sit up.' He wrote the *Playboy* and it *did* make 'em sit up. He said that at the first night not a word could be heard after the first three minutes. All had to be in dumb show. Later he had policemen to chuck out the worst rowdies. Then the theatre was empty. But he kept open, playing to £2 or £3 a week. He stopped all newspaper advertisements and hoarding advts. and kept on. He used to invite the audience to collect in the first row of the stalls. He lost many of his friends and has never got some of them back. After 6 months the newspapers asked for seats. He said they must pay. They said they wanted his advts. back. He said they would have the advts. on condition that they didn't say in the paper that his theatre was empty. He would let them slang his plays and his players, but not say that his theatre was empty. Then the hoarding people came and made peace. He won out. It seems that Yeats, Lady G[regory] and Synge were directors at this time.

This man was a hero and never shows. He is full of creative ideas about the theatre.

Comarques, Friday, September 19th. – *Sacred and Profane Love* was produced at the Playhouse, Liverpool, last Monday 15th, at 7.30. The audience laughed when Iris Hoey called out 'I cannot bear it' as the hero was playing the piano. True, the playing was appallingly bad. This ruined the first Act Sc. 1. Act 1 Sc. 2 went perfectly. The hold of the play gradually increased on the audience, and at the close an emphatic success was undeniable. I took a call because I had to. Then I had to take a second call. A thing I never did before.

London, Tuesday, January 6th. – At the Garrick last night Mair told us that he was absolutely sure that Shaw had not been an ascetic. Also he said that, in reply to an American criticism to the effect that when talking about love G. B. S. did not know what he was talking about, G. B. S. wrote to the paper to say that few people could possess greater practical experience as amorists than he possessed. This found us very startled and Anthony Hope incredulous, but Mair reiterated that he was quite sure. As to Shaw's amorism. It occurs to me that only a practical man would have written the 1st act of *Man and Superman*.

January 11th. – Symphony concert yesterday at Queen's Hall with Sassoon and E. M. Forster. Henry Wood having a chill, Frank Bridge conducted in his place at a few hours' notice. After Schubert C major symphony, much applause at such good conducting at such short notice. Members of the orchestra applauded their conductor, and there was general mutual applause. Sassoon said: 'I often wish when all these mutual compliments are going on they'd give the composer a show. Instead of pointing to the orchestra, why doesn't the conductor hold up the score and show it to the audience.'

London, March 9th. – Lately we have seen 3 revivals. *Arms and the Man* seemed better than it did 25 years ago. Very fine. Shaw's title to be the modern Molière not so rocky as I had thought. On the other hand *Pygmalion* is on the whole poor. Most of the characterization is quite rotten, and wilfully made so for the sake of art and eloquence. The last act is foozled. Mrs Campbell was superb. There is still nobody else to touch her. Last night *The Admirable Crichton*. Excellent. I liked it better than when I first saw it, much better.

London, Wednesday, March 10th. – Philippe and Hélène Berthelot came for dinner last night. Berthelot said that he read from 11 to midnight. Then worked from 12 to 3 writing out his telegrams, and got up at 7.30. He had done this for six years – I think he said without a break. He talked exceedingly well, indeed perfectly, rather in the manner of Cambon. All his judgements seemed to be quite detached and fair. But you could see he was the official, crafty, urbane, and also good-natured. He told several funny stories, two pathetic ones, quoted *mots*, quoted poetry; and poured my best champagne into a tumbler of water; didn't smoke; and left at 10.30, having given us a most finished entertainment.

On the other hand, he never once showed the slightest curiosity about anything whatever outside his own sphere of action – not the slightest. He had a great notion of Ll. George's agility of mind, and quickness to grasp new ideas. He said that among the big men at the Conference, Clémenceau was the only one who thought only of his country. (True, I imagine. But I wish he had thought of it differently.) He was politely fierce against Hoover, while recognizing his value. Of Wilson he said that during the war he had all his immense correspondence from persons unknown to him classified regionally etc., and got local people to report on the senders, and thus arrived at a notion of what public opinion was in each district, and suited his political arguments to that district, and thus in the end managed to bring U.S.A. into the war. I thought this rather good, but Berthelot despised it, and implied that a truly great man would convert the state of public opinion by means within his own mind, not employing machinery.

As a fact, Berthelot has little use for public opinion. He said: 'On peut toujours s'asseoir dessus.' He said that Wilson had got on by failing at everything: the Bar, university, New Jersey, etc.; and that some people *did* get on like that: which is true. His judgement on the man's double quality – idealistic, and yet ruthless in affairs – was excellent. But he didn't seem to realize that this judgement doesn't dispose of the Americans and of their future predominance. You can understand the secret disdain of such a highly-cultured, broad-minded, efficient, conscientious and industrious man, descendant of a great father and the finest civilization, for the crudeness and mental slovenliness of representatives of U.S.A. and even of England. And he gave us a great show.

London, Tuesday, March 16th. – Saturday. Knoblock's play *Mumsee*. Little Theatre. After the first night he cut off the last (fourth) act entirely. Which leaves the play ending in a raw stump. It is astounding how people can do these things, with apparently no sense of the fact that they are butchers.

London, Saturday, March 20th. – Yesterday morning, after careering in the park after play-ideas and catching them, I went to Neville Lewis's show and bought a small picture of a woman suckling a child (portrait of Madame Litvinoff) for 15 guineas. Clifton, with whom I had a talk, told me of the times when Johns could be bought for 10 guineas – and damned few buyers. He said he had once sold a very large pastel of John's for 10 guineas to a woman and had never heard of it since.

I heard yesterday that the first week's receipts of *Sacred and Profane Love* in New York were over 16,700 dollars. This easily bangs *Milestones* and all my other records. My royalties on that week exceed £350. My faith in the theatre as a means of artistic expression was of course instantly re-established. It would be.

London, Sunday, March 21st. – Yesterday morning I wrote the first scene of 2nd act of the play which for the present I am calling *Caspo* [*The Bright Island*]. It turned out more vivacious than I had expected but then I took the precaution of inspiring myself with the spirit of Italian 'Commedia delle arte', and I used one or two more of its jokes. The success (apparent, any-how) of *S. & P. Love* in New York gives me hopes of one of my other plays being soon produced there. I find the elation caused by a 16,000 dollar week in New York wears off in about 24 hours, but it faintly reappears at intervals.

London, Thursday, March 25th. – I went down to see E. last night about her affairs and especially about the efforts being made by the landlady to turn her out of her house. I had a strong impression of the acute misery caused to people by the shortage of houses. It seems that agents have notices fixed on their doors: 'No unfurnished houses or flats of any description to let under £160 a year.' I also had a strong impression of the misery among demobilized girls, many of whom can get neither work to do nor rooms to sleep in. City people, it appears, instantly turn down any application from a W.A.A.C. or W.R.E.N., etc., City people are always very imitative. I went and came back in a bus, between 8.30 and 11. I suppose that few of the people in the buses thought that their lives were hard; but I thought so.

Comarques, Wednesday, March 31st. – On Sunday, performance by the Stage Society at Hammersmith of Ashley Dukes's translation of George Kaiser's *From Morn to Midnight.* This play, though mostly ineffective and very mad, improved as it went on. It had ideas. It showed how all English and French dramatists are in a rut. Its last scene, saving of souls at a Salvation Army meeting, was strikingly good.

London, Wednesday, May 5th. – I went for week-end to Beaverbrook's on Saturday and returned on Monday. Max has now two crazes – playing tennis all day, – and sleeping at night in the garden. He gave me the full history of his relations with his father, as material for my next 'big' novel. (But I'm afraid I shall have to write a little one first.) He also promised to tell me stories of 'deals' as material for short stories. Especially Strathcona's life in England.

He had a series of Mutt and Jeff cartoons in which Ll. G. and Bonar Law were Mutt and Jeff, and Ll. G. was always playing tricks on B. Law. He said that in the end Law asked him to stop this and he stopped it. Ll. G. expressed curiosity earnestly to see these things, and so Max asked him and Mrs Ll. G. to come to Cherkley with several other Ministers, to see them on his private screen, and Max got an orchestra, which cost him £25. Ll. G. saw the whole lot. Max said it was an ordeal for him (Ll. G.) and that Mrs Ll. G. was very subdued during the rest of the evening. Practically the whole Bonar Law family came down in batches while I was there. All perfectly delightful – papa, 2 girls and 2 boys.

Monday night: *Mary Rose*, Barrie's new play at the Haymarket. Tedious. The papers for the most part hailed this work as a great masterpiece.

Last night. *The Skin Game*. Galsworthy's new play at the St Martin's. This play may be a melodrama, but it is a very good one indeed and it holds you absolutely. It is very well acted. It is a tale, an incident, whose effect depends on a coincidence, and it has no general significance. The writing and the observation are excellent.

Comarques, Monday, May 10th. – I spent the week-end in doing gratis work for other people. Alterations and additions to *The Beggar's Opera* for Hammersmith, a prospectus for the *New Statesman* and a descriptive sketch of H. G. Wells for W. Rothenstein's new book of drawings. I also finished the proofs of *Body and Soul*.

I read Atkins' and Ionides' *A Floating Home* all through. It is a very good book indeed. Some of my illustrations to it are fair and some are merely awful. I read most of Aldous Huxley's *Leda*. The first poem in it is the best modern poem I have read for years. This last week I have read Ernest Newman's book on Gluck. It is a youthful work, published 25 years ago, and written in style very much less sure than his present style, but it is the goods.

Comarques, Saturday, May 15th. – Wednesday I went down to Bournemouth to see Rickards, and I returned on Thursday. Glimpses, through Rickards, into a vast world of sickness and tragedy – a whole world, complete in itself, and looking on angrily and resentfully and longingly at our world. The fact is that Rickards has stood very admirably this trial of being all of a sudden cut off from our world and all that he so extremely *savoured* (rather than *enjoyed*) therein. So has Mina Rickards. He grumbles terribly, but he has stood it, and his judgement has remained sane. On Thursday night we took Richmond to see Sacha Guitry and wife in *La Prise de Berg op Zoom*. Episodically very amusing. But nothing whatever in the play. Sacha is really a better actor than an author. He is really very good. Yvonne Printemps young and fairish. It was rather pathetic to see the once young and worshipped Suzanne D'Avril playing the small and purely farcical part of the *ouvreuse* in the 2nd act. *L'assistance était très snob.* I took pleasure in pointing out to sundry acquaintances in the foyer that what we were seeing was really nothing in particular, and that the whole season, artistically, depended on Lucien Guitry's interpretation of his son's clever second rate boulevard plays. The acting generally, however, and the production, were without question superior to English ditto.

Comarques, Monday, July 12th. – I finished the second act of Eadie's play yesterday afternoon at 7, having written 1,500 words of dialogue in 3½ hours. This is work. I was extremely exhausted. I took my Sunday to-day. Drove to Clacton this morning; but had no interest in it. Weather full of heavy thundershowers with hurriedly hot interludes of tropical sunshine – reminding one of Conrad's equatorial landscapes. Beneath all my work and occupations, I have been getting information as to yachts for sale. This is really interesting. I must have a yacht rather bigger than I ought to have. This will give me the new interest and anxiety which I want.

Comarques, Monday, August 2nd. – Having begun my play, now called *The Love Match*, on 1st July, I finished it on 31st ditto. The stuff in it is all right, I think. But I should not be at all surprised if Eadie declines to take up the option for which he has paid £200.

Yesterday evening I finished *La Chartreuse de Parme* and immediately began *Le Rouge et le Noir*, of which I have already read over fifty pages (8 a.m.). The Chartreuse is very great. It is only in reading such parts as the escape from prison that one sees that the technique of the novel has advanced. This part is not fully imagined; it is very well imagined up to a point, and very well invented; but the physical acts of escape are not as well rendered as Stendhal probably intended them to be. However, the wit, the power, the variety, the grace, the naturalness and the continuous distinction of this book will want some beating. In reading Conrad lately, I sometimes had a sense of effort. Not so with this, which I have now read three times. The opening of *Le Rouge et le Noir* has the air of being *très ingénue*; but after 20 pages you see *avec qui vous avez à faire*.

Royal York Hotel, Brighton, Saturday, August 7th. – On Thursday I saw two of the finest yachts afloat. *Iolanda*, which I have often admired at Cannes. The other yacht was the Duke of Westminster's *Belem*, lying in the Medina near to *The Wanderer*. A converted French merchantman. Fantastic luxury; but real taste. I got some ideas from it for *The Wanderer*. A lovely ship. Allen said the Duke had spent well over £100,000 on her, and that £35,000 would buy her; which probably meant £25,000. The wages bill must be £700 a month. She appears to be used for only about a week or so a year. This is a social crime.

I think I should fancy more than any of these boats the *Shenandoah*, a 3-masted schooner, with a big beam; she floated on the water like a duck and looked superb. When we went out in a launch to inspect the motor launch that goes with *The Wanderer*, we went close by the *Shenandoah* and it was sickening to think she wasn't mine.

London, Saturday, October 9th. – Yesterday afternoon I went down to Cambridge to stay a night with Rivers and see to Richard's [his nephew] induction into Clare College. Train full of undergrads and relatives. Tea at Rivers's. Then by 'backs' to Clare where I saw Richard's rooms.

I dined with [W.H.R.] Rivers in St John's hall. A 'short' dinner, too short, and professors etc. rather dull. Too cautious; too pedagogic. Another professor there, agriculture. I forget his name. His chief interest seemed to be the history of the barley plant. Went on with him to Rivers's, where there was another psychologist (psycho-analyst) who had just been on a visit to Freud. Freud speaks English perfectly. Talks little. Gets the 'patient' to analyse himself. Was told afterwards that a good psycho-analyst would charge 300 guineas for a case, which might employ one hundred hours. I went to bed hungry, and woke up so hungry at 3.15 that at about 5 I got up and searched for cake and found it. Three undergrads to breakfast, besides Richard. But among them only Davison (poet) talked. He *did* talk well. Rivers's delightful personality!

London, Tuesday, October 19th. – At Siegfried Sassoon's suggestion we went last night to a chamber concert. Haydn, Beethoven, Schumann. I made notes of it for a chapter in my new novel. Seemed thin, and too small for the hall. Anyhow I was bored. Ottoline Morell was there. Distinguished features. In fact a personality. She left with us after the Beethoven. Siegfried, delighted with the music, would not leave till the end.

London, Thursday, October 21st. – Rivers came to lunch at the Reform on Tuesday. He and Shufflebotham were talking about miners' eye-diseases, etc. and Rivers said that the danger factor on the nervous system had never been taken properly into account. Shufflebotham said that he had been preaching it for years. Shuff said that you could always distinguish miners from potters on their way to early morning work. Miners had an apprehensive look. Potters would whistle on the way to work; miners never. It appears that someone has just pointed out in *The Times* that if you put the mines in order of frequency of accidents, and also in order of majorities for strikes, the two lists coincide! All this of course, so far as the miners are concerned, is chiefly subconscious. Shuff said that of course boys voted for strikes. They had not had time to become accustomed to the danger, and the instinctive reactions were very strong.

I got frightened about the opening of my novel *Mr Prohack* yesterday. But on reading it through I thought it wasn't so bad.

London, Saturday, October 23rd. – At Reform on Thursday. Sassoon, with Jascha Heifetz violinist and his pianist. Something distinguished about Heifetz. Very young. A gold collar-pin and a pearl scarf-pin. I went with those three to a concert of Josef Hoffman at 3 p.m. They said he was the finest pianist in the world and that there was no good second. This is his reputation in America. (They are both – Heifetz and his accompanist – markedly Americanized.) Hoffman certainly played magnificently, but the programme was not a good one.

London, Sunday, October 24th. – Four orators in Hyde Park. One: a sort of imitation working man, old, on political themes. Good crowd. Extremely dull. Two: an Oriental preaching Islamism in fluent English with exaggerated R's. Extremely dull. Three: a young man preaching I don't know what, though I listened several times. Monotonous gestures. Extremely dull. Four: an evangelistic scene. A little man with a big nose, and a group of attendants including 5 or 6 dull women. Bad singing of bad hymns. Extremely dull. Still, he did say: 'When I lived in the country and worked on my farm the girl came out and shouted (very loud) *"Mr Way."* *"What?"* *"Dinner."* Ah! That was a good moment. But God's dinner is better than that. On the farm I wanted a fresh dinner every day. God's dinner lasts for ever,' etc.

London, Wednesday, October 27th. – I finished the fifth chapter of *Mr Prohack* yesterday morning, and corrected all the proofs of the E. A. Rickards book in the afternoon – and they wanted a lot of correcting. When they were done I suddenly realized that I was exhausted and that the top of my head was coming off. Jascha Heifetz concert at Queen's Hall. M.'s one idea as soon as the concert had begun was to depart again. I thought Heifetz was a marvellous performer, with a lovely tone, but his interpretation of César Franck's sonata did not excite me.

London, Tuesday, November 2nd. – I concocted a film plot yesterday evening in the streets between 5.15 and 7.15, after spending most of the day in worrying about the proposals and cast for a revival of *Milestones*. I first heard of this affair on

Wednesday last, from Eric Pinker on the phone. He had just heard of it; but negotiations had previously been going on between Eadie and Bright (on behalf of Knoblock). I refused to agree to Eadie being the producer, and wanted to cable to Knoblock. Miss Nerney, however, learnt on the phone from Bright that Knoblock had left no address and that Bright had a power of attorney and that Bright agreed to Eadie being the producer. So I agreed.

On Friday evening Eaton came to see me and assured me that Eadie would produce it all right, which I much doubted. He also showed me a copy of his letter to Eadie in which he indicated that there would be no trouble about the casting and that I should only have to be formally consulted. On Monday I learnt from the Pinkers on going to see them that Bright and Vaughan had fully discussed the cast on Friday. Why they didn't ask me to join in I don't know. I then got Eric Pinker to send to Vaughan for the cast and he brought it up to me here yesterday at 3 p.m. The only 'name' in it was Eadie's, with possibly Harben's. I told him to say that I insisted on Haidée Wright for Gertrude. I said that a failure of this revival would damage the play for ten years, that the bulk of the players were unused to London, and that everything centred round the star, whereas there never has been a star in *Milestones*, and I wanted some balance to the star, in the shape of a first-rate actress in the most important woman's part. I said that Haidée W. had a good figure and could make up for the first act as least as young as Eadie, and that she was perfect for the other acts.

London, November 8th. – Difference between London and provinces. I have several times noticed in provincial theatres and music-halls that the men in the audience do not stand still when the National Anthem is played. They do not even take off their hats (or caps). In West End theatres the observance of the protocol is still absolutely strict.

London, Tuesday, November 30th. – I read Lawrence's new novel, *The Lost Girl*. It would be absolutely great if it had a clear central theme and comprehensible construction. It doesn't end; it stops. But it is very fine indeed, the work of a genius. It held me. I read it in less than 24 hours.

London, Saturday, December 11th. – This morning at 12.30 I finished the writing of my first film. I have temporarily called it *The Wedding Dress*. It has taken 25 days, out of which I was ill on 7 days and did nothing whatever. I should estimate that the MS. is about 10,000 words.

London, Christmas Day, 1920. – Two thoroughly bad nights, full of the church clock. Still I wrote over 4,000 words of my novel in 3 days, with lots of preoccupations.

· 1921 ·

London, Saturday, January 1st. – I did over 5,000 words of my novel on Tuesday, Wednesday, and Thursday; but owing to shortness of sleep none of it yesterday or to-day. Last year, I published *The Log of the 'Velsa'* and *Our Women. Sacred and Profane Love* was produced in America and India.

I wrote 145,100 words.

I had over 600 and probably at least 630 theatrical performances during the year. The returns for the colonies and the provinces have not yet all come in; and the amateur performances are not counted in this total.

London, Monday, January 10th. – To-day I lunched with George Moore at 121 Ebury St. Nice London house, with fine pictures. A marvellous Claude Monet and ditto Constable. I said 'So you have two Manets.' He said 'I am the only man in London who has two Manets.' Not true, of course. The house was very neat and well kept; but in the nicely furnished embrasure on the half-landing, I saw a collection of hat-boxes etc. hidden in a corner.

Moore said that even *I* used French words sometimes in writing, and that he objected to it. I said I never did. He cited the word 'flair'. I told him it had become English. He wouldn't have that. He was curious about the financial side of letters. Like other people, he could not believe that I can't get my plays produced.

He said that when Bernstein had a play on the stocks he went to a manager and said to the manager: 'The play will be finished on such a date. You will pay me so much. I shall have so much for scenery etc. I shall be allowed to engage artistes up to so much weekly. I shall conduct the rehearsals. *You* will be permitted to come to the last 3 rehearsals.' He assured me this was true, and that the manager would (at any rate officially) know nothing about the play till the end. Moore has no use for Hardy or Conrad. He spoke of 'Hardy the Villager, Conrad the Sailor', etc.

London, Thursday, January 27th. – A desolating night on Monday at the New Theatre, to see Matheson Lang in Thurston's *The Wandering Jew*. Terribly old fashioned and ugly, but his acting very good. Lang wanted to buy *Don Juan*; but he insisted on doing his own scenery and producing. Also he would only pay me half my demanded terms. So I told Eric Pinker to call it all off.

Wednesday, Norman Mackinnel came here for tea and bought *The Love Match* on my terms. He asked me to try to get Gladys Cooper for the principal woman. I wrote to her at once.

London, Sunday, January 30th. – I bought another complete Tchekoff for this flat yesterday. Couldn't do without it any longer.

London, Monday, February 14th. – Thoroughly indisposed for a week. But immediately I began to feel better I began also to feel that I could finish up that damned novel in no time.

London, Sunday, April 17th. – I was too much worried with *The Wedding Dress* film to write anything here. I finished the entirely new version of the film to-day, 27,400 words, and feel relieved.

During M.'s absence in France and Italy I have been doing a lot of dancing – 3 dances a week, and going to bed late, and with results on the whole good.

London, Tuesday, April 19th. – I finished Strachey's *Queen Victoria* this afternoon. It is only a sketch, and the part dealing with the widowhood (40 years) is really too outliny. The style seems artificial often, and the brilliance sometimes fails. Still the thing is on the whole very brilliant and very readable.

London, Wednesday, April 27th. – In the night I finished the tenth volume (just out) of Tchekoff. Apart from 'Ward No. 6', the only long story, I think the best thing in it is 'The Frost'. It struck me on re-reading 'Ward No. 6' (for the 3rd time) that this tale is not at all like any other tale in the volume, and that there are very few Tchekoff's like it in manner in any volume. In places it seems to have been written under English influences. It is a most terrible story, and one of the most violent instances of Tchekoff's preoccupation with Russian slackness, and corruption.

London, Saturday, May 7th. – Futile reflection about *Mr Prohack* most of yesterday; but I got the ideas at night. I arose early this morn and had written another 600 words before 8.15 and 1,000 before 10.30. To-day we go to Thorpe, and on Monday I go to the yacht.

London, Friday, May 20th. – Yesterday was what can be lawfully called a full day. After a late night dancing I made my tea at 7 a.m. and worked. Correspondence and advising M. about her Anglo-French Poetry Society, and receiving Robert Bion (who arrived on Wednesday from Paris) took me till 10.45. I went out for an idea-collecting walk and returned before 11.30. I wrote only 300 words by 12.30. M. and I had to leave at 12.45 to lunch at the Lovat Frasers' and meet Bruce and Karsavina at 1. Karsavina has a perfectly marvellous charm. She is shy and rather reserved. Dressed in nice colours. This lunch was quite all right. No nonsense about it. And I liked Bruce.

London, Sunday, May 22nd. – George Moore for lunch. He is very prejudiced, especially on the old subjects of James, Conrad, and Hardy, but extremely interesting, though longwinded. He said he much wished our acquaintance to continue. He said that Christine was the finest cocotte in literature, and that I must have lived with her, and actually witnessed the Sunday afternoon kitchen scenes, etc. I don't think he believed my denial of this and my statement that it was all invented, including Christine. I didn't tell him that when I was hunting about for a physique for Christine I saw Madame R. accompanying her husband at a concert, and immediately fastened on her physique for Christine – sadness, puckering of the brows etc. Moore told me he was writing five short stories about celibates.

London, Monday, May 23rd. – After dinner, M. and I walked in Hyde Park for an hour, and saw the rhododendrons, the amorous couples, the avenues, the *grues*, and heard the band. It was a very beautiful and amusing evening.

London, Wednesday, June 15th. – I began to write the last chapter of *Mr Prohack* at 3.57 yesterday and wrote 1,200 words by 6.30, being then perfectly exhausted, though I had written easily. My health was all wrong, as it generally is when I'm finishing a book. Alistair Tayler came to dinner, and we (including Marguerite) went to Harriet Cohen's concert. Very good playing. The modern music came out pretty well, but there was nothing first class. I was never really 'held' for more than a moment at a time. I ought to have been at the concert at Queen's Hall hearing Gustav Holst's *Planets*. All this because I liked Harriet Cohen's physical style and her playing.

London, Friday, June 17th. – I finished *Mr Prohack* at 3.57 yesterday afternoon. Last night Cochran dined with me, and at 10 p.m. we went to see *Petrouchka*. The dinner was to discuss the idea of me writing a revue with Lucas for him.

London, Sunday, October 30th. – I left the yacht on Oct. 1st, and came here. I had kept the log regularly. But here, owing to conjugal worries, I could not possibly keep this journal. On Tuesday 18th inst. I consulted Braby as to the marital situation. I determined that nothing should be done until after M.'s recital at Lady Swaythling's on 19th inst. This was the last evening I spent with her. Braby sent for her on the Thursday. She wrote him on Thursday night confirming her desire for a separation. Yet on Friday she asked me to take her to a concert! I told Braby about this, and he wrote suggesting that she should go and live somewhere else.

On Saturday morning 22nd inst. I went to the Tate Gallery so as to be out of the house. When I returned she had gone, but I did not know this until the next day!

London, Wednesday, November 23rd. – On this day the two parts of the deed of separation between my wife and myself were formally exchanged by our solicitors, and the matter is complete.

Yacht Amaryllis, Nice, Saturday, December 3rd. – I arrived here on Wednesday morn 11.1 to join Bertie S[ullivan] on his yacht. Magnificent morning. Cloudy afternoon. Continuous rain on Thursday and Friday. Gradually clearing to-day with some sunshine, and rather warmer.

La Tosca last night. Theatre, very ugly, full of provincial people and Americans. The bulk of the French women fat and plain. Also the same for the chorus in the opera. The story of *La Tosca* childish and made more childish by the 'production'. Excessive ugliness of the 1st act *décor*, church scene. Also of last act, top of tower, with the ridiculous sky border and side pieces. 2nd Act (Palazzo Farnese) not much better. Crucifix on back wall, placed there *à propos des bottes*, but you knew that it would be used before the end of the act, and it was, to put by body of murdered Scarpia. The childishness of the thing positively revolting.

This afternoon we went into the Jetée Promenade. Another casino on a vast scale. Dancing there was better: but no *chic*. True, the season has barely commenced. Views of town as we drove after lunch in search of cigars very imposing and fine. I was really impressed in the warm evening air. Double rows of trees in electric light, etc.

Amaryllis, Nice, Sunday, December 4th. – I began to write *Lilian* at 3.30 this afternoon, having walked about most of the morning. Sea-front, Jardin Public, food at the Café of the Casino Municipal, home exhausted – collecting and arranging ideas. The Riviera is not a place that I can walk in without fatigue. The others drove over to Beaulieu. I wrote partly in saloon and partly in my cabin, and had done 1,200 words as the clock struck 7.

Lovely sunshine this morning. Cloud and some rain this

afternoon. At 9 p.m. stroll round into Jetée Promenade with Biron and home by Place Masséna. A warm night.

This morning I found that while the new town was very Sunday, commerce seemed to be proceeding very busily in the old town. At Jetée to-night a lower middle-class crowd, not too full. Immense blaze of electricity. The Casino Municipal was brilliantly lighted and doubtless a packed crowd within; but deserted without. Not a soul sitting on the *terrasse* of the great café.

Amaryllis, Nice, Wednesday, December 7th. – Last night at the opera *Les Huguenots*, with Gramer (tenor – not bad) and Gellay (soprano – bad) – the worst operatic performance I think I ever saw. It showed up the marvellous absurdity of the operatic convention. Female hags, really and visibly old, in chorus; also men nearly as ugly and equally wooden. The ballet comic in its puerility and ugliness. Many principals in the cast of course. Tenor good, but a putrid actor and a *fat* of the worst description in his self-complacency. Groupings idiotic. Orchestra bad. Intonation 75% bad. The thing left the audience very indifferent except for a few high notes.

It is wonderful how in these performances some individual will be found to cry 'Bravo' at any imitation, however feeble, of a showy thing. This happened at the end of a *pas seul* of the most mediocre sort. When a song pleases at all, the *pleased* at Nice will begin to applaud before it is over. The theatre itself, showy in an old-fashioned conventional sense. 3 tiers of boxes, or apparently boxes, with the royal box occupying 2 tiers in the centre – like the Costanzi at Rome. Usual decorations. Heaps of room for orchestra. The auditorium and audience were like the performers and the performance. Seen 1000 miles off they would look like the real thing.

Provinciality of Nice at this season passes description. I couldn't make out a single well dressed woman, and very very few either young or pretty. The dowdiness in general was dreadful. We left after Act 3 and walked home. It was a pleasant change to-day to go to Monte Carlo. By motor bus, very luxurious. 8 francs inside and 6 out. 50 minutes lovely ride. Marvellous weather. Few on the terrace before lunch. One or two ogling *grues*, and a few really well dressed women. Marvellous sunset for 30 minutes. Then dark. A very agreeable day. 600 words before starting.

Amaryllis, Nice, Thursday, December 8th. – 1,400 words to-day.

The clock of the church opposite our stern strikes the hours twice, the second time about 2 minutes after the first. I suppose the people have to be reminded that the hour actually *has* struck and that time is not standing still. Detail characteristic of the regional failings.

Yacht Amaryllis, Cannes, Friday, December 16th. – I played chemin de fer after dinner under Bertie [Sullivan's] tuition and lost 200 francs. At the table there were more women than men. Two lovely women came in later to another table. The status of some of these women is mysterious. They do nothing but play, and if they are cocottes they must do their business very slowly. If not cocottes they must be *femmes entretenues*, or very near it. But a number of them are too old to be *femmes entretenues*, though perhaps not too old to be cocottes. Gamblers are very ingenuous. They believe in such things as the effectiveness of a *faux tirage*, of *cartes fait exprès* to change the luck. They constantly talk of how near they were to winning a large sum – if only the bank had won one more time; etc. As if they were not always very near to making a large sum, and that the nearness of the big win was not the very essence of the charm of gambling.

Amaryllis, Cannes, Monday, December 26th. – The band that plays on the Croisette is the most *petit bourgeois* thing you ever saw. Chiefly middle-aged and old men. Townsmen. No string instruments. Dirty old music of the French al-fresco concert variety – and never straying out of the accepted convention. Round about the Casino through various windows in the morning you can see rehearsals of various things to be done. Opera. Choruses. Band, etc.

Joel's yacht *Eileen* came in the other day and left this morning for Naples with the family on board. His display of deck electricity is very showy, as at Deauville; but it is a great yacht. The *Lorna* came and left. *Finlandia*, *La Résolue*, and *Sita* (a very old Rothschild yacht) are now here, and next to them – us. Splendid weather most of the time; but damned cold sometimes in the morning. Still, no overcoat required to go across to the Casino on Xmas night. Still reading, slowly, *The Brothers Karamazov*.

Amaryllis, Monte Carlo, Tuesday, December 27th. – Yesterday lunched with Sholto Johnstone Douglas to meet Jean de Reszke and wife. De R. is 71, fat, but looks decidedly younger. When he came in he said 'Ah! Vous voilà enfin. Ma femme ne parle que de vous. Elle vous lit toujours,' etc., in a teasing tone. He acts and relates and makes jokes the whole time. Full of life. Delightful with children. Pleasantly *rosse*. His wife, Breton, aged nearly 60, slim as a girl, beautifully dressed in black. Full of *chic*. Very beautiful even now. *Rêveuse, sentimentale, pessimiste* (through having lost her son in the war, I think). Quite enchanting.

Amaryllis, Monte Carlo, Monday, January 2nd. – Great sunshine. Too tired to work, I went on to the Terrace to think, and the first person I met was the Mrs B. with whom I had arranged to dance this afternoon. Shortish, slim, pretty, *bien habillée*. She had a dog. She said her husband went to early service while she took care of the dog, and she went later while he took care of the dog. This vaguely disturbed me. I rashly said in talk that I never went to church. Did I believe in a Supreme Being? Yes. Did I believe in the divinity of Christ? No. Did I believe in the Bible? Parts of it. How could I only believe in parts of the Bible? And so on, showing the most dreadful crudities of thought, accompanied of course by absolute certainty of being right. She was soon telling me that once one believed that the English were the Ten Lost Tribes then the whole Bible became perfectly clear, and one could see that all its prophecies had been or were being fulfilled. Further, that the second coming of our Lord was expected about 1935, and then the Jews had better look out for themselves, and there would be a thousand years of peace. Thirdly, that all the great historic dates of the world had been engraved long in advance in a secret place beneath the Great Pyramid, and they were all correct. They could be seen by anyone who understood how to read them. ... She tried to get me to church with her (room at Grand Hotel). However, I shall dance with her.

Amaryllis, Cannes, Friday, January 27th. – I finished writing *Lilian* on Tuesday last at 10 a.m. Since then, as usual after these feats, I have been ill, chiefly in bed.

Amaryllis, Cannes, Tuesday, February 7th. – I calculated the other night that the big table (50 louis départ) took 2,900 frs. every ten minutes, and therefore that it must make about £140,000 in the season. Some other people told us that the

Casino calculated to make an average of 30 louis per day out of each person who played. A bank manager here told us that a number of rich men (including Guggenheim) started to play at 2 a.m. with total resources of probably about 5,000,000 frs. They played till 7 a.m. when each person announced that he had practically no money left beyond a few thousand francs. It had all gone into the *cagnotte*. And of course if you play long enough all the money must eventually reach the *cagnotte*. The percentage is probably much bigger than at roulette or 30–40.

Saturday, September 29th. – Savoy Dinner, given by the Savoy to a few journalists and Sassoon and me, to introduce (privately) the new 'Savoy Orpheans' the wonder-band. Temple in chair (as publicity manager) and Blumenfeld on his left. Talking about Hannen Swaffer, Blum said he was very clever and had been in Blum's employ on the *Express* about twenty years ago; but Blum had sacked him because he wore blue undershirts. He sat down to the table to write and exposed his blue undershirt to the wrists, and Blum stood it as long as he could and then sacked him. Probably quite untrue, but Blum told it very well. The Orpheans are about twelve in number and for the most part play strange instruments all looking like silver and gold. The piano has two manuals with a harpsichord attachment. Black trumpets – Conductor a Britisher. (No doubt to smooth things over with the Ministry of Labour who always object to importations of labour.) They played bad music well. 'You see the man the second from the right,' said Temple, 'that's Count G., the finest saxophone player in the world. Nine out of ten people won't know he isn't an ordinary fine player, but the tenth will, and the tenth will make the fortune of our band, which has been collected from all over the world. You see that thing under Count G.'s chair. It's a bird-cage. There's a canary in it. He left the bird in New York. It fretted. He cabled for it. It is the only canary that has crossed the Atlantic alone. Count G. gets £83 a week. The band costs between £430 and £460 a week.' (I had guessed £200 a week.)

Alhambra, Saturday, October 6th. – Richard and I went to see Rastelli, juggler, Italian. Very good. But a shade monotonous in invention. He did some of the Cinquevalli tricks, with a soft ball, not a hard. One of his best was juggling with two balls by his head alone. His finest thing was juggling with eight discs (not for long) while doing something with his head – I forget what.

Griffiths Brothers with a horse now, not a donkey, were side-splitting. So was Potter, a 'comedian'.

Apathy of audience to all the good things. Applause, but not enough.

Slow motion film of Carpentier *v*. Beckett. Very impressive. Like doom. Sort of inevitability. Beckett slowly falling. The towel floating into the ring, etc.

Gloominess of Alhambra and stodginess of audience compared to my recollection of 1889. Yet probably no real difference.

Friday, October 12th. – Tania [Harriet Cohen] said, discussing her new repertoire: 'The Chopin Mazurkas are patriotic. The Polonaises are political. I shall play them in a political manner.'

Newman Flower told me that C. K. Shorter went down to see Hardy and asked to inspect his manuscripts, which were stacked in boxes in an attic. Having inspected them C. K. S. said: 'I'll have the lot bound for you.' Hardy agreed. The manuscripts were bound but very cheaply and badly indeed. Before sending them back C. K. S. wrote: 'I think you said you'd give me two manuscripts.' Hardy kicked at this but agreed to give him one – *The Return of the Native*.

·1924·

Tuesday, January 1st. – Chelsea Arts Club Fancy Dress Ball. Seemed to be fairly well organized on the whole, though it was impossible to get supper without standing in a crush on stairs for a very long time. The supper was free. The light refreshments downstairs were not free. Still, one got them. All boxes occupied. 3 or 4 thousand people I should think. Beauty of building. Commonness and poverty of most of the costumes. I was disappointed too in the female beauty. Orchestra goodish. Processions and stunts rather poor. Fantastic noises. Some drunks. I saw few friends or acquaintances. On the whole a mediocre show, I was glad to get away (1.20 a.m.). My chauffeur seemed to me to be a much superior person to most of the revellers. In fact it struck me as being somewhat under-civilized, below the standard set by ordinary standard conventions of style, and rather studio-ish.

Friday, January 4th. – Yesterday, highbrow tea at Ethel's [Ethel Sands]. Logan Pearsall Smith and L. H. Myers (the author of *The Orissers*) and young Marjorie Madan and me the guests. Myers is a thin dark man, *silencieux, un peu précieux*, but apparently of a benevolent mind. Certainly a highbrow; L. P. Smith also. L. P. S. started the affair by saying that he had been asked by a publisher to make a list of 23 books of *permanent* value published in the 20th century. He read us the list, and several times amiably altered it according to our criticisms. He had no use for Hardy, and I had little for H. James. Then we went on to make a similar list of French books, and it was not nearly so good.

I went on to a dinner at Sinclair Lewis's timed for 8 o'clock. The talk at the end of the dinner went to old C.P.R. days, and the careers of the famous Van Hoorn and Jim Hill. Lewis thought of it as an idea for a novel: which I should say it was. Lewis has a habit of breaking into a discussion with long pieces of imaginary conversation between imaginary or real people of the place and period under discussion. Goodish, but too long, with accents, manner, and all complete. He will do this in any discussion; he will drag in a performance, usually full of oaths and blasphemy. A most striking contrast between the dinner and the tea. The latter all bookishness and what is called, I believe, culture. The former all life and scarcely any bookishness or culture at all.

Lewis soon began to call me 'Arnold', and, once begun, he called me 'Arnold' about 100 times. He has things to learn, but I like him. He showed me the first typescript of his new novel – all blue and red with millions of alterations, – a terrible sight.

Tuesday, January 15th. – Yesterday afternoon I suddenly decided that I couldn't proceed with my story about Elsie until I had been up to Clerkenwell again. So at 4.50 I got a taxi and went up Myddleton Square. Just before turning to the left into this Square I saw a blaze of light with the sacred name of Lyons at the top in fire, far higher than anything else; also a cinema sign, etc., making a glaring centre of pleasure. I said, surely that can't be the Angel, Islington, and I hoped that it might be some centre that I had never heard of or didn't know of. Certainly its sudden appearance over roofs was very dramatic. However, the old chauffeur said of course it was Islington. Rather a disappointment.

Myddleton Sq. with its Norman windows of its 4-storey houses, and church nearly in middle, with clock damnably striking the quarters, was very romantic. I had to correct several of my memories of the architecture. I walked round the Square gazing, and going up to front-doors and examining door plates and making notes under gas lamps (very damp and chilly) while the taxi followed me slowly in the mud. Then I drove up to the Angel and saw that it had truly been conquered and annexed by the Lyons ideals. Still, it was doing good up in Islington, much good. Compare its brightness and space to the old Angel's dark stuffiness. I got home at 6.30 and I had been in other worlds, though less than two hours away in all.

Wednesday, January 16th. – Lunched yesterday at Thesiger's to meet Princess Marie Louise (daughter of Princess Christian). She married a Prince Albert of Anhalt, lived in Germany nine years, then got a separation. A woman of 51, dressed in mourning for her mother. Everyone called her 'ma'am' or 'madam' in every sentence, except me, and the women curtsied to her, and Thesiger said the only thing insisted on was that he should meet her at the door when she came.

Her lady-in-waiting, Miss Hawkes, was there too. Marie Louise kissed her heartily when they met. Seemed a fairly sensible woman and pretty wise. Said nothing in particular but said it neatly, used of course to deference, which she received in plenty, though Thesiger teased her the whole time. Still, I was glad I had not been effusive when she wrote to me about the Queen's Doll's House twice, as I might have got dragged into St James's Palace, which I should have hated, I know.

Friday, January 18th. – Emerging last night with Duff Tayler from Garrick. A very damp and chilly night – 'struck through you'. Stopped by a fairly well-dressed man of fifty or so. A woman with him walked on. She was very soberly dressed. Too dark to see properly. 'Excuse me speaking to you, but are you a member of the Garrick.' 'I am,' etc. (Duff left the talk to me.) 'I hope you won't be angry,' etc. 'Needless to say that if you're a member of the Garrick, you're a gentleman. You won't be angry. You're looking very serious.'

'I'm a serious man.'

'You're an author or something.'

'No, I'm just a man.'

'But all you Garrick fellows are celebrities of some sort... ? Now that lady there is my wife. She *is* my wife. We're in a deuce of a hole. Really in a hole. I'm a friend of W. B. Maxwell. You know him? Now if he was in this club, it would be all right. But he isn't. I'm a gentleman. Public school man. My brother is a General at Cardiff, that is to say, he's really a Brigadier-General. Willie Maxwell will tell you. I must introduce her to you' (making a move, which I discouraged). Many more prefatory remarks, and me getting colder and colder, and Duff putting in a word or two now and then. 'Now if you could oblige me with a little – just until the bank opens tomorrow morning. Give me your name and I'll leave the money for you in an envelope to-morrow. I'm a gentleman. You can trust me . . . ? Otherwise my wife and I are in for a night out.'

'I'm afraid I can't do that,' said I. He didn't seem very disappointed.

Strange how these people can hope for success in cadging. He probably haunted the entrance to the Garrick all the evening. Duff said that his object in wanting to introduce his wife to me was to get hold of my name. The man had a weather-worn face. Spoke quite well, and was undoubtedly what is known as a gentleman. It was a hell of a nasty night, though not actually raining at the moment. The wife was waiting about 100 yards up the street. I could see she was dressed in brown. A most deplorable case, the case of this man.

Saturday, February 2nd. – Yesterday, lunch at Savoy with Reeves Smith, Rupert Carte, Thornewill and Temple. They showed me over the hotel.

The waiters' tips are put in a *tronc*, and divided each week into *parts* (French word). Some men get a little over 1 *part*, and some as low as ⅛th of a *part*. A *part* may mean £8 or £10 a week. It appears that if any waiter is cheating he can usually be detected, by the law of averages. The waiters have their own clerical work done; but it is checked by the hotel, 'to see fair play'. The maître d'hôtel takes no share in the tips. In the credit department, I found that all mistakes on the wrong side, in bills, if waiters' fault, have to be paid by the waiters.

I heard that the Savoy alone took in receipts a total of a million a year, about £3,000 a day.

Chambermaids keep their own tips individually. Ditto valets. Valets do a business in clothes-pressing, etc. The charges for these go on the hotel bills, but the money goes to the valets. Door-porters pool their tips.

Tale of the head of the cloak-room; been there for ages; remembers people's faces, often without troubling as to their names. He took an overcoat from an old gentleman, and gave it back to him at the end without a word.

Guest: How did you know that this is mine?

Employee: I don't know, sir.

Guest: Then why do you give it to me?

Employee: Because you gave it to me, sir.

Kitchen. Head Chef under thirty. Worked his way up. Wore a natty little white cravat without collar. Stores. Fish in tanks. The man who calls out the orders as they come down is called the *aboyeur*. I didn't see a great deal of special interest in the kitchens, except the patent washer-up.

Power station. Artesian wells. Geared turbines. Power for carpet-sweepers, pumping, etc., etc. The Power station looked like the stoke-hold, rather, of the *Lusitania*. Run by oil now. Ventilated by vast draughts of cold air through trumpet-like things. Water heaters for both.

Graph Office. (*Capt. Jack.*) Graphs for various receipts. In summer receipts for rooms go up, and restaurant receipts go down. Londoners away in summer. Hence there are two publics. The travelling, and the home publics – very distinct.

Audit Dept. Every bill separately checked – but afterwards. Every query on them has to be cleared up.

Printing Office. All menus, cards, programmes, and large bills. In their spare time they do the hotel's commercial printing (such as order forms).

Repairs department. I didn't see this. But they plan all their big carpets there. However, I saw through a window in the side-street the room where 10 to 12 women repair the hotel linen every day.

Laundry. Clapham. I didn't see it. An American expert said it was undoubtedly the finest equipped laundry in the world.

Bedroom and suites. 6 guineas a day for double bed and sitting-room, bath, etc. 9 guineas for two bedrooms and sitting-room. It pleases visitors best that the rooms should be if anything too warm when shown. Thornewill had given orders previous night that one suite should not be let, so that I might see it at my ease.

Sunday, February 3rd. – On Friday Denison Ross produced a theory that all art sprang from the contemplation of the veining of marble. He spoke also of pictures in fires and in clouds and said how much these were superior to human early efforts (he knew this last was rot). He referred to the celebrated ugly marble in grill room of Holborn Restaurant, called the 'Gorgonzola'. He said he had seen in this a great battle, and he was sure it represented the great battle in which the Gorgons overthrew the Zola system.

Monday, February 4th. – Yesterday, walking on Thames Embankment near Grosvenor Road, met Sidney Webb and wife. Beautiful morning. They were quite happy strolling along. Of course I stopped them. I said to Sidney, 'Well, how do you like things?' (meaning the first Labour Government, being in the Cabinet, etc.). He said, 'Oh, I think it's a jolly lark.' Then they asked me rather anxiously what I thought of the Cabinet – that was their first question – and my answer pleased them. Discussed various individuals. Told me how people were impressed by the really business-like qualities of the new ministers. I said, 'Evidently they are business-like – the praise is quite justified.' 'Well,' said Mrs Webb as they left, 'they *do* work. You see they've no silly pleasures.' I said, 'I hope they have; I hope they have!' She wouldn't have it. And as they walked off Sidney said, about 'silly pleasures', 'And here she is taking me out for a constitutional.' Evidently he didn't like that. Clearly these two are never tired of their job. And they have no pleasures except their job, and no distractions except perhaps reading novels.

Tuesday, February 5th. – I finished *Lucien Leuwen* on Sunday. Two pictures of society, at Nancy, and in Paris. At Nancy, military, social, political, passional. At Paris, political, social, flirtatious. It develops really into a political novel, and Lucien's excursion to Caen and another place to influence elections on behalf of a minister makes the Paris half provincial again. It must be one of the best and truest political novels. And as regards the local aspects of national politics (intrigues of prefect, etc., and those for or against him) it must be about as true to-day as it was in 1830. The whole thing is almost savagely ironic. All very fine. This is Jean de Mitty's edition (1901) *'reconstitué sur les manuscrits originaux'*. Highly serious that one chapter, and that one of the most important – (Lucien's return to Nancy to see his worshipped Bathilde de Chasteller, who he thinks has had a child) – is entirely indecipherable in MS. and is therefore omitted. I should have thought some expert could have made out the more than usually changeful cypher or cryptogrammic form in which Mitty says the book is written and this chapter particularly.

Friday, February 8th. – Last night, 1st performance of *The Way of the World* at Lyric, Hammersmith. I have seen two rehearsals and the performance of this play, and still do not know what the plot is, nor have I met anyone who does know. Further, the balance of the play is astoundingly neglected. There is a very long (and good) scene in first act preparing the entrance of Petulant, and of course preparing an audience to believe that Petulant is the chief character, whereas Petulant does nothing whatever in the play, and might, so far as the plot is concerned, be left out. The two chief characters in 1st act are not as they ought to be Mirabell and Fainall, but Petulant and Tony, the character played by Playfair (I forget his name – Sir Wilful's half brother). And so on.

The play suffers through the proper names abounding in the short 'i' vowel sound and other shorts. Mirabell, Millamant, Witwood, Wishfort, Wilful. One gets confused.

The last act drags terribly, and is enough to kill any play. It seems to me that Congreve had something of the superior and really snobbish artistic negligence of Wilde and Byron. Anyhow his play suffers. It is celebrated; but it cannot hold the stage because of its crude and inexcusable faults of construction. Were it well constructed, it would easily rival Sheridan and Goldsmith.

What liberty was allowed to unmarried girls in that period. If Millamant was not a widow – and I never understood that she was (same for Marwood), they must have had a great deal of licence.

The performance and production last night were admirable. The play will fail, but it must add to the prestige of the theatre. Edith Evans as Millamant gave the finest comedy performance I have ever seen on the stage.

Saturday, February 9th. – Last night I told Walter Roch we would go home by bus instead of taxi because it was more interesting. He agreed. We had to wait 5 minutes in Piccadilly for a 19 or 22 bus. While waiting a very little oldish, spinsterish, thin, misshapen, stooping woman came slowly along, carrying two large neat parcels, strapped together, with a string handle. She was neatly dressed, polished shoes, but misshapen and queer – probably about 45. She could walk with great difficulty a few yards only, using all her might to lift the bulky double package, and then stop and rest and start again. She seemed so exhausted that I went up to her and asked her if she wanted a bus. She said 'No,' but I didn't think she meant it. She then said she had to get to Holborn and that 44 bus went there. I said: 'You're on the wrong side of the road,' and I almost picked up the package to carry it across Piccadilly for her. She said she didn't want a bus, hadn't any money. She seemed to me to be too neat and self-important and obstinate for me to offer her the fare.

Then in the bus we saw a respectable man kiss a little girl. She got out and left him.

So that we were rewarded for our bus ride.

Wednesday, February 13th. – Last night, performances by students (actors, actresses, orchestra and conductor all students) of two one-act operatic things at Royal College of Music. I was given a seat right at back of long, low 'Parry Opera Theatre', next to the Director's chair, which remained empty for some time. Then Sir Hugh Allen bustled up in the dark. Light tweed suit and a vigorous, active air. I rather liked him. You could see he was on his own dunghill. He showed me the stage. The scenery was appalling in its infantile ugliness, and ought not to have been permitted. We were too far off to hear and see the first opera (a scene from *Martin Chuzzlewit*, awfully good) and for Armstrong Gibbs's and A. P. Herbert's *Blue Peter* we got seats in the front row and too near. But even then the words could not be well heard owing to bad elocution. Aveling, the registrar, clutched on to me; he began on highbrows. He said the students were all perfectly mad on (what he called) highbrow music. Never talked about anything else. Evidently he resented it. I suppose he meant all the post-Brahms composers. I must say the Dickens Opera was stuffed with cleverness (D. Martin Wood, composer), not modern but damned ingenious and graceful. It really held both Duff and myself.

Saturday, February 16th. – J. B. Priestley's article on me in *London Mercury* for February. After quoting from *The Author's Craft*:

'With the single exception of Turgenev the great novelists of the world, according to my standards, have either ignored technique or have failed to understand it. What an error to suppose that the finest foreign novels show a better sense of form than the finest English novels!'

He goes on himself:

'What an error indeed! The fact is, of course, that the art of fiction as practised by the great novelists *is* technique, and any other "technique" is either some inferior method or a mere catch-phrase of the pontifical critic.'

This is a bit thick. It is easy to show where very many of the great novels fail in technique (*Anna Karenina*, e.g.) and where they could have been improved if the author had had the advantages of Flaubert, de Maupassant, or even Tchekoff. They are great in *spite* of carelessness, and their carelessness is often notorious. I thank heaven I have always gone in for technique. And *The Pretty Lady* and *Riceyman Steps* are both, in my opinion, jolly well constructed and *done* books.

Monday, February 18th. – At Harold Snagge's yesterday and day before. Basil Lubbock (author of *Round the Horn before the*

Mast) told various of his adventures in two wars and in Klondyke and as a seaman. He said, and repeated, that he had met only one or two British cowards. Practically everybody was brave in danger. He expected shell-shock, and also 'panic' affecting a number of people together.

Either he or Snagge told of some of the methods at Ford works. When the employees come in and hang up their street things, the hook is whisked up high in the air, and does not come down again till shutting-off time, so that nobody can prepare to go in advance. Also a man had been employed for some time and thought he was doing quite all right, when the manager sent for him and told him he could leave as they didn't want men like him. He asked why. 'Look at these photographs,' said the manager. One snapshot showed the man stooping to speak to a fellow workman as he was passing from one spot to another. The other showed him looking into a doorway which was forbidden. I should want very high wages for work in these conditions, I think.

Tuesday, February 19th. – First night of first playing of *Back to Methuselah* last night at Court Theatre. 'House full' boards outside before the performance. The affair was a *solennité*. But not quite the usual kind of 1st night. Walls of box dead black and of stone. We could see the empty orchestra, and the nakedness of Adam and Eve. Curtain going up announced by a sort of clash of a cymbal. I was very bored by the play, I could see nothing in it; neither action nor character nor a sermon nor wit. The game of finding new words played by the characters seemed silly. It was too far round to go to smoke in the interval, so we stayed in our tomb. In the second act I went to sleep and had to be wakened for fear a snore might be heard on the stage. A most depressing night.

Tuesday, February 26th. – First night of *Kate* (or Love will find out the way – Good God!) at Kingsway last night. It fell flat in the audience. The applause exclusively friendly applause. The thing was killed by a perfectly rotten book.

The plot was unfollowable and the words terribly dull. No one that I saw in the audience thought other than that the thing was a frost. We went behind to M. Gordon's dressing-room. Full of flowers and bonbons (costly) and 2½ bottles of champagne which I was asked to open. I opened one. Completely different atmosphere. Marjorie after her great effort, needing praise and optimism, and getting them from half a dozen people. Difficult to know whether these artists really believe in a success, when any grain of common sense should tell them that the thing was bad and failed to please. A woman saying, 'I'm *sure* the stalls liked it.' Me saying: 'Delightful, you were splendid, Marjorie.' (Well, she was, but had nothing to do.) 'Beautiful production,' and so on. All praise. No criticism. Not a hint as to badness of book. We go. On stairs I meet Donald C. Well, he asks me my view. I tell him I like the production (I don't – yet we are very intimate), music, performances (yes, true). I give a slight hint as to badness of book. He likes it all right. But supposing I told him book was bad enough to bust up any show? We drove homewards, Dorothy and I, and say again and again that the thing is hopeless. And in scores of cabs and autos radiating from the theatre to all points of the compass people are saying the same thing. But the artists and the aged authors of the book are trying (not successfully) to convince themselves that the thing is a success. This is a 1st night sample of many 1st nights.

Monday, March 3rd. – At Ciro's last night. D. seemed to have caught a chill and she complained that the hot room was very cold. 'It's very draughty,' said she. 'I can't feel any draught at all,' said I. She said: '*It's when the waiters pass.*'

Thursday, March 6th. – German film last night at Polytechnic Cinema. One has the idea that all films are crowded. The balcony here was not 15% full. Front row, where Duff Tayler and I were, 8*s.* 6*d.* for 1½ hours' entertainment. A gloomy place, with gloomy audience. No style or grace in them. All lower middle class or nearly so. The hall tricked out with a silly sort of an ikon, illuminated, of Death, to advertise or recall or illustrate the film. The orchestra most mediocre. Played all the time, and three performances a day! Hell for the players I should think. Also the horrid habit of illustrating certain points musically, or noisily. The clock must strike, etc. And a special *noise* as a sort of *leit motif* for death. Lastly three small common Oriental mats (probably made in England) laid in front of the screen on the stage to indicate that much of the story was Oriental. The captions, etc., were appalling, and even misspelt, such as 'extention', 'Soloman' etc. The phrasing! Good God. *The City of Yesteryear* meant, I believe, the cemetery.

Tuesday, March 11th. – I lunched with Donald Calthrop yesterday. I knew the Kingsway *Kate* was a failure. He showed me the figures. He had been away for the week-end. Motoring up yesterday morning he had had an idea for a revue. He had seen that it would be better for his backer (who had written him decisively that he would finish up in three weeks) to close the theatre at once and spend what he would have lost in producing a cheap revue (no scenery).

His notion was to produce this revue in less than three weeks. True, it is not yet written. He asked me if I would edit it. So I said I would, but on the understanding that he took a month to do it in. We went through all the items he might get at once, and the authors whom he could approach at once. The revue was to be called *Pass the Port, please* and the nature of it was that some people are dining together and instead of going out they amuse themselves, and then call up the servants to help them in amusing themselves. The servants are headed by Sidney Fairbrother, whom the backer had engaged for another three months yet at £50 a week. I said the backer hadn't yet agreed. In fact he knew nothing about it. Well, D. C. said he would see the backer that afternoon and phone me at 7 p.m. I stayed two hours' nearly with him. He phoned me at 7.25 saying that the backer was very interested, and could he see me to-day? He is to lunch with me to-day, and that is how theatrical business is done.

Wednesday, March 12th. – Phillpotts's rustic comedy *The Farmer's Wife* at Court Theatre last night. This play is, really, far less naïve than the vast majority of West End society plays. Far less. The cynical wisdom of the 'hind', 'Churdles Ash', is much better than that of Pinero's 'Cayley Drummles'. The plot is neither more nor less conventional than West End plots, while the characterization is immensely superior. I liked most of the play. So did Dorothy. The love scene in the last act between the farmer and his servant was really beautiful. Yet I asked Herbert Griffith (*Observer*), 'Do you like this play?'

'No.' He certainly did not. He could see nothing in it.

I asked George Mair (*Evening Standard*), 'Do you like this play?'

'No.' He could see nothing in it.

These people could see nothing in *The Farmer's Wife* because it was rustic, and dealt with a life of which they knew nothing and for which they cared nothing. Eden has put a lot of careful observation of manners into this play.

No place, taken in a certain way – in its weak spots – is more provincial than the West End.

Friday, March 14th. – Yesterday, Reform lunch. Talking about gambling. It was defended by James Currie and even by Lord Buckmaster. Stated to be the one distraction of the people. There is, however, fornication. Apropos of all this, when I was coming home from Hammersmith in the Tube yesterday evening, two workmen got in, one about 35 and the other 18 or 20. They carried paint pots and 'turps' pots wrapped in paper and covered at top (paint pots, i.e.) with paper with a hole for brush handle to poke through. Dirty. Shabby. Dirty hands. Dirty caps, with big peaks. The young one wore black leggings. They pushed the cans as far as possible under seats. The young man was smoking a cigarette. As soon as they sat down each of them pulled a new packet of chewing-gum from his pocket, stripped off the paper, broke the packet in half and put one half into his mouth. I didn't notice any actual jaw-motion of chewing. The young man kept on smoking. The chewing-gum business was evidently a regular thing, and much looked forward to. Obvious satisfaction on their faces as they opened the packets. After a few minutes the young man pulled a novelette from his pocket and went on reading it.

Tuesday, March 25th. – Last night at the Colefax's Ethel Sands said that on Sunday night she was in bed at 9.30 and slept without a break till 8 o'clock. Arthur Colefax said that he would sleep fourteen hours without a break if he was not called. He was called every morning. He liked a little snooze before dinner. Now last night *I* had what I call a goodish night for me. 12.30 a.m. to about 2.55 a.m. Then about 3.15 a.m. to 5.45 a.m. Then a few short snoozes, totalling perhaps 40 minutes at the very most. In all 5½ hours. I don't think I have ever had to be called, certainly not for 20 or 30 years, even for the most urgent or early occasions. I can always be sure of being awake for anything in reason.

Friday, March 28th. – Edith Sitwell last night told me of the feuds in the verse world. Osbert is always planning some literary practical joke against someone. Siegfried Sassoon won't speak to Osbert now because (he says) Osbert will never leave him alone. He won't speak to Edith, because Edith will not stop Osbert doing his tricks. 'But what can I do?' said Edith. In revenge, Sacheverell Sitwell swears he will never speak to Siegfried again. It appears also that either Siegfried won't speak to Robert Graves or vice-versa.

Monday, March 31st. – I met George Moore last night at a Phoenix performance. He said he wanted me to go and dine with him and that he would tell me about *Riceyman Steps* – a lot of things that I don't know (he said). Then he told me. He said it was the only really objective novel ever written, and very original. (I knew from others that he thought very highly of it.) He said, 'It has no form whatever, *no* form. It is not very carefully written – it is adequately written. It has no romantic quality. Yet it holds you. A bookseller crosses the road to get married – that's all. It is disturbing to think that hundreds (he should have said millions) lead their lives just like that. The book is the FACT (he emphasised the word several times) and that's all.' Then he repeated about great originality, lack of form etc. ... Considering that in my opinion it is very well constructed. ... !

Saturday, May 10th. – I saw Sir Edward Elgar at the Garrick the other day. I said I was working hard. He at once said, 'Ah, you work because it pleases you; we poor men work because we have to.' He seldom talks to me without mentioning his poverty and my riches. I suppose this is natural, and I expect I should do it in his place. *I* have a grievance, and it is that I sleep badly, and I am always mentioning it. 'Do you sleep well?' I asked him: He said he did, generally. He said that for thirty years he had had 'a tea-machine' in his bedroom, and if by chance he woke up and didn't think he should go to sleep again easily, he at once got up and made tea and did one or two hours' work. I said I couldn't work in the middle of the night. 'Not original work,' he said, 'but there is generally other work waiting to be done.'

Friday, May 16th. – Max [Beaverbrook] told the following last night. He had bought the story from a divorce detective for £50 but dare not use it. A woman consulted a divorce detective about her husband's apparent infidelity, and the 'tec said that before doing anything she had better cease to live with him, as if she lived in the same house she might 'condone' his offence and so endanger a divorce. She said she didn't want a divorce, she was very much in love with her husband, and she only wanted to know who the other woman was.

The 'tec at first refused the case, then took it on. The woman then told the 'tec that her husband was in the habit of going away for week-ends, never saying in advance that he was going to stay away, but always telegraphing that he was detained. One night while he was asleep (after return from a week-end) she went through his pockets and found a letter from a house agent by the seaside to say that he could have possession of a certain house; also a cloak-room ticket, Victoria Station. The ticket was for a smallish bag. The 'tec and the lady went together to Victoria, and got the bag, which was locked. The 'tec pulled apart one side of it, and bloodstained stuff was disclosed. They left the bag at the cloakroom. 'What can this be?' the 'tec in effect asked. 'Nothing,' said the lady. 'My husband goes fishing and he's probably put a wounded fish into an old shirt or something.' And she went on: 'Now, you're in *my* service? You're in nobody else's?' The 'tec agreed and she reiterated the fact and he positively agreed.

Sometime later she rang up the 'tec and said: 'My husband has just left for Victoria in a taxi. You had better watch him there and if necessary follow him.' The 'tec replied: 'Something grave has occurred, and I must ask you to come here to my office at once, and bring a woman friend with you. Most important.' He insisted. She arrived at his office at 6.30. The 'tec said: 'I'm sorry to inform you that your husband was arrested for murder at 5.55 at Victoria.' The lady said: 'You villain. You scoundrel. It is you who have sold him to the police. Yet you swore you were in my service only.' The husband was now of course in prison.

I was in the Park yesterday thinking about a short story, and saw a woman on horseback with an old man who had a striking resemblance to Cunninghame Graham. The woman stopped her horse and spoke to me. She said I shouldn't remember her name and I didn't. She then introduced me to Cunninghame Graham. C. G. didn't hear. 'Who are you?' he asked. 'Ah,' he said, 'I didn't recognize Mr B. in a hat. The photos of him –' I complimented him and asked how he was. He said, 'As well as possible under the reign of MacChadband.' Prejudice against Labour showed itself instantly, and you could see that the Labour régime was very much on his mind, since it leaped out at the first opportunity. I stuck up for Ramsay MacDonald. He said that the Clydesiders and especially Kirkwood, always called him MacChadband (because he preached so much). I said he was a very decent fellow. 'So was Judas – a very decent fellow!' said C. G. and went on a bit about Judas, larkishly.

'Who told you that, C. G., about Judas?' I asked. He hesitated and said, 'I – I got it out of the Talmud.' I said, 'I see, I withdraw. You have the better of me.' He stretched out his hand to say good-bye. A sporting sort of cuss.

Saturday, May 17th. – Lilian Braithwaite lunched with me yesterday at Kettner's. She told me that when her daughter Joyce received a certain play to read, with a view to playing a part, she said to her mother, 'Well, I don't see how they *can* ever produce such a thing. It's too awful, absurd' (or something like that). Lilian also read the play and came also to the conclusion that the play would never be produced because it simply couldn't (not that I attach too much importance to the views of actors on plays and parts). However, the play was somehow produced, and it was a most dreadful frost. The curious thing is that the libraries made a *deal before the first night* (Why? Why couldn't they wait a day?) on the strength of Marie Tempest and Marie Lohr being in the cast. As if any names ever saved a hopeless play or even a very bad play. Producing may save a pretty bad play, but acting never. So I think. The Library Committee (supposed to consist of the greatest experts in public stage-taste in London) must have seen a rehearsal or so, or at any rate read the play.

Last night to Lena Ashwell's 'Once a week players' performance of Shaw's *The Devil's Disciple* at the Century Theatre, Archer Street, North Kensington, produced by Beatrice Wilson.

Beatrice said she had had to produce the play in ten days, and they always did plays in this period. They dispensed practically with props and scenery. Just a few tables, chairs, window-frames, door-frames, and curtain. Same furniture throughout, whether for a general's headquarters or a widow's modest home. Three soldiers stood for a 'square' of soldiers at the execution, etc. Everything very poor and cheap; but nicely done – not overstepping the modesty of nature – and the play held you, except the last 5 minutes which were very poor. A fellow named Henry Oscar played the lead. Evidently of much experience. Handsome. He did very well. Has done

Shakespeare tours. The dialogue is exquisitely written – better than Shaw is writing now, I think. Less glittering, but as pure and fine as Congreve.

I contrasted all this poverty with the great costliness of our Drury Lane production, with its lavish advertising, etc. Dean is producing *London Life* with the most notable skill. You would say he knew everything about plays and producing. Yet the taste of people generally fails somewhere. He wanted me to introduce into the part of the Prime Minister Holyoke (played by Henry Vibart and supposed to be a mixture of Asquith and Balfour with a touch of Rosebery) the words 'Wait and see'. I refused absolutely at once. Imagine the cheap roar which would follow such a despicable sally.

Monday, September 8th. – Alex Erskine's consulting-room. Neurologist. He has told me wonderful stories, which I believe, of trance states, etc. He had a youngish subject to go to sleep in my presence. After I had gone, he said to the subject: 'Did you see into that man's (my) mind? What did you see?' (This was while the subject was awake.) The subject said: 'His mind is like this. If you want to stop his stammering, tell him to stammer like hell and insist on his stammering.' I thought this was rather good. I have always noticed that when I practised Coué-ism on myself, the impediment got worse.

Nevertheless, under Erskine's daily suggestion, and reading many times and saying many times daily to myself: 'I have *perfect* confidence in myself. I am *never* nervous. I have *complete* control over my speech,' the impediment gets less. In seven séances Erskine has failed to put me to sleep. But I have gone off once or twice for a few seconds; only the slightest noise or movement or touch wakes me up.

Wednesday, September 10th. – T. S. Eliot came to see me at the Reform Club last night, between two of my engagements. He wanted to interest me in Virginia Woolf's reply in his *Criterion* (2nd reply it really was) to a few remarks of mine about character-drawing in fiction about a year ago in *Cassell's Weekly*. He wanted a contribution on the subject. I said I would do one, probably in the form of fragmentary notes, but that I wouldn't give a date for delivery and I would make it a reply to her. Pale, quiet, well assured. He works at Lloyds Bank, in a department of his own, 'digesting' foreign financial and economic journals. Interesting work, he said, but he would prefer to be doing something else. He edits the *Criterion*, and writes, in the evenings. I said to him: "I want to ask you a question. It isn't an insult. Were the notes to *The Waste Land* a lark or serious? I thought they were a skit.' He said that they were serious, and not more of a skit than some things in the poem itself. I understood him. I said I couldn't see the point of the poem. He said he didn't mind what I said as he had definitely given up that form of writing, and was now centred on dramatic writing. He wanted to write a drama of modern life (furnished flat sort of people) in a rhythmic prose 'perhaps with certain things in it accentuated by drum-beats'. And he wanted my advice. We arranged that he should do the scenario and some sample pages of dialogue. I found him extremely sound in taste. He had excellent views about the 'Virginia' school of fiction. He had discovered Pauline Smith's stuff in the *Adelphi* for himself, etc. I liked him much more than ever before.

Thursday, September 11th. – I was thinking about what T. S. Eliot and I had said about character in fiction. A character has to be conventionalized. It must somehow form part of the pattern, or lay the design of the book. Hence it must be conventionalized. You can't put the whole of a character into a book, unless the book were of inordinate length and the reader of inordinate patience. You must select traits. You must take many traits for granted, and refer to them, as you do and must refer to them, in a way to show that they are conventionalized. If you wanted to get at total truth you'd only get a confused picture. Question: Does a novelist want his characters to remain in the mind of the reader? Some novelists don't. But I do, for one. Dickens's characters remain in the mind. They may perhaps be too conventionalized, too simplified. Same for Thackeray – Dobbin and Amelia. But they remain in the mind. No novelist can always be creating absolutely

new, or fresh, characters. Balzac used the same frame of conventionalization over and over again. His titled amorous
dames many of them of the same pattern. So did Shakespeare.
So did Scott. This implies a form of conventionalization. Then
half-critics say, when they observe the necessary conventionalization, that there is no character-drawing at all. The
thing is to produce an impression on the reader – the best you
can, the truest you can: but some impression. The newest
despisers of form and conventionalization produce no impression at all.

Monday, September 15th. – About *Uncle Spencer*. This is the
1st book of Aldous Huxley's that I have really liked. Character drawing in it, for the first time in his books. Uncle Spencer
is *drawn*, emphatically. But technically the story is clumsy.
Why an uncle at all? It serves no purpose. Why a nephew?
Why is story told in 1st person by nephew? Serves no purpose.
And for the 2nd part of the story, after nephew leaves Belgium
at beginning of war, it is a positive hindrance to convincing-
ness, you feel all the time that the nephew could not possibly
have known all the details of gesture, thought, etc., which he
relates. (Same with Conrad.) The prison stuff is well done.
The little music-hall star is well done. The story nearly ends
artistically. Aldous doesn't finish; he ceases. But another
perfect page and the end would have been good. He shirks the
final difficulty and so there is no end. Same with the next best
story *Little Mexican*. No end to it. But the character drawing
of the N. Count is good. *Fard* is a Tchekoff story. But the
feelings of the maid when mistress tells her to rouge herself
to hide her tiredness are shirked.

More about novel writing and character drawing. You
couldn't fill in a whole character except in a book of enormous
length. The young ones don't seem to me to 'select'. They
shove in pell-mell whatever happens to strike them. They
don't construct even a character. Then they think they are
truer to life: but they aren't. Description of faces is futile.
Waste of time. Give the reader something to hold on to, and
then let him fill in for himself.

Tuesday, September 23rd. – Aldous Huxley came yesterday afternoon to do what he had called on the telephone 'pay his homage'. He looked older and more distinguished. His clothes seemed to be Italian and in material if not in fit very nice. Altogether he looked better and talked more easily. We agreed on nearly all literary questions except the value of his *Antic Hay*. He likes that book, thinks it has a point to it. He seemed to agree with my few criticisms of *Uncle Spencer*. He told me some funny tales about Fascism. One friend of Mussolini's made 40 million lire in two years. He had four very big motor cars of the — Company. It was found out that in exchange for these cars he had let the company off taxation for two years – had promised to do so and *had* done so. The consideration for this great act seems rather trifling to me. Also he insisted on an edict enforcing the little red glass reflectors on the backs of bicycles. The cabinet was not in favour of it, but he got it through, apparently behind their backs. I told Aldous there was bound to be a big rumpus in Italy soon. He thought there was too, but he couldn't see quite what was to be done against 400,000 well-armed Fascists, the only power in the country.

Friday, September 26th. – Max Beaverbrook rang me up last night and said: 'Arnold, I want to tell you. The *Daily Express* has been offered a biography of you written by Mrs A. B. They wanted to make it a condition that we should treat the offer as confidential, secret; but I absolutely refused to do any such thing. So I'm telling you. Our man has read it all through and likes it. Says he wouldn't mind anyone saying of him in his lifetime what is said of you in the book. If you have any objection I won't buy it: but if you haven't, I'd like to.' I reasoned that if the *Express* or any other paper refused it, M. would put the refusal down to me and would be accordingly resentful. She would never understand the awful bad taste of the whole thing, whether accurate or inaccurate, praising or blaming, etc. It is bound to be published somewhere; it is bound to make people think that I am partner in the bad taste. But if it is to be published I would sooner it be published by someone who is very friendly and who will take care that nothing offensive appears in it.

Saturday, September 27th. – Max rang me up again yesterday about M.'s life of me. He said he had now read it all through, and it was unadulterated praise. The parts describing me at work were good and interesting: the literary criticism dull. He said he would certainly put a prefatory note at the beginning, to say that she had been separated from me for some years.

Without that (said he) the thing would be 'intolerable', as anyone not in the know would think I had been conspiring with her to make some advertisement for myself.

Wednesday, October 1st. – *The Great Adventure* played to £1,610 last week – its best week. But it is coming off on Oct. 18 because the receipts fell for two weeks earlier (in the run) to less than £1,200 a week. Harrison had the right to give me notice to terminate the run. And he did so, not believing in the chances of the play. He was justified, though to my mind a little panicky. He made contracts with McKinnel and others for Galsworthy's play, *Old English*, and he must keep them, or it pays him better to keep them, or he thinks it pays him better to keep them.

Thursday, October 2nd. – Osbert Sitwell lunched with me yesterday at Reform Club. By arrangement, Swinnerton joined us. Before lunch S. Sassoon came up and said: 'Can I lunch at your table to-day?' (In pursuance of my reproaches that he would keep by himself in the club) I said, 'Certainly. You must. Osbert is coming.' Sort of silly feud between him and Osbert. S. S. drew back but I made him come. A little occasional acerbity in S. S.'s tone at times, but it was quite all right. At the end I made S. S. see Osbert out of the Club.

Wednesday, October 8th. – Walking in Fulham Road yesterday morning I saw in a slatternly chemist's shop a section of window given to 'Yeast is life. Vitamines mean health. X— Yeast

Tablets. .... A lightning pick-me-up' guaranteed (or money back) to aid headaches, etc., in 5 minutes, flatulence, etc., in 5 to 10, stomach trouble in 10 to 15, flu cold in 24 hours. I went in and bought some – probably because I used to take yeast and it may have done me a certain amount of good. I didn't know what was in the tablets (beyond yeast). I knew that for many years I had tried all sorts of remedies and that not one of them had succeeded with me. Yet, as usual, I had hope again. I believed again, etc., etc. I took stuff blind again. This indestructible (though often destroyed) faith in quack medicine advertisements is a very interesting and perhaps almost universal trait. I took a tablet. Felt nothing. But about tea time I felt a rather wonderful change in my organism. After tea I took two more tablets – or was it before tea? Anyhow I felt very much better. I took two on going to bed, and have had the best night for many weeks. In fact I slept 5¾ hours, of which 3¼ at a stretch. I felt I could do with more sleep; but I couldn't get it. However, I have much more energy and optimism to-day.

Thursday, October 9th. – Friendships made between young women on the telephone   solely. I have come across more than one instance of this. They like the tones of each other's voices and the things they say. And the friendship grows. Then comes an invitation to tea or another meal. 'Do come.' 'I should love to' etc. I wonder what the results are. But I never hear. This method of companionship (sightless) is very queer.

Tuesday, January 20th. – One of the main things, at my age, is to avoid strain – 'pushing forward' (as you do when you are in a taxi and are getting late for an appointment). Nearly all my life I have been keeping to a time-programme, and I have been doing it until quite recently, and have carried programmes through in spite of neuralgia and such obstacles. I think that now this method results in less instead of more work. On Sunday afternoon, after two hours' work with Knoblock on *Mr Prohack* in the morning (with neuralgia) I gave up the bit of re-writing that I had meant to do in the afternoon, and stayed in bed all afternoon, and of course felt much stronger. In fact towards six I was really inclined to clear off some small oddments, including a 300-word of appreciation of Thomas Hardy for *Harpers*, which I did, all right.

Yesterday morning my scheme was to re-write the end of Act II of *Prohack* in the morning. However, I had a sense of rush and strain even before breakfast, and so I became placid and gave myself all day to finish Act II, and telephoned to Knoblock suggesting that he should put off our appointment to proceed with Act III from 3 p.m. yesterday to 11 a.m. today. He agreed. I finished the Act easily at 7 p.m. The sense of strain had gone, and though I had neuralgia all day, I felt better, and had quite a fair night and began to do letters and oddments at 8 a.m. in good form.

Wednesday, January 21st. – Anthony Hope told me last night at Lady Russell's dinner party that on every first night Henry Irving gave an immense champagne supper to about 300 people – journalists and friends. Also that all sorts of people had free entry to the theatre on any night – and if no seats they stood. You only had to know Irving or Bram Stoker or Loveday in order to be let in, without any trouble. Hope had the *entrée*. Irving also had a heavy permanent salary list. Hope said that his sister-in-law Suzanne Sheldon was engaged by Irving by the year, but never played for more than 3 or 4 months in the year. Hope said humorously that all subscription lists were opened by Irving as a matter of course by 'Henry Irving, £105'. And so on. I asked how Irving could live. Hope said he thought he did not make anything out of the Lyceum, but made large sums on tour and in America. There must have been a chronic state of hard-up-ness. Hope said that towards the end Irving had the beginnings of a great success with *Richard II*, and then fell down and hurt his leg, and couldn't play. They tried Herman Vezin, etc., but nothing would work. However Irving left £10,000, which surprised Hope, who expected only a schedule of debts. He said that Irving would never pay a royalty to an author, because he would never give to anyone even the theoretical right to inspect his books. His attitude towards the author was the old one: 'Send for the fellow and we'll tell him what we want him to do.' He would pay as much as £1,000 – but not more – without difficulty. Hope said that Bram Stoker came to him, Hope, more than once, suggesting that he should write a play, but Hope wouldn't write without a royalty and Irving wouldn't pay a royalty.

Tuesday, January 27th. – Lee Mathews brought Komisar-jevsky to dinner last night to discuss *The Bright Island*, which K. is to produce for the Stage Society. He doesn't look above forty. A nearly bald head. Nervous. Shy. Melancholy. But he soon warmed up under treatment, and I found he could laugh like anything, especially at the amusingness of his own ideas for producing the play. I liked him.

He said he worked under the Soviet for some years. The work was interesting, but the conditions appalling. He had to produce two or three purely propagandist plays each season as a condition of being allowed to work at all. All his house-hold possessions were taken from him. His valuable library was taken and given to some public library. When he got to Western Europe he hadn't a cent or any possession.

Saturday, January 31st. – Last night to *Jitta's Atonement*, adapted (nominally 'translated') by Shaw from the play by

Trebitsch. Fulham Grand. This play made a very deep impression on both of us. Shaw has taken an obviously conventional and machine-made play of Trebitsch's, left the first act in all its conventional competence, 'situation', and dullness, and then in the 2nd and 3rd Act treated the development of the theme realistically and wittily. The effect is simply electrical. The play wakes up, the artists wake up, and the audience wakes up. Enthusiasm obtains.

The mere idea of starting on a purely conventional 1st Act and then guying it with realism and fun, shows genius. In the other Acts there is some of the most brilliant work, some tender, some brutal, and lots of the most side-splitting fun that Shaw ever did – and he is now approaching seventy, I suppose. The 'hysterics' scene of laughter between the widow and the mistress of the dead man is startlingly original. The confession scene between the mistress and the daughter of the dead man is really beautiful. The fault of Shaw's changes is that the husband of the dead man's mistress, a shallow person in the 2nd Act, quite suddenly in the 3rd Act becomes a wit and a practical social philosopher of the very first order – a Shaw at his finest. There was a very good audience, and any quantity of appreciation and delight. And this in spite of very, very little good acting and a great deal of very bad acting.

Wednesday, March 11th. – *Spring Cleaning* at St Martin's Theatre, by Fred Lonsdale. There is a lot of wit in this play, and the opening scene, wherein a lot of decadents and homosexuals, etc., come in to the hero's house for cocktails is very ingenious and well managed. Afterwards there is nothing that seems real, save an odd remark. The 'great' scene in the 2nd Act where the hero introduces a prostitute to his wife's dinner party is not in the least convincing, and the prostitute (well played by Cathleen Nesbitt) is like no prostitute that ever was. All the 2nd Act is absurd. The 3rd Act, scenes between husband and lover chiefly, is equally false, but it is saved, partly, by some fine lines and by Ronald Squire's acting as the lover. This Act owes everything to Squire. On the whole perhaps not a totally wasted evening. But I don't know. If the play runs for a long time I shall be surprised. I should think it would peter out unexpectedly. My theory is that a play which pretends to be serious and is not will not run for very long though it may make a great splash at the start. A spurious play may run if it is dull and all alike. However, the whole subject is very complicated.

Thursday, March 12th. – The head of the little dancing school, where I am daily being taught to dance, came in to watch me being taught yesterday. He said to me: 'What you want is courage, decision. Don't be afraid of 'em (women). Remember they have to do what you want. You've *got* 'em. And it's the only time you *have* got 'em.'

Monday, March 16th. – A 6½-hour-night last night after a week or so of bad nights. Well, I was in a high state of nerves yesterday. Barrie and Eliz. Lucas were dining at Savoy Café last night, and afterwards he took D. and me with Eliz. back to his flat. He said an extraordinary thing had happened to him. A man who had never written a play before sent him a 1-act play, which he, Barrie, passed on with a strong letter of recommendation to a management, which management accepted it the next day, and is to produce it next month. I showed Barrie my praise of the last act of *Dear Brutus* in yesterday's *Observer*. He agreed with my remarks on the easy-ness of 1st Acts. He said a play of his of which only the 1st Act was good was *What Every Woman Knows*. He said he wrote that Act in two days. The 2nd Act took weeks, and the 3rd Act took months.

Thursday, March 26th. – I was walking in Selfridge's basement yesterday afternoon, idling between two appointments, when I met Selfridge in rather old morning suit and silk hat. He at once seized hold of me and showed me over a lot of the new part of his store. Cold-storage for furs – finest in the world. Basement hall 550 feet long. Sub-basement with a very cheap restaurant where they serve 3,000 to 4,000 customers a day. He introduced me to the head of his baby-linen department: 'Here is a gentleman wants things for three of his children, one is three months, another ten months, and another a year old.' Then up his own private lift to the offices and his room, where I had to scratch my name with a diamond on the window – with lots of others. He showed me a lot of accounting. Then downstairs to book department. Fine bindings, etc. His first remark was, taking up a book: 'Human skin.' I had to hurry away. He kept on insisting that it was wonderfully interesting. And it *was*.

Monday, April 6th. – Some weeks ago Mrs S. M. recommended to me some anti-fat pills made and sold by a chemist at Nice. The course was six boxes. I got the six boxes from Nice and began. Mrs S. M. positively assured me that they were quite harmless and very effective. After I had taken a little more than two boxes, I began to notice that I perspired very freely and also was short-winded after any exertion. Also that my heart made a too loud noise and was rather irregular. So much so that I could not sleep on my left side on account of the thumping row. Fjellsted, my masseur, told me my heart had been affected by something – he thought it was due to veronal, of which I had taken one dose for insomnia. (By the way my sleep grew heavier but much more broken, and no better as regards total quantity.) I hadn't and haven't told him about the anti-fat pills as his feeling against all pills is so strong.

I then sent for Dr Griffin. He examined me and said my heart was organically quite all right, but that it had been upset by the pills and that I must at once cease to take them. He came a second time on Sunday, and said that the improvement, though noticeable, was very slight. I still have to walk upstairs very slowly and to avoid any physical strain. Dr. Griffin had the pills analysed. The analysis on the box (in accordance with French law) says: 'Iodothyrine', 'Hypophyse', 'Surrenales', and 'Génesiques'. He said that the quantity of thyroid (cheap) was larger than in the formula, while the other things (more expensive) were less than in the formula on the box. He said that I oughtn't to take medicines without consulting him. And of course he is quite right. It is perfectly staggering the idiotic things even a wise man will do.

Tuesday, April 7th. – Max Beerbohm, with others, dined here last night. I hadn't seen him for ten years (at the Reform Club). He was more delightful than ever. His mind is sound right through; and he is often witty. Some people have told me that he would dine out and say nothing but the most ordinary things. Last night he said scarcely anything ordinary. He was unaffected, modest, and thoroughly wise, and made a great impression on everybody. After the Maughams and the Parsonses had gone he expanded even more to Kathleen Long, Dorothy, and me. I asked him what kind of cigarette he preferred, Eastern or Western. He said it didn't matter. He just took whatever came. He didn't care about many things, and as soon as he owned something that he had wanted it ceased to please him.

His age proved to be 52, whereas mine was 58 in May next. He said he *wanted* to be 58 – every year was a conquest. He did *not* envy young people; in fact he felt sorry for them. Their lives also were precarious. They might die any day, and if they did die – what a suck-in for them! How much they would have missed – without knowing it. He said he had no feeling for London. He liked to visit it, but only on the condition that he could leave it and return to Rapallo. He said that he couldn't possibly have the romantic feeling for London that I have, because he was born in it. 'The smuts fell on his bassinette.' Whereas *I* could never lose the feeling of the romanticalness of London. He told me that I was in his new series of 'Old Celebrities meeting their younger selves', shortly to be seen at the Leicester Galleries. The legend under the drawing of me was:

> *Old A. B.* Everything worked out according to plan.
> *Young A. B. My* plan.

What a depth and width of criticism of me in this!

Tuesday, April 28th. – I went to Chinatown last night with Beaverbrook and Ashfield. Pennyfields is the name of the chief

street, Limehouse. We went to the Limehouse Police Station
first. It took us exactly fifteen minutes to drive there from
Ciro's. Great change in a short time. We saw some 'curios' (as
the Chief Inspector called them) first. Explanation of 'Fantan'
and 'Pluck Pigeons'. The first seems a purely childish game in
which the bank pays 2 to 1 winnings on a 4 to 1 chance.

Then out with the Inspector to Pennyfields. No gambling
after 8 o'clock, he said, usually not later than 7. We entered
two Chinese restaurants (11 p.m.) where lots of people were
drinking tea. Humble people. All very clean and tidy indeed,
and the people looked decent. A few nice-looking prostitutes
– chiefly Jewesses. Nearly all houses closed. Some windows,
said the Chief Inspector, were always shuttered. 'They don't
like the light.' Glimpses of curtained bedrooms higher up.
We went into a Chinese Music Club, where four men were
playing Mah Jong and one strumming a sort of Chinese guitar,
with very large string-pegs. Their singing nights were Wednesday and Saturday. A suggestion that they should sing was
not well received. They were very polite but didn't want us.
We were to have seen the Chinese Chapel, where the religion
of Confucius is practised; but it was locked up.

Then we went into a pub (closed) and found one or two old
topers (friends of proprietor's) drinking stout after hours. We
were taken upstairs and there saw a wonderful collection of
Chinese carving of all sorts – chiefly picked up from sailors.
Lastly, return to police station. No prisoners. Cells marvellously clean and sanitary. Steam heating. Temp. must be 63 at
least. Plank bed, white as a yacht's forecastle, but a pretty comfortable pillow: one rug. On the whole a rather flat night. Still
we saw the facts. We saw no vice whatever. Inspector gave the
Chinese an exceedingly good character.

Wednesday, April 29th. – Noel Coward lunched with me
yesterday and answered all my arguments in criticism of *Fallen
Angels*. He said that he wrote it in five days, and *The Vortex*
in four days (or three). When he once began, he worked
straight through. He showed much intelligence. He said he
meant to write a *really* good play, and a *really* good novel. He

has a little house in Majorca, where he is going with his mother. And in the Autumn to play in *The Vortex* in New York. I was pleased with him.

Monday, May 11th. – On Friday, at lunch at the Vineyard, I had my first long serious detailed talk with Max Beaver[brook] about political material for my novel *Lord Raingo*. It lasted just 1½ hours. He was marvellously effective and efficient. He didn't need to be told what sort of stuff I wanted. And he gave way at once when he was on the wrong tack – for me. He has exactly the right sort of imagination, and a very powerful and accurate one. He can invent pieces of plot to fit certain incidents, and is just as interested and as effectual in the matter of women as in the matter of politics. I got an immense amount of stuff. So that was all right.

Yesterday afternoon I taxi-ed up to see Barnsbury, so well spoken of as a curiosity by W. Whitten. It is a curiosity. The Sphinxes and little Cleopatra needles in front of the porticoes of a long row of houses in Richmond Rd are too marvellous. There is quite a lot of other Empire ornament round about here. Barnsbury Square is very good. And so is Malvern Terrace. The taxi and D. and I attracted attention, and while we were strolling around a nice polite (and no doubt curious) boy (Jewish) came up and asked me if I wanted 'Miss Galway's house'. It never occurred to me to ask who Miss Galway was. I should have liked to know.

Tuesday, June 2nd. – Yesterday I began on the political part of *Lord Raingo*, and had to go cautiously. But I did 1,200 words with increasing confidence. A heavy day's work anyhow. Olga Lynn brought Rudolf Kommer, Reinhardt's right hand, for tea. He wanted to see me. He told me some things I didn't know or had forgotten. He said that *The Great Adventure* had been produced in Vienna and failed – owing to production. Also published in book form in Berlin.

Wednesday, June 3rd. – Rudolf Kommer said on Monday that though the actors were better in Germany and Austria than in England, nobody there could play 'the English gentleman' as quietly as it ought to be played, and that I should find all performances of my plays 'noisy'. He spoke of 'English gentlemen' with great admiration and respect, as of something unattainable.

Monday, June 22nd. – On Saturday I returned from 17 days' yachting. Not two minutes' rain in the whole time.

To-night *The Cherry Orchard* is transferred from the Lyric, Hammersmith, to the Royalty. This I think marks a definite turn in public taste towards true plays. I have been remarking this turn for some years, but managers seem to be quite blind to it.

When Fagan produced *The Cherry Orchard* for us at the Lyric, we thought it ought to be done but did not believe in it. The first performance was splendidly received. But we did not believe in it. On the Thursday after the first performance (Monday) none of us believed in it, and Fagan met the directors and agreed without argument that the thing was a failure. But a few days later he was believing in it (by reason of the enthusiasm of small audiences), but the returns were still awful, and the loss heavy. Then the returns enormously improved. Loss became a profit, and to-night this most disconcerting and original play is going in a sort of triumph to the West End, where no manager would have looked at it a month ago. All this is owing to N. Playfair having seen it done at Oxford, and being firmly backed by me in his desire to have it done at the Lyric.

Wednesday, June 24th. – When I saw the above play again at the Royalty on Monday, in a by no means full and rather apathetic and not at all first-night audience, I was struck still more by the power and beauty of the play. I remember Jacques Copeau coming to me during the Stage Society performance of *The Brothers Karamazov* in a state of nervous gloom and exclaiming: 'Ces malheureux artistes!' and asking me why I hadn't warned him or done something; whereas I didn't know anything about the performance.

The revival of *The Beggar's Opera* last night at the Lyric, Hammersmith, was an affair of *prodigious enthusiasm*, and well done in some ways. Here is an absolutely English thing, understood by English artists, and done by them excellently well so far as the limitations of their gifts would allow. The music is lovely, heavenly sometimes, and the dialogue always brilliant. Also it is daring and bawdy, with robust ideas about life. This is in my opinion one of the most wonderful entertainments I have ever seen.

Salzburg, Saturday, July 11th. – I have not seen a well-dressed person in this lovely town. Day before yesterday we went up a lift to the 'Café-Wein' Restaurant on a mound of the Mönchberg. It is just opposite my window on the other side of the river but about 300 yards farther down. The lift takes about a minute and in that minute a marvellous change has taken place. You see the entire town at your feet, and the surrounding country gets itself into proper proportion. The centre of the town is a mass of domes and towers, which I have certainly not yet unravelled. We dined at the said Café-Wein restaurant, but indoors because it began to rain, and rained heavily and kept on raining with one short surcease, which we used to get down again in. I reckon the current of the river is doing 4 knots all the time. In flood it must do a lot more. A few punts are tied up to the banks here and there, doubtless for transport, but how they are manoeuvred I can't guess. Much of the baroque architecture is fine. The Mozart House is a lovely building. There seems not to be a single decent drapery shop in the town. I mean of the women's kind. The dresses of the women attest this. It is really a very remarkable fact.

Thursday, July 16th. – These *aussichts* of Alpine stuff leave me definitely rather cold. Visited the Kurhaus on the way back to the hotel. Vast and gloomy – especially the restaurant where an 'Alpine evening' was to take place last night. Feared it and avoided it, and dined at the Mirabell Garden Restaurant where also I had lunched. At lunch, Jerskny, director of the Blue

Bird troupe, had a table, with several of his artists; they were
extremely jolly and giggled like anything. At night: music.
Waltzes and operatic selections. Electric light; hence theatrical trees; dogs playing with each other; outsiders staring; girls
carrying beer all the time; a girl wheeling round and round a
thing like a perambulator containing all sorts of confectionery;
she did this for two hours and was still doing it when I left.

Friday, July 17th. – About 4.30 went up to Hoher Salzburg.
A very Margate-ish crowd; indeed the same sort of crowds
everywhere. They stream into the town daily. Coming home,
I met Kommer; or rather he stopped me and offered me a
piece of paper. For a second I didn't know him. He had inquired at all the hotels for me (including this one) without
success. He had then gone to the police, who informed him
at once that *E.A.B.* was staying at the Oesterreichischer, and
gave him a bit of paper to that effect; this was the paper he
was exhibiting to me in the street. Kommer told us that the
modesty of Asquith's country house 'The Wharfe' was one of
the things that struck him most. Said it couldn't happen anywhere else. Asquith had been P.M. for eight years. He said
that in any other country a man who had been P.M. for eight
months would retire rich. He said he was now working on the
German version of *The Great Adventure* and that Reinhardt
would do it in both Berlin and Vienna. Probably some delay
as there was great row between German managers and German stars. The managers had decided that no star should get
more than £15 a night and the stars had struck. He said that
the actor who took Ilam Carve made as much as £100 a night
because he took 25 per cent. of the receipts.

Saturday, July 18th. – Max Reinhardt's schloss, Leopolds-
kron, about ten minutes' drive from the town, is a really huge
house, with magnificent views of Alps on one side, and the
Hoher Salzburg fortress on the other. So fine as to be scarcely
credible. The house was built by an archbishop-prince about
1700 or 1680. Vast. Vast rooms. I mean really vast. We dined
in a tiny dining-room that you could scarcely see, only it was

larger than my ditto at home. The real banqueting room would have held 12 or 20 such rooms. Reinhardt's private suite – study, bedroom, bathroom, and dressing room – is simply colossal, – like a dream. The dressing room would occupy twice the space of my drawing rooms together. The finest rooms are the chapel and the big reception room over it. I should say that each of them is 30 or 35 feet high at least. Not a single room was really finished off complete, except the big reception room.

Kommer said that Reinhardt has a mania for building and transforming. He has no use for a finished place. We saw a lovely music room, nearly finished, upon which a Salzburg artificer had been at work for ten years. Reinhardt is seldom there. In theory he is there for 4 months in the year; but in practice he is generally away from it. At the moment he is in Venice. He spends all his money on it. The profits of the Denver *Miracle* built an enormous semi-circular wall round two thirds of the estate. It is a good wall.

He is incurably lazy about everything except producing itself. Kommer said he had known him for twelve years and worked closely with him for four years, and had never received a letter from him or seen his writing. No intensity of urgency could make Reinhardt write a letter, or (it seems) even dictate one. Telegrams were his method of communication. He said R. was a very quiet, very modest, very shy man, with no knowledge except of his own subject; but *full of sense*. He never had known him to say anything foolish. Also he was never a bore.

Monday, July 27th. – Kommer took us to *Orpheus aux Enfers* at Stadt-Theater. I had never seen this before. The music is delicious. So is the plot. The production was terrible, and I don't see how it could have been better in the circumstances. I calculated that the stalls, full, held about £20 only. To which Kommer retorted that the actors didn't get more than 3 million kr. a month (which is about £9 sterling) – at most. I asked: 'Is it worth while doing things when they have to be done so badly?' He said: 'Why, of course! For instance here;

they do everything. In May last I saw even Galsworthy's *Windows* here.' He then recounted what the theatre meant to him in his native town (Czernowitz, Eastern Austria), when he was a schoolboy. He said it coloured his whole life. They did everything, very badly, and he saw everything. He said: 'I couldn't *walk* to that theatre. I had to run there.'

Czernowitz is a small town, but it had a municipal Academy of Music, and the director of the Academy wrote a serious opera. Nobody outside Czernowitz wanted to produce it; but Czernowitz wanted to produce it, and did. After the first performance (or the 2nd or 3rd) the Burgomaster came on the stage amid terrific applause and presented to the composer 1,000 gold ducats in the name of the town. Fancy such a thing in England! Kommer said that all these small theatres (about 400 in Germany or in Germany and Austria) are the origin of talent. Reinhardt started at Salzburg. Some actors look on a place such as Salzburg as the final goal of ambition, after having played much in inns and similar fit-up places.

Tuesday, July 28th. – Kommer came at 6.45 and we were to have gone to a rehearsal of *The Miracle*, but there was to be no choir that night, he found, so we didn't go. I was determined to dine one night at the Horn Hotel with the golden sign, and we went there last night. The food was excellent and cheap and the wine excellent. We talked about the organization of the people's pleasure. Kommer quoted Chesterton as saying that since Dickens no one in England had cared for the people's pleasure because the Tories hated the people and the Liberals hated pleasure. Kommer pointed out how in Continental cities a young man could get decent civilized pleasure for almost nothing, especially in Berlin, Paris, and also in the smaller cities such as Salzburg. But not in London. When he was young in London there was nothing. Everything closed early (it closes earlier now) and there are only the night clubs even now, and they are not for the poor. We have the loveliest river, and it is not organized. The restaurants and cafés are rotten, and not *accueillants*, no choice of food and the food bad, little music, and it is so difficult to get to the places – you have to change and do all sorts of things. In places like Vienna, Berlin, and Paris, all such places are easy to get to (especially in Teutonic countries) and the entire population goes out to them on Sundays.

Friday, July 31st. – Wednesday morning, collecting ideas, I went for a walk down stream on left bank and up stream on right bank. Plenty of life going on on these banks; dogs playing in shallows; a dog being caught in current and carried down at a great pace and ultimately getting across. Boys playing in shallows. Fishermen. Old people on benches chatting and making fat poodles sit up too long. Poor women sewing and knitting. Fairly well-to-do young mothers with perambulators, and occupying a whole bench with piles of sewing work and spending a large proportion of time staring admiringly at the baby. Young girls in converse. Water cart (motor) rushing along and creating at first a prodigious dust. I got ideas for my next section; but returned home with the beginning of neuralgia. I worked in afternoon, but my neuralgia got worse and worse, and I stopped after 800 words.

Sunday, August 2nd. – On Friday I was still suffering so much from the effects of neuralgia that I could do no work. Shopped in the afternoon, and went to see a German film in the evening; it was very bad, as bad as the weather.

I finished *The Kellys and the O'Kellys* yesterday morning: Trollope's 2nd novel, written at the age of 34. This novel is consistently excellent, and Algar Thorold's introduction to it is absurdly trifling and inadequate. The characterization is admirable, strong, true, and sober.

Thursday, August 6th. – At night, with Kommer, to a rehearsal by Reinhardt of *The Miracle*, at the Residenz. I saw a little insignificant man in the gloom which covers the floor, but not the upper spaces, of the vast room; and it was Reinhardt. For an instant he seemed *quite* insignificant. Then at once you saw he was not. He stood well on his feet, had fire and authority, and yet was always quiet and smiling. I was much impressed by him. I also liked much of the acting. This rehearsal was an experience. It lasted till 11 p.m. A dreadful night to drive about the streets in a fiacre behind a very old white horse and a very old driver.

Friday, August 7th. – This hotel is very well run. The staff seems to be very cheerful; but most people seem to be cheerful in this part of Austria, and I think that the hours of the staff are very long. So far as I can see the young boys here work at least fourteen hours a day, and they seem to be here every day – Sundays included. I see a boy-waiter working at 9.30 at night who sometimes brings me my breakfast at 8 a.m. and who probably begins work actually at 7 a.m. The chamber-maid here, who is very good indeed, – well I have seen her about in the corridors at 6.35 a.m. and she is also about at 10 p.m. The other evening she went out with an elderly woman – probably her mother; a night off, nice to witness, but also rather pathetic.

Tuesday, August 11th. – This morning I went to a rehearsal of von Hoffmansthal's *The Great World Theatre* in the still far-from-finished Salzburg Festtheater. I asked him when he wrote the play. He said in his funny clipped English: 'I wrote it in 1920 (or 21?). There was Bolshevism in Munich and Bolshevism in Buda-Pesth. We Austrians were between the two. I said "Shall we turn Bolshevik?" and I said " No I think we shall not." Partly because we have a certain natural common sense, and partly because we have been living happily for hundreds of years. So I wrote the play.' The little speech was rather touching and very charming. All the acting at this rehearsal was admirable.

Tuesday, September 15th. – W. J. Locke last night at the Garrick said he had practically a life contract with Hearsts for serials, going on till 1932. I said if I offered a story for a serial they always wanted it altered. He said with him, never. Once he had his hero try to commit suicide. Hearsts said that they had a strong Baptist connexion, and that readers might object to the hero having a tendency to suicide, and would Locke turn it into an accident (motor car, it was). He did so. On another occasion they wanted the end of a story altering. He said: 'If you can get one of the clever young men in your office to alter it I shall have no objection.' Of course Hearsts left the thing alone. On another occasion they wanted a tale altering. He replied by cable: 'Wife won't let me.' He said he worked between 10 p.m. and 2 a.m. and never at any other time. His first story (a short story £2 10. 0.) appeared in *London Society* in 1882, in the same number as an instalment of Wilkie Collins's *I say No*. This is what they call a 'link'.

Wednesday, November 11th. – I finished Part I (including all the political stuff) of *Lord Raingo* on Monday afternoon, to my great relief. While doing this I could not be bothered to write journals or do anything that I was not absolutely compelled to do. 83,000 words of the novel are now done. Beaverbrook has read all but the last 4 (short) chapters, to vet. it for political correctness, and he is enthusiastic about it, thrilled by it. He only found one small slip in it (about the time at which it would be possible for Raingo to leave the House of Commons after hearing a debate). He found another slip; but it wasn't one. He made two suggestions, one for altering the wording of a telegram, and the other in a form of address. It is *marvellous* to me that I have been able to do all these complicated politics without once getting off the rails. I can scarcely believe it.

Hotel de Russie, Rome, Friday, January 1st. – Three Madonna churches in Piazza del Popolo. I went into two this morning at 11 a.m. At S. Maria del Popolo, fine church with two good chapels, lovely design, and some good baroque, mammoth music and choir. Quite a congregation. All the high altar lit up by electricity like a booth at a wakes. At S. Maria del Monte Santo, two altars were being served at once. More gorgeous priests. Congregation spread over the floor on chairs, anyhow, as at a drawing-room meeting. Collection being made by a dwarf in a short white thing over black; dirty face; very dark.

Later I went into the same church (S. M. del Popolo). Another Mass afoot, but the electric illuminations of the high altar had been extinguished. Why? A larger congregation. We made out the paintings by Pinturicchio, Raphael, etc., and sculpture by Mino da Fiesole. This church ought to be seen again and again. It shall be. We drove up to the top of the Janiculum Hill, for the view of Rome at sunset. It was marvellous, rose-tinted; then the sun disappeared, and the show was suddenly over.

One of the chief curses of Roman street life is the hooting of the motors. Incessant and peculiarly strident. If it isn't altered the population will develop some nervous disease.

Tuesday, January 12th. – We went to the Doria Gallery this morning. Badly hung pictures. Badly lighted. The galleries narrow and terribly over decorated. The collectors seemed to have had a sure taste for the second rate. But there were several very fine Breughels – small, second rate Claudes and Titians, and a lot of filthy stuff.

Thursday, January 14th. – Neuralgia all night. I finished Gerhardi's *The Polyglots* in the night. This work is too long, lacks shape, and has a few short passages of merely silly jocosity, but as a whole it is individual, original, comical, touching, and full of flavour. In the night I also read a lot of *Candide*. The most amusing novel ever written.

Tuesday, January 26th. – I finished *Lord Raingo* at 5.30 p.m. to-day, having written 2,000 words in the day. Total length: 130,200 words. I liked the last chapter. Very tired.

Friday, January 29th. – I read *in* the first number of the *New Criterion*, in which are some weird things, including one by Gertrude Stein, out of which I could make nothing; and not much out of T. S. Eliot's essay on what a review ought to be. Aldous Huxley's story 'The Monocle' was good in detail, but had absolutely no plot, and is really only a sketch. Perhaps he meant it for a sketch; only I think he meant it for a short story and failed to bring it off.

Wednesday, February 3rd. – After tea I went into S. Maria of the Miracles in the P. del Popolo, because it was open, and I was too feeble to walk. All at once in a different world (with the lounge of the Russie just across the street). Church scarcely lit. A few people, chiefly old and poor. A choir boy or acolyte moves about, bowing to altar every time he passes in front of it, lighting a bit of electric light. Then a bigger acolyte, a tall man, appears, and climbs up and does things to the altar. People come in, like the others chiefly old and poor and mainly women, but a few aged men. The priest comes with hands together, and kneels at altar, and begins to chant and the congregation gives the responses. I should say quite twenty minutes this goes on. It is wonderful how the congregation remembers the responses. Meanwhile the boy, having left bell-ringing to priest, begins to light tall altar candles by a light on the end of a long stick. He has difficulty with some of them. Somebody hidden behind the altar helps with a still longer stick – uncanny effect of this longer stick moving about without hands. At last all lighted. An older priest, only in black – no ornaments, has come and sat at a desk within the choir. Church now lit. Very effective. Then an organ (? American) in a gallery strikes up. It is awful. Also a small hidden choir, equally awful. A tremendously long and monotonous choral business. I left before it was over. I had been in the church 50 minutes at least.

Thursday, February 4th. – Night moderately bad. Finished 'Fathers and Sons' article for *Sunday Pictorial* at 6 p.m. At 11.20, D. and Martin Wilson and I went to Palatine Hill, and saw (chiefly) the views therefrom – and especially the dome of St Peter's, like a pearl (really, in the soft light). It was a wonderful humid day for colour, and of course it rained before we reached Ranieri's for lunch. Livia's house, Tiberius's palace, etc. It seems that in the garden on the top, the State grows all the old Roman plants. I began to get tired *immediately* I began to walk about seeing sights. After lunch I ached in every limb, and I still ache, and I have neuralgia. It is always the same.

Monday, February 8th. – After waking about once an hour from midnight to 5 p.m. I arose at 6 and wrote the first scene of a new sensational, comical, moralistic larkish novel, and have been completely exhausted during the rest of the day.

I have gone back to reading Stendhal on Rome. A relief. This book is always interesting.

Pisa, Tuesday, February 16th. – At 8.30 a.m. I received a note from C. K. Scott Moncrieff asking to see me and offering to show me things in the town. He came at 11.30. Lame, quick, fussy. Very talkative (smartishly) and rather nervous at first but not later. He said that Lucca was only twelve miles off. This was on our way to the cathedral. I wanted to turn back at once and get a car for Lucca, which had always been romantical to me on account of a chapter in Heine's *Reisebilder*. We couldn't get a car in the town. All had gone or were going to Viareggio for the Carnival.

At Lucca we got a *carrozza*, and went through the town at walking pace, and saw cathedrals and churches. Very fine and distinctive, and Moncrieff a good guide. A rich town, prosperous, clean, self-contained and self-sufficient. More so than

Pisa. The oil business and farming must be money-making. But I asked for the Bagni di Lucca, made fascinating to me by Heine – and they were twenty miles off. So I was baulked there. At San Frediano, Lucca, it was interesting to see the altar where Francia's *Entombment* once was. Who pinched it and put it in the National Gallery I don't know.

Hotel Miramar, Genoa, Wednesday, February 17th. – Pisa. Duomo in morning. As Ash Wednesday, service going on. Large audience of choir boys and *écoliers* and a few schoolgirls and old people. Many guests of various ranks. The parson began to preach, got up full speed in about twenty seconds, and then never paused or even hesitated for a word for half an hour. Then he sat down and wiped his face, and then, still sitting, talked to the congregation about a collection. When you were close by he was perfectly audible. Twenty yards off you distinctly heard two voices, and still farther off you heard three or four voices, a babel of voices, all furiously arguing or wrangling. It was a most curious echo effect.

Genoa, Thursday, February 18th. – I am not very keen on *The Pilgrim's Progress*. So far it is too full of minute 'similitudes', which are tedious. I doubt whether I shall finish. The question is: Do children read it all? Or do they skip the morality and theology for the more active parts? I doubt whether the book is holding its own in the public esteem to-day.

Saturday, March 6th. – I have returned to reading Stendhal's *Promenades dans Rome*. Then I sat in garden, and thought out next chapter of my novel. We just got back to the hotel at 1 p.m. for lunch. Neuralgia. I slept fifteen minutes, and woke acutely nervous and still neuralgic. I went into D. and said: 'I can't sleep, and I can't work either.' She said: 'Perhaps you can begin packing my valise.' She was sewing. I made no reply, but returned to my room and began to write. I wrote 1,100 words – a complete chapter – in seventy-five minutes, and then felt better.

Hôtel Bristol, Paris, Wednesday, March 17th. – We drove to
André Maurois's house at Neuilly. Nice ground-floor flat with
garden and two children (boys 4 and 5); the daughter aged 12
had gone to her *cours*. Portrait of the dead mother on table in
drawing-room. She was beautiful. Something tragic about this.
Maurois, slim, slight, Jewish; charming; with an open mind;
interested, admirably urbane.

Sunday, March 28th. – After tea we went to the film *The Sea
Beast* at the New Gallery; the idea being taken and slaughtered
from *Moby Dick*. A filthy and preposterous thing and humiliating to watch. John Barrymore the chief interpreter. A
dreadful Hollywood girl as the heroine; obviously chosen for
her looks, which were dreadful. This film really did annoy me.
We didn't see it all. The immense hall was by no means full;
especially the dearest seats were nearly empty when the Barrymore film started (it was a continuous performance). The films
of the Boat Race and the Grand National were not bad. The
Grand National seemed to be all falls. It seemed most brutal,
and I was minded to write an article about it. Also about the
Boat Race, which ruins the hearts of so many youths. No. 5
in the Oxford crew this year collapsed before the end, and I
expect that his heart will never be the same again. Of course
he is branded, with pity, in the papers. He even had headlines.
He must have had quite an agreeable week-end.

Wednesday, April 21st. – I have begun to read *Rhoda Fleming*.
Goodish. But he *will* make all his characters talk smart or
epigrammatically, and every now and then he foolishly tries to
justify this smartness by some psychological explanation.
Some of the dialogues are very tedious and untrue. Still, there
is stuff in the book.

Thursday, April 22nd. – I meant to go out for an aimle
walk, and then I saw that it was the Private View of the Seu
pictures at the Lefèbre Galleries, so I went there. The Seu
pictures want a lot of seeing to appreciate. In the big pict
Poseuses, one thing that strikes you is the loving patienc

the execution – equalling Memling's, e.g., the pictures were badly framed, but according to Seurat's own ideas.

To the New Gallery to see the new Jannings film, *Vaudeville*. It is very fine, despite a simple and rather crude story. All the pictures make 'designed pictures'. I should say the prisoners' exercise was inspired by Van Gogh. Even the empty interiors are like Cézanne. The close-ups are wonderful in design.

Tuesday, May 4th. – To-day was the first day of the general strike. Many more motors about. I walked round to Victoria, which was shut up (both stations) one small entrance guarded by policemen. I heard someone say that a train had gone somewhere during the morning. Yet in the vast empty stations Smith's bookstalls were open. So were (outside) the cafés. The populace excited and cheery, on this 1st day of the strike. No evening paper. News from the Wireless at very short intervals, $\frac{1}{2}$ hour intervals at night up to midnight. I should think that nearly all theatres would soon be closed. Already to-day there has been a noticeably increasing gravity in the general demeanour.

Saturday, May 8th. – I've been reading *Le Lys dans la Vallée* lately. I've read about 140 close pages, and I don't think I shall read any more. A few pages here and there are really good. And the story is designed, organized, constructed. But the book is ruined by sentimentalism and *sensiblerie* and eloquence. There are no chapter divisions and many of the paragraphs are far too long. I wouldn't mind the dialogue being stilted, but I object to its awful eloquence. Never was there a woman, really, as angelic as Henriette, and if there was she ought to have been abandoned to a brutal and licentious soldiery. Yet when I first read this novel, perhaps thirty years ago (in a rotten English translation) I enjoyed it immensely and thought it was a masterpiece. I fear Balzac is going to pieces. The last time I read *Le Curé de Tours* even that seemed to be rather thin and tedious in parts. Ditto *Le Père Goriot*. I suppose I must try to read *Splendeurs et Misères* again. If that won't pass, I'll try

Cousine Bette, which I think is the finest Balzac, and if that won't pass I shall denounce Balzac as a back number, to my extreme regret.

Tuesday, May 11th. – I am still sticking to my point with everyone that the calling of the general strike is a political crime that must be paid for. Also that the general strike is revolutionary, that is, aimed at the authority of the Government. How this can be denied when the Unions Council has the infernal cheek to issue permits to goods and vehicles to use the roads and railways, I cannot understand. As if anybody could possibly need permission to use roads except in a revolution.

Wednesday, May 12th. – The general strike now seems pitiful, foolish – a pathetic attempt of underdogs who hadn't a chance when the over-dogs really set themselves to win. Everybody, nearly, among the over-dogs seems to have joined in with grim enthusiasm to beat the strike. The Doctor called yesterday morning, and even he had been working at 'criminal investigations' for the Government. (He spoke of deaths resulting from East End rioting.) Willie Maugham was working at Scotland Yard till 8.30 of a night – I don't know what at. Special constables abounded.

Thursday, May 13th. – Everyone is still preoccupied with the strike, or rather with what is called 'The new strike'. Duff Tayler told great stories of his adventurous journeys on the Tube trains driven by swagger youths in yellow gloves who nevertheless now and then overran the platform with their trains, or pulled up too short. Also of University porters with gold cigarette cases and an incredible politeness and fatherliness towards you for your safety. Maugham was what he called a 'sleuth' at Scotland Yard. A police car was sent for him always. The first night he worked all night from 11 p.m. to 8.30 a.m. He said the last few hours, after the dawn, were simply terrible, and he couldn't see how he would ever be able to get through them. I don't know what a 'sleuth' is.

Amberley, Saturday, May 22nd. – Lovely weather. I walked up on to the Downs in the middle of the morning. Sun. Prospects. Three teams of horses rolling a field. Hawthorn everywhere, a little red, all the rest white. The most insistent phenomenon, however, is the song of birds. You hear that everywhere and practically all the time. I hoped there was going to be a cricket match in the village field close by this house; but there wasn't. Nothing except a few children using the swings.

I finished *Cousine Bette*. It holds you throughout, but it is very high-flown and sentimental, and the good women are far too good, and the bad a little too bad. It becomes melo-dramatic in the end. The 'Brazilian' is used in a manner very effectively dramatic towards the end and at the end. I then began Dreiser's *An American Tragedy*, a book of immense length – 2 vols. 900 pages or more. Written in a very slatternly way; in fact dreadfully written. Seems ordinary at first, and in the main is ordinary; but after 40 pages it does begin to hold you. The fellow has a large sense of form, and an eye for things that count with the imagination.

Sunday, May 23rd. – Dreiser's *An American Tragedy*. I have already read 150 pages of this novel. The mere writing is simply bloody – careless, clumsy, terrible. But there is power, and he holds you, because his big construction is good. The book quite woke me up last night, just as I was going off to sleep.

Tuesday, May 25th. – I heard definitely from Marguerite this morning that she would not agree to a divorce. Couldn't work. I went out for a short walk, past the castle and through fields. The spectacle grew more and more lovely. Suddenly I came to the river Arun and no bridge. A ferry which is not available during day, but a man happened to be on the spot, and he ferried me over. At Bury church I learnt that it was three miles to Amberley, unless I went back by the ferry. I wouldn't go back by the ferry. I therefore walked the three miles, and got back at 11.45, tired but in much better health. Also I had picked up some ideas for my novel *en route*. I despaired of doing any work, but about 5.30 I came upstairs and wrote 700 words: A triumph of will over pain and pessimism. At intervals I read Phillpotts's latest classical fantasy *Circe's Island*. It is very easy to read, but not at all classical. It is just a vehicle for his philosophy of life. Fine humour in spots, and a certain agreeable general saltiness.

Monday, May 31st. – I was reading about Scott's methods in *The Times Lit. Suppl.* on Sunday, and it seems he wrote the last chapters of *Woodstock* at the rate of one chapter, or about thirty printed pages, a day, consecutively. Well, it is almost miraculous. It must have been 5 or 6,000 words a day. And once written the stuff was not re-read or looked at, at all, until the proofs came in. If I could write anything like that I should only work six months in the year. I suppose it's true.

Wednesday, June 2nd. – After lunch I finished *An American Tragedy* by Dreiser. This book must be 250, or 300,000 words long. Taken as a whole it is very fine and impressive. He has held it together everywhere magnificently. It has no humour, and lots and lots of original, true psychological observations.

Thursday, June 3rd. – This afternoon I read through the first 20,000 words of *The Vanguard* and corrected them. Not good: not utterly evil. I have now written 40,000 words – half of it.

Saturday, June 5th. – While I was working here in my bed-room, I saw a funeral come up, four men carrying a coffin on their shoulders, and some nice flowers on the coffin, and a few black-clothed villagers of both sexes behind. I wrote a few words, as it seemed, and I looked out again, and the people were coming back, minus the coffin, much disburdened, and feeling easy and free. The burden had been put down in the grave in a very short time.

Tuesday, June 8th. – This day the hatching took place in several of the four nests of house martens under the south eave of this house. To-day I saw in the June number of *La Nouvelle Revue Française* an advertisement of *Le Spectre*, by Arnold Bennett. I expect I wrote this about 27 years ago. Nobody thought anything of it, and I didn't. And yet the very high-brow N.R.F. chooses it to begin its campaign for 'imposing me on the French public'; (according to the words of Gaston Gallimard, who has now written to me twice). All of which is very strange.

Wednesday, June 9th. – After a little hesitation, I set to work on a new chapter of *The Vanguard* and wrote 1,800 words in just three hours (3 o'c. to 6 o'c.). It meant ten words a minute throughout, and really more than that, because at 4.15 I made my own tea (or rather my own verveine) and partook of the same in a leisurely manner with brown bread and butter. And all this after a rotten bad night. Pride! Vainglory! In the evening (when it rained tremendously) we paddled down to Mrs Glenister's bungalow. At the end of the evening, she turned on the loud-speaker wireless, *Valkyrie* in the room. I don't seem to be able to get over the amazing magic of this wireless device. The music seems to come to you from nowhere, and you wonder where it has been hiding while waiting for you to want it.

Thursday, June 10th. – I have now worked myself into a spell (which may prove short) of mass-production in *The Vanguard*. I wrote 1,100 words before tea to-day in less than 90 minutes, and another 500 words after tea in about 30 minutes. All this, for me, is very quick work, though Trollope beat it practically the whole time, and so did Scott.

I read about half *The Ghost* yesterday. It begins brilliantly, but is not so good later on. But it is all fairly good and an excellent performance for a first book (as I believe it was). I am still puzzled by the N.R.F. beginning their publication of my novels with this book, but I am less puzzled than I was before. *The Vanguard* is better than *The Ghost* in truth to nature and in skill of handling material, but that it is fundamentally better in creativeness and verve, I doubt. Neither of them is more than a fantastic lark, nor pretends to be more.

Friday, June 11th. – John Cowper Powys walked over the downs from Burpham to-day, and arrived before noon and stayed till after 5.30. He was delighted beyond measure when I spoke very highly of Dreiser's *An American Tragedy*. He said Dreiser was very susceptible to praise. He said that Dreiser had sold the film rights of the novel for 50,000 dollars. Powys is a very sentimental man in many ways. He was rather in favour of the general strike, but gave in instantly to my argument that it was right to squash it; but I expect he is in favour of it again by this time. He has very fine literary taste, except when it is misled by his few prejudices. I asked him about his days (not evenings) in provincial cities in America. He said he did nothing except walk about. He wanted to work, i.e. write, but couldn't work in hotel bedroom; at least had not seriously tried to. I told him I had written lots and lots in hotel bedrooms and he said that he should try. An untidy fellow, of very great charm.

Wednesday, June 23rd. – My ideas were not sufficiently creative for me to go on with the next chapter of *The Vanguard*; so I went on correcting the last 30 odd galley proofs of *Lord Raingo*. I finished these immediately after lunch. Some portions of Part 2 I think are dull, and lacking in drama, being merely descriptive if taken separately. I may, however, be wrong, as I was very tired while correcting them, I was tired physically as well as a bit mentally.

I fiddled about until nearly 6 p.m. in the afternoon, and then wrote 1,000 words of *The Vanguard* in less than 90 minutes. I ached all over with something rheumatical.

Sunday, June 27th. – I finished reading *Pierre*. This novel is not equal to *Moby Dick*; but it is full of very fine things, and a most remarkable book. Melville's idea was the grand romantic manner, and when he succeeded in it, he *did* succeed. His humour, too, is very rich. I think he must have been influenced by Rabelais, though there is nothing Rabelaisian in the book. The pity is he gets so many incidents improbable, when with a little more invention and trouble he might have made them quite probable. Nevertheless I think it is entitled to be called a great book – even if *manqué* here and there.

Thursday, July 8th. – I finished *The Vanguard* to-day at 4.15, having written 5,500 words of it in two days. I began the work on 8th February in Rome; it was very seriously interrupted by the birth of Virginia, and I wrote the 10 or 12,000 words of it all over afresh, and I'm glad I did it. I wrote the last two-thirds of it here at Amberley in 44 days. I have never worked more easily than during the last six weeks.

75 Cadogan Square, Friday, July 16th. – The other day Philip Nichols was urging that it was undignified for me to write for Sunday papers, etc. But I argued him out of it. I have rather a passion for a big public and plain subjects.

Friday, July 30th. – I drove to the Tate Gallery and saw for the first time the basement galleries containing many dreadful Sargent water-colours and a whole collection of modern French small pictures, including Braque. I also heard one of the Tate lecturers, not so good as the one I listened to the other day. This was a younger man, and much more of a finicking highbrow. He was talking of Romney, and rather severely. He said that 'Romney was often vulgar – that explained why he was so fond of Emma' (Hamilton). True, perhaps, but this young man's style was far too condescending.

Saturday, July 31st. – I walked to Victoria after breakfast, just to see the sight, which was worth seeing. The Bank Holiday crowd was about the size I expected. Long, thick queues in various places of the station, both inside and outside. But all quite orderly. And the sight of the 3rd class Pullman was satisfactory. Although far more people travel now than 40 years ago, they travel far more comfortably and with more dignity. I saw no crushing and crowding. Nevertheless it must be quite an enterprise to take a family away, with all baggage, on the Saturday before Bank Holiday. In the late afternoon, when I walked down King's Road as far as

The World's End, there was proof that most of London had stayed in London. The side streets of King's Road are at least as interesting as the main road itself. I suppose painters don't paint them more because they can't get a calm 'sitting'.

Saturday, August 7th. – I found a new way of getting to the Tate Gallery, via Victoria and thence by tram. It has taken me some years to think of this, but I have thought of it. With luck fifteen minutes will cover the whole thing. I heard part of a good but too detailed lecture on Hogarth as a storyteller, and then devoted myself to the Blake drawings, which I have always avoided here hitherto. What terrific stuff. These in their largeness and simplifications are quite as good on inspection as any for the novelist who is trying to move on a high plane.

Sunday, August 8th. – I felt that I must have some adventure. It was a very nice afternoon, with threatening clouds. I hurried out and taxied to St Paul's. Immense flock of tame pigeons on the piazza, being fed. A congregation (sparse) assembled inside for a service. I then took a bus for Hackney Wick. I thought that would do as well as anywhere. But before I got to the Wick I saw buses going in the opposite direction to Blackwall Tunnel, which I had never seen. So I got off, and took one of these latter, and went all down the Burdett Road into East India Dock Road to Poplar, and I saw big steamers and even a fine 3-master, and a huge home or hostel for sailors. Incidentally the top of the slope leading to the tunnel. The thoroughfares are superb in width and very clean, and I noted lots of very interesting things. The East End keeps on till you get to Aldgate when it stops all of a sudden, and you begin to see Theatre Ticket Agencies.

Thursday, August 12th. – I had a great desire to go and see what the other side of the river was like opposite the Tate Gallery, and so, by tram and bus, I went. What a quick change there is immediately you cross. Stone setts instead of wood or asphalt. *Many* more horses than the N. side. Much more noise, more dirt. More physical labour. There are various big factories just close to Vauxhall Bridge, not to mention the railways. A great press of road traffic. Semi-slums. I walked up several semi-slummy streets, such as 'Italian Walk'. Then I went back over the bridge – at once calmness, quiet, and no horses. Very dramatic.

Monday, August 16th. – At 11 a.m. I suddenly went off to the Oval to see an hour of the 5th and last Test Match. Crowd very quick to take up every point. Every maiden over cheered, for instance. Women fainting here and there. Attendants to look after them. Cricket cautious and very slow. Great roar when Woodfull's wicket fell. Heat of the crowd. Great difficulty of seeing anything at all, even by tiptoeing and craning.

Monday, August 23rd. – I have been reading *A l'ombre des ieunes filles en fleurs*, and I still maintain that it is a bit on the dry side, though very good. It doesn't impassion *me*. I shouldn't care much if I didn't read any more of it. It lacks juice. It has almost no concern with anything except analysis of views and feelings – especially snobbishness. No landscapes, no furniture, no corporate life. No general 'feel' of things. This sort of business satisfies Walkley, but it could never satisfy me, in a novelist.

75 Cadogan Square, Thursday, August 26th. – At 11 a.m. I bussed and walked up to Charing Cross Road and bought *Lamiel*, a novel by Stendhal that I had never seen, and couldn't remember ever having heard of. [After lunch] I bussed and walked to Hammersmith for the Lyric Board meeting, where I was told that the author of *Tommy, make room for your uncle*, composed in 1876, had come into the theatre to hear his own song sung, and was pleased with the performance thereof. Such is life.

Sunday, August 29th. – I seemed to spend a great deal of time reading Wells's *William Clissold*, of which I nearly finished the first vol. I also nearly finished Stendhal's *Lamiel*.

At about 5.15 Dorothy and I went out for a City excursion. We drove to St Paul's Cathedral first, of which the front was in the usual Sunday mess; a fearful litter of paper, and kids feeding the birds, and hawkers: all extremely untidy, slatternly, etc. Even offensive. The inside was as it was the last time; but I saw the dreadful Watts's pictures. Also *The Light of the World*. It is all pretty dreadful, and I suppose it will remain so for years – until the repairs are at last finished. Something ought to be done about the front space on Sunday afternoons.

Monday, August 30th. – I finished reading *The World of William Clissold*, Vol. I, and I thoroughly enjoyed it; it held me; I read it with gusto. So in the evening I wrote to Wells and told him so.

Hotel Commercio, Venice, Wednesday, September 1st. – After a long journey (beginning as regards this day with a heavenly breakfast at 7 a.m. in the train and brightened by the sharp self-consciousness which one has after a bad night, and proceeding by Lakes Maggiore and Garda) we arrived at Venice at 5.21, only six minutes late. We plunged straight into a gondola. We liked the Hotel Commercio because it is not in the least the *genre Palace*. The scene on the Piazza, and in the small square (giving on the Canal) where the big band was playing, were simply marvellous at night. Unique.

Friday, September 3rd. – [Edmund] Dulac assured me that he had promised Puccini some old Chinese tunes for *Turandot*. He forgot the matter, and Puccini wrote and reminded him. Dulac then composed some Chinese tunes himself, and sent them, and Puccini used some of them. Then to *terrasse* of Florian again. Lots of acquaintances. Band playing Wagner on a marvellous temporary bandstand in centre of Piazza. Sudden shower of rain. *Terrasses* emptied in a moment, and colonnades crammed. The band seemed to have been magically dissolved away by the rain.

Saturday, September 4th. – I had an appointment with Alf Mason [A. E. W. Mason] at Florian's at 11.30. Alfred and I went off in his gondola to see the Accademia. A fine gondola all black and gold with the funny extra furniture of a chair to match. Very comfortable. I was rather disappointed with my first view of the Accademia. The pictures seemed to be too exclusively Venetian, and I could not see Titian's *Assunta*. We stayed there till exhaustion set in, and then went by small canals to Ristorante Bonvecchiato for lunch. Picturesque and good. Then we walked and got lost, until suddenly I saw a street I knew, close to this hotel. But I could not have found my way back to Bonvecchiato though it could not be more than a third of a mile off.

Saw Mrs Lindsay in the Florian colonnade and she re-introduced me to Lady C., who wanted me to exert myself to get the O.M. for George Moore. She said that Balfour was favourable but would never actually do anything to help anyone.

Saturday, September 11th. – We went to the Scuola di San Rocco to see Tintoretto and Titian. It is, however, impossible to see these pictures owing to them being very dark and hung between great windows which dazzle the eye and darken the pictures. So we couldn't appreciate them. Two great thrills to-day. The Bellini altar piece (tri-partite) in the Frari church this morning, and this afternoon we went to the Giovanetti palace, and saw Giorgione's *Storm* (of which I keep a reproduction in my bedroom). Marvellous! Un-human. So rich and full and harmonious. Finer than I had hoped for. The palace has a tremendous series of communicating salons, with a huge ball-room. All heavily furnished, with much ugly stuff, but rich. The hundreds and hundreds of candles had been turned to electricity.

Wednesday, September 29th. – Michael Morton came by appointment to see me at 6.30. He said that *Riceyman Steps* had been refused by practically everyone in the West End, except Leon M. Lion. Lion was prepared to do it (as he was having a great success with Galsworthy's *Escape*); but he would only begin it by a series of six matinées, and he would get it into an evening bill if it succeeded at matinées. Lion instanced the case of *Tiger Cats*. He gave four matinées of this and lost £900; then, after an interval, put it into the evening bill and made £5,000. Morton believes in him. He says he is sure he wants to do fine things. Lion has a brother in the City, who said to Morton: 'I haven't read this *Riceyman Steps* play, but I believe it's a fine thing, and I'll back it with my money, and I don't care if I lose over it.' Lion is to play the miser. A month ago I should have said that the notion of Lion playing the miser was absurd, but after seeing him in Galsworthy's *Escape*, I should say that he could play it very well indeed.

Sanclu Hotel, Ramsgate, Saturday, October 9th. – I read about 50 pages of Osbert Sitwell's first novel, *Before the Bombardment*. It is inscribed to 'dear, good, uncle Arnold from a nephew'. Well, it is difficult to read. Very brilliant, or perhaps 'rather' brilliant: but it doesn't seem to have much form, and much individual interest. The man *describes* characters instead of showing them.

Sunday, October 10th. – Drove to Sandwich. A really antique feeling about this place. Streets such as Delf Street. Most curious the moment you begin really to think about it inquisitively. Happily a few barges get there still, up the stream, and seem to live in fields. All churches round here are closed on Sunday. We got into the one at Sandwich because some unfortunate children were imprisoned there for the afternoon service, but the fine church at Minster was closed; reminding me of my Sunday visit to Truro to see the monstrosity of a cathedral there: which was closed entirely.

Wednesday, October 20th. – I went first of all to Charing Cross Road; but couldn't find any book that I really wanted to buy. I bought one or two little brochures on French and German painters, and a copy of the *Calendar* with a grotesque article by D. H. Lawrence in dispraise of Wells's *Clissold*: a terrible revelation of Lawrence's childish and spiteful disposition.

Thursday, October 21st. – I began to read *Brunel's Tower* as a beginning for my essay on Phillpotts's novels for his limited edition.

The Wellses, the Robert Nicholses, Geoffrey Scott, and Alec Shepeler came for dinner. This party went off admirably well and was a great lark. Wells is quieter than he used to be, and Nichols is even noisier than he used to be. There was a lot of argument between him and H. G. Wells in which H. G. was quiet and effective. Geoffrey Scott is a very good talker, and very charming. He really has a brain, and isn't afraid to give its results to you at once.

Friday, October 22nd. – I finished reading Phillpotts's *Brunel's Tower*, in the afternoon. It is done in the classical manner and tradition, but needs a relief of which there is no indication. I now have two others to read before I can write the introduction to the *édition de luxe* of his novels. It is interesting to find, in the copy of *Brunel's Tower* which he lent me to read, how he has perceived, ten years after writing the book, that it was too long and might be cut with advantage. This copy is marked in red ink for the printer of the new edition, and I should say that a good 50 pages have been cut out of it: which here and there makes it rather awkward to read.

Saturday, October 23rd. – At 12.15 we drove down to Cherkley to lunch with Max [Beaverbrook]. Max asked me if I would write a weekly article on books under my own name for the *Evening Standard*. I didn't give a definite answer, but what I said and didn't say was not far short of a consent.

Tuesday, October 26th. – Went to Tchekoff's *Three Sisters* at the Barnes Theatre. Well, I was bored frequently. Did I enjoy myself? No, not on the whole. Was I uplifted as I had been by an even gloomier play, *Rosmersholm*? No. It seemed to me that often the author was wilfully pessimistic. He is certainly very monotonous, and all his plays that I've seen have the same tone. A decent Philistine man, sitting just behind us, said at the end of the second act that he had been disappointed and bored. But he liked Act III better, and Act IV still better. On the whole Tchekoff had succeeded with him.

Saturday, October 30th. – I began to think more seriously about the plan of my new novel [*Accident*]. I had already got the moral background for it: the dissatisfaction of a successful and rich man with his own secret state of discontent and with the evils of the age. I wanted a frame. I walked about three miles this morning, and about a mile after tea, without getting a really satisfactory idea; then as I was lolling in my 'easy' about 6.30, I suddenly thought that I would extend the rôle of the *train de luxe*, which I had thought of for the scene of the opening of the story, to be the scene of the whole of the novel – so that the entire time-space of the novel will only be about thirty hours or so. I didn't go any farther than this; I had enough for the day.

Tuesday, November 2nd. – Beaverbrook and Jean Norton came to lunch. I agreed with Max to do a series of book gossip articles for the *Evening Standard*, beginning next week. Then I rushed off to Wardour films, and spent a final $2\frac{3}{4}$ hours on *Faust*, finishing it except for passing proofs of titles and choosing some types. Thorpe asked me to do their next film, *Carmen*, and said I had done splendid work for them and been very patient. I said that I had lost money on *Faust*, in the sense that I could have earned more by other work in the same time. True. But the advantage of doing titles is that they involve no brain-strain.

Thursday, November 4th. – We were ten minutes late for dinner at H. G. Wells's, and H. G. himself was eleven minutes late. The Shaws were there, and Frank Wells, and Marjorie Craig (H. G.'s morning secretary) and the Leonard Woolfs. Both gloomy, these two last. But I liked both of them in spite of their naughty treatment of me in the press. Shaw talked practically the whole time, which is the same thing as saying that he talked a damn sight too much. After dinner he and Dorothy and Virginia Woolf and H. G. formed a group and never moved. I formed another group with Charlotte Shaw and Jane Wells, and never moved either. I really wanted to have a scrap with Virginia Woolf; but got no chance.

Saturday, November 6th. – I forgot to put down a thing I heard Edmund Gosse say at the Sitwell lunch on Thursday. He said, in reply to a remark: 'Who is James Agate?' Considering that Agate is the dramatic critic on the *Sunday Times*, of which Gosse is the chief literary critic, and that they are both weekly contributors. ... André Gide sent me one of 25 author's copies of *Le Journal des Faux Monnayeurs*. This gave me the idea of keeping a journal of my next novel. I may do it. But I ought to have begun it a month ago.

Easton Glebe, near Dunmow, Sunday, November 7th. – A lovely, a heavenly morning; very clear and sunshiny. But very damp underfoot. I breakfasted with Jane Wells at 9.15 and then others came down. Then H. G. and I and D. went for a walk in Easton Park and the grounds of Easton Lodge, and saw a heron on the lake, and heard from H. G. a résumé of Lady Warwick's political life, wrong in certain details. We came back, and H. G. and I changed, and all six of us played ball games for 50 minutes. Fine lunch with 3 ducks and a hot apple pie. After which, sleep, which enabled me to miss the tennis. There was some tennis and some bridge and some Schubert trio on the gramophone, and some yacht talk, and some tea – with rose leaf jam. The day (outdoor) was now over, and all we had to live for was the fireworks postponed from wet yesterday evening. H. G. disappeared for about 90 minutes after tea. We thought he was reading or asleep. But at midnight he told us that he had suddenly had the ideas for continuing a novel that he hadn't touched for a month, and so had gone on with it.

Sunday, November 14th. – I corrected my article on E. Phillpotts, for his limited edition. I think very little of this critical exercise: I hope it will help to sell the edition; but I doubt whether anything will overcome the general public objection to peasants in fiction. This was always strongly against Hardy's success too. If Phillpotts had dealt with the bourgeois, he would have been accepted as one of our leading psychologists. However, it doesn't matter; anyway he has made the public accept two bucolic comedies at once.

Tuesday, November 23rd. – I wrote a letter to the *Daily Mail* in reply to Birkenhead's criticism of *Raingo* in that paper, and I signed it before I left home. After I left, the *Mail* telephoned that they would like an article at 2*s*. a word, as well as the letter. They said the letter was too good to lose. So, by telephone from the theatre, I agreed to both. I much enjoyed writing both the letter and the short article.

Monday, November 29th. – I didn't finally wake up till 7.58, very rare occurrence, as I had had very few breaks during the night. *Daily Mail* article by Birkenhead on me, in which he practically accused me of lying.

I went downstairs and wrote my reply to Birkenhead in the form of a letter to the *Mail*. When I took it to Miss Nerney she said that the *Mail* had telephoned for an article: so I crossed out the Sir, and Yours truly, and called it an article and charged £60 for it.

Wednesday, December 1st. – When I opened the *Daily Mail* this morning I found that Birkenhead had made no further answer to me; so the incident is now, I suppose, closed. The press has been very generally in my favour. I had prepared some heavy artillery to kill him if he had continued the fight.

Mary Borden wrote an article in the *Standard* (as a retort to my criticisms of her) advising the young to take no notice of the work of H. G. Wells and myself. She is a clever woman, and was clever enough to ignore my criticisms of herself.

Thursday, December 2nd. – I walked all the way to the Savoy Hotel for the dinner of the Other Club. Birkenhead came in, and we were very affable to one another, and everybody laughed about the just finished scrap between us in the *Daily*

Mail. Afterwards he was most friendly and asked me to lunch with him alone. Reading was in the chair, and the dinner was the most agreeable that I remember of this Club. Churchill and Jack Seely came in very late, long after dinner. Churchill said to me: 'Receive the congratulations of Tom Hogarth' (over my row with Birkenhead). There was a great deal of *Raingo* throughout the evening.

Sunday, December 5th. – Walter Sickert and wife (Thérèse Lessore) and Cobb and Schuster and Wylde dined with us at the Royal York. Sickert (now aged 66) was in great form, especially towards the end of the dinner and later when we all came over to this hotel and sat in our sitting room. His wife was very quiet and dark and sweet, but far less quiet than when I sat next to her at dinner at Ethel Sands's a year or two ago. Sickert said some fine, sound things. He explained to us exactly why he liked Leader's pictures. But his pose is increasing of admiring the public as a judge of heart. I said that what he said was only half true, and he said, 'Yes, but there is a great deal in it.'

Monday, December 13th. – To the Hotel Cecil for the grand political Liberal Party dinner in honour of Vivian Phillipps, chief whip and organizer of the said Party. Earl Grey in the chair. It was quite lively at our table. Grey made a very good and really weighty speech of 45 minutes. Nearly all the white-haired politicians behaved as usual at these things, just like kids – pleased to death at the slightest 'hit', or comedy platitudes. Beaming all the time.

Monday, January 3rd. – Left at 10.45 p.m. and reached the Robert Mayers's, Cumberland Terrace, at 11 p.m. for a reception given by them to the members of the jury which decides what new works shall be produced at the International Music Festival. They are here (5 of them) for a week, and have to weed out 200 modern works. Arthur Bliss was there, and very lively; also Calvocoressi; also d'Aranyi, looking most distinguished. But the chief draw for me was Bernard van Dieren, whom I had never met. Apparently about forty: looks frail and good-humoured and a bit sardonic. A marvellous brain. He indulged in an argumentative scrap with Bliss, who also is very intelligent, and beat him hollow. I was obliged to tell them that I never could argue. I liked van Dieren very much; or rather I admired him very much.

Friday, January 7th. – To the Royal Academy for the Belgian-Flemish picture show. The Belgian masters are magnificent, but none of them – not even Rubens – ranks with the biggest Italians. Memling, van Eyck, and Breughel are the best. I was sitting in front of the Breughels when Laurence Binyon came up and said: 'Don't you think Breughel is the finest painter in the world?' He isn't, but I was very pleased, because I've been saying this ever since I saw the small Breughel seascapes and things in Rome.

Tuesday, January 11th. – I walked to the Carlton Hotel to meet Colonel Fitzhugh Minnegerode, Leader representative of the Magazine Section of the *New York Times*. Minnegerode had been twenty years in the American army, and had lost the greater part of his regiment at Verdun. He told me the funniest story I have ever heard about a writer. At d'Annunzio's place, somewhere in the north of Italy, the servants have the strictest orders when they meet the master in or about the house, to drop instantly whatever they may be carrying, and

to put one hand and forearm over the other. Whatever it is –
a tea-tray with glasses, *e.g.*, must be dropped on the floor.
So that now the servants have instituted a private 'heralding'
system. A man carrying anything is preceded by another, and if
the former meets the master he crosses his arms, and the
latter gets quickly out of the way. Minnegerode said also that
in the architecture somewhere there is an unfinished column,
and d'Annunzio says that that column will be finished after
Ireland is completely free.

Hotel Tyrol, Innsbruck, Saturday, January 22nd. – Eventless
journey. The Wagons-Lits conductor of our coach said that
conductors depended solely on tips. He said it was all right
when the train was full, but not otherwise. He said that 50
francs was a fine tip. People gave 30 and 20; even 10 and even
5. He said Americans demanded the most attention and gave
the smallest tips. He had an idea that tips were not given in
America.

Wednesday, February 9th. – To-day I read in the *Continental
Daily Mail* that George Sturt ['George Bourne'] was dead.
This death produced no effect of sadness on me at all. George
had been ill and half-paralysed for many years, and I don't
think I had seen him at all for about sixteen years. When I did
see him I drove down to Farnham, and he asked me to keep
my car and chauffeur out of the way lest it should constrain or
frighten or embarrass, or something, his household. And I had
to eat at the inn. I understood all this perfectly well, however,
and I had a couple of hours' fine time with him, chiefly in his
garden. His later books, so far as I read them, were not as good
as his earlier. I remember that when I started to keep a journal
– it must be over thirty years ago – I made up and bound (in
cardboard, etc.) the volumes myself. (I had them bound in
calf later.) I showed the first volume, scarcely written in, to
George. George said: 'If you'll bind me a volume like that,
I'll keep a journal too.' So I did. Afterwards he kept on keeping a journal, but in large volumes. I think that he had made
notes before, but he had never kept a journal. Of course all

these notes and journals were the material of his books in a quite exceptional degree.

Thursday, February 10th. – I saw by chance in the *Nation* a wonderful description of a thunder and hailstorm at a popular resort on a mountain top, by D. H. Lawrence. He can do it sometimes. In fact he can d—d well do it sometimes.

Sunday, February 13th. – Idle in the grand manner to-day. The Huxleys came for lunch shortly after 1 o'clock, and we had a very good lunch, and I drank beer, and it did me no harm. This is the first time I have drunk beer without suffering for it for about eighteen years. The last time I drank it was at a restaurant at or near Baia; it made me ill instantly. The time before that was about sixteen or seventeen or eighteen years ago in a café in the *place* where are the theatres Sarah Bernhardt and Porte St Martin, after seeing Sarah Bernhardt in some rotten play; it made me quite ill for twenty-four hours.

Monday, February 14th. – Aldous Huxley is getting more and more into the habit of using such words as 'inconceivable', 'incredible', 'fantastic'. These three are his favourite words, and one of them comes into nearly every sentence. His general knowledge is extraordinarily good. In fact it is inconceivable, incredible, and fantastic.

Hotel Ruhl, Nice, Tuesday, February 22nd. – We were due at H. G. Wells's, Quartier St Mathieu, Grasse, for lunch. It soon began to rain. Nevertheless the continuously mounting drive to Grasse was very beautiful. Little seems to have changed in that region in the last five years. Nor at Grasse either. The rendezvous with H. G. was for noon in the *Cours* at Grasse. We arrived precisely at twelve, and he was there, signalling, in a big doggy overcoat with the collar turned up, in the rain. Plenty of mud. We left our car and got into his Citroën. Drive of about ten minutes, narrow curving, up and down, thoroughly bad little road. He has the *dépendence* of a larger house, but is building a house of his own on the opposite side of a little valley. Odette Keun came rapidly down-stairs to greet us. She enveloped us in welcome. The 'feminine touch' all over the place. Excellent lunch, Provençale, with appreciable garlic in it. An original lunch. We went over to see the new house in process of construction. Well, H. G. designed it himself and got an architect to 're-draw the plans'. What he would call a jolly little house. But it wouldn't suit me. Rooms too small, and windows too large, and no tradition behind the design. Still the open-air rooms will be very 'jolly' for eating and sitting about in. Much charm in the situation. We greatly enjoyed this visit. It was very invigorating in every way.

Hôtel Bristol, Paris, Thursday, February 24th. – We walked along the Rue du Faubourg St Honoré. Lovely shops. Beauti-fully arranged. Marvellously arranged. This fact strikes me more and more. You may wander afar off to see old quaint quarters of Paris; but they are not more artistic than these modern shops in the middle of the much-despised modern shopping Anglo-American quarter.

I read in Paul Morand's *Rien que la Terre*. This book does not seem to me to be anything very remarkable – at best you can call it remarkably bright, variegated journalism. This is the last of the six French books which I bought in Paris on the day we left for Cortina. I have now read or sampled them all. The best is certainly Aragon's *Paysan de Paris*. I gave it to the Aldous Huxleys. De Castellane's *Comment j'ai découvert l'Amérique* is very interesting and alive for the most part, and contains a few rather profound things. But on the whole I haven't read anything really very startling since we left Eng-land. I doubt whether I am in fact very fond of reading. I always *look forward* to reading. But the realization is less satis-factory. I soon tire of it.

Tuesday, March 1st. – I read a good bit of *Si le grain ne meurt* in the night. The *souvenirs d'enfance* are beautifully done. I am liking this book, of which Gide has sent me a copy of the special *tirage* (50 copies) of the *nouvelle édition*. Certainly I have learnt a little about the newest French literature since I left England. Gide said yesterday that he should speak to Gaston Gallimard to find out why the N.R.F. was so silly as to begin the French translations of my works with *The Ghost*.

Thursday, March 3rd. – I drove down to the Institut de France along the quays, and then walked slowly back as far as the Rue du Bac, looking at the book-boxes. I only bought one book, *Les Moments Perdus de John Shag* by Gilbert de Voisins, which Gide had specially recommended me. It was marked '*Service de la Presse*', 8 frs. instead of 12, and its transparent paper envelope had not been violated at all. There were a few other books I might have bought, but I didn't want to carry them, or I knew I shouldn't read them, or something.

I then walked on to the Restaurant Lucas, where Maurice Baring gave a very good lunch to Dorothy and me and a Russian exile named Dimitrieff Momonoff, a sharp-nosed man with a good grey beard, speaking good English. Unfortunately he had not been reading the new Russian authors, except Leonid Leonov, whom he specially recommended to me. He said that *The Death of Simon Fuge* was in the Tchekoff style, though probably written before I had read Tchekoff. There is something in this. Maurice said I had never written the sort of plays I ought to write and could write. Something in this, too.

Wednesday, March 9th. – I walked up to the Reform, and lunched with Page, Gardiner, Roch and two others. Discussion of Churchill's book [*The World Crisis, 1911–1918*]. Everyone praised it as a *tour de force*, but said it was by no means always honest, and certainly wasn't history, inasmuch as it was obviously written to prove that Churchill had been right throughout the war. Personally, I think it is a bit better than that.

Thursday, March 10th. – Went to the dinner of the Other Club at the Savoy. It was a small but a particularly good meeting. I had Ned Lutyens on my left and Archie Sinclair on my right, and Churchill opposite me during the last and best part of the evening. I referred to Charlie Masterman's criticism of his rhetorical style, and in particular of the phrase about pistols drinking blood. Churchill at once said: 'What about taking arms against a sea of troubles?' He said that when he wrote that phrase he had pistols actually by him (for some reason which I forget).

Saturday, March 19th. – I went to the Goupil to see Stanley Spencer's big *Resurrection* (15 ft long). It contains over 60 figures. It is a sincere and highly emotional affair. I respected it, liked bits of it, and was not pleased with it as a whole. Some of Spencer's sketches and smaller pictures were very original. *Resurrection* is the talk of London at the moment.

Monday, March 21st. – I've written 20,000 words in the last twelve days. I had to order the meals and wrestle with the French cook this morning. Also I had a highly disturbing letter from F. C. B. about a wild project of his for coming to London; which upset me. So that by 10.30, although I had had a very calm pre-prandial time (from 6.30 to 8.30), I was beginning to have a headache and felt *dans tous mes états*. I went out for an idea-finding walk, and got to the South Kensington Museum and sat down in a corner, and no sooner had I done so than four workmen came to disturb me by moving trestles. No sooner had they gone than the ideas came to me in a vague but satisfactory rush; and I walked straight out again. Exactly at 12 sat down to work and at 12.35 had actually written 700 words. It seems as if nothing can stop me from working just now.

Saturday, March 26th. – Fair night, vitiated by over-smoking. However at the end I received from God just over $2\frac{1}{2}$ hours of unbroken sleep, and at 5.45 accordingly felt restored to health. Before dressing I wrote a little opinion, at the request of the *Sunday Express*, about the pirating of Joyce's *Ulysses* by one Samuel Roth. Into this I contrived to insinuate the opinion that Joyce is a very important figure in the evolution of the novel.

Tuesday, April 12th. – Drove to Reform Club, and began lunch, by myself. H. G. Wells, who joined me, said that he had lost the art of reading. He got restless if he read for long. Perhaps his eyes – but I know it isn't his eyes. Because I'm just the same, and I know it isn't my eyes.

Grand Hotel Continentale, Rome, Saturday, April 16th. – The train was always punctual and arrived at Rome exactly at the appointed hour, 8.10 p.m. Not a bad achievement for an international train. I got a porter at once, and he carried my stuff across the Piazza to this hotel. I was served by a middle-aged kindly waiter evidently alcoholic, though not drunk at that moment.

Then put on my overcoat and went for a walk round the big church S. Maria degli Angeli close by. Squeaking trams on curves. Many hotels here near the station. Then I walked into the station, in which one of the chief departments was apparently the Militia 'Commando'. I went to bed at or before 11, having eaten a bit too much. Nothing much on the train journey here, except that I read *Brothers Karamazov*. Third or fourth time of reading. Yes, fourth time. I read it slowly to savour it. It is very great and masterful. An Englishwoman, fattish, sixtyish, very energetic, had the *cabine* next to mine. She talked at length to anyone she could get hold of about Mussolini and her interview with him and the greatness of Italy, rottenness of France, and muddledness of England. Loud voice, very tedious. A Fascist, carrying the insignia, and the official card with photograph. I had to sit opposite to her at lunch. She tried hard to get up a talk, but I beat her off. All her ideas were wrong. But if anything evil happened to her in Italy she might well change them all. Her acquaintance with Italian customs and Italian was such that when she got her lunch bill and saw 'Tassa di Bollo' at the foot of it, she called the waiter and said she hadn't had any *tassa*. She talked French volubly and not well.

The sunset round about Civita Vecchia was richly marvellous. Such a thing as you couldn't see in England. The whole day was lovely, and quite warm. Lovely bright leaves and blossoms on the trees everywhere. Especially after emerging from the Mont Cenis tunnel, and later it was marvellous.

S. Domenico Palace Hotel, Taormina, Sicily, Monday, April 18th. – No restaurant on the train between Naples and Sicily. The car-conductor made black coffee in a little kettle at the end of the corridor. I had two cups with great joy at 8 a.m.

We got to S. Giovanni fairly on time (9.35), but fiddled about some time in getting carriages 3 abreast on the steamer-ferry. It was raining. I walked about on the steamer itself, unovercoated in the spitting rain. The crossing took exactly half an hour. We were 20 minutes late on leaving S. Giovanni. But the restaurant had been hooked on, and a hungry lot of us rushed into it and began eating before the train left. I had already eaten two apples and an orange and I said to myself, I wouldn't eat much else. But could I resist eggs and bacon? I could not. I ate all there was. This was after 10.30. It didn't seem long before we were at Taormina, where nearly everybody got out. The San Domenico bus was soon full. The climb up to the hotel is terrific. I should say 5 or 600 feet, and when you are in the hotel dining-room you look down on the sea almost perpendicularly. The hotel seems really to have been a monastery.

Hôtel des Étrangers, Syracuse, Thursday, April 21st. – Lovely morning. We drove down to Taormina station and caught the 10.18 for Syracuse, which was ten minutes late. I saw a four-master as we entered the town. I said to Kahn: 'She's here.' But we couldn't be quite sure; I might have seen a four-masted trading schooner. The guide awaiting us at the station said that no yacht had come in. We drove to the port, and there was the yacht all right – a magnificent object. Thrilling. We went on board and were greeted by Captain Davies (a Chester man), very young for the post, I thought. We looked over the state-rooms and saloons. Highly satisfactory. Beautiful. The artists were thrilled by the yacht. So was I, only more so.

We went to the Hôtel des Étrangers (Casa Polliti) which

overlooks the port, and Kahn engaged rooms there. I insisted on some of them having a cup of tea before we rushed off in a terrific haste and pother of dust to the Greek Theatre for a performance in the Greek convention of Aristophanes' *The Clouds*. I expected to be bored by this, but was not. It was very impressive as much by itself as by its surroundings. All classic, legendary, history. Good acting of the play. Clear enunciation heard at a great distance. Fine dancing. I understood all of a sudden the classicalness of the classic drama.

Yacht 'Flying Cloud'. Course about E. Friday, April 22nd. – We all went out soon after ten to the Museum, and saw two fine statues, including the Venus Anadyomene, and a finer earlier one in bronze, and some vases, including a few Greek indecencies; then to the catacombs, very large, but not very interesting; they seemed to me, oddly, to have been made stuffy by the residence of Christians in them; then to the Latomia, the second one, finer even than the one we saw yesterday.

'Flying Cloud', between Sicily and Cape Matapan, Saturday, April 23rd. – I was chatting with the Chief Officer on the poop before 6 a.m. Perfect morning. Saw one sail, a brig, about ten miles to the north going westward. Saw nothing else all day. There was a slant of wind, and I reckon that the ship was making 3 or 4 knots under sail only. Four sails set, 2 topsails, 1 top stay-sail, the sky-sail and three jibs. Bridge has been played nearly the whole day. And it has been a simply magnificent day. Captain Davies said that he was not a yacht-captain but a captain in a yacht. Well, the yacht shows it.

Hôtel Petit Palais, Athens, Monday, May 2nd. – Not an attractive city; but a very good and very small hotel. The first person I saw was Arthur Rubinstein, in a bath-gown, just out of his bath. He joined us at lunch and talked all the time. Kommer called him a traveller in music, and enlarged on this definition very well indeed. We went to the National Museum. The pre-Phidias things were the best. I made up a theory out of this, which I shall use. We then drove to the Acropolis. Dust. Great heat. The Acropolis and the Parthenon fully sustained their reputation. The spectacle was really overwhelming. Also the Anterior room in the Acropolis Museum was equally overwhelming. What sensations! Extreme exhaustion. But after tea, despite this, Kommer and Dougherty and I went out shopping, but didn't get all the photos we wanted. They don't exist in Athens, being out of stock. We were recommended to get them in Florence!

Lloyd Triestino Steamer 'Féodora' between Athens and Constantinople, Saturday, May 7th. – After many delays, we drove to the town of Piraeus. Quite a big town, with some streets terribly shabby and slatternly and badly paved, and others rather handsome. After quite a long time we reached the port, and it was quite a port, full of steamers. The ship left at 5.48, only 18 minutes late. Lovely afternoon and dusk. Smooth sea. Light wind. Lovely view of Piraeus on leaving, and marvellous views of the Acropolis half an hour later.

The general atmosphere of the ship was *très sympathique*. A heavenly night. Our lot played just as much cards as usual.

Pera Palace Hotel, Constantinople, Sunday, May 8th. – The sight of the Dardanelles, which we entered about 8 a.m., had a strange solemnizing effect. Not, however, on those who were still in bed, or on those who stuck in a corner of the smoking room and played bridge.

'Flying Cloud', between Kalakolo and Corfu, Sunday, May 15th. – I learnt that the string of beads which so many men carry is used merely to employ the hands, apparently thus soothing the nerves. It has no religious significance. The village of Kalakolo was decorated for some fête of the Virgin, and on a high terrace we saw males dancing, and the sound of an instrument like a bagpipes came to us.

The moonlit scene, as the yacht passed between Cephalonia and Ithaca was marvellous, both in romantic quality and in beauty. I got all the card-players out to see it.

Friday, June 24th. – N. X. came to see me at 9.30 about his critical position. Can't get work. Only earned £23 last month. Has shaved off his beard in order to look younger, and so on. Even at this interview, which was supposed to be very serious, he could not keep to the point. He would fly off to odd, trivial matters which had nothing whatever to do with the point, and I had to bring him back to the point again and again. However, it is very easy to criticize a man who has got himself into a mess. I gave him a few ideas for money-making to think over. He left at 10.10. After this my thoughts were miles off my work, and I scarcely hoped to do any. However, by tenacity, I got my thoughts back, and between 11.15 and 12.30 I wrote 600 words of a new chapter of *Accident*. I corrected two articles for Hearsts, and then had time to go out for a walk before Noel Coward came for tea. Noel was very bright and good and sensible, and talked much sagacity to Dorothy. He told me that he had started a novel and written 25,000 words but had destroyed it because it was done too hastily and carelessly. He said he *had* to write a play quickly (and that he wrote *Hay Fever* in three days), but he had now found that this method wouldn't do in a novel. So he was going to start again. I haven't had a really good night for weeks. However, my work is now going a bit better. I got figures from Flower about book sales to-night. *Raingo* has sold over 29,900 copies, and *The Woman Who Stole* sold 548 copies last week – over 12,000 in all he told me yesterday. So that I was rather pleased. Apropos of my article in the *Daily Mail* to-day, practically everybody I met referred to it. There can be no doubt that no other paper gets into so many hands. In fact everybody seems to make a point of at any rate looking at it. The price of the English-speaking world rights for that 1,200-word article is £270. Highest I ever got, I think.

Sunday, June 26th. – We drove off down to Bray, to Leo Schuster's Elgar concert at 'The Long White Cloud'. A great crowd of cars and fashionable persons in the music-room and the purlieus thereof at Schuster's. The programme was entitled 'Homage to Elgar'. A nice thought of old Schuster's.

We sat, among Sitwells, just outside the barn-like doors of the music-room, and I soon got cold. I spoke to Elgar and he said, when I praised his part of the entertainment: 'The silences are good, anyhow.'

Thursday, June 30th. – Harry Preston gave a dinner at the Green Park Hotel for the Walker-Milligan prize fight. Desolate sight at Olympia. Thousands of empty seats. Charles Cochran gloomy. Harry Preston had been deceived in his seats and was *most* gloomy. However, Cochran changed them and we got magnificent seats. The world-championship fight – Walker *v.* Milligan – was the most exciting I ever saw. Milligan was soon done in. Walker won tremendously. And yet he got scarcely a hand (being American) whereas Milligan, smashed to bits and tottering (with stitches in his lip), was terrifically cheered. This because of Milligan's mad pluck. Walker crossed himself before fighting.

Wednesday, July 6th. – I walked quickly, with perspiration, in hot sunshine, to get ideas for *Accident*, and reached the Tate Gallery. I thought I would look at the Conders. No sooner was I in the Conder room than Aitken, the director, came along, towing Lewis Hind and wife and two young men, one at least of whom was a son of Mitchell Kennerley. Then, when I had shaken myself free, Aitken, who is a very nice fellow, came along again to me and took me along to see the big wall decorations, by a young man named Whistler aged 21, in the refreshment room – decorations still far from finished. I enjoyed them.

We went on to Holland Park Hall to see Lenglen play tennis. Sparsely filled. The men's singles (Cozelin and Kinsey) were fine. Women's singles poor, because Lenglen (*v.* Dewhurst) had nothing to do. Cozelin is an exceedingly fine player. I should like to see him against Tilden. Another thing that I should like to see would be Lenglen against a man – I mean a really good one, a first-rate man. She would be beaten, but it would make a fine show, and would restore the public perspective. Lenglen is short and walks well, though with a rather peculiar step.

Monday, July 11th. – George Arliss came at 4.30 for tea and to discuss Edgar Selwyn's scenario for *Lord Raingo*. He had been sufficiently interested to do a scenario of his own, and after much talk he said that he would re-write his own scenario. An attractive, very 'sound' fellow of about 50 or 55, with the true actor's face. Quiet, firm, no frills, no theatrical gush whatever. He said he was frankly old-fashioned as to the art of the theatre. Liked the old. Thought the new no good. Didn't think there had been any progress, or ever would be.

Sunday, July 17th. – Thomas Bodkin came for lunch. He was a great friend of the lately assassinated O'Higgins. Said he was a great man. Said that even if the murderers were caught they could not be tried by a jury because juries would be too frightened by threats of murder to convict them. He said the whole thing was very grave.

Tuesday, July 19th. – I went on with *Accident* to-day morning and afternoon, and finished it about 6.30 p.m. I didn't care much for the last 300 words. Total length 67,300 words. I felt gloomy as usual when I had finished it.

Tuesday, July 26th. – Bishop of Liverpool wanted me to contribute to a series of little books which will be meant to help to show some sort of design, order, divine origin in the world, 5,000 to 10,000 words each. I said I would contribute a booklet if he could suggest to me some subjects which appealed to me. Tall, dark, muscular chap, decided, clear tones and movements. A ready smile at a joke. I liked him. I saw him out.

I then read the first pages of Wells's *Meanwhile*, which arrived this morning. Dorothy Massingham came to dinner, and we talked personalities about our friends. I took her to see Lonsdale's *On Approval* at the Fortune Theatre. Not a bad first Act in a very old-fashioned 'smart' way, with some very good jocular lines. In the first entr'acte in came Elizabeth Bibesco and a young man. She said she hoped the first Act was not the best act. I said it would certainly be the best act. She had merely arrived one hour late for the play.

Easton Glebe, near Dunmow, Wednesday, July 27th. – H. G. Wells called for me at 10.6 instead of 10.15 to 10.30 as he had said, and drove me down to Easton to see Jane. First part of the drive in heavy rain. When it cleared up we stopped and had a drink at a pub on the edge of the forest, gin and ginger-beer. We arrived at 12.6. Jane had just got downstairs. She is carried down, and wheeled everywhere; but she walks a few steps. H. G. had said she was better, stronger; but she didn't seem to me to be so. Jane keeps an eye on the house. She had just arranged for the servants' holidays. The following people came in during the afternoon; the Byngs, Mrs Davies, Lady Warwick (with an astounding hat), Peggy Gibbons (Frank Wells's fiancée) and Lady Mercy Dean, the young mother. Bridge first. Then tennis. Wells joined in both. Nobody for dinner except 1 nurse. H. G. went upstairs to spend 15 minutes with Jane, and then came down, and we talked till 11.10. At the end he made tea for himself. We discussed his wife, his servants, his sons. He was in favour of me politically running *The World To-day*, and said that whatever I undertook I should succeed in.

Wednesday, August 3rd. – Went to see the *Metropolis* film at the Élite Theatre. Sickening sentimentality. Many good effects, spectacular, spoilt by over-insistence. A footling story. No understanding of psychology of either employers or workmen. 'Adapted by Channing Pollock.' Good God! What captions. Enough to make you give up the ghost. The theatre was very nearly empty.

Friday, August 5th. – I wrote part of an article in the morning for *Evening Standard*. Komisarjevsky and wife came at 12.30. She is Austrian. They talk Russian when alone. She learnt it in nine months. Agreeable and pretty and melancholy. After five hours' acquaintance she told me all sorts of things about the disadvantages of her life in London. 'Lost in Kommy', etc. They lunched with us. We drove over to Winchelsea.

We had tea at the Beach Café. Not bad. Sort of lady-waitresses. We asked for salt. The waitress cried: 'Salt – whatever *for* ?'

Wednesday, August 10th. – We drove over to Winchelsea at noon. Lunched with the Robert Nicholses to meet Arthur Symons and wife. We had met wife in Paris with the Sutros about 18 months ago. Arthur Symons, a little very pale white-haired man, prim. He is full of reminiscences of French and English authors, especially French. Verlaine and Baudelaire and Villon he considers to be the three greatest French poets, – the rest not comparable. I rather liked him. He is in every way a 'little' man, but with real taste and refinement.

Friday, August 19th. – Reading of all the letters I have received from George Sturt. The scene begins in 1895. This is for the introduction which I am to write for his posthumous work. These letters are extremely good, and many of them ought to be printed in full. They made me feel sad, somehow; because I saw in them a reflection in commentary of the history of all my literary life – over thirty years.

Saturday, August 20th. – I read Ostrovsky's play *The Suitors*, which Komisarjevsky wants to begin with at the Court Theatre. It is a good, quiet, old fashioned, and very *Russian* comedy of manners, with all that damned Russian incapacity and financial corruption – which we are so sick of in Russian manners. It would have no chance whatever on the London stage. People would wonder what the hell it was all about.

Sunday, August 21st. – Bernstein, the 'business man' in Komisarjevsky's and our 'Sloane Productions Co., Ltd', which is to run at the Court Theatre in the autumn, was to have come down for lunch to-day. He arrived – scarcely hoped for – at 3.25, and stayed for tea. He proved to be all right, *sympathique*, young, some artistic perceptions and some artistic blindnesses. Thus he could see *nothing* in *Malbrouck s'en va t'en guerre*. Before dinner I read Merezhkowski's *Paul 1st* and decided that it would do for the Court Theatre. To-night I wrote to this effect to both Komisarjevsky and Bernstein. On the other hand, Ostrovsky's *The Suitors* is a hopeless thing for the Court Theatre or any London theatre. I have been very gloomy; I began to be gloomy yesterday. Dorothy pointed out to me that my liver is out of order, and I think it certainly is.

Thursday, August 25th. – I walked on the front at Winchelsea, watched bowls and thought of the plot of my next story 'Under the Hammer', for about 1½ hours.

I finished reading *Coningsby* on Tuesday. It is a sad welter. No construction. Very little cohesion. Too much eloquence. But there are good things in it. It is very rich and varied. The big interview between Monmouth and his grandson Coningsby towards the end, written in a very inflated style, is excellent in force and effectiveness – the convention of it being once granted. Much of the political criticism is good, and much of it very epigrammatic and amusing.

Saturday, August 27th. – I thought fruitfully about my story 'Under the Hammer' for 90 minutes in the morning.

Sunday, August 28th. – I meant to begin my short story 'Under the Hammer' in the afternoon. Then I finished the Masterman thriller, and I couldn't concentrate on my own story, so I wrote an *Evening Standard* article on thrillers, etc.

Monday, August 29th. – During the afternoon and evening I was much held by Julien Green's *Adrienne Mesurat*. This is a very fine novel – but I've read only half of it yet. It is the most 'holding' French novel that I've read for years.

Friday, September 2nd. – I wrote 1,100 words of 'Under the Hammer' in 1½ hours. Great going.

Considering I only slept 2 hours last night I was in astonishing creative form to-day.

75, Cadogan Square, Sunday, September 4th. – We had an appointment with Komisarjevsky and Bernstein here at 7 p.m. We decided that the 2nd production at the Court Theatre should be *Mr Prohack*, subject to Golding Bright's approval on behalf of Knoblock. Komi and Bernstein only left at 8.20 when Dorothy happily turned them out.

Thursday, September 22nd. – To Apollo Theatre to see Strindberg's *The Father*. Met Nelson Keys there, who said he was still looking for a play and was going to America to look for one. Very disappointed with *The Father*. It is the work of a madman, inconsequent, loose, too quick, too slow, sort of shaking all the time.

Tuesday, September 27th. – Mrs Patrick Campbell and Komisarjevsky came for lunch – in order to meet each other. Komi said very little. Stella talked tremendously, and very well. Her ideas are exceedingly sound, and in spite of all that I have heard about her naughtiness, she seems to me to be fundamentally good-natured. Then I went over to the theatre to see a rehearsal, having previously learnt – but only by my own enquiries – that the directors' meeting supposed to be arranged for to-night had not been arranged at all. I was rather glad, as this would give me an extra 90 minutes at least for my work. I stayed at the rehearsal [of *Paul I*] till after 5, hearing Mrs Pat's excellent criticisms.

Friday, September 30th. – I went to the first dress rehearsal. It started an hour late. At 6.25 the last act was only just begun. To the Gate Theatre (held at the Ettlinger Theatre temporarily). 1st night of Paul Green's *The Field God*. I stayed till just before the last scene began. Farmhouse stuff. Goodish dialogue but not *really* true. Anyhow a change from the West End drawing-room stuff. It had moments of truth. But the thing is really nothing but a chronicle play. No genuine construction or artifice. Just a tale. Nicely produced. I rather liked the light being centred on the middle of the stage. So that people walking along down stage showed only like black silhouettes. But this of course was quite as untrue to life as any other form of lighting.

Friday, October 7th. – In morning I corrected and revised and cut Act I of *Mr Prohack* and in the afternoon I did the same to Act II.

Then we went to Bauer Concert at Wigmore Hall. It was simply magnificent.

435

Sunday, October 9th. – I walked 2¾ miles in Battersea in the morning – lovely morning – and saw the aviary, which is rather poor, and then came home and began on Act III of *Mr Prohack*. After lunch I attacked Act III again. I must have done three hours of really concentrated work on it during the day. I was very tired.

Monday, October 10th. – I finished the revision of Act III of *Mr Prohack* before lunch, after a walk in the Park. As a fact it needed less work on it than I had feared. I then had to go at once to Jane Wells's funeral. Lots of people there, and only one man in full mourning. The Wells family and wives were not in mourning. Shaw had an amber handkerchief and no overcoat. Number of really A.1 people present, very small; which shows how Wells kept out of the 'great' world and how the great world is not practically interested in Wells. T. E. Page read the funeral oration (written by H. G. himself) very well. This oration was either not well done, or too well done.

Saturday, October 15th. – Madame Komisarjevsky was to arrive at 3.30 to play duets with me. I was fully awake at 3, and so I thought I would just begin my next week's *Evening Standard* article. She came at 4.15. By that time I had nearly finished my article. We played Haydn and Schubert. She read very well, and said that she had never had a lesson in her life. She said that Englishmen were not interesting. I contradicted her, and offered to show her lots of interesting Englishmen. She said she much wanted to see them.

Monday, October 17th. – Rehearsal of *Prohack* at Court at 11. Nearly everybody late. However, I saw the 1st part of Act III gone through for the first time, and decided that, with cutting, it would do very well indeed. Komisarjevsky came for tea, and we went through Act III except the end; all right except cutting. But he wanted a change of construction in Act II, which rather troubled me.

Queen's Hotel, Manchester, Wednesday, October 19th. – Came to Manchester by 11.50 a.m. arriving at 3.40 for performance of *Flora* at Rusholme.

Thursday, October 20th. – I took the 12.5 back to London, which went through the Potteries. The sight of this district gave me a shudder.

Saturday, November 5th. – Went off to hear Pouishnoff give the last of his six pianoforte recitals of Chopin. Quite a good audience. What fame – Chopin's – to stand six consecutive evenings after 100 years!

Wednesday, November 16th. – I dressed, and went off to entertain Major and Mrs. Whittall at the Yacht Club. It is a fact that between 8.15 and 10.15 or 10.20 I never once remembered that the first performance of *Mr Prohack* was going on at the Court Theatre. The Whittalls left about 10.35. I smoked a cigarette, after a cigar, and then drove down to the theatre. The curtain had just fallen. It kept going up again while I was in the wings or near the wings. Much satisfaction in the wings, on the staircases and in the dressing-rooms. Charles Laughton very pleased with himself, as he had the right to be, seeing he had had a great triumph. Everybody who 'came round' professed the greatest enjoyment of the play. I almost believed in a success. Especially as, going into the theatre, I saw Komisarjevsky outside in the dark entry. I said: 'Is it all right?' He said: 'Oh yes, it's all right.'

Thursday, November 17th. – I read all the morning press notices of *Prohack* at breakfast. *Express* good. Most of the others gently praising, tepid. *The Times* most depreciatory. Board Meeting of Sloane Productions, Ltd, at 2.30. Bernstein, who had not liked the play when he read it, was really very enthusiastic about it in performance. Dorothy had bought the afternoon papers, all of which were encomiastic.

To the Reform Club, and met Geoffrey Russell on the steps as I was entering. He said I was going with him to hear Liszt's

Faust Symphony at the Philharmonic concert. So I went. Heard the last movements of a Brahms pianoforte concerto played by Arthur Schnabel. He is a very fine player.

I got back to the Court Theatre before the performance was over, and heard the end of the play from the Royal Box with Whitaker, the manager. The public laughter was very reassuring, and I felt more optimistic about the future of the play.

In the afternoon I had written a character sketch of Masterman, the news of whose death I had had in the morning.

Monday, November 21st. – Disturbed night; dreamed much. I seldom dream. I did some work to-day for a change. I began my new short story at 10.30 after a walk, and wrote 600 words of it in about an hour. I then set off in the rain to St Margaret's for the funeral service of Charles Masterman. A lot of people there. Ll. George following the coffin. I didn't like the sight of him there. At 9 I was at Mrs Masterman's discussing her affairs with her. I promised to set on foot a scheme for collecting £4,000 for education of the three children, all of whom I saw.

Saturday, December 3rd. – I decided at early morn to go to Gladys Beaverbrook's funeral to-day. I drove off in the car at 1.40, and got to Mickleham, scene of the funeral, at 2.25. So I drove on to Dorking and through Dorking and came back, the car having taken a wrong turning, just as the hearse and procession was arriving at the lych-gate of the churchyard. I went in and Castlerosse joined me, and I saw Baxter, Blumenfeld, James Dunn, Raymond Thompson, and a whole lot of Max's secretaries, clerks, etc., etc. The entrance of the coffin, covered with really magnificent wreaths, was moving. Max was leaning on young Max's arm, and looked quite old. Chopin's funeral march – not equal to Handel's. *Abide With Me* at the end. This hymn is quite a good poem. Then the coffin goes out again, and a scene of terrible damp cold at the graveside, and our hats off, and Lord Ashfield only just up that day from a chill. These funeral rites in an English winter are absolutely barbaric. I met Max at the gate, and was so moved, unknown to myself till the moment came, that I could not speak to him.

Tuesday, December 6th. – I attended the dinner of the P.E.N. club to Lion Feuchtwanger, and sat next to him, and was pleased with his personality. He is evidently well-used to publicity. He said that his Berlin secretary said that he spent one hour in writing and the rest of the day in business, making contracts, and seeing people. Rebecca West was in the chair, and she didn't say enough. Feuchtwanger spoke very satisfactorily in very bad English. I went over and talked to May Sinclair, whom I hadn't seen for sixteen or seventeen years. I also went over to Mrs Aria. She said: 'You haven't kissed me.' So I kissed her – for the first time.

Thursday, December 8th. – Feuchtwanger came for tea at 4.40. Also Hugh Walpole. Feuchtwanger looks just like a cat. He talked about himself almost the whole time. He is certainly very intelligent.

Sunday, December 11th. – Mrs P. Campbell came for tea at 5.30 and made a terrific outpouring. She said: 'If you want to keep me quiet give me a cigar.' So I gave her one. Later, she went out into the Square smoking it. Her energy seems quite unimpaired. She now wants to produce and play in *Flora*. She arrived with a great scheme all complete. She read the play about a year ago or more, and saw nothing in it. Now she reads it again and sees everything in it. I discussed a few things with her and left the rest to Pinkers.

I finished *Monte Cristo* at 11.30. On the whole this is a wonderful book. The end is too hurried, especially considering the immense leisureliness of all that precedes it. Many explanations are lacking.

Thursday, December 29th. – Splendid health. I have now cut my breakfast down to four or five kinds of fruit (raisins, orange, apple, lemon and prunes) plus two cups of tea, and two pieces of rye-bread. And little or no meat for lunch. I then walked along the Embankment to the next bridge West and down along King's Road, and then wrote 750 words of my 'Millionaire' article in $1\frac{1}{4}$ hours at most. Lunch at Reform Club with Gardiner and Tudor Walters. I like Tudor more and more. Sir John Brunner and Vivian Phillipps joined us in the smoking-room. Talk about our own defects, and about the characters of politicians. I came to the conclusion that what Liberal statesmen lacked is courage. This applies to Walter Runciman, Herbert Samuel, and Asquith, and John Burns.

Friday, December 30th. – We went to lunch with Ruth Draper who has a little house in Charles Street, belonging to an American named Chubb. Present: the Alan Herberts, and Mrs Phipps, sister of Lady Astor. She was full of Bernard Shaw's conversational liveliness. She is very lively herself and I liked her. Ruth Draper again talked to me about writing a play for her, and I promised to write to her about such a play.

I have now cleared up all the work I have to do this year. In actual production it has not been quite as large as last year, but it has been quite large enough. And the financial results have been the best for many years; also the financial prospects for next year are good.

Sunday, January 1st. – I read myself to sleep with *Peter Simple.* Yes, it is very good, but it seems to be all the same – the old picaresque stuff. Oddly, Marryat brings in another quite long story told by another young naval officer to Peter, about his life, a few years earlier. There is no contrast between the two. Just an idea that occurred to the author, I suppose, when he was hard up for an idea.

I have made only one good resolution: to write more legibly.

When I met Barry Jackson this morning on the Embankment in the snow, he was wearing snow-boots, as I was, but no overcoat. 'Ah!' he said, pointing to my boots, 'we're the same.' He is the blandest person I ever met, I think. A sort of veiled voice – *voix blanche.* He said how well I looked. I said how well *he* looked. 'That's my glass of orange juice,' said he, beaming. He did look very well. He admitted that he had not of late been losing money in the theatre. Even after deducting the losses of his various failures, Phillpotts's two great successes showed him a profit. About his forthcoming production of *Macbeth* in modern clothes, he said he was afraid it would, so, prove too *grim* for modern audiences. He said he was having the greatest difficulty in getting a Macbeth.

Monday, January 2nd. – I took Mrs Masterman to dine at Sovrani's new restaurant in Jermyn Street. Lucy Masterman told me a lot about Charles, their children, and the Asquiths. She has a pleasingly sardonic yet affectionate tongue. She said to me once again: 'Charles always said: "If you're really in a hole, go to A. B. He's the one".'

Thursday, January 5th. – I corrected typescript for one hour, and then walked up to Piccadilly Circus and back, thinking further over my scheme for a play for Ruth Draper. I got this scheme into order, and wrote to Ruth about it immediately after lunch. I find I can think best when I am in a street of shops, now. I like more and more looking at shop-windows. Could not get decent rest owing to the noise of workmen next door. I arose, and did a further instalment of my *World To-day* article, about the Riviera, writing it with zest and ferocity.

I read a lot of *Peter Simple*. It has apparently no form, but it is very good indeed otherwise. It does give a picture of naval life, and its moral backbone is excellent. I was very gloomy this morning, reflecting that life ought to be give and take, but that I gave without taking. However, at night I was cheerful again. Odd!

Saturday, January 7th. -- At Dorothy's urgent request, I went over to the Court Theatre. Atmosphere of the last night of a run, but, although no other theatre has yet been obtained, we trust it is not the last night of the run. Evelyn Cochran came round after the performance, and Charles was *really* enthusiastic about the play. He said he hadn't liked a play so much for years. Evelyn said she had never seen Charlie so happy in a theatre. He also liked the acting. It seemed impossible not to believe that this play, in the West End, and *kept* on for a bit, should not develop into a very great success. All the packing up had to be finished in Dorothy's dressing-room. More good-byes. Sally, the dresser, is really a very nice old woman, with a voice as thin as a piece of paper. We got home at midnight. Then searchings in larder for food for Dorothy.

Monday, January 9th. – We went to the first night of Barry Jackson's new Court season, *The Adding Machine*, by Elmer Rice (American). I feared the worst for this play, but it turned out quite well. It has the misfortune of having two subjects – first one and then another, and it is under-produced. But the writing and satire, and some of the expressionist stuff are quite decent. I enjoyed myself.

Tuesday, January 10th. – I am now getting to the end of *Peter Simple*. There is a wonderfully sly bit of social satire in this work; comic description of a negro religious meeting in Barbados, followed immediately by a comic letter from an Irish priest. The juxtaposition shows that there is nothing to choose between the nigger parson and the Irish priest.

Saturday, January 14th. – I walked to the Leicester Galleries and on the way thought of a great idea for a modernized version of *Faust*. I mean I thought it out in some detail. I had thought of it yesterday. To-day I ordered a literal translation of Goethe's *Faust*.

At Leicester Galleries a show of drawings and lithographs by Matisse. Compared to the price of his paintings the drawings were very low priced. I bought one drawing, 25 guineas, and two lithographs. Also a show of paintings by John Armstrong, which are causing some stir. I wasn't quite startled by their excellence. I had a talk with Armstrong, who was looking quite spick and span in relatively new clothes. He said, in reply to my questions, that he had been chiefly influenced by Carpaccio (a Venetian painting of which he had never seen the original) and Signorelli. Also Picasso.

Monday, January 16th. – I had to lunch early in order to go to Hardy's funeral at Westminster Abbey. It was all done very smoothly and calmly. Music good. South transept not full. In the morning I had written a letter to the *Daily Express* animadverting upon the distribution of tickets for this affair.

John Galsworthy as pall-bearer made a magnificent figure.

Tuesday, January 17th. – Formerly in my life I was always pre-occupied by my insomnia and my digestion. I only rarely think about my digestion now – it is so good – but I am still terribly pre-occupied with my sleeping. I walked to the Metropole for the Dramatists' Club lunch. Pinero in the chair. Quite a muster of members because Pinero had been ill. Coward and Malleson appeared for the first time – new members. Coward said to me: 'Don't leave me, Arnold. I feel so strange here. I'm on the verge of hysteria among all these people.' He sat on Pinero's right with Barrie next to him.

When Barth was reading the minutes at the end, I said 'Bad grammar, I regret to say.' The sin was 'None ... were.' But Barth couldn't see it, and others couldn't. I think only Barrie saw it. Yet all were authors.

Saturday, January 21st. – I walked to South Kensington Museum, and had a look at the British Water Colours, which I had not examined before as a whole. Well, I think that Cotman is the best of them, easily. Peter de Wint I like less than I did. He gets pretty and his colour is often not agreeable. Brabazon, clumsy and groping, is still the most interesting of the moderns. Indeed I couldn't see anybody else who aroused any emotion in me.

Sunday, January 22nd. – Battersea is a different world. I saw on a *Sunday Express* poster: 'Hardy's last novel, by Sir Edmund Gosse.' It seemed terribly absurd there. How many people in Battersea Bridge had heard of Hardy, or of Gosse, or could get up any interest whatever in a last novel though it were written by God himself? It is a gloomy drab street, with most repulsive tenements, a big technical institute, an open gramophone shop (with a machine grinding out a tune and a song) and an open 'Fun Fair' sort of place (a shop with the front taken out) and a few small boys therein amusing themselves with penny-in-the-slot machines.

Tuesday, January 24th. – To the first night of Behrman's (American) *The Second Man* at the Playhouse, in which Noel Coward is playing. Good first act. Noel Coward was admirable. Dorothy learnt from Peacock that Laughton must be either re-engaged or lost to-morrow morning. Much against my wishes, she telephoned to ask for capital. It wasn't capital we wanted for the continuance of *Mr Prohack*, but a small theatre at a reasonable rent.

Thursday, February 2nd. – Rather wearing, visits from relatives whom you scarcely ever see, and whose course of existence is separating more widely from you every year, and has been so doing for over 30 years. It is in fact desolating.

Saturday, February 4th. – Bernard Shaw came for lunch. He and Dorothy talked theatre all the time. He said that the first preliminary to her going in for theatrical management and acting was a divorce between us. He was very quiet, chatty, sensible and agreeable. He went up with us to Harriet Cohen's Henry Wood orchestral concert at Wigmore Hall, and by chance had got a seat next to ours. We all enjoyed this concert. The hall was full. I dozed off twice, being very fatigued and sleepy, but still I enjoyed it. We drove home in rain. Shaw left us to get exercise on foot. Dined at the St John Hutchinsons: Ethel Sands, Roger Fry, and W. Gerhardi. Fry was in great form. His latest notion is that Delacroix, though a great man, was not a great artist.

Tuesday, February 7th. – I was just going out on a secret mission when Dorothy came in so that I had to hurry like anything to my destination, which was in Eaton Place, and even then arrived after Father Vincent McNabb, O.P., had begun his 'spiritual conference' in a West End drawing-room to a pretty full audience in which I was the only man. I liked Father McNabb. He looked about 50. Very refined face and voice. Good enunciation, with unembarrassed pauses for a word or a sentence. Very soft-toned. Rather restless. Subject: Parable of the Vineyard. He said some good things; but his chief effect is that his bearing and mood compel you to think about spiritual values. I was certainly impressed. It was Maurice Baring who told me to go and hear him. Lasted half an hour. Then the Father came down from his low rostrum and passed along the front row, where I was, and I saw that he was much older than I had thought. Everyone remained seated till he had gone. He went out as it were furtively, as if self-conscious. He was in a monk's dress.

I finished *Tess* yesterday. It is really a very impressive masterpiece; and its faults are quite trifling. I was wrong to say in the *Evening Standard* that it is not among Hardy's five best.

Thursday, February 9th. – I went out for a walk and wrote 1,350 words of a *Sunday Pictorial* article, before lunch. After dinner I read 'Desolation', Pauline Smith's new short story. Very fine. And I finished correcting the MS. of my article and of a short story finished some weeks ago: 'The Seven Policemen'. Not very good.

Friday, March 2nd. – Mildred Temple, Lang's London representative, told me that Pauline Smith's story, 'Desolation', was very fine, and she personally loved it, etc., etc., all the usual stuff – it was a little too gloomy for them. I reasoned seriously with her; told her she had spoilt my evening and refused to dance with her.

Saturday, March 10th. – George Doran came to lunch, and after lunch in my study he began talking about the idea he had given me last year for a novel based on the tragic life of Ernest Hodder-Williams. I said I liked it, but couldn't handle it yet, as I was more attracted by a scheme for a realistic novel about a big luxury hotel. I shall probably begin it as soon as I have finished my play.

Wednesday, March 14th. – Went to see Chaplin's film *The Circus* at the New Gallery, where I joined a party. Fairly good film: a few fine moments in it, really funny, and some dull parts; the end had pathos with distinction. Then all of us in three or four cabs to Sybil Colefax's for supper. A lot of stage nobs came in: Coward, Du Maurier, Leslie Faber, Oliver Messel. Wells came. Victor Beigal sang Viennese popular songs superbly; Noel Coward sang his own songs extremely cleverly. Viola Tree and Oliver Messel gave side-splitting imitations, and I concluded the programme.

Wednesday, April 11th. – During the holiday [at Sidmouth] I read all the 520 pages of *The Moonstone*. It is a very good detective novel, one of the best. It holds you throughout, and it has some fun in it. The method of narration – personal narration – is unsatisfactory, because all the narratives are so obviously written by Wilkie Collins. A few failures in *vraisemblance* – e.g., how could an officer of the police force be *paid* for his services by a private person (Lady Verinder)? Still, a good book, though entirely *terre-à-terre*. Collins has some good observations about life, and some hard things to say about women. One narrator says: 'Women have no principles.' This is misleading but true. He ought to have said 'general principles'. To which he might retort that every principle, by the very nature of it, is 'general'.

Thursday, April 12th. – Bad night. Thorpe, of British International Films, and Dupont, the German producer of *Vaudeville* and *Moulin Rouge*, came to see me about writing a film story about Piccadilly, under the title *Piccadilly*, for Dupont to produce; I agreed to write, and promised the first sketch for Tuesday.

We dined at 7.35 and went to *The Man with Red Hair*, with Charles Laughton in it. We arranged beforehand that I should leave after the second act in order to go to bed early. So I did, though with reluctance, because the 2nd Act interested me, and I had a desire to see the 3rd.

Saturday, April 14th. – I had a bad night, very, but I was determined to write the story of the film for Dupont, and I wrote practically all day. I never went out of the house till night, and didn't dress until I dressed for dinner. I finished the thing by about 5.30.

Monday, April 23rd. – I went out, and in Hyde Park I met W. J. Turner. He said that life could and did 'maim' a man. I replied: 'Very rarely.' I said that it was well to remember that nothing happened to a man outside his own head, and that therefore if the mind was under control, etc., etc. I left him suddenly, saying that though apparently idle I was busy working. I got back home at 11.40 and began Act III of my play, and by 12.50 had written quite a lot.

Sunday, April 29th. – I wore my new house-suit from Sulka's. As I wanted to wear it all morning, I decided not to go out. It is so magnificent that I felt rather shy about showing it to the nurses. However they gave no sign of stupefaction.

Sat in the Park a bit, and listened to the band under Charles Godfrey. Then I walked on to the Park orators. Socialist and Anti-Socialist. The Socialist was the best; he held his audience and made me laugh. Salvation Army lass preaching Jesus. Awful. A speaker of the 'Catholic Evidence' society. Large crowds at each pulpit.

Thursday, May 24th. – Finished the whole film story, just under 17,000 words, at 12.30. I began a fortnight ago exactly. This has been the most strenuous fortnight I've had for years.

Wednesday, June 13th. – I was at the Memorial Service to Dennis Eadie at St. Martin in the Fields at 12.30. Sat with Mason and Miss Stevens. Then Viola Tree drove me to the Garrick Club so that I could see Gerald du Maurier about my (Faust) play. Gerald offered to accept my play without seeing it. I refused the offer; but promised to do the play as quickly as I could.

Saturday, June 16th. – Eugene Goossens and Alick Shepeler came for dinner. Eugene began to play and sing our opera *Judith.* He has evidently set out to do something not too incomprehensible. Better than I had expected. Dramatic. Effective. My libretto seemed quite good. He talked of a production at Covent Garden next year.

A young girl from Liverpool called yesterday afternoon, with a packet which an uncle in Peking had charged her to deliver to me personally. So she had come from Liverpool on purpose, though some weeks ago I had told her she mustn't. She seemed resentful against her uncle; said she knew nothing about the matter and couldn't understand her uncle. I opened the packet. It contained simply the documents of a British government official at Peking deeply possessed of a grievance about being dismissed from the Salt Administration, and an appeal to me to see that Justice was done. Pathetic.

Monday, June 18th. – I proceeded with the play. I don't feel convinced of its excellence as a show for a large public. And I really doubt whether I will ever do another. Career as a dramatist closing!

Thursday, June 21st. – I finished writing the (unnamed) play on the Faust theme about 11 a.m. I was very exhausted.

Wednesday, July 18th. – I finished re-reading *Mansfield Park*. This is a fine novel. One or two pages of Zola's or rather Huysmans' realism in it. Also at the end she refrains from killing Edmund's elder brother so that Edmund may come into the money, and the title.

Le Touquet, Tuesday, July 24th. – After dinner, I began to re-read Baudelaire. I was much struck in Baudelaire by the recurrence of the word *'ennui'*. In one place he says that it is the child of 'incuriosity'. Something in this, but not everything.

Wednesday, August 15th. – Pinero came up and asked me how my rehearsals were going on. I said I hated rehearsals, dealing with a lot of hypersensitive and sometimes conceited persons; watching what they did, etc. Pinero said: 'Yes, and watching what they don't do, and you want 'em to do, and what they leave out.' Pinero is the most charming old man I know. Met Marie Tempest and spouse in a car just outside the Club. She asked me to go and see her in the new play. Another charmer, but capable of ferocity.

Thursday, August 16th. – I am reading Lawrence's *Lady Chatterley's Lover*. He is the most original novelist now writing, except James Joyce.

Tuesday, August 21st. – During the morning I put down 11 titles for the play, and in the end everyone agreed on one title *The Return Journey*. Whereupon this title was officially given out to Louis Nethersole the press-agent. The rehearsals went quite well: three acts out of four nearly done. I gave lunch to Gerald at the Green Park. He insists on a particular cocktail, anchovies, cold roast beef, no sweet, no cheese, beer, and a couple of ports, and then goes off and works again like the devil.

Saturday, September 1st. – I walked to the St James's Theatre but seeing a crowd still in front, I walked round St James's parish for a bit, and entered the stage door at 11.27. I found Gerald du M. alone in his dressing-room. He seemed fairly content, but not enthusiastic at all, about the reception. Reception on the stage, champagne, etc.

Monday, September 3rd. – I reached the St James's Theatre at 11 a.m. Everyone was pretty gloomy, except me. They pretend to despise critics but they attach extraordinary importance to everything the critics say. Gilbert Miller was cheerful, and he and I upraised these spirits. By 5 p.m. they were quite cheerful, and dreaming of an 'enormous success'; and so on. I was on the stage for six hours during the day, making minor alterations, and changing the business at the end of the last act, and rehearsing the same.

Imperial Palace Hotel, Annecy, Thursday, September 6th. – There are one or two fine mountains in full view (7,000 ft or so) but I found it impossible to be enthusiastic about lake scenery. It is like living in a picture postcard, especially when there is full sunshine. The steamer calls at all sorts of places, little places. Menthon was the best. We stepped off at Duingt because Noel Coward had given such an enthusiastic account of it to Dorothy. Not bad, but suffering from the disadvantage of being seriously cut off by hills from the sun both east and west. Noel must have been there in love, some hot August.

Friday, September 7th. – We drove into Chambéry. The arcaded street is good architecture and unspoilt. Rousseau must have seen it just like that, and the people the same too – except for their clothes. Provincial ceremoniousness when friends meet on footpath. I doubt if you could see it in England. A rather 'petty' people, I thought; but naturally so. How could they be otherwise? We liked it all. The cathedral itself is not much – roof good, Genoese-decorated walls not good. But it is nice and small, and one has a pleasant change from big cathedrals. The elephant fountain is not *sympathique*. Quantities of old architecture, corners, squares, little old shops. We came back by the mountain route, etc. Very fine scenery, good roads, full of hairpin turns; vast vision of a wall of cloud (and a rainbow above it or in it) hiding the highest mountain.

Monday, September 10th. – To the Hall of the League of Nations for the afternoon session. It is a biggish hall, absolutely awful acoustics, in the ex-Hotel Victoria. Atmosphere (mental) rather like the House of Commons. Physical atmosphere simply terrible; hot, stuffy, odorous of people in the *première galerie*, for which Duff had got us tickets. Briand had orated in the morning, and they all said it was *marvellous*. But in the afternoon we saw nothing marvellous. We saw him record his vote – he is now a hunchback – on the admission of new nations to the Council. These were Persia, Venezuela – I forget the third. This business of voting on new admissions took a long time. Before that there had been statements about new rules. At the end of the declaration of the vote, the Chairman declared an interval of ten minutes. On the floor of the big Chamber, delegates and secretaries moving about and coming in and going out (especially at the back of the platform) the whole time. My general impression of the League was that something is being done there, despite the appearance of tedium and slackness.

Wednesday, September 26th. – I have at last finished D. H. Lawrence's *Lady Chatterley's Lover*. It is *foncièrement* indecent, but not pornographic. Some of it is very good, and some awful in dryness. Generally speaking, the lechery scenes are the best.

Thursday, September 27th. – Lunch at the Reform. H. G. Wells came upstairs later and Gardiner being rather boastful I offered to play him a tennis match on the hard court in Cadogan Square for a quid. He took it on. He also offered to play Wells after he had played me, and Wells took that on too. The matches are to take place on Wednesday at 3.

Friday, September 28th. – Noel Coward telephoned he couldn't come to lunch. Reginald Turner telephoned he was in bed with a cold and couldn't come to lunch so that only the Bernard Shaws and Jeanne de Casalis came. This lunch was very successful and Shaw was in better form than I have seen him for a long time past. Charlotte Shaw plays the rôle of the super-celebrity's wife with much tact.

Wednesday, October 3rd. – Preparations for tennis with Gardiner and H. G. Wells in Square. Gardiner came shortly after 3 and Wells a little before his appointed time, 3.30. Both middle-aged, grave, jocular, voluble. They changed their clothes up in my room. Our ages, A. G. G. 63, H. G. W. 62, and me 61. I beat Gardiner 6–5, and then he thought he should only play one set with me as he had to play Wells. He beat Wells 6–2. He then played Wells again and beat him 6–2. The last was only a fun set. I was told that there was betting at the Club – all against me. I took £1 off Gardiner and Gardiner took £1 off Wells.

Friday, October 19th. – I wrote 1,000 words of short story before noon. I then walked two miles and then drove to the Garrick Club, where du Maurier lunched with me. He practically wanted me to rewrite Acts II and III of *The Return Journey*. I told him I couldn't, but gave him leave to fool around with the play.

We reached the Ravel Concert at the Aeolian Hall 20 minutes late, and Ravel himself came into the vestibule. We talked a bit. This concert was extremely satisfactory. It seemed to me to be *all* good music.

Friday, November 2nd. – Worried by my film *Punch and Judy*, I walked out for an hour and got ideas and came back and wrote another scene. Then at 2.15 I drove in a studio car to Elstree to see some shooting of the *Piccadilly* film. Full crowd. 300 guests in the famous club. The colouring of the dresses was not at all distinguished; but this doesn't matter on the screen. Each item was filmed five or six times. Endless trouble taken. Considerable heat from *terrific* blaze of electric lamps.

Sunday, December 16th. – Terrific day. The best I have done for years. Nearly 5,000 words. I dined at the Savoy. The millionaire owner of a number of papers came up to me and I didn't know him. I asked him: 'Who are you?' He said he wanted some *really* good stuff for X. He said my article in the first issue had done them a great deal of harm, and asked why I had attacked Lloyd George, and Ll. George wanted to know. Considering that I had not mentioned him, or indicated him in any way, or any other politician, I said that this was a bit thick. I said I didn't know whether I could think of any subjects; I had too much to do. He said he worked harder than I did. I said 'You don't!' 'Don't?' said he. 'Don't,' said I. 'Don't?' said he. 'Don't,' said I. I gazed at him. His eye fell.

Monday, December 31st. – This year I have written 304,000 words; 1 play, 2 films, 1 small book on religion, and about 80 or 81 articles. Also I lost a full month in rehearsals, and a full month, no, six weeks, on holidays.

London, New Year's Day. – Up to a few years ago you could not advance the cause of anything without a banquet more or less expensive. Nowadays you do it to cocktails. The change is for the better. The new method takes a shorter time, and less alcohol is swallowed. I am not in favour of cocktails; but the harm of them is exaggerated by the godly. The amount of spirituous liquid in a cocktail is trifling. The mischief is that people – especially the young – do not confine themselves to one cocktail. At this very party I was talking to a famous man. He said, while drinking a cocktail: 'Cocktails are a great evil. My second daughter is nineteen to-morrow. She went out to dinner the other evening and when she came home she confessed that she had had five cocktails before dinner.' I said: 'But you ought to forbid it.' He said: 'But how can I forbid it? I do forbid it. And they come home and cheerfully announce that they have had five cocktails! You can't put your girls in prison. There it is. That's where we are today.'

The cocktail craze will pass. And perhaps by the time it has passed we shall know the origin of the word. A cocktailed horse is, I believe, a horse which has had its tail docked. Hence its tail flounces out gaily. Hence it has an air (quite spurious) of vivacity. Hence a cocktail ought to be so-called because it gives you the jolly feeling of a horse with its tail up. But actually *is* it so-called for that reason? Nobody can say.

All I know with certainty about the cocktail is that it is a source of considerable income to caterers and bar-keepers. Even in a respectable club a cocktail costs a shilling. In a first-rate fashionable hotel it costs half-a-crown (ten francs in France). The material of a cocktail surely cannot cost more than sixpence: a liberal estimate. Add another sixpence for overhead charges – again a liberal estimate – and the hotel is left with eighteen-pence clear: a net profit of 150 per cent.

London, January 3rd. – Royal Academy Private View of the Dutch Exhibition. I sat gazing at a superb seascape by

Breughel. One of the highest authorities on the graphic arts in London came up to me. I had not seen him for a long time. Did he salute me, ask me how I was, say he was glad to see me again, or do any of the things usually done on such an occasion? No! Without any preliminaries he burst out passionately: 'Don't you think Breughel is the finest painter that ever lived?' I said: 'Yes, I do.' 'So do I,' said he.

He said it, and in a way he meant it. But he would never have dared to write it. Still, I loved him for saying it. His written appreciations of art are always calm, careful, measured, judicial. Reading them, you would think that he was incapable of passion. One might even be excused for thinking that he was not a man, but a pair of scales. His impulsive exclamation to me proved that he was a man, had a beating heart, could let himself go and 'damn the consequences'. Fortunately with me he was safe.

Of course at this Private View I met lots of celebrities. What chiefly struck me about them was the likeness they bore to their caricatures. Some of them exceeded their wildest caricatures. (English caricatures are not cruel enough.) Celebrities always deprive me of my naturalness. Either I begin to tease them or I am tongue-tied. When I met Chaliapin, on the stage of the Paris Opera, after his first performance there, I could not think of a word to say to him. Nor, apparently, could he think of a word to say to me. I just looked up at him, and he just looked down at me. Then some kindly person drew the giant away.

London, January 4th. – My only good resolution for the New Year was to read Thomas Love Peacock, one of those classical, established English authors whose reputations are invulnerable and whom nobody reads. So I got a set of his works at once, but not without difficulty. Curious that I could not get a set in a uniform cloth binding! The first bookseller whom I approached had apparently never heard of the author of *Crotchet Castle*, etc. I chose *Gryll Grange* to read, and I read it in the odd moments of two days. Well, Peacock had no gift for plot; a considerable gift for the narration of an episode, but little gift for joining his episodes together. As with so many English novelists, he had not taken the trouble to learn his job. The thing is the wildest fantasy. Young hero living in a tower with seven lovely serving-maids, sisters, each of whom has a plain, bucolic, ultimately successful swain. Everything beautifully pure. An audacious modern novelist handling such a theme would certainly have got himself into trouble.

I should not be surprised if *Gryll Grange* is the most learned novel in the English language. The elderly hero, Dr Opimian, is a great man and a great scholar. The very numerous quotations from the Greek, Latin, French, and Italian are admirably translated, and the general style of the story is admirable. The book is mature, mellow, urbane, civilized, and ironic without bitterness. I kept saying to myself: 'This book is ridiculous, but ridiculous with nobility.' Peacock must have been a distinguished character, if excessively odd. I did not see any potential Meredith in *Crotchet Castle* when I read it many years ago. But I see potential Meredith in *Gryll Grange*. Dr Opimian is the spiritual ancestor of Meredith's Dr Middleton, but finer – and possibly even more erudite. *Gryll Grange* is richly suffused with learning – learning carried with what elegance and what ease, displayed with what readableness! The most prodigious scholar might read it without humiliation!

London. – At lunch at the Club yesterday two University men and classical scholars, Dr A [T. E. Page] and Mr B [J. A. Spender], talked about the great Benjamin Jowett. They agreed heartily that Jowett's translations of both Plato and Thucydides were extremely unsatisfactory – difficulties not faced, the Greek not accurately rendered, and the style not good. Mr B, a famous editor, said that Jowett, whom he was under at Oxford, was a very rude man. Mr B was asked every term to a solitary lunch or a solitary dinner or both, with Jowett. Jowett would not speak. Mr B tried to talk, of course very intimidated. Jowett would greet his remarks with such replies as: 'Think again! That is a very silly remark,' and so on. Mr B's only reward for these apparently purposeless purgatories was an occasional invitation to one of Jowett's celebrity parties. Jowett was a great snob, and loved collecting celebrities. Mr B recalled one dinner-party at which both Tennyson and Browning were present. Browning walked with him about the quad afterwards, and was most affable and interesting. Browning said to him: 'They've given Tennyson a peerage, and me a Fellowship of Balliol. I prefer the Fellowship.'

Jowett, it appears, wore a dress-coat (I mean in the daytime) to the end of his life. I said that this must have been one of Jowett's self-advertising stunts. Someone said not; but both Dr A and Mr B agreed that it was, and that the old man knew exactly what he was doing and realized the advertisement value of all his remarkably bad manners and rude if witty sayings, which were passed on from mouth to mouth. Mr B said that the secret of Jowett's prestige was that, despite his lack of first-rate scholarship, he was a great man; also a disagreeable man. He preached sermons which were very well attended, – sermons which bore hardly on undergraduates. Jowett's chief plank was the importance to the young of planning out a career as a whole. He was always at this. He would say to undergraduates: 'After you leave here you have forty years before you.' Etc.

In Surrey. – I know nothing about racing. Forty years ago I saw the Derby. Or rather I didn't see the Derby; but I was on Epsom Downs on Derby Day in the midst of an innumerable crowd of persons many of whom didn't see the Derby either. Since then I have seen a country-meeting or so, a Dublin meeting, and various meetings on French racecourses, though with no interest beyond the mere general spectacle. However, to-day, in a country-house, my host [Lord Beaverbrook], an owner of race-horses, began to talk vividly about racing people. He described the woman who, when she had won, talked to herself the whole time as she drove home, saying nothing comprehensible, just babbling and gabbling, half-unconsciously. The terrible evening gloom of those who had lost, and could afford to lose. The still more terrible gloom of those who had lost and couldn't afford to lose. He said that the betting 'system' of most of these people was to back (what they deemed to be) absolute certainties, and then by way of embroidery to make a few very long shots – 50 to 1 affairs. He said that they lived for nothing but racing. They talked to all the jockeys, all the trainers, and even all the stable-boys whom they could come across.

But there was another variety of racing people – especially at Newmarket – who went in for racing simply because it brought them within 'exclusive circles'. They would have preferred to hobnob with exclusive intellectuals; but lacking the brains necessary for the intellectual business, they courted the smart turfites, entertaining lavishly, etc., solely in order to be in 'society'. A woman present questioned the existence of this latter variety; but my host named instance after instance, and the woman yielded. He said that when you had 'big thing on in a big race', the thrill during the race was unique. He named a very famous and experienced owner and said that this middle-aged cosmopolitan celebrity literally shook with excitement in such circumstances.

Paris, February 9th. – I went to the Variétés to see the great outstanding success *Topaze*. Theatre packed, and just as dirty and frowsy as when I first entered it in the year 1903. (But in those days the first four rows of the stalls were reserved to the male sex. This rule no longer obtains. The earth does revolve.) I had tickets, which were duly examined and approved by the four gentlemen in shabby evening-dress who sit at the entrance of every Paris theatre. But we couldn't get our rightful places. Two *ouvreuses* differed about the geographical situation of them. At the end of the first act we were expelled from the seats allotted to us. More *ouvreuses*. More arguments. We got other seats. At the end of the second act we were expelled from our new seats, and passed a quarter of an hour in disputation. Just as the curtain rose on the third act we were put into our rightful places, not without a lot of trouble. These wandering hostilities rather marred the play for us. Still, I thought it a very fine play indeed. It finished at midnight. Rain. No taxis. I walked along the boulevard and looked into several cafés. In each of them I saw British intellectuals forgathering.

Brighton. – I came down here to rid myself of the obstinate neuralgic sequelae of a quite mild attack of influenza. Also for the purpose of getting an idea for a short story. Despite entertaining, and being entertained, and free indulgence in the most agreeable and (to me) most pernicious of all alcoholic liquids, champagne, I attained both objectives in three days. Of all the circle in which I 'move' I think I am almost the only person who likes Brighton. The sole thing I object to in Brighton is the penny-in-the-slot machines on the piers. Brighton has character, as the man who made its fame had character – but *his* character was evil. I have spent months and months in Brighton, and I thought I knew the place, especially the 'Lanes'; but to-day I found a second-hand bookshop previously unknown to me. I went in there immediately and discovered some plays of Labiche, an author of whom the bookseller had never heard – so that I got the plays cheap! I bought twelve books for £1 15s. This episode gave me no idea for my short story, but it certainly did something to cure my neuralgia. Later I went for a ride along the shore on the Electric Railway. Years ago the proprietor of this railway gave me a season-ticket for it because he liked one of my books. An example which might advantageously be followed by the G.W.R., the L.M.S., the L.N.E.R., the S.R., and other systems.

London. – I returned from Brighton and developed an entirely new kind of neuralgia, the fourth kind since my influenza. A man brought his niece for tea, and was witless enough to tell me that I looked tired. My latest neuralgia at once became acute. And yet doctors still begin all their treatments at the wrong end, dealing with the body first instead of with the mind first.

Blue Train. – Fog in the Channel. The ship crept forth from Dover Harbour at the rate of about a yard an hour. Three look-outs, and I made a fourth. I met various friends and acquaintances, and we all found it advisable to go below and drink champagne. (In my time I have slept on board ship for one hundred and twenty nights together, and my experience is that I prefer the worst storm to a fog at sea.) Delays apparently endless. Yet, such is the margin which the Southern Railway keeps up its sleeve, we arrived at Calais almost to time. We arrived at Paris exactly to time. The newest Blue Train is a marked improvement on its predecessors. But the railway track is no better than it was. Nor the food, whose sole merit is that it is not English. And as usual the train got later and later the further it penetrated into the slack South. So that we reached our destination sixty minutes behind time, and for no discoverable reason except negligent sloth. And when we did arrive on the Riviera with the fabled ideal climate, everyone was full of unimaginable tales of twelve inches of snow and the destruction by frost of hundreds of thousands of trees.

Antibes. – All around the Domaine des Charmettes are vast nurseries in which flowers are grown wholesale. Tens, perhaps hundreds, of thousands of blossoms under roofs of glass, with flaps that can be raised or lowered, and straw-matting which is put on the glass-roofs or hung in front of the same. Any single blossom exhibited in a drawing-room would look beautiful and really be beautiful. But seen in the mass these blossoms lose their attractiveness by losing their individuality. They are like prisoners thronged together in an internment-camp.

Antibes, April 10th. – Motor accident. A car in front of us stopped without signalling, and we ran into its petrol-tank, which crumpled up like cardboard. An old German couple occupied the first (totally disabled) car. Tremendous Babel of English, French, Italianate-French, and German tongues. The German couple, frail and pathetic, were ready to weep amid the odour of spilled petrol. I took them into my car, and we soothed them and undertook to drive them to Mentone, where all Germans stay and always have stayed. I feared the French police, with whom one can do nothing – except in the north of France. The French chauffeur wanted to be indemnified for everything: the smashed tank, the spilled petrol, the transport of his car to Mentone, and his loss of wages while the tank was being replaced. I made the wildest promises to him, swearing upon the sacred memory of my ancestors to fulfil them, and all sorts of things. He said: 'I trust you.' I said: 'You may.'

We got away. As soon as we were beyond the boundary of the municipality in which the accident occurred, I breathed more freely. Within their own districts the police can summarily detain your car after a collision. But once outside the district of an accident neither its police nor any other can lay upon you the hand of violence. This is the only good thing I ever heard of French road-law. In due course I wrote to my insurance company, and from that moment I heard no further word of the affair.

Mediterranean Islands. – A party of sixteen of us had been having a long and magnificent picnic which included motor-boating from the mainland, bathing, motor-boating from one island to another, enough walking, some dozing, and bouillabaisse the equal of which I have never eaten in Marseilles. This was the only picnic I have really enjoyed in my life! On principle I object to picnics, when they comprise a meal. I prefer a table and chairs for meals, and I think that most men not immature would agree with me. Women are different. Women prefer discomfort – up to a point. And anyhow, they have little righteousness in food. They would sooner eat bad food amid picturesqueness than good food in a prosaic room. This picnic combined picturesqueness with very good food, which food more than compensated for the unsuitability of the earth's surface as a chair or triclinium.

In the late afternoon we embarked for and reached the second island, whose buildings were limited to a café-restaurant and a monastery. We noticed that the sea was less tranquil than earlier in the day; but the island was only a couple of miles from the mainland, so that a few waves could not matter. A long dinner-table had been set for us in the open air near the somewhat primitive café-restaurant. The sun was descending. The wind was rising. The dinner was excellent, but it was eaten with a deal of sand which the wind persisted in blowing across the table, although the table was under the lee of the café-restaurant. We could hear the wind violent in the trees, and we could see the trees yielding, deferential victims of violence.

The dinner ended in deep twilight. We returned to the covered *terrasse* of the café-restaurant and drank at another long table. It grew dark. Somebody, unaware of the influence of words on the imaginative, carelessly used the word 'dangerous'. The chief organizer said lightly: 'Pooh! I will telephone for the regular passenger-steamer to fetch us.' But the social atmosphere was changed. Nothing, said some, could be safe in the sudden, mad Mediterranean storm. We were marooned for the night. As the oldest seafaring man present, I was invited to decide whether or not we should make the voyage. I said, 'Yes, we must make it.' But my decision had no effect on the minds of about half of the picnickers.

By this time there was a bridge-party, also a baccarat-party, at work, and everyone was visibly beginning to feel tired. No beds in the café-restaurant. The organizer said that he would send up to the monastery and ask the monks to lend us mattresses for the women. The proposal was not received with approval by the women. Some of them remarked with false gaiety how jolly it would be to sit up all night and play cards and watch the dawn and so on. The general feeling was against departure. What interested me was the psychological explanation of the real reasons for or against departure. These were certainly not the avowed reasons. There were three real reasons. The card-players were absorbed in their games, and wished not to be disturbed. The alarmist section had passed from the normal into a highly nervous state which no rational arguments could affect. If the *Mauretania* had come to fetch us, this section would still have jibbed. A third and small section, to which I belonged, wished to depart because a programme is a programme and should be adhered to. This section insincerely laughed at the alleged risks. It would not admit the risks even to itself. It would sooner accept risks than default on a schedule. Some people are like that. Then news arrived that the steamer refused to come, on the plausible excuse that the crew had departed to their homes; but that our own motor-boat was coming. I said: 'Well, if the motor-boat can safely come, it can safely go.' In the high wind and in black darkness I stumbled along uneven ground, and got into a quagmire and out of it, to the little harbour. I could see the whiteness of foam. I saw the motor-boat make three attempts to enter the habour, and fail. It succeeded at the fourth, and cheers were heard. I returned to the café-restaurant still scoffing at danger.

Then news arrived that the captain of the motor-boat had said definitely that we could not leave. Relief of the card-players! Triumph of the nervous section! Defeat of the schedule-keepers! I remained silent. I would admit nothing. In about an hour and a half, which seemed like eighteen hours or days or months, the news arrived that the captain of the motor-boat had said that the storm had fallen enough to allow us to depart in safety. All were openly relieved – for among the card-players fatigue was conquering the gambling spirit – except the nervous section. The nervous section would not trust the captain's wisdom. It spurned the argument that, assuming the captain's readiness to risk our lives, he would not risk his own. It slandered the captain, asserted that he must have had several drinks and got himself into a reckless mood and lost his judgement. But the nervous section was borne down, though it had to be dragged, protesting, to the boat.

We did depart. The extraordinary Mediterranean was calm again. And now the nervous section refused to admit that it had been wrong. Fortunately all were very hungry. About 2 a.m. we reached a night-restaurant where a nigger was saxo-phoning with an intensity that rendered conversation impossible. No matter. Nerves had vanished. We ate and danced. We reached our beds, some fifteen miles off, at 4.45 a.m., after escaping a motor accident by mere miracle.

London. – I went to St Bartholomew's Hospital this afternoon to visit a relative. I cannot remember ever having been in a hospital before – except war-hospitals behind the Western

Front and in London. The size of these civil hospitals is positively intimidating. St Thomas's is a town. The London
Hospital is a town. And Bart's is a town. But the largest institution I ever saw was a lunatic asylum – in Yorkshire. One is
told that the London is the largest hospital. It does not seem
any larger than St Thomas's or Bart's, or as large. When one
thinks that there is somebody in supreme charge of Bart's,
with the whole weight of the huge organism on his or her
shoulders, one is glad not to be that person.

When I go into a very large organism, I am always apprehensive of the formalities, filling up papers, submitting to
cross-examination by puffed-up guardians at the gate and so
on. At Bart's there were no formalities. The king of the porters gave me a brief sketch of the geography of the place. I
passed through courtyards and corridors and up palatial
staircases and walked direct into the right ward. I saw my
relative at once, and went straight up to him; nobody challenged me, and I breathed again.

My relative told me with pride that Bart's was the oldest
hospital in the world. Perhaps it is. Remarkable how inmates
of an institution immediately identify themselves with the
institution and take pride in it.

He related how for two days he had silently wondered why
salt was not served to him with boiled eggs. At last he had
discovered, by chance, that the salt was put in the egg-cup
under the egg. No one had told him. No doubt the nurses had
assumed that everyone would know a thing like that!

The ward was fairly large, and contained a variety of cases.
I saw a small boy of 6 or 8 years, suffering from rickets, imperfect appendix, and other troubles, being led out by a nurse.
There was pathos here. But to my relative rickets and troubles
of the appendix were common and totally uninteresting
diseases. Whereas his disease was a genuine and exclusive
curiosity, and doctors came specially from distant parts of the
hospitals, walked through miles of corridors, in order to
inspect him. He at once became intimate with doctors.

When I left the hospital the king of the porters nodded to
me as an old friend. I stood outside, and gazed at the immen-

sity of the buildings. I walked as far round them as I could, and tried to estimate how many beds were within. And how much suffering, pain, anguish, loneliness, insomnia. The streets of the district had a strange, callous air.

London. – The managing director of a large hotel, equally expert in cookery, wine and cigars, told me at a banquet that all the true Bordeaux in the world came from a single stretch of country thirty miles long by six wide, north of Bordeaux. The quality of its grapes depended on the combined influences of general climate, sun, and soil. The same vines would not produce the same grapes if planted anywhere else in the world. It was easy for me to deduce that only a small percentage of wine described as Bordeaux really is Bordeaux. And I know that large quantities of wine produced in such *départements* as Tarn-et-Garonne are not merely sold as Bordeaux but are called Bordeaux in the district itself. The director was full of piquant information about wines. He said that Germans will pay at the rate of as much as £3 a bottle for certain Rhine wines *in the wood*. He said also, in regard to claret, that connoisseurs will differ completely as to the value of a particular wine, or year, when the price gets beyond 25*s.* a bottle. In other words, up to 25*s.* a bottle you can be sure of getting value for money, but after 25*s.* you only get individual preference for money. Whereas with German wines you can get quality as to which all connoisseurs will agree, proportionate to prices far exceeding 25*s.*

English Seaside Hotel. – We lunched here, and had to wait half an hour because the place was packed. All the waiters were old, but decent and efficient; the head-waiter particularly; he looked like the Archbishop of Canterbury. The lunch was good and not dear. Four shillings a head.

Afterwards I inquired at the office about suites for the summer. A middle-aged dame was in charge of the reception-office. She was kindly, but marvellously *non possumus*. She assured me that *no* applications were ever, or ever could be, considered until after Easter was over. *All* applications must be in writing. *All* suites were the same: one double bedroom, one sitting-room, one bathroom. The inclusive charge for two people was twenty-six or twenty-eight guineas a week. Extra bedrooms could be had; but not adjoining a suite. This was absolutely out of the question. Single rooms would cost, inclusive, ten or twelve guineas a week in the season. *No* reduction for a baby two years old. Babies counted as adults.

The lady put every obstacle in my way. At last she said I ought to write to the manager. She was, however, in sole charge of the office, and the place was crowded with lunchers. I only made my inquiries at the office because an attractive tariff-booklet had been handed to me with the bill. The charges stated in the office were decidedly higher than those stated in the booklet.

And yet British hotel-keepers wonder why English people are so unpatriotic as to go to the continent for holidays.

Very Large Hotel in a Very Large Provincial City. – I had to myself a small but officially 'double' bedroom with private bathroom. One pound per day. The bathroom, which did not need it, was centrally heated. The bedroom was not heated. I had to have a fire all the time. No bells. All orders in rooms had to be telephoned. The service, however, was efficient and worked smoothly. A writing-desk, but no waste-paper basket. When I arrived on Sunday afternoon the room felt stuffy. I tried to open the windows, but totally failed to make either of them budge. Obviously they had not been opened since they were painted, which was certainly not yesterday. I telephoned for the valet. A porter came. He also totally failed to make either window budge. He fetched another porter, and between them with immense effort they managed to open one window. The easy-chair had lost a castor. I got this remedied. I also got a w.p. basket.

London, April 23rd. – I went to see the famous 'coloured' play, *Porgy*. Considered as a play it seemed to me to be negligible. Considered as a noise of wailing, singing, and praying it was far from negligible. Considered as a 'production', it was certainly very elaborate and complete; Marmoulian, the producer, is held to be in the foremost van of theatrical producing. But I could detect scarcely any modernness in the innumerable realistic detail of this production. I should call it of the school of David Belasco. I remember seeing the Belasco production of a feeble sentimental drama at the Belasco Theatre, New York. At the beginning of one act, a clock struck the hour; then, a few moments later, another clock struck the hour. 'Truth to life – what!' This is what in those days in New York they called 'realistic' production. If the play itself had had the tenth part of the truthfulness to life shown by the two clocks, it would have marked an epoch in the history of the stage. But the play hadn't – nor the hundredth part.

London, April 27th. – Final of the English Football Association Cup. The streets were full of charabancs carrying football enthusiasts, men and women, to see the sights of London before seeing the match. The Albert Memorial had great popularity. And indeed as a fact there are much worse architectural evils in London than the Albert Memorial. I see one rising skyward in the vicinity of Park Lane. Most of the visitors had conspicuously labelled themselves. One charabanc bore the announcement: 'Reckitt's Canister Factory.' I admired this *esprit de corps*, this industrial pride. There was something fine in it. The day, however, was remarkable to me for a reason entirely unconnected with football. Years ago I bought, together, a lovely complete edition of the *Memoirs* of St Simon, and a lovely complete edition of the works of Rousseau, who is supposed to be responsible for the French revolution and all subsequent social progress. I had often read St Simon, but never Rousseau. I took down the *Confessions* and began to read them. Big stuff!

I ought to have read the *Confessions* long since. They have the feel of a classic of the first order. What measured wisdom! What close and intricate psychological observation! What impartial truth! In these matters we have learned nothing new in a century and a half. If the *Confessions* were written afresh in a staccato, devil-may-care style, without verbs and commas, and signed by a young American or Irish name and dated from Paris, they would become a best-seller in two hemispheres.

London, April 29th. – *Tristan and Isolde,* conducted by Bruno Walter. Well, I prefer the bourgeois quality of the Vienna Opera to the brazen smartness of Covent Garden on a truly smart night. Not that Covent Garden was wholly smart tonight. Since we have begun to take an intelligent interest in music, Covent Garden has never been wholly smart. There is always a large admixture of genuine enthusiasts whose understanding of music surpasses their understanding of clothes. I left at the end of the second Act, not because I wasn't enjoying the performance (which was superb, except for the tenor), but because I was determined to go to bed at a reasonable hour. The megalomania of Wagner is shown as clearly in the excessive, the inhuman length of his operas as in his ruthless demands on the services, financial and other, of his friends. Only ill-balanced, one-idea'd persons can enjoy the last act of a Wagner opera as well as the first; for the reason that man's capacity for appreciation is limited. Louis of Bavaria would listen to *Tristan* twice in one night. But Louis was mad. Every first-rate performance of the best Wagner operas is attended by a number of people nearly as mad as Louis.

London, May 27th. – My birthday. I celebrated it by going to Portland Place and undergoing what for some inexplicable reason is called a thorough 'overhaul'. I had been warned that every man over fifty ought to be 'overhauled' every few years, whether he thinks he needs it or not. Dire maladies may unobtrusively begin their awful work within you, and develop and develop quite unsuspected, and then suddenly declare open war on you, and you are dead before you are prepared for death. Moreover, had I not been suffering from chronic insomnia for many years, and must not insomnia have a cause? And so on. The advice seemed sensible. As regards insomnia, my overhauler suggested that I should take a drug, 'medinol', every night for three months or six months. Yes, such was the advice I paid for!

London, June 5th. – I received the detailed report of my overhauler, via my ordinary doctor, in accordance with medical etiquette. There was nothing the matter with me at all. Blood pressure right. Heart very fine. Lungs very fine. Arteries suitable to the age of 32 instead of 62. The liver somewhat less brilliant than the other parts of the body, but still an excellent specimen of this great organ. No light thrown on my chronic insomnia. As a fact, another doctor, not professionally consulted, had once uttered to me the final word about my insomnia: 'It's simply this,' he said. 'You happen to be a bad sleeper.' I have never got beyond that!

London, June 25th. – Another oath broken. After some fantastic experiences at my own first-nights, I had sworn never to attend another. But when I told the authorities of Covent Garden that I should not be present at the first performance of the Goossens-Me opera *Judith*, there was such horrified, outraged protest that I accepted a box on the spot. And there I sat on the first-night, hiding behind a curtain, and surveying the crowded house. My highly nervous state was mitigated by the realization of the unquestionable fact that I was not Eugene Goossens, exposed defenceless to the public and conducting the orchestra. I kept carefully in the box, but well-intentioned friends and quidnuncs would insist on visiting me both before and after the performance. I had not the courage to tell them that, with the important exception of loud and prolonged applause, all an author wants on a first-night is to be left alone. I paid what I was afraid would be a state visit to the prima donna. But it was not in the least stately. After I had kissed her hand we forgot ceremony and were realistic with one another about all manner of things, and laughed like girl and boy.

London. – Dinner and interview with a star film-director. I was told that he was the finest and the most successful film-director in the country. I had never seen anything of his on the screen. A youngish man, with a clear, penetrating voice, trained no doubt to make itself heard in the immensities of studios, but more than adequate for a dinner-table. I had written and sold a film scenario, and at the request of the purchasing firm the director was considering the same.

At first he assumed the air of a puissant lawgiver. When resolutely tackled, however, he changed the air for another one, and we became almost equals. He argued on the following lines: 'Now the hero of your story is a financier. Now would a street-barrow woman in Hoxton understand about getting an overdraft at a Bank? That is the test, the street-barrow woman in Hoxton. Is office work and typewriting romantic? *Is* it? Now if we could have the story lowered in class, if for instance you could make the financier a ring-master in a circus, now that would be colourful. What we want is colour.' And so on in similar style.

I argued him out of every point, and soon his principal phrase was, 'Oh! I agree.' But though he agreed point by point, he did not agree in the least on the whole question. I yielded on nothing. He yielded on everything, and said at last he would think the matter over. But I was quite certain that he never would think it over.

The purchasing firm had specially commissioned me to write a story that did not resemble the ordinary film-story. They knew my more notorious books, and desired a story in the manner and on the plane of those books. I had asked them if they wanted truth to life, and they had replied that truth to life was precisely what they did want and that on the screen truth to life was coming more and more into fashion! Audiences were getting tired of sobstuff, etc. I now perceived that, if audiences were getting tired of sobstuff, film-directors were not.

When we had thrashed the story all to bits and neither he nor I had anything more to say about it, he grew communicative about himself, in reply to my questions, and revealed himself a regular figure out of film-land. He said: 'I can never begin work until about eleven-thirty in the morning. I have a glass of sherry then, and that starts the flow of ideas. You must have the flow. The film must move rapidly, and so your ideas must come rapidly.' An odd argument, but I don't think he could see any flaw in it.

I found that in order to impress him I had to boast. Hence I did boast. I called down rather sharply one of the head-waiters who had been too curt with me. This episode obviously increased the director's respect for me. When the interview was over he said he should not require his car, and amiably offered to send me home in it. It was a magnificent, a glorious car, the car of the legendary film-director. I thanked him and said that I might just as well go home in my own.

London. – Authentic revelations about the central adminis-tration of justice in Ireland before Ireland, or part of her, became a Free State. A Lord Justice of Appeal had to wear on state occasions a court dress with a train. One Lord Justice named to me bought his dress third-hand for £50 from a second Lord Justice who had bought it from a third Lord Justice, its original owner, who had paid 250 guineas for it. The dress was destroyed in the destruction of the Four Courts by the rebels. The Government asked Lord Justice No. 1 what compensation he wanted. He asked for £200 and got it. A train needs a train-bearer. Lord Justice No. 1 did the usual thing: he appointed a relative to be his train-bearer. This boy had to bear the train four times a year for about half an hour each time. Salary £100 per annum.

Apropos, my informant told me that in the glorious old days of the Exchequer Division the judges thereof had the patronage of various sinecures (£1,000 to £1,500 a year each) and that they invariably appointed their fellow-judges to these sinecures. And my informant also told me that the Irish Attorney-General, before the rule of Sinn Fein, had to see all indictments at a fee of three guineas apiece, and that his income from this source had been known to run as high as £25,000 in a single year. I received other similar information, but nobody would believe it in print. I have allowed it to slip my memory. Some day perhaps I shall obtain equally startling stuff about the financial idiosyncrasies of Sinn Fein.

Italy. – An English bank is inhuman or godlike. Its attitude towards ordinary customers implies that it is conferring a favour upon them by doing business with them at all and that they ought to consider themselves indeed a fortunate lot. It cannot or will not recognize that it is a mere shop for the sale of monetary facilities, and that there are rival shops. That it exists for the convenience of its customers, and not vice versa, is an idea which apparently seldom occurs to it.

Now French and Italian banks are human. They are very human. I have done plenty of business with French and Italian banks. Yesterday I went into a typical large branch of an Italian bank; and everything happened according to precedent. Italian banks close from 12 to 2. Such a system would not work in England, but it works smoothly enough in both Italy and France. At ten minutes past two the numerous staff comes strolling casually in from its lunch, smoking cigarettes. Italian bank-clerks seem to be unable to do business without tobacco. And why should they do business without tobacco? Tobacco is humanizing. Their manners are exquisite; their charm is notable.

At the first guess I went to the right counter, behind which some half-dozen clerks were more or less busy in a cubicle. I presented a cheque – not a foreign cheque, but one of the Bank's own cheques. I furnished evidence of identity. I was most urbanely received. The entire half-dozen young males showed a friendly interest in me. Then I said: 'I want this money in English sterling.'

'*Sterlina!*' exclaimed the youth attending to me, astounded. 'Ah! We must go upstairs.'

He escorted me upstairs to another and a vaster room. He telephoned to the cashier downstairs: 'Have we fifty pounds in sterling?' A pause. The clerk smiled. Yes, the Bank had in its coffers fifty pounds in sterling. Then began the filling up of forms, with carbon duplicates. A tremendous affair. My full name, the name of my father, my permanent domicile, where I had come from, where I was staying. Then I started to endorse the cheque, which required two separate signatures. With perfect tact, the clerk stopped me.

'Excuse me,' said he. 'The signature on the front of the cheque ought to have been written before you came into the Bank.'

'But I will sign it in your presence,' said I.

'Ah, sir! We have our rules.' Then followed a long palaver among the staff.

'I must consult the Director,' said he.

He departed to consult the Director, who presently arrived to see me. The manners of the Director were marvellous: a lesson to all Britons. They were comparable to those of the late Lord Chaplin, whose social deportment I have never seen equalled – in England. The Director agreed with me that I might perform the first signature in the Bank itself, and left me with an enchanting bow and smile. Then the second signature. Then more forms which had to be signed. The clerks were in continual consultation as to procedure.

'Now we will go down to the cashier,' said my special clerk. 'I will accompany you.'

We descended to the cashier. A third signature was demanded. In all, I wrote twelve signatures. But I got the sterling. I also got humaneness, charm, and courtesy. Also my affair had engaged the attention of eleven clerks and the supreme Director. At the close everybody appeared to be very pleased and relieved. On everybody's face was an indication that a miracle had been accomplished. I myself felt that a miracle had been accomplished. True, it had taken thirty-three minutes: but a miracle it was. I went forth into the hot blinding sunshine of nearly three o'clock. All this happened in an illustrious city where tourists are as common as flies; and in my view it was quite as interesting as any of the city's storied monuments.

Lago di Garda. – The hotel-pension is quite the best I ever stayed in. A former Archbishop of Canterbury is reported to have said, as to food: 'All I ask for is a plain but perfect table.' We had what the Archbishop of simple tastes asked for. And everything else about the place was perfect, including the service, which was rather super-perfect, for the reason that, having arrived long before the hullabaloo of the summer season had set in, we had the entire hotel to ourselves.

The hillside above, like the garden, is as steep as a roof. The faint sound of a bell descends from its hidden verdurous height. I drive up. It is a severe climb, even for a car. An interminable succession of acute hair-pin bends. I reach at last a village, San Zeno di Montagna. The altitude is marked on a wall, 700 metres odd – appreciably over two thousand feet. Every Italian village has five profane phenomena: a cobbler's, a barber's, a general store, an unkempt café or so, and a municipal decree written on paper, signed by his Worship the Mayor, and affixed to the façade of a prominent house. In other respects San Zeno di Montagna seems to be uncorrupted by the latest civilization, save for a young woman or two nicely shod and with coiffures whose elaboration has cost time if not money. The church goes without saying. It holds nothing to astonish, unless you are capable of being astonished by a large portrait of San Zeno himself in modern stained glass. A workman has taken out one of the windows and, perched on the sill, is working with a noisy hammer thereat. The village priest, under an umbrella, promenades to and fro, keeping a prelatical eye upon him. A few indifferent inhabitants, no doubt the oldest or the fattest, move slowly around the slatternly, dusty, half-ruinous hamlet on their vocations agricultural or commercial. The two cafés are empty.

The great fact is the sun overhead, much too bright to be visible, shooting down cataracts of hottest light. Millions of insects unseen whirr and creak, as though their machinery needed lubrication. I look through the boughs of an untidy orchard, and see the changing sheen of the vast surface of Lake Garda beneath me, the largest and the least spoilt of the North Italian lakes. Over thirty miles long; ten miles at its broadest and a couple of miles at its narrowest. North, west and east it is shut in by mountains, quite a number of them rising to seven thousand feet. And at the foot of these thirty or more villages. Several of them towns, with dubious imitations of grand hotels, white tram-cars, Kodak shops, and emporia for the sale of English and German newspapers. The population of one town attains five thousand. And half-way up the ranges lie large villages, with no hotels, no nothing except cobbler's, cafés, barber's, small stores, and mayoral ukases. Perilous roads hang like cotton threads on the slopes; and five miles of them are as one inch.

And rising very high above all this, range behind range, the naked summits of the coloured mountains, never climbed, never approached, utterly immaculate. An immense quantity of the earth's surface in Italy is wasted by nature, serves no purpose save to impress the unaccustomed eye. Impress the unaccustomed eye it certainly does. The scenery is lovely, majestic, the scenery of a dream or of a picture-postcard. The eye can discover in the distance naught but a dreamy, hazy, ideal beauty conceived on a terrifying scale. If beauty and terror are the desiderata of the artist, here he has them, incredibly combined.

The lake is empty. Not a steamer in view, not a barge in view. Only one islet (but there are two still tinier islets out of sight to the north). This is called the island of Garda. I saw it close yesterday. It belongs to the Borghese family. Of course it would – or to the Scaliger family. It has a stucco palace on it in the worst taste, and a whole little street of appurtenant out-houses in better taste. Apparently the palace is uninhabited; but you never know. It is not 'open to the public'. The leases of some historic Italian palaces contain a clause compelling the tenant to deliver his drawing-rooms one day a week to the common gaze – for a trifling fee. But the Borghese family are superior to such rules. The island has a queer reputation. Not so very many years ago a Borghese princess fell off a terrace parapet while watering flowers and was drowned in the sea of the lake. People spoke of suicide. Soon afterwards the next tenants, an amorous pair, were drowned out of a boat in a squall. Thereupon the rumour of a Borghese suicide suddenly became an accepted myth. Nobody could deny that the unhappy princess did not fall off the parapet, but threw herself off in despair. And the island was accursed, fatal to human life. There the island lies, a glistening spot hung between the sea of sunshine and the sea of the lake.

Verona. – Juliet's home-town, I suppose some would call it. The phrase takes the edge off romance, and I designed it to do so, determined as I am somehow to vent my rage at being shown Juliet's house, a picturesque and untidy tenement, with balconies certainly too high for love, unless Juliet was a trapeze acrobat, accustomed to hanging head downwards by her toes.

This was not Juliet's house, for the sufficient reason that so far as authentic history shows, there never was any Juliet. It seems that Shakespeare took the story of Juliet from an Italian fiction, performing in the process his customary feat of making a silk purse out of a sow's ear; and that he chose Verona for her habitation because of its agreeably sounding name. There not having been any Juliet, there could not have been any Juliet's house. Hence to label a building as Juliet's house, and to draw the special attention of simple-minded tourists to it as such, was an act of unscrupulous fraud, which the city authorities ought to have firmly and publicly disowned. The thing is as barefaced a swindle as the alleged tomb of Agamemnon at Mycenae.

Still, Verona is not a mean city. The first view of the vast old reddish Castle, with superb bridge to match, after you have passed through its triple enclosure of walls, is exceedingly impressive. Also the place is unspoilt. It exists now as it did exist. The hoof-marks of the globe-trotter are not upon it. The streets are narrow, with very few new monuments, and without vistas. (True, the traffic is directed by policemen with white batons, derived doubtless from London via Paris via Rome and Milan.) The main street is forbidden to all wheeled traffic. The famous Herb Market, where the original frescoes on the façades of the houses largely survive, makes a truly romantic spectacle. The one defect of the Herb Market is that the supply therein of the modern staff of life – I mean oranges – is both insufficient and inferior.

And the citizens are unspoilt children of the Renaissance, ingenuous, provincial, violent in face and mien, unpolluted yet by their brief contacts with the touristic horde! We were the only Anglo-Saxons to lunch at a purely Italian restaurant under the immense arcade of the old Bourse, where the waiters dashed to and fro in ordinary suits, arguing with one another, and being charmingly explanatory to their strange guests. We took coffee at the best hotel, and tea at the other best hotel; and both were pretty third-rate – according to touristic conventions. I liked that, especially as the tea was good and the coffee was good. You seldom or never get a first-rate hotel in an unspoilt town. First-rate hotels arise on the ruins of the primitive.

I was pleased, too, to see that no concerted effort had been made to utilize socially or touristically the fearsome river Adige, on which the city is situated. Not a terrace on its banks; not a café with a river view. Evidently the citizens regard the swift-flowing Adige merely as an impossible stream. They have imprisoned its turbulent water between granite walls, and then just left it to rafts and lumbermen. The principal open-air cafés are all in an inner square, where you can see girls walking and officers walking (Verona is the headquarters of an army-corps) and the inhabitants behaving naturally and self-unconsciously, as they do in Seville.

At the lunch hour there is an enormous rushing outbreak of bicycles, which though dangerous to limb are less so than automobiles and belong more to the historic past. Neither English nor French is spoken in the dark and cavernous shops. And as for the Post Office, which you reach by a splendid balustraded stone staircase in a splendid courtyard, it may be called Renaissance in its routine as in its architecture. The employees appear to say to each other: 'Funny thing! Here's somebody wanting a money-order! What next, I wonder!' All which is delightful and touching – in homeopathic doses. The huge Roman gateway, the huge Roman amphitheatre –

well, you can study them if you so desire. The inhabitants
negligently tolerate them. And if you have been travelling a
lot, you yourself are as sick of gateways and amphitheatres as
of churches. I remember an old retired wealthy industrial
Frenchman remarking: 'Italy would be tolerable if it were not
for its public monuments.'

You leave Verona, after your first visit, with an impression
of tremendous beating sunshine and of a general higgledy-
piggledyness. The people have the phlegmatic indifference of
Englishmen at home. They may just have heard of Shakspeare.
If they have heard of the fabled Juliet they assuredly set her
down as a wanton wench, imperfectly guarded, who deserved
all she got from destiny.

Bergamo. – Travel is full of startling contrasts: one of the
most startling is that between the richly decorated, idle
luxury of the large Italian liners in the port of Genoa, and the
slums and never-ceasing toil which surround the port. Not
for a single hour in the twenty-four is the port quiet. Another
contrast is that between the magnificent suburbs of Milan and
the squalid suburbs of Genoa. The splendid straight smooth
roads radiating from Milan easily surpass those of London or
Paris. The periphery of Genoa is terrible. Why? Genoa is a
very important place, and is indeed called, justly, the 'city of
palaces'. One hears that the relative rise of Milan is due to the
influence of a certain Alpine tunnel. But there must be a more
complex explanation than that.

And yet another contrast. We sat in one of dozens of large,
too-musical cafés in the centre of Milan. All full; and the pavements full, and the tram-cars. Tremendous babbling crowds,
of which an extraordinarily large proportion consisted of
smartly dressed young men. An enigma of the life of big cities
is the multitudes of young men therein who apparently are
free to enjoy themselves at four o'clock in the afternoon. (But
you do not see them in London, nor in Manchester nor
Glasgow.) From the cafés of Milan we walked a few yards into
the cathedral. Hardly a soul on the measureless desert floor of
the unornamented house of God. And after the sunshine

glitter of the streets and squares, the sacred interior seemed to be in that final stage of dusk which immediately precedes black night. Darkness and utter silence. In a distant corner, an altar was lit with candles that gave an effect as of fireworks in the heavy gloom. The sudden change made you think, almost overwhelmed you.

But it was at Avignon that I encountered the greatest contrast. I do not care much for Avignon. It is over-visited. The Palace of the Popes is not worthy of its reputation, and the inhabitants are not sympathetic. They must suffer dreadfully from the mistral. I once suffered myself from the mistral in Avignon, and I shall not forget it. The mistral is a wind to destroy nobility of character and dry up the milk of human kindness.

We stayed in one of two largest touristic hotels. The evening heat was very oppressive. The hotel was full of assorted British and American accents. Not a 'foreigner' in the building except the mistral-cursed staff! I often wish that all Anglo-Saxons (except me and my companions) would have the decency to stay at home and leave the continent of Europe uncorrupted by their presence and voices. The crowded dining-room of that infernal hotel was more Anglo-Saxon than London, and much more Anglo-Saxon than New York.

We fled from it, and in about three minutes were in the square of the populace. Some Anglo-Saxons would have the effrontery to call it the native quarter. The large square was a most soothing spectacle. All cafés, theatres, cinemas. The mundane name of Esther Ralston written in electricity on a façade, and under it two black-robed Italian young women taking their ease in wicker-chairs and gossiping with a man in evening dress who bent laughingly over them. The young women must have been ticket-girls of the cinema, and the man may have been the director. Groups of natives drinking and chattering on the *terrasses* of the cafés. Crowds of natives sitting or sprawling on the hot pavements; and many children among them, including a baby of one and a half or so, who propelled himself to and fro on his basis with considerable skill. The hour was ten-thirty. French children seem never to go to bed. Yet they are beloved, petted, cared for, and look well. Evidently the British method of rearing is not the sole satisfactory method.

We had a glimpse of a corner of the Palace of the Popes, just beyond an open corner of the square. The architecture, scarcely visible in the night, rose majestic above house-roofs: as mighty and magical as a stage-set by Gordon Craig. The vision drew us up to another great square, dark and quite empty, and then into the public gardens on the far side of the Palace. We heard the ringing of a bell. A guardian arrived and turned us out of the gardens jocularly, and locked the heavy gates behind us. Eleven o'clock had struck.

Back in the first square, where everything, infants included, was proceeding just as before, we sat down on the terrace of a café, and ordered drinks, polluting the nativeness of the place by our touristic aspect and deportment. When we reached the hotel, it was dark, and the gate was locked, and we had to ring more than once for readmittance into Anglo-Saxondom. Anglo-Saxondom was in bed and no doubt as fast asleep as the heat would allow. Our sightseeing fellow-guests had missed the most interesting sight in Avignon.

Montluçon, July. – I was looking for rooms in a hotel near the railway. As the landlady and I went along a corridor upstairs, I said I hoped the noise of trains could not be heard in the bedrooms. 'One hears nothing,' she answered positively. She opened the door of a room, and a tremendous engine-shriek met us, seeming to drive us both back from the threshold. She shut the door, and tried another one, and we were met instantly by another tremendous engine-shriek. She burst out laughing. I laughed too. If she had not proved her sense of humour I might have walked straight out of the hotel. But her sense of humour kept a customer with a sense of humour. I got quiet rooms at the back.

Montluçon is rather an ordinary provincial town, which probably few stay at except business men and the benighted. But it has a somewhat elaborate system of traffic-directing policemen. Provincial towns, both in France and Italy, seem to glory in the profuse provision of agents of order; also in one-way streets. Municipal snobbishness: that is what it is. Traffic-directing policemen and one-way streets are clear proof of the existence of a large volume of traffic. Moreover, small towns must imitate large towns and the metropolis. At Montluçon we asked a grim, sardonic policeman the route for Le Puy. He gave us an answer than which nothing could have been more wrong. After two miles we had to return into the town. One of us said that the incorrect policeman had acted from mere provincial maliciousness, hatred of the tourist, etc. I would not agree to this explanation. Obviously the policeman could not admit ignorance. He just made a guess and the guess happened to be a bad one. We asked another policeman. He said: 'Follow the high street *and ask again of the fourth policeman you see.*' We did so and were saved.

Poitiers, Saumur, Angoulême. – At a restaurant entitled the Chapon Fin, I had one of the most wondrous meals of my existence as an eater. And not too dear. Poitiers is only a small town, and yet the largeish restaurant was full of lunchers all doing themselves exceedingly well; and few tourists among them. Of the few tourists the most astonishing were two English or Scottish sisters. They ate at length, and never spoke to one another. One had a book and the other a newspaper. They ate truly distinguished food, dish after dish – and they read.

Saumur is an enchanting town, full of fine domestic architecture. Angers is an enchanting town, full of fine domestic architecture. So is Angoulême. But all three are very provincial.

Fontainebleau, July. – Yesterday I visited Fontainebleau. Another of those châteaux! All French châteaux are not on the Loire, and this one is not. It is very nearly on the Seine, which is beautiful here, especially a little higher up, at its confluence with the Loing. The French have not yet quite learned how to exploit either of these rivers for pleasure. What they chiefly do is to sit on them in a moored punt and fish with perfect futility for hours. The barge traffic, however, is interesting.

Thanks to the facts that Napoleon liked Fontainebleau more than any of his other residences, that he imprisoned the Pope there for nearly two years, and that he abdicated there, under stress, Fontainebleau is probably the most popular chateau in France, just as its superb forest is the largest. Every ten minutes throughout every day of the week, a party is conducted by a guide through the showy portions of the chateau; and as the tour takes about forty interminable minutes there must be three or four parties *en route* at once, each dominated by a guide who says the same things in the same words eight or ten times daily. These guides surpass actors in that they seem never to 'dry up', and never to 'fluff'. True, the runs of their sedate performances must easily beat all theatrical records.

The mischief with their work is that they are evidently bound more strictly than other château guides to a time-schedule, a schedule which leaves no margin for leisure or caprice. You are moved inexorably on, for the parties behind you are hurrying near, and the concourse of visitors in the waiting-room is always growing, and growing impatient. The guide is succinct – he has to be – except when he indulges you in childish details, such as the exact number of different woods used in a complex parquet floor.

The rooms, as usual in châteaux, are badly planned, often dark, and often inconvenient. The darkest and the smallest, and the most inconvenient are those of queens; the most spacious are those of royal mistresses. Characteristic of masculine and feminine human nature! As surely as you enter a noble interior, so surely will you see the proud initials of Diane de Poictiers innumerably repeated in gold on the walls. Nearly all the rooms are cruelly overcrowded with furniture. Much of the original furniture is stored away in hidden depositories of the château, whose appearance would be improved if still a great deal more furniture were stored away. Though there are lovely things here and there, the general effect is one of an overpowering sumptuous vulgarity.

Last year a French journalist, novelist, and wit, Pierre Mille, put the silly-season question: What would have happened if on the 15th August 1769, Letitia Romalino, wife of father Bonaparte, had given birth to a girl instead of a boy? It may be said with certainty that one thing which would have happened would have been a marked decrease in the dreadful imperial ugliness of the château of Fontainebleau. Two of the most appallingly rich chambers in the world are Napoleon's throne-room and his bedroom – with the cradle of the King of Rome, whose misfortunes began with the sinister formidableness of the poor little dear's Empire cot.

I have a considerable affection for the Empire style, of which I bought a houseful when it could be bought for half nothing. But the excesses of the style are terrible, and Napoleon preferred the wildest ornate excesses. I had not beheld the interiors of Fontainebleau for twenty years, when it was far less visited than to-day. I enjoyed it less than ever. My estimate of Napoleon's culture – if he had any – was less than ever. My sympathy for the unhappy members of his court – read the devastating memoirs of the gradually disillusioned Madame de Rémusat – was keener than ever.

Brittany. – Yesterday I was lunching in a strange hotel where I had never been before and to which I shall never return, seeing faces and hearing voices of mysterious human beings called waiters who knew me, and whom I knew, for an hour only. And while I was sitting in the lounge drinking coffee, and looking round at the expanse of the golf-links, whose existence is the sole cause of the existence of the hotel, I saw a procession moving slowly towards a windowed shed in a corner of the course. This procession consisted first of a policeman, second of a stretcher borne by two men, and third of a group of followers. Upon the stretcher I could make out nothing but a rug and a pair of heavy boots at the fore-end of the rug. The stretcher disappeared into the shed, at whose door the policeman stood on guard. The group of followers remained outside, staring. The number of starers increased. Then members of the hotel-staff went out into the hotel-garden and stared. And I stared. Then a waiter came up to me and without being asked for information said: 'It is an Englishman, military. He was on the cliffs near here. He fell into the sea. They have just removed the corpse.'

'An accident?' I suggested. 'Oh, yes, sir. An accident, without doubt. The cliffs are dangerous.' When I left I passed close by the shed. The starers had disappeared, but golfers were golfing on distant parts of the course. Curiosity had exhausted itself. The door of the shed was open and the policeman stood in the doorway.

To-day I was informed positively that the affair was not an accident, but suicide. The English military officer was known on the coast for his peculiarities; a letter had been found ... relatives were arriving from England. Yes, it was all very sad, very regrettable. A charming man, he was, though peculiar and of solitary habits. Etc. etc. What stuck in my mind was the pair of heavy boots protruding insensate, callous, ugly, from the fore-end of the rug ...

Brittany, July. – At 4.30, though the dawn has furtively begun, the lighthouse about five miles off is still flashing its red sector over the deep dusk; two flashes, a pause, two flashes, a pause, and so on without end. And the other lighthouse, about ten miles off, is flashing its white light. (Men on those lighthouses probably dozing!) The character of the sky cannot be determined in the gloom, except as far as it is indicated by a total absence of stars.

I lean over the balcony, seeing naught save the warning lights, and reflect upon the reactions between my fellow-creatures and myself. Or rather, I do not reflect, for at that hour my mind is incapable of sustained logical thought. I muse, vaguely, meanderingly, reaching however the clear conclusion that the desired goal of moral perfection is still somewhat distant, and that I am often maladroit in my social relations and lacking perseverance in the pursuit of righteousness. In short, that there are better men on the revolving ball.

At 6.15 all is light, and the lighthouses – nightwatchmen – have retired to rest and total invisibility. Every detail of the golf-course, where nature has been defaced in order to make gratuitous difficulties for the golfer, is plain to the sight. With my glasses I can even decipher the numbers on the white boxes of the teeing-off platforms. The restless sky is dark and terrible with steely menaces. The little flags on the putting-greens are fluttering desperately in a south-west wind. Not a soul. Not a sound.

Then a fox-terrier comes ambling along on some secret and no doubt sinister enterprise of his own, and disappears. He is the first soul. Then a youth on a bicycle free-wheeling down the gritty, bituminous road in front of the hotel. He jumps off at the door of a small building of which part is employed for the profitable business of the golf-professional. I look away; I look back; youth and bicycle have vanished. Then in the distance of the links I see two workmen separately approaching. Their paths are unnecessarily devious over the turf. I expect the paths to converge and the men to meet and talk, near the hotel. But no! The paths do almost converge but curve apart again, and the men give not a sign of being brothers in the same worldly boat. Perhaps they are preoccupied with house-hold afflictions and the harshness of the coming toil. One continues up the hill rising to the north-west; the other enters the same building as the youth.

Work is beginning somewhere. A tiny fishing-boat stands out to sea, heeling over at moments to a squall. Work there! Then an aproned man appears underneath me from the portals of the hotel, shouldering a carpet which he lays out flat on the grass and sweeps vivaciously with a besom. He folds up the carpet in the same old folds, and carries it within again, trailing his besom. I look down on the balconies below me. Most of them are encumbered with highly-coloured bathing-costumes and white towels. The sun blindingly appears for a single instant between black clouds, and retires for the remainder of the day.

A man perched amid the whirr of a motor-mower is now operating on the putting-greens. Then a smart motor-car approaches. '*Voilà papa!*' says a voice. A lady in a peignoir, with a small child on her lap, is sitting out on a balcony near to mine. The car comes to a stop in front of the hotel, and a smart man, for whom the chauffeur has respectfully opened the door, steps down. 'Say good morning to papa,' says the voice. 'Good morning, papa,' squeals the small child. The smart man looks up, as in a daze. He descries his wife and child. 'Good morning, little one,' he answers in a tender tone, and walks into the hotel, followed by the chauffeur with his bags. And the lady and child disappear from the balcony. Where has that man come from, to arrive so smart and blithe at 7.15 a.m.? Heaven knows. Later, while I am still wondering, I hear a knock at my door. I leave the balcony. The chambermaid, black and white, all smiling and fresh, and bearing a tray, enters the bedroom. 'Behold your complete tea, monsieur!' says she. 'Thank you, madame,' say I. She is a mere ten minutes late. I smell the unique, the revivifying odour of tea. I pour out the tea. I fall on the rolls and butter. The day has at last really begun and the world is fully alive once more.

Dinard, August. – We are perhaps too often unjust in our moral judgements. When I suggested to the manager of a hotel that 8 francs was a bit high for a simple bath, what I really and indignantly meant was that the charge was an outrageous ramp. The manager very mildly explained to me that he himself paid 5 francs to the waterworks for a cubic metre of cold water, and that the average bath meant half a cubic metre of water. He then had to bear the cost of heating the water, pay interest on the cost of the bathroom installation, pay wages for cleaning the bathroom, pay for the laundering of the towels, and provide for his overhead charges. I recalled a statement of the most efficient hotel-manager I ever met to the effect that his overhead charges came to 52 per cent. of his turnover. Thus, if he bought a bottle of wine for 4s. 10d., he must sell it at about 10s. to save himself from loss. ... I admitted that perhaps 8 francs for a bath was not such an outrageous ramp after all.

London, August. – Yesterday evening I took the night-boat to England. Late at night I had a heart-to-heart talk with the steward. Like most stewards he was a pale, thin, quiet man.

'Do you get any sleep at nights?' I asked him. He answered: 'Well, sir, it depends on the season and the passengers. Sometimes *we* (never 'I') get a bit of sleep. But of course it's night work. If I'm lucky I'm off duty at nine in the morning, and when I'm in England I go home to my wife and family, and sleep.'

'But holidays?' I asked. He answered: 'Well, sir, *they* give us a week's holiday in the year.' 'But Sundays?' 'We work Sundays as well as weekdays.' I said: 'But do you mean to say you work every night in the year except seven?' He answered: 'Yes, sir. It's all the same, week in, week out. Of course it's monotonous, but that's the conditions and we accept them.' I said: 'But you ought to have a night off a week and a fortnight's holiday.' He smiled: 'Well, sir. That's what it is.' 'Well,' I said, 'it ought to be altered.' He said, indifferently, fatalistically: 'Yes, sir.'

He was a very agreeable and soothing man, but, though yet young, he had sunk into a groove extremely deep, and had apparently lost all divine discontent. He lived the life of a monk – and of a shuttle, to and fro, to and fro. Saw many dawns, but rarely the midday sun. Now and then an afternoon movie, never a theatre. He was cut off from mankind, except for glimpses of his family and the nocturnal society of his fellow-stewards. To me his existence presented itself as terrible, and the worst of the affair was that to him his existence was perfectly ordinary.

I retired to my cabin and slept. At five-thirty the next morning he came all bright into the cabin with my cleaned shoes and some fruit – and apologies for disturbing me! I bade him good-bye on the quay. Probably I shall never see him again. And in less than fifteen hours I have forgotten his features.

At Sea, August. – I am in an ocean steamer, a liner. I said to my steward: 'How early can I have my breakfast?' He said: 'Any time *you* like, sir.' 'Yes,' said I. 'That's all very well, but when do you start work? I don't want to inconvenience you.'

He said: 'I am called at five and on duty at half-past five, sir.' 'Every morning?' 'Yes, sir.'

I began to be interested. I asked: 'But when do you go to bed?' He said: 'Eleven o'clock every other night, and ten o'clock every other night. Sometimes I manage to get off at nine-thirty.' I said: 'But do you get enough sleep?' He evaded the question. Here was a seventeen- or eighteen-hour day, seven days a week. I did not care to question him further. I knew that he was on duty all day, because whenever I rang the bell he answered it. I did not inquire about his holidays. Like the steward on the cross-channel steamer, he was pale and thin and meek! but a trifle less meek, and certainly more sturdy, morally. This is the day on which 'everyone' in England either has gone to the north or is going. There seems to be some truth in the adage that it takes all sorts to make a world.

At Sea, August. – The same steward further informed me that if the interval between two voyages did not exceed four days, the Line kept him on. But if it exceeded four days, they got rid of him. He was anticipating an idle interval of three months soon. 'What do you do then?' I asked. He said: '*We* go on the dole, sir. The Line sometimes loses good servants, sir, that way. We ought to get a small retaining fee.' At the price of a small retaining fee, he seemed quite willing to be thrown out of work whenever it suited the Line.

London. – Some people have odd notions of romance. I have. When the dailiness of the domestic atmosphere oppresses me in the afternoon, and what I am writing seems flat and getting flatter, I sneak out of the house and go to a Dairy Company's tea-shop in King's Road, and order a pot of China tea and read *Les Nouvelles Littéraires*, and neglect *Les Nouvelles Littéraires* in order furtively to watch my fellow-wassailers. A tea-shop is a wonderful place, in a high degree romantic. The people who come in and go out. The girls together, feminine. The men together, masculine. The men who would no more think of taking their hats off in a tea-shop than in a railway station.

The different tones in which orders are given. The different demeanours which the same attendant will adopt towards different customers. The staid supervisors. The slatternly dishwashers peeping forth now and then. The cash-girl eternally in her cage, and in the draught from the ever-opening and ever-shutting door. One talks of the romantic quality of Paris cafés. They are prose compared to the free-verse of a London tea-shop.

Moscow, August 28th. – I went to the opera, and saw an Act of a most tedious ballet, alleged to be modern, but in which I could perceive nothing but a futile spirit of reaction. My new novel, which I have been on the edge of commencing for a year past – without having commenced it, was worrying me into a fever of apprehension. My whole future seemed, and seems, to depend on the quality of that novel. I had the idea for it years ago. I saw the thing vague, but magnificent, tremendous, the greatest novel that ever was or could be written by anybody. Then I lost it. I mean I lost the creative mood for it, and couldn't regain the mood. Then, later, I began to see the thing afresh. I pieced two plots together and made one. I saw the chief characters, and the chief incidents, and the climax. The trouble was, I still could not regain the creative mood for that particular book. I saw, but didn't feel. Everything was there except the breath of emotional life. The spectacle of the ballet extinguished in my inefficient noddle the last glimmer of hope.

The next item on the programme was an Act of Rimsky-Korsakoff's opera, *Sadko*. I'd never seen *Sadko*, and I doubt if I had met anyone who had seen it. Anyhow, I knew Rimsky was not a really first-rate composer, only an agreeable melodist and a terrific swell at orchestration. I expected little from *Sadko*. But I had a surprise. The music was so close to being first rate that I was unable to tell the difference, and the performance was marvellously fine. Something of the old autocracy had survived into the Soviet autocracy. Before the Act was half over, my novel was coming back to me in quite the grand manner. I could listen to the opera and think about the novel simultaneously. I felt the creative mood permeating and enveloping me. Hope returned, higher than ever. At the end I applauded with the enthusiasm of a youth. *Sadko* was my salvation.

Oslo. – Only when you see the provincialism of Oslo do you appreciate the wonderfulness of Ibsen. It was as manager of the theatre at Bergen that Ibsen learnt for himself more about the stage than any other dramatist in nineteenth-century Europe. Now Oslo is a capital; it has three times the population of Bergen; it is much nearer the cosmopolitanism of Sweden. If Oslo is provincial – and you may even call it parochial – to-day, what must Bergen have been like in those early years when Ibsen, directing its theatre, formed his ideas and planned his schemes for the rejuvenation of the drama? Whence came the inspiration which enabled him to make all the plays of the continent seem petty, parochial, and ingenuous in comparison with his own? This is a mystery which cannot be explained, and certainly Ibsen himself could not explain it. I doubt whether any creative artist ever can satisfactorily explain his causation.

I remember the time when Clement Scott in the *Daily Telegraph* used to attack Ibsen violently, to shoot him to pieces with epithets. (Ibsen never seemed to notice that he had been shot to pieces by the most influential dramatic critic in the biggest city in the world.) The mildest of the charges brought by the angered Scott against Ibsen was that he was parochial. In those days, thirty or forty years ago, I was indignantly anti-Scott. Ibsen parochial! The notion was grotesque. But to-day I do have a glimmering of what Scott was driving at. In a way Ibsen *is* parochial. (So was Aeschylus, and so was Thucydides.) It was like Ibsen's immense cheek to assume that the élite of Europe could be interested in the back-chat and the municipal and connubial goings-on in a twopenny town of a sort that nobody had ever heard of. Ibsen's assumption nevertheless proved to be correct.

Yes. Ibsen was parochial, even in his finest plays of contemporary life; but he lifted parochialism to the mundane and the universal. Read or see Ibsen's social dramas without pre-judice, and the still small voice within you will say: 'But I know that town and its inhabitants. I have lived in it, and among them. I *am* living in it.' Fundamentally, we are all living in Bergen.

London. – Talking familiarly at lunch with a London police-magistrate, I asked him: 'Do you really like your work?' He said: 'I love it. I'm never bored by it. I shall be at it even this afternoon, much to the annoyance of counsel, who would prefer to be watching the race for the Schneider Trophy. It was always my ambition to be a police-magistrate, and I'm very happy in the job.'

'But,' I said, 'isn't it a bit monotonous? Same sort of cases recurring again and again, and so on.'

He said: 'You might think so. But the fact is, no two cases are alike, and no two cases have to be treated in the same way. There's no monotony in a police-court – at least there isn't for me. A police-court is all human nature, and I haven't yet found that human nature is monotonous. Now yesterday I had a case. Two old gentlemen, aged sixty-five and seventy, quarrelling about a waistcoat valued by A at ten shillings, and handed over by A to B for safe keeping. Both these gentlemen resided in a Rowton lodging-house, and earned a precarious living by addressing envelopes. A demanded the return of the waistcoat and B wouldn't part. B made excuse after excuse, until A came into court with his grievance, demanding the waistcoat, or in the alternative ten shillings cash. I discovered that B has been wearing the waistcoat – no doubt he had none of his own – and that it was no longer absolutely clean. I de-cided that the waistcoat was worth five shillings, not ten, and I ordered that the waistcoat should be handed over within a week, or five shillings paid. A then said to me: "I hoped your worship would make a specific order for payment in cash, because, as the waistcoat has been in wear by Mr B since April, it would not be satisfactory to me to have a *restitutio in integrum*." '

A tragedy hidden somewhere behind those last three words!

London, September 25th. – What generally spoils long novels is the untimely supervening creative fatigue. This happened to *The Heart of Midlothian.* It is a calamity which the author has very little power to prevent. Heaven in its wisdom decided to give you a certain amount of strength. You cannot increase it. Towards the end of a race, if you are tired you are tired, and there you are! Nobody can pour a quart out of a pint pot.

Lots of good novels fall away a few score pages before the end. Readers say: 'The author scamped this last bit.' He usually didn't. He was at the end of his creative strength. He may have had, and probably did still have, reserves of invention, ingenuity, perseverance and conscientiousness; but his *power* was exhausted. He had been guilty of only one artistic sin, the sin of miscalculating his creative strength. No work on earth is more trying than creative writing. As you write the first words you are self-conscious. When you finish the first page of manuscript you think: 'I have so-many hundred more pages to write. Every one of them has to be written, and every one of them must be good. Every one of them must be the best. No letting down.'

I reckon that this novel will fill 900 pages of manuscript. How do I reckon? I don't reckon. I just know. Experience has taught me pre-knowledge. When I began *The Old Wives' Tale,* I announced to the domestic hearth: 'This novel will be 200,000 words long, divided into four equal parts.' Well, it was. The new novel will be 150,000 words long, and probably not divided into parts. I think I have now grown out of dividing novels into parts. To-day such a division strikes me as a bit pompous. I know the main plot, but by no means all the incidents thereof, though I have a few titbits of episodes which I shall not omit. The episode of the gloves, for instance, which I found in and appropriated from the *Journal* of the brothers de Goncourt. I know the three chief characters, but by no means all the ins-and-outs of them. They won't alter – I would never allow any character to get the whip-hand of me – but I shall fill them out. I know the 'feel' of the novel. That won't alter, either. And I have the whole of the material for the novel; and it is indexed, in a notebook. I would sooner lose fifty pages of the manuscript than that notebook. If I did lose it, I think I should be capable of abandoning the novel for ever. And yet I leave the notebook lying about.

I have been fighting for years against the instinct to write this particular novel. About thirty years ago I was taken to the Savoy Hotel for tea, came out, went home, and wrote *The Grand Babylon Hotel* in three weeks of evening-work. *The Grand Babylon Hotel* was a mere lark. The big hotel de luxe is a very serious organization; it is in my opinion a unique subject for a serious novel; it is stuffed with human nature of extremely various kinds. The subject is characteristic of the age; it is as modern as the morning's milk; it is tremendous, and worthy of tremendous handling. I dare say it's beyond me. But nobody else has caught hold of it, and if I am not audacious I'm nothing. To-day I wrote three pages. 897 left to do! The thought is terrifying. Any serious novelist will agree with me as to the terrifyingness.

And when I have finished it and corrected the manuscript and corrected the typescript and corrected the slip-proofs and corrected the page-proofs, and it is published, half the assessors and appraisers in Britain and America will say: 'Why doesn't he give us another *Old Wives' Tale*?' I have written between seventy and eighty books. But also I have only written four: *The Old Wives' Tale*, *The Card*, *Clayhanger*, and *Riceyman Steps*. All the others are made a reproach to me because they are neither *The Old Wives' Tale*, nor *The Card*, nor *Clayhanger*, nor *Riceyman Steps*. And *Riceyman Steps* would have been made a reproach too, if the servant Elsie had not happened to be a very 'sympathetic' character. Elsie saved *Riceyman Steps* from being called sordid and morbid and all sorts of bad adjectives. As if the 'niceness' of a character had anything to do with the quality of the novel in which it appears! But authors are never satisfied.